Working with the Person
with Schizophrenia

Working with the Person with Schizophrenia

THE TREATMENT ALLIANCE

Michael A. Selzer
Timothy B. Sullivan
Monica Carsky
Kenneth G. Terkelsen

NEW YORK UNIVERSITY PRESS
NEW YORK AND LONDON

Library of Congress Cataloging-in-Publication Data
Working with the person with schizophrenia : the treatment alliance /
Michael A. Selzer . . . [et al.].
p.   cm.
Bibliography: p.
Includes index.
ISBN 0-8147-7891-7
1. Schizophrenia.   2. Psychotherapist and patient.   I. Selzer,
Michael A., 1934–   .
[DNLM: 1. Physician-Patient Relations.   2. Psychotherapy.
3. Schizophrenia—therapy.   WM 203 W9266]
RC514.W63   1989
616.89′82—dc20
DNLM/DLC
for Library of Congress   89-8971
CIP

New York University Press books are printed on acid-free paper,
and their binding materials are chosen for strength and durability.

Book design by Ken Venezio

Contents

v

Preface

About ten years ago a former teacher of mine, Leon Shapiro, called to offer me "the job you've always said you wanted." Leon, who had just been appointed Medical Director of The New York Hospital, Westchester Division, was asking me to create and direct a long-term treatment unit for chronic schizophrenics. "A kind of asylum," he suggested "with, of course, unlimited opportunity to teach." It was this last phrase, as he well knew, that made this an offer I could not refuse.

For the next eight years, I lived out my wish to work intensively with this very special population, surrounded by colleagues whose eagerness to learn was sufficient to overcome the challenges posed by the inpatients' (apparent) indifference, withholding, rejection, and hopelessness. In thinking back on that time, what stands out is the degree the staff maintained comraderie. Despite the discouragement, fright, and helplessness the patients engendered in us, we maintained our curiosity. Discussions of clinical issues were lively and intense, frequently ending without a consensus having been reached—this despite the fact that there was considerable group pressure to present a united front to the patients. There was a continual pressure to come to closure, to define what the "right thing" was and then do it. The complexity of the problems, however, did not allow for absolute, party-line solutions, and the need to keep issues open was respected. In most instances, we came to learn that, however much we wished (and needed) to feel responsible and in charge, we lacked precise answers. To be sure, our own anxiety often led us to impose our beliefs on the patients, but they quickly showed us how ineffectual we were.

Over this near decade of trial and error, students came and went. Three in particular stood out in terms of their dedication to, persistent inquiry about, and affection for their patients: Monica Carsky, Tim Sullivan, and Ken Terkelsen. When I began to think about writing this book, it seemed natural to ask them to collaborate once again—to put on paper some of the experiences we had shared. As we talked about what the focus should be, the issue that surfaced again and again was the question of forming an alliance. How does a partnership emerge? What contributes to its development? What information do we, as professionals, need in order to begin trying to create such a partnership?

We focused first on what had allowed us to maintain an exploratory attitude in the face of all the clinical demands to provide quick solutions. Gradually, through our reminiscences, we recognized that, without having been aware of it, we had been guided by a common set of principles that had never been explicitly articulated.

The task then became one of setting down this model and illustrating it with clinical examples. We hope that the liveliness and enthusiasm that marked our work will be shared by our readers.

A word about authorship. The concepts in this book are, in large part, derived from our clinical experience. The actual writing summarizing that experience, was assigned to particular authors. Each of us contributed to the introduction. Chapters 1, 2, and 3 were written by Drs. Sullivan and Selzer; chapter 4 by Drs. Selzer and Sullivan; chapters 5, 6, 7, and 8 by Drs. Carsky and Terkelsen. We hope the reader will see this book as a collaborative effort.

MICHAEL SELZER M.D.

Acknowledgments

The New York Hospital, Westchester Division, Extended Treatment Service was the laboratory in which we created, tested, and modified the ideas that came to form this book. We owe a debt of gratitude to the staff and patients, all of whom played a crucial role in shaping our thinking. In that sense, this book is a collaboration of hundreds of people.

We wish particularly to thank Dr. Robert Michels, Chairman of the Department of Psychiatry at Cornell, Dr. Otto Kernberg, Medical Director of the Westchester Division, and Dr. Richard Munich, Chief of the Extended Treatment Service.

A special thanks to our secretary, Cheryl DelMastro, who managed to decipher four different styles of illegibility while maintaining her composure.

Finally our editor, Kitty Moore, wins the endurance medal of honor for being patient, supportive, and never critical when we perpetually missed our deadlines.

Working with the Person
with Schizophrenia

Introduction

The last thirty years have been a time of great progress in schizophrenia research and treatment. Advances in psychopharmacology have enabled patients who would have once been doomed to a lifetime of insanity to live with a minimum of psychotic symptoms. This development has transformed our view of the nature of schizophrenia and set in motion a wide-ranging reassessment of the arrangements of care. Once viewed as the result of external stress on an otherwise healthy psyche, the disorder is now seen principally as a biochemical illness. The great asylum hospitals, regarded for a century as optimal habitats for patients with schizophrenia (1), are being closed or converted into short-term treatment centers. Previously considered the principal source of the disorder, families are now courted as primary caregivers and encouraged to collaborate with clinicians in promoting the patient's return to community life. An array of community-based supportive services has surfaced as towns and villages that shunned these patients begin to see them as disabled citizens with a right to live alongside the rest of the community.

1

Although these advances have altered the course of the syndrome, those receiving treatment still do not "get better" in the usual sense of that term. They experience what we have come to call a remission of symptoms. They are no longer insane. They have left the institutions. They have rejoined their families. But the great majority continue to suffer from loss of vitality and interest in ordinary activity and from inability to achieve and maintain a sense of competence, dignity, and meaning in their daily lives. Even though they reside in communities, they are not altogether like their fellow citizens, and rarely do they belong wholeheartedly. No longer inmates and no longer acutely ill, they are not well.

For patients and their families and their doctors, the absence of aliveness, the inaccessibility of dignified social roles, and prolonged, even life-long dependency on others are central concerns. Patients (2–3) and their relatives (4) complain bitterly of the adverse effects of medication on their vitality and reject the very treatments that open the way to life in the community. Frustrated doctors (5) mount often fruitless attempts to persuade patients to adhere to the prescribed treatments. Investigators search for less bothersome ways to use existing drugs (6–8), for new drugs with less troubling side effects (9), and for ways to understand noncompliance (10).

Gradually, as drug treatment has brought the psychotic states under better control, attention has turned to these quality-of-life problems. In the early 1970s, the practice of referring to many of these clinical phenomena as the negative symptoms of schizophrenia emerged (11). Largely because of recent successes, professionals and the laity alike have assumed that these phenomena can likewise be understood in biological terms and that they will give way to advances in drug treatment. Beginning in the late 1970s, investigators working from this perspective developed methods of codifying the loss of vitality (12) and advanced a variety of psychobiological models to account for it (13–18).

All of this notwithstanding, our experience and that of others involved in day-to-day care of patients in community and hospital settings continually compel us to take the view that these human beings are very active forces in their own right, exerting unnoticed and unmeasured influences on the course of their illnesses. Moreover, it is apparent that the status of patienthood, which often requires participation in a great many disagreeable clinical encounters and even more painful encounters in the open community, significantly contributes to the loss of vitality and of dignity. Yet it appears that few professionals are aware of the quality of life problems of our patients, and they are certainly not oriented to dealing with them. The relative dearth of available literature and research supports this view. In our daily work, our routine encounters with hospital staff and community workers demonstrated their pervasive tendency to speak of the patient as merely a victim of a biological illness. In addition, families have championed the biological perspective, searching for better drug treatments and often appearing uninterested in human measures that might have an impact on the patient's quality of life. In short, all participants have seemed intent on applying medical treatments—on seeking to extinguish symptoms without giving any particular attention to the impact that the illness and the treatment was having on the sufferer or to the adaptive responses (or survival strategies) employed by patients to cope with their predicament.

This volume grew out of a felt need to give voice to our patients' experience of losing access to the kind of predictable, benevolent, rewarding involvements that make up life for most citizens and to speak of the implications of that perspective for the study of chronic schizophrenia and especially the negative symptoms of the illness. Our aim, however, is not just to call attention to how hard it is to live with schizophrenia. Rather, we hope to elucidate a method of talking with patients adapted to daily encounters with people struggling with the effects of schizophrenia, whether that work is proceeding in hospital or community settings, in clinical or rehabilitation facilities.

The method elaborated in the chapters to follow draws heavily on the premise that an understanding of the sufferer's experience of the illness, of the treatments applied thus far, and of what the sufferer has lost and what future he or she hopes for is critical to the quality of the alliance between oneself and the sufferer. This kind of understanding goes far beyond the conventions of diagnosis and, we believe, complicates in no small measure the pursuit of conventional treatment methods.

While the importance of forming a treatment or therapeutic alliance is stressed in some texts and training programs (19–23), it is easy to be misled about the nature of the relationship one has formed with a schizophrenic individual. Some individuals appear thoroughly negative, refusing attempts at contact and declining treatment efforts unless coerced into institutions, where they often repeat a pattern of withdrawal. Others "take to the road." Another very large group of persons maintain some degree of contact with family and clinicians, but refuse to follow advice or to fully engage in what those others feel would be the best type of treatment or rehabilitation program. The alliance often feels tenuous, shifting, and is full of surprises, and the clinician and program personnel may grow frustrated or feel hopeless, perhaps even ending their efforts with that particular person. Even an apparently strong working alliance with a schizophrenic individual may be, unknown to the clinician, built upon delusional or distorted expectations and perceptions, whose disappointment later leads to a rupture of the relationship, a rupture that feels as mysterious as it is unanticipated to the clinician.

Yet our experience suggests that partnerships can indeed be formed with even the most apparently negativistic persons, provided the clinician has as an initial goal the understanding of the person's subjective experience. This requires the clinician to keep in check, at least temporarily but often for long periods of time, the need to diagnose according to objective standards, the wish to influence behavior as an end in itself, and the impulse for therapeutic zeal. The formation of a treatment partnership with the severely disturbed and demoralized person requires the clinician to become the person's collaborator. Evidence of this collaboration may appear only in tiny, subtle ways, seemingly light-years away from the mature doctor-patient collaborations to which we are accustomed from work with less beleaguered individuals.

When we speak of a treatment partnership at this level, we are referring to a form of cooperative venture (the nature of which will be exemplified in the chapters to follow) in which two individuals undertake some activity in a spirit of shared interest and mutual respect. The clinician's overall goal is that the patient should be able to have a life that is "better" in some way that is meaningful to the patient—more autonomous, enjoyable, and gratifying in relationships and activities and less constricted by the illness. Specific treatment recommendations—to take medication, to go to a day program, to see a psychotherapist—are always subordinated to the goal of a better life as defined by the patient. Just as the clinician may initially need to infer what the patient's notion of "better" is all about, so too must he or she infer how the patient will experience the treatment recommendations in terms of the patient's broader goals. A therapeutic collaboration is one of many relationships we form to get along in life, but the individual struggling with schizophrenia is simultaneously more in need and more frightened of such help than most. Thus, we must start with simple, basic assumptions about why we are meeting with this person.

The formation of an alliance requires the satisfaction of at least two conditions: First, the sufferer cannot be so frightened or pained as to refuse all contact, and, second, the clinician has to become truly involved in an effort to understand, even when this is an unpleasant experience. Part of wanting to form a relationship entails seeing the other as a human being struggling to live, no matter how appearances may belie this perspective. The clinician must respect the adaptive intent of the other's behavior and beliefs, even when these appear senseless or self-destructive.[a] For a schizophrenic individual, preserving dignity may be more important than endorsing everyday perceptions as reality, and the loss of a world-view that, while delusional, affirms one's significance may feel like too high a price to pay for access to the disappointments and demands of ordinary life. Apathy may represent a very active attempt to avoid the pain of involvement with others and to protect an inner life held sacred by the schizophrenic individual who has in so many other ways lost the ability to automatically carry out the cognitive and emotional functions that make us human and make life worth living (24).

To develop this relationship, which will pave the way for a future treatment alliance, the clinician needs curiosity about the other person's experience, including the person's experience of the self, the illness, and the clinician, among other things. The clinician hopes to find an arena in which patient and therapist can collaborate: a discussion, a mutual exploration, a project. Often this involves identifying an area of enjoyment or one of pain that the sufferer decides to share or one of uncertainty or conflict in the person's inner world; it involves any area that can be designated as a discussion topic of mutual interest.

As an example, consider the following. The case of a young man with schizophrenia is presented at a conference in a psychiatric hospital. He has had several prior stays and reluctantly returned for what others saw as severe deterioration in his functioning. The presentation reveals that the patient is totally withdrawn and apathetic about all aspects of the treatment program in the hospital. The staff have drawn on what is known of his educational attainments and his interests in repeated efforts to coax, cajole, or tempt him into programs for recreation and rehabilitation, all to no avail. The trainee presenting the case is clearly frustrated and pessimistic, as is the rest of the staff.

In the conference interview with a consultant, the patient ignores his doctor and his special nurse and assigns these roles to others in the room. The consultant comments that there is another nurse who believes that *she* has been working with the young man, rather than the nurse he has pointed out, and there is some bland discussion about these differing views of reality. The consultant, believing the patient's pointed omission of his special nurse indicates his involvement (albeit conflicted) with the nurse, then asks the patient, "What do you imagine this other [ignored] nurse might be feeling?" The patient offers the view that the nurse might feel hurt and that only a cruel person would put her in such a position. The consultant then suggests that, someone who was fighting for his life might do this to the nurse, for reasons of his own having nothing to do with cruelty, and only with survival. The patient breaks down in tears and suddenly seems human and vulnerable, in sharp contrast to the picture of numb, aloof withdrawal he had previously been presenting. Alerted by this unexpected revelation, the staff begin to discuss ways to deal with the patient—now seen as a more complex individual—with more interest and more hope.

The consultant's openness to the young man's experience was based on the assumption that schizophrenic individuals seek security, survival, and protection of self-esteem even when these efforts are not evident. In this case, the consultant's validation of the patient's wish to survive, even if it meant engaging in hurtful behavior and in distortions of external realities, enabled the temporary formation of an alliance within which the patient could relate momentarily as one suffering human being to another. To form a reliable treatment partnership, this moment of unity and aliveness would have to be repeated in a stable relationship over time, but the evidence that it was possible helped the staff to avoid limiting assumptions about the implications of the young man's negativistic stance and withdrawn behavior for the future.

There are, of course, myriad barriers to the kind of understanding exemplified in this vignette. People living with schizophrenia have commonly encountered numerous others who have revealed a commitment to behavioral change long before they displayed an interest in the direct personal experience of the sufferer. These prior encounters, whether inside or outside clinical domains, have often taught the sufferer to be wary of self-revelation. In addition, there are the many effects of the illness itself on the sufferer's ability to get him- or herself understood, the effects of grief for what is lost and despair about the future, all of which diminish the sufferer's capacity to engage wholeheartedly in conversation about his or her experiences. There are also constraints posed by the needs and prerogatives of institutions. And, of course, there are pressures of time, money, and the expectations of improvement. Compounding all of these issues, there are the sufferer's many and constant fundamental human needs—for personal comfort, for concrete provision of food and housing—any of which may intrude unexpectedly into and interrupt or capsize the dialogue, but which nevertheless must be attended to in the service of fostering the sufferer's belief in the clinician's humanity. Finally, there is the impact of the story on the listener, including certain powerful impulses generated in the listener—to observe from a distance rather than be with, to mend, to flee the inquiry. Thus, even given a certain dedication to the task, the sufferer and his or her interested listener are both hard pressed to create and sustain an interpersonal field within which this kind of understanding can evolve. With all these barriers, it is small wonder that we understand so little of the inner world of our patients with schizophrenia.

The primary obstacles to the formation of this kind of alliance are conditions that forestall the development of empathy. Either the person suffering from schizophrenia or the individual he or she encounters can be the primary source of any given obstacle. Society views individuals with mental illness, especially schizophrenia, as alien and sometimes dangerous. Although these aspects of schizophrenia are exaggerated in the media, they do form a cultural context that tends to militate against clinicians developing a view of the individual with schizophrenia as a suffering human being with ordinary needs. A similar effect derives from the common view of schizophrenia as a mysterious malady that inalterably transforms the individual into a caricature of humanity—as in the common notion that schizophrenia refers to a "split" personality. The idea that schizophrenia is an illness with its roots in the biology of the brain and which affects the personality in complex and largely invisible ways is made more difficult to grasp by these popular oversimplifications.

Modern clinical training about schizophrenia has begun to incorporate information about the neurophysiological aspects of the illness and the benefits and risks of the medications used to treat its symptoms. The idea that family and community support is important to the long-term course of the illness is widely accepted now. What is very often not taught explicitly is how to understand and deal with the aspects of the illness that do not respond to medication or to social supports. For example, the negative symptoms of schizophrenia have come more to the attention of clinicians in recent years. The practicing clinician who has learned only to record symptoms and to prescribe medication is at a serious disadvantage. Again, however, the implicit message in much contemporary clinical training encourages the clinician to distance him- or herself from the patient: the doctor is well; the patient is sick and needs to take the medications. The possibility that the doctor could, and perhaps should, try to understand the sick person's subjective experience and use this understanding to maximize treatment results or to change the goals of treatment altogether is a more threatening proposition. It is also one that may never even occur to traditionally trained practitioners, for whom the idea of the effect of psychological variables on treatment response and course in schizophrenia is a new one (25–27).

Obstacles to full understanding of the experience of having schizophrenia are also created by the patient and others with whom he or she lives. For example, social pressures may demand the use of explanations of negative symptoms that ignore psychological variables, attributing all such manifestations to laziness or to biological deficits. Similarly, the schizophrenic person's idiosyncratic interpretations of events will be the subject of criticism and exasperation because they seem so unrealistic or so demanding of special awareness by others. Family members have their own strong feelings about having a schizophrenic relative, feelings they may manage by mixtures of denial and acceptance of illness, anger, sadness, disappointment, anxiety, and avoidance, any one of which can interfere with their efforts to form the kind of partnership with the patient that we are espousing.

Intertwined with these processes are the schizophrenic person's own intensely mixed feelings about being understood. Very frequently, the patient will provide some hints about personal wishes and fears, only to retreat behind distracting symptoms, withdrawal, anger, negation, provocative behaviors, or a wall of indifference. As we have noted earlier, the schizophrenic individual often feels that revealing a wish to be understood is tantamount to inviting intrusion and relinquishing control over his or her life. For one whose sense of sovereignty is already weakened, the usual response is vacillation between involvement and negation of involvement, between revealing and obfuscating.

The clinician may have correspondingly mixed feelings about how much interest he or she has in a schizophrenic individual's subjective experience. While a capacity for empathy is frequently a prerequisite for the choice of a career as a clinician, the attempt to empathize with a person who is delusional is a special case. It produces a great deal of distress, as a rule, commonly evoking distancing maneuvers that are supported by culture and training. The clinician who would work with patients with schizophrenia must possess or acquire an unusually high degree of tolerance for ambiguity and uncertainty. At the same time, clinicians of various disciplines could be helped by a model that could inform a variety of therapeutic interventions and encompass the varied and inconstant expression of the illness.

Prior models have failed to resolve a crucial issue: how to understand the relative contribution of biological and psychological variables in the production of the schizophrenic syndrome. This failure has at times been a consequence of biased assumptions about the illness and at other times been due to a lack of adequate scientific information. An unfortunate result has been the development of two different camps (the purely psychological and the purely biological), each of which views schizophrenia from its own isolated perspective.

In recent years, this division has been exacerbated for various reasons, but one in particular. It has been demonstrated that pharmacologic treatments are effective in ameliorating certain aspects of the illness. At the same time, psychotherapeutic interventions have failed to demonstrate their efficacy in a statistically rigorous fashion. Few converts have been made to either cause. Instead, increasing rigidification has polarized the field into two positions: adherents to the biological treatment model and those who advocate a psychotherapeutic model. Most unfortunate has been the failure to arrive at a consensus for developing and using a model that incorporates both perspectives.

Differing views on treatment are reflected in differing notions of etiology. Those who view schizophrenia as essentially an illness responsive to biological treatments see the various manifestations of the disorder as immediate consequences of biological abnormalities and all symptoms as having a physiologic etiology (28–29). This position is represented in particular by those who divide schizophrenic symptomatology into positive and negative symptom syndromes (30–32). They view positive symptoms as the product of the toxic physiologic disorder that underlies schizophrenia and all negative symptoms as the consequence of cerebral deterioration and consequent functional deficits. This view is frequently supported by references to biological studies that demonstrate the many perceptual and cognitive difficulties experienced by schizophrenic patients as well as to those studies that demonstrate increased ventricular brain ratios on CAT scans in chronic schizophrenics. The studies that demonstrate apparent reduction in cerebral mass are used in particular to support the view that chronic schizophrenics with negative symptoms are simply suffering from a chronic dementing process. The negative symptoms of the syndrome, those that most vex clinicians, families, and researchers, are seen to be "deficit" symptoms of a progressive deteriorating mental illness, a concept similar to Kraepelin's first projection of the irreversible downward decline of dementia praecox.

Those who espouse psychotherapeutic interventions have tended to ascribe many, if not all, of the symptoms of schizophrenia to underlying psychological conflicts, often due to developmental traumas that have given rise to a schizophrenic psychological state. Major writers such as Winnicott, Searles, Frieda Fromm Reichman, and Otto Will have been the forerunners of this view. Most often, the theories postulated a psychological trauma relating to maternal-infant interactions or other disturbances in object relations. These pathologic interactions are hypothesized to impair the individual's capacity to tolerate intimate relationships because of his or her fears and wishes regarding boundary disruption. This intensely ambivalent attitude toward merger compels the individual to reject relationships as well as most social interactions. This view focuses on the way in which schizophrenic symptoms appear directed to distancing the individual from others, denying meaning in relationships, and tending to focus on autistic absorption, rather than purposeful other-directed activities. It assumes, for example, that such distance from others is a psychological state for which the individual ambivalently strives.

The manner in which these two points of view have been elaborated in the past two decades has led to polarization rather than resolution. Adherents of the biological model view the psychotherapy literature as farfetched, unscientific, founded in speculation rather than empirical observation. They also denounce psychological theories about schizophrenia as neglecting the biological input for which scientific research has established a place in any model of this illness. By the same token, psychotherapeutically inclined clinicians and researchers view the biological model as unnecessarily pessimistic, saying it deanimates the patient and leads to treatment programs or styles that inadequately address patients' experiences. These clinicians believe such programs offer little in the way of understanding patients' psychological states and fail to give a sense that they can control and affect their lives in ways other than simply accepting the treatments psychiatrists prescribe. They complain that, at a theoretical level, the biological model does not allow for or recognize the possibility that psychological reactions or indeed psychological conflicts play a role in at least some schizophrenic symptoms. And clinicians also criticize the biological model in its extreme form for its dictate that patients adopt a passive role in their treatment.

Clearly, a model of schizophrenia must include an understanding of and reference to the biological disorders that have been demonstrated. At the very least it must allow that many of the symptoms may be secondary to the genetically acquired and perhaps developmentally elaborated illness. We believe, however, that such a model must at the same time address the psychological experience of the individual who struggles to adapt to and, where possible, control rather than be controlled by the core physiologic disturbance. Thus it must allow for the possibility that some of the symptoms may be a consequence of psychological reactions to the disorder. Such a model would provide a more complete picture of the illness and the patient, which we believe is necessary for optimal treatment and research efforts. In seeking to treat an illness that attacks the very core of what makes us human—the capacities for intimacy, communication and thought, and productivity—we fail if we ignore any of these functions. An ideal model would generate hypotheses about ways to allow the individual to experience a sense of self-esteem and control over his or her life, as well as hypotheses about which symptoms might be amenable to psychotherapeutic intervention, in particular those that heretofore had been poorly responsive or unresponsive to biological interventions. It should also predict ways to most successfully combine biologic and psychosocial treatment efforts.

Why a model at all? Without a conceptual model stipulating potential treatment goals and how change occurs, it is difficult to assess the efficacy of any intervention. If we are not clear about the relative contribution of psychological and biological variables and do not have a model to tease out those issues, then we are handicapped in our capacity to construct research to assess psychotherapy, pharmacotherapy, or rehabilitative efforts. In attempting to assess the efficacy of a particular drug, for example, it would be essential to study or control for psychological variables as well as biological ones. Although we know that most positive symptoms respond well to medication, negative symptoms, such as amotivation, frequently prove refractory. This could be construed to be due to the patient's difficulty in acknowledging that he or she is ill. In this instance, if the patient could be helped to acknowledge and accept the illness, he or she might manifest a positive response. In addition, research suggests (33–35) that insight into illness increases the patient's compliance with medication. Perhaps this would be due, in part, to the fact that an insightful patient may be more gratifying to work with and would therefore motivate the doctor to be more invested in the treatment. Perhaps this increased involvement of the clinician would then make the patient a more active participant. Clearly, other interpretations of the patient's behavior are possible. Our point here is that with the current level of our knowledge, nonbiological factors need to be carefully considered and studied in our treatment and research efforts, especially since the biological component has not been clearly delineated.

There appear to be subgroups of schizophrenic patients who exhibit varying degrees of symptomatology and different patterns, with differing levels of severity (36–37). As has been shown in research with other diagnostic groups, outcome assessment is a highly volatile variable that is dependent on one's being certain that one is dealing with appropriate and comparable cohorts of patients. A conceptual model combining knowledge about both the biology and psychology of schizophrenia can also help to establish a useful nosology of the disease itself, permitting the delineation of those psychological and phenomenological variables potentially important in differentiating subgroups of patients.

In establishing a conceptual model that integrates biological variables with an understanding of the psychology of the schizophrenic patient, the term "functional deficits" is an especially limiting one. "Deficit" connotes a degree of finality and irreversibility and pessimism and may, in fact, be misleading when applied in particular to the negative symptoms expressed by the schizophrenic patient. Such a term suggests that the patient is mentally dead or incompetent. This is a damaging notion when it dominates the thinking of anyone working with an individual with schizophrenia, for it treats the patient as merely the unfortunate recipient of some dread malady and avoids the possibility of identifying areas of struggle within the patient regarding these very issues of competency and awareness. Furthermore, as we hope to elucidate in the conceptual model that follows, some of the negative symptoms of schizophrenia, while appearing to reflect functional deficits, may in fact be a consequence of compensatory adaptive psychological functioning in response to the illness, which precipitates the production of the schizophrenic syndrome. In any case, until there is more convincing evidence to the contrary, areas of suboptimal functioning in schizophrenic patients can be examined for possible psychological variables in the hope that there may be an opportunity for more productive adaptation leading to greater autonomy and improved self-esteem.

In summary, we are interested in adding to biological models of schizophrenia a metapsychological model that integrates the individual's subjective experience with his or her biological substrate. We believe this is necessary because in few other conditions does the individual's personality and reaction to the illness become so intimately interwoven with the manifestations of the disease. The patient's awareness that he or she is ill and his or her feelings about accepting help from professionals are key variables in the disease, as important as the very condition that affects the ability to perceive, think, and trust others. While some might speak of a person who suffers from schizophrenia as they speak of a person who suffers from some other disease, here we talk about an illness that pervades the person's experience of self and of life in general. Learning about how this person experiences life is crucial, we believe, to planning adequate treatment and evaluating our efforts.

After we present a model to provide a framework for looking at individuals with schizophrenia in this way, in subsequent chapters we will outline ways to perceive and respond to patients' active efforts in the various clinical contexts of evaluation, somatic and psychological therapies, hospital programs, management, and rehabilitation.

What these seemingly disparate clinical contexts share is a requirement for a "treatment partnership." In order to engage in any kind of therapeutic endeavors with a schizophrenic patient, it is necessary to consider the person's ability to collaborate with the clinician. To assess this ability and to foster a working partnership, we believe that the clinician must be committed to understanding the subjective experience of the schizophrenic person. This includes the experience of this illness in its biological and psychosocial manifestations, its impact on others, and, very importantly, the patient's attempts to adapt to the illness in ways that preserve his or her self-esteem. These adaptations, which may seem unhealthy or inappropriate or illogical to the outsider, are not to be lightly dismissed or thoughtlessly challenged. They represent the schizophrenic person's attempts to hold on to his or her humanity and to cope with and seek to influence the environment while in the throes of an illness that threatens to upset what makes us human: the ability to feel, to think and plan, to trust and care about others. The clinician's responsibility is to listen for these messages of human concerns, to hear them as guides to understanding what the individual needs and wants and how the clinician can help.

1

A Model for
Understanding Schizophrenia

This book aims to provide clinicians with the means to understand their schizophrenic patients and the skills necessary to engage those patients in treatment. We do not intend to present a model for psychotherapy, although our views are based on work with chronic schizophrenic individuals in supportive psychotherapy, as well as in directing inpatient treatment programs. Our focus will be on the therapeutic relationship with the schizophrenic individual; its characteristics, vicissitudes, and idiosyncracies and its central importance to any therapy.

Because of the disorder's effect on thinking and behavior, the affected individual experiences and manages relationships in ways that provoke frequent misunderstanding by and confusion in others. To avoid making inaccurate and misleading assumptions, the clinician must not only understand the disorder but also the individual's reaction to it. The psychological response to schizophrenia must be studied in the patient's manifest and also implied communication. This approach is crucial, for the subjective, psychological reaction to the illness best informs us of the patient's capacity and motivation for treatment. The deciphering of the patient's communications depends on our familiarity with the issues that typically concern schizophrenic individuals, our comfort with the intense feelings they arouse in us, and our willingness to recognize similar (as well as different) experiences in ourselves. To this end, the following chapters will explore characteristic themes encountered when working with schizophrenic patients and develop a framework for comprehending them.

Recent literature (1–2) has described the limitations of empirical descriptions of psychiatric disorders, including schizophrenia, and underlined the importance of identifying theoretical bias in any conceptual model. DSM III-R, as a kind of empirical model, while aiding in defining more distinct groups of phenomenologically similar individuals, has not brought clarity to the muddle of symptoms and signs associated with schizophrenia, and it is limited by its emphasis on empirical phenomenology. Such models have been unduly influenced by the diagnostic emphasis on the flagrant symptoms of the disorder—that is, delusions and hallucinations, initiated by Bleuler and perpetuated by Schneider and others. The attempts of Crow and others (3–6) to divide schizophrenic symptoms into two categories ("positive" or "negative") and further to delineate two distinct schizophrenic syndromes, while able to claim empirical support, suffer from an excessively reductionistic spirit and as yet have not furthered the treatment of schizophrenia.

Investigators have tended to categorically describe the medication-unresponsive symptoms of schizophrenia as "negative symptoms" (7). (One notable exception is Wing, who has drawn attention to the role of the patient's reaction to the illness [8].) It has often been suggested that these symptoms represent "deficits" in neurological functioning, perhaps associated with a neurologic syndrome, and dementia. This conceptual approach makes broad and unsubstantiated assumptions about the etiology of a complex syndrome, whose symptoms may be multidetermined. Though there is accumulating evidence of brain pathology associated with schizophrenia, the literature has not conclusively demonstrated that "psychological" factors are irrelevant to symptom pathogenesis (9–10). The complex behaviors represented in the "negative" symptom syndrome are too readily seen as mere expressions of frontal lobe pathology. Nevertheless, it is likely that disturbances in frontal lobe functioning are implicated in the phenomenology and, probably, etiology of schizophrenia, since most schizophrenia patients have some disturbance in cognitive performance (11–12). These areas of dysfunction, though significant, do not support the conclusion that broad, irreversible cognitive deterioration is the rule in treated schizophrenics nor that the varied and variable "negative symptom syndrome" is entirely the result of neurologic deficits. It is not even clear that the "negative symptom syndrome" is an entity.

Recent research (13–17) suggests a more reasonable view of the schizophrenic syndrome, where "positive symptoms" (hallucinations, paranoia, agitation) are seen as functionally and neuroanatomically distinct from discrete yet profound disturbances in subcortical, frontal, and prefrontal cortical brain activity. These latter "deficits," which may conceivably vary in severity, can explain many of the symptomatic features of schizophrenia: impairment in task performance on problem-solving; becoming overwhelmed by excessive stimulation from the environment; difficulty processing the emotional complexities of interpersonal relationships; and ineffective use of learned patterns of coping with stress or challenges (18–20).

If this accumulating research is accurate, then it begins to explain part of what clinicians see in their work with schizophrenic patients. There still remain the perplexing problems of amotivation, apathy, avolition, and withdrawal, which are often such a prominent and discouraging aspect of the syndrome. Such symptoms may be revealed to be due to further, as yet undiscovered, discrete neurological deficits; in some patients they may be part of a depressive syndrome. Our thesis is that in many patients these "negative" symptoms are part of the psychological reaction to the illness process itself. Furthermore, denial and the often associated convictions stemming from delusional interpretations of events represent, in part, a psychological response to the illness. Although distorted ideation originates in physiologically provoked perceptual distortions, delusional symptoms are the consequence of a complex elaborative and integrative psychological process.

The essential hypothesis of our model is quite straightforward:

1. There is a complex biological basis to the schizophrenic disorder.
   a. There are also secondary, physiologically determined phenomena (e.g., depressive syndromes).
2. Significant aspects of the "symptomatic picture" of schizophrenia are manifestations of psychological responses to the disorder or efforts to adapt to it (however well or ill), involving the innate resources of the mind and demanding of the clinician an understanding of cognitive mechanisms and "psychodynamics" (which we would consider an aspect of cognitive functioning).
   a. Social behaviors, which include relationships with caregivers, are heavily influenced by these psychological reactions and are often a major barrier to effective engagement in and motivation for treatment.[a]
   b. While all behavior, or mental activity, may ultimately have a biological basis (i.e., we are not attempting to "separate" psychological and biological processes), it is useful to think of some aspects of the schizophrenic patient's mental life as part of the "normative" process of adaptation to stress.[b]

With this conceptualization of the disorder, we can devise a rational approach to the treatment of the schizophrenic individual with any modality:

1. Those symptoms that we know to be physiologically stimulated and for which we have somatic treatments (usually medications) are first treated appropriately and with respect for the complicated effects of these treatments.[c]
2. The symptoms or behaviors that "remain" after such treatment are addressed according to the following priorities:
   a. Efforts are made to determine if symptoms or behaviors have a cognitive or psychodynamic basis and are worked with accordingly.
   b. Those symptoms and behaviors that are persistent, not currently remediable with somatic treatments, and not available to work within a cognitive, behavioral, or psychodynamic paradigm are clarified and studied carefully, and efforts are then made to help the patient adapt to these limitations (e.g., prefrontal cognitive disturbances that impair instrumental role functioning).

The preeminent focus for all clinicians, however, must be to establish and maintain the treatment alliance. This is an ongoing task and often must precede other efforts, particularly in the case of the "noncompliant" patient. Among other goals, the treatment philosophy must communicate to the patient the idea that he or she can be understood; that the "illness" represents but a part of his or her mental experience (although a dominant and pervasive influence); that he or she is not utterly debilitated, helpless, or to blame for what has happened.

As clinicians, we must provide patients with a model of effective coping, which assumes their participation and contributes to their self-respect. Our treatment programs should help patients achieve an available, plausible understanding of themselves. At the same time, we must take into account that the patient's view of his or her psychotic experiences has been heavily influenced by the intensity of those events and the patient's perception that the hallucinations or feelings of suspicion are or were accurate. The "truth" is indeed never so simple as "our way" or "their way." The patient's rendition of reality must be respected as the most accurate representation of his or her inner experience, and, therefore, as a crucial source of data for teaching us about the patient's frame of reference, which is a necessary first step in establishing an alliance.

Many treatment programs are limited in effect because they do not address these concerns. The schizophrenic patient is too often given prescriptions, whether for medication, rehabilitative treatments, or other therapies, without a concomitant effort to help him or her understand why or how the treatment will help and without placing the "prescription" within the context of the patient's subjective experience. Clinicians are inhibited in this regard by their uncertainty of the most effective means of coping with the patient's denial or delusional convictions. The matter is too often resolved by attempting to convince the patient that his or her perceptions or beliefs are simply wrong and that the clinician's view must be accepted. Conflicts, noncompliance, or passive compliance characteristically arise from such confrontations. The treatment alliance is further strained when, in the face of serious impairment in some aspects of the patient's cognitive functioning, as well as dejection, resentment, and consequent withdrawal, the clinician or therapeutic staff assume that the patient is globally impaired and beyond help. Therapeutic despair is then not uncommon and often unavoidably communicated to the patient through the clinician's withdrawal or avoidance or through an expression of resentment toward the patient for rejecting his or her efforts.

In any treatment, as we attempt to establish a basis for collaboration and to educate the patient about himself or herself, we will encounter several obstacles. The patient may, under the influence of overwhelming paranoid attitudes, mistrust our intentions. What we are describing may represent an unacceptable narcissistic injury. To the degree that schizophrenic individuals are aware of their inability to control their mental life, our confronting them with this fact may occasion feelings of horror, humiliation, and hopelessness. Any treatment experience is potentially quite difficult for the schizophrenic individual, who may manifest distress through increased paranoia, oppositionality, or withdrawal rather than overt acknowledgment of sadness or fear of what is happening. It is also true that the patient may experience relief that someone appears willing to openly confront what he or she, and others, have sought to conceal or avoid.

Much of what we discuss will be relevant to the work of psychotherapists attempting to interest and maintain schizophrenic individuals in treatment. But we chose to write this book about treatment alliance because we felt it to be a crucial, yet often unappreciated, component of all treatment paradigms. Psychotherapy may have an important, even pivotal, role in the maintenance of the treatment alliance with the chronic schizophrenic individual, but all therapies require a treatment alliance, and clinicians of every discipline face the same stresses and obstacles in working with this patient group. Multidisciplinary treatment represents the only possible approach to the treatment of schizophrenia—no single therapy can address all of the problems posed by this illness. It is therefore critically important that practitioners have available a model of the disorder and of the treatment philosophy and goals and understand the basic workings of the treatment alliance so that consistent treatment efforts can be applied.

UNDERSTANDING THE CRISIS IN THE TREATMENT ALLIANCE

Treatment of the schizophrenic individual usually begins with the assessment and pharmacological amelioration of such symptoms as hallucinations, agitation, and disorganization. Later stages of treatment focus on the patient's difficulties in social and occupational functioning. Poor outcome, or noncompliance, is usually seen to be the consequence of "positive" symptoms that are too-little responsive to medications or the debilitating effect of severe "negative" or "deficit" symptoms. While this formulation may, in some cases, be true, we have found in our own work that outcome and compliance are more dependent on the nature of the treatment alliance than on any other single variable. This is, to a degree, a conceptual distinction, because the nature of the treatment alliance is certainly influenced by the prevailing symptomatology and the severity of the illness' manifestations; however, the distinction is not a facile one because disturbances in the treatment alliance implicate psychological mechanisms that are also distinct from "positive" or "negative" symptoms. In addition, although attention has recently, and appropriately, been focused on the "negative" symptom syndrome, failure to appreciate the importance of the treatment alliance will hamper clinicians' attempts to engage these patients in rehabilitative or other treatment strategies.

The treatment alliance is especially troubled by the persistence of delusionality or irrational denial (which are often associated). Clinicians struggle to cope with these phenomena that often limit the effectiveness of the treatment process. What seems most troublesome is the difficulty in persuading patients to reconsider their firmly held views. Patients can often hold apparently contradictory positions (e.g., "My problems were caused by people who were torturing me because I was evil," and "I'm afraid there's no cure for me"), yet still resist acknowledging the utility of medications, the value of hospitalization, or of after-care treatments. One factor explaining the intensity with which delusional ideas are held may be the nature of the physiological-perceptual experience, such that the individual experiences these distorted "facts" and "events" as real. Irrational (sometimes delusional) denial, however, reflects not only distorted perception but the fear of profound narcissistic injury.

In our experience, virtually all patients who present with a delusional view of themselves and their experience or with dense, irrational denial are also unable to relinquish their convictions, to change their point of view, at the start of a treatment program. Some patients will persist in their distorted view of the world throughout their treatment; but such patients, though not all perhaps, can nonetheless develop a workable treatment alliance and participate effectively in treatment. To accomplish this, clinicians must be able to identify the obstacles to the treatment alliance and have in mind strategies for engaging the patient, either despite the obstacles or sometimes by using these apparent barriers to our and the patient's advantage.[d]

Three broad patterns of maladaptation characterize troubled treatment alliances. These may represent an individual's maladaptive responses to the illness rather than symptoms of the illness itself. We will note them here and discuss them in greater length:

1. Maladaptive Resentment or Grandiosity
   a. need to blame others for plight, often coupled with rage and envy toward the world, which combine to successfully keep potential helpers at a distance; unrealistic estimation of ability to manage self and symptoms (e.g., 'I can stop my symptoms if I want"; "I choose to retreat into fantasy"; or "I am above earthly matters")
2. Delusional Conviction or Denial
   a. persistent belief in a view of events that precludes, in whole or in part, participation in treatment [e.g., "I am already dead"]
3. Demoralization
   a. apathy, amotivation, withdrawal

As we noted earlier, these represent responses to the symptoms of the illness, which have a direct and significant impact on the patient's interpersonal functioning and on his or her attitude toward treatment efforts. Although each behavioral or cognitive pattern is influenced by the characteristics of the illness, these complex phenomena have significant psychodynamic components.

To facilitate our consideration of these concepts, we will present three vignettes of patients who manifest symptoms or behaviors that present challenges to the formation of a treatment alliance. Each case is slightly different and suggests unique problems and different solutions. All are drawn from our experiences in working with schizophrenic individuals in supportive psychotherapy.

Case A: A Dialogue from Two Perspectives

A woman in her early thirties presented with a ten-year history of psychotic symptoms, frequent suicidal ideation, and poor treatment compliance. Neuroleptic medications were able to bring about only partial remission of her symptoms and had not affected her suicidal intent. Antidepressant trials were equally limited in effect. She had not previously been seen regularly by any clinician, nor was she ever engaged in psychotherapy. She was bright and articulate and had a mild thought disorder that did not significantly impair her communication skills. Nevertheless, her life had been seriously disrupted by her illness.

At the time she first began to experience symptoms, she was married and considering graduate school with an eye toward a future career in academics. At that time, while separated from home by many thousands of miles and facing the strains of a new marriage and some financial difficulties, she began to experience a sense of mistrust, a feeling of being watched, as well as disturbing premonitions that suggested she had some foreknowledge of important world events. She gradually became convinced that she had powers of prophetic perception and that she possessed information that could affect the course of world events. She began to interpret statements made on the radio and television as containing messages to her from international agencies. As she remembers, these statements made over the media were unambiguously directed at her. She subsequently became convinced that her home was under electronic surveillance because these agencies were desperate to know what she knew.

Her marriage deteriorated in part because her husband was

troubled, even angered, by her suspicious concerns and also because she became anxious and withdrawn, uncertain and socially
uncomfortable. She was divorced soon after, was on her own,
terrified and despondent for a time, then lived with her parents
until the time of admission. She had a few prior hospitalizations,
precipitated by suicide attempts or threats. Despite her intelligence
and educational background, she was able to work only when in
settings where the expectations would rarely threaten her. She
found that she became extremely, unmanageably anxious when
supervisors were critical or impatient. When workings as a sales
person, irritable or difficult customers would provoke similar, disabling anxiety. If faced with a problem for which she had no ready
answer, she was terribly frustrated to find that she could not reason
out a solution. It was as if she were quite stupid, though she was
not. She felt helpless and confused, frightened that she seemed
unable to use her intelligence. She said she felt tortured all the time
and was intensely mistrustful. She hoped there might be an answer,
a way to stop the torture. At times she wondered if she were crazy,
but then felt convinced that her perceptions had been accurate all
along. She did believe she was losing her mind, but as a consequence of perpetual mental torture rather than mental illness.

On admission to the unit, she described this past history as if it
had happened to someone else. However, when she spoke of the
early days of her marriage and of her initial happiness and sense of
peace, she became sad and said that she felt angry at herself for
having let all of that happen to herself. She said this despite the
fact that in the same interview she acknowledged that she still
believed that these events (her premonitions, the electronic surveillance, etc.) had really happened. The interviewer at that time did
not ask her to try to resolve the incongruity between her statement
that she was responsible for her plight and her conviction that
those events had really happened to her. Believing that the patient
could not, at that time, reflect on her (unconscious) uncertainty
about the veracity of her delusions, he chose to begin by focusing
on her tendency to blame herself for events that were clearly not
under her control. She acknowledged that this had been a lifelong
characteristic and had first appeared in the context of her relationship with her mother.

Several weeks later, the patient asked the therapist how he understood what had happened to her. He told the patient that, based on her statements and his ongoing observation, he thought she had suffered a prolonged psychotic episode. This would be hard for her to acknowledge, he went on to note, for a variety of reasons, one being that acceptance of her illness would make it harder for her to blame herself. "You'd rather think of yourself as bad than ill. That way you can continue to beat up on yourself."

On hearing this, the patient was initially distraught, not the least because, once again, she had been unable to find someone who would support her view that she was persecuted. For some time, her treatment focused on her need to blame herself and her anger at her therapist for accepting rather than punishing her. Gradually, though not endorsing the "illness" model, the patient began to demonstrate interest in the coping strategies presented to her and listened while her therapist described how feeling suspicious or experiencing troublesome mental events (hallucinations, premonitions) need not paralyze her.

She learned about managing anxiety and stress with medications as well as through other techniques. The staff presented their understanding of why it was hard for her to solve problems by pointing out the role of anxiety and demoralization and suggesting that it was possible to find a way around these impairments and to find jobs that did not lead her to confront them as often. She also began to consider that her suspicious views of others might be based on distortion and that others' behaviors could be explained by less malignant motives than those she had imagined. She and her therapist devised "tests" that could help her to evaluate people's motives, to see whether a less suspicious attitude brought about better relationships and better predicted people's behavior.

Case B: An Agreement to Disagree, and Yet Work

A man in his late twenties had been ill for several years and, despite a number of hospitalizations, had not been able to recover any meaningful involvement in social relationships or in work. He had several times been treated in day programs and halfway houses but usually dropped out after a few months. He would then live in an apartment alone or with a friend for several months without purposeful activity, subsisting on welfare until he manifested a worsening in his symptoms that would require his rehospitalization. Most people working with him had given up and described him as a "burnt out schizophrenic."

A clinician began to work with this young man in an attempt to help him realize his potential and make use of his evident personal attributes, which included a remarkable warmth, generosity, and persistent faith in himself and others despite all of his difficulties. After one year in once-a-week outpatient supportive psychotherapy, he presented a complaint about someone who had insulted him in public. At the time of the session, the patient had been living in a half-way house and engaged in a day program for one year. He had recently decided to look into obtaining training in a field in which he had had prior experience.

Throughout the year, the patient and his therapist had had many discussions regarding how they might separately understand the patient's experiences. These included recurrent auditory hallucinations, ideas of reference, and delusions that during sleep he had left his own body and performed various criminal acts about which he now felt guilty. It was not without precedent, therefore, that on this instance the patient asked the therapist how he ought to respond when a stranger in a department store said to him without provocation, "You helped 'Son of Sam' perform all those killings." The patient had considered confronting, even assaulting, his accuser or calling the police—the latter idea least favored because he was afraid they might believe the other man.

The patient had previously accepted as a possibility the idea that sometimes he heard things that were a product of his own mind and that, in particular, his experiences of moving outside of his own body might not actually have happened. Nevertheless, on this occasion, when the therapist suggested this possibility to him, he became defensive and said that it was impossible that he had made up what was said to him. The therapist pointed out that having a hallucination did not mean that one "made up" the experience for it would certainly seem as if it had actually happened. They discussed ways of understanding how hallucinations occur and how they are perceived. Nevertheless, the patient insisted that the event actually took place. The clinician acknowledged that he could neither convince the patient nor prove what had happened, and so he asked the patient how he could be of further help. The patient said he was troubled by the implication that he was evil. The therapist reviewed their history together, emphasizing the therapist's experience of the patient as a caring and generous person who, although capable of anger and resentment, had shown no evidence of the outrageous tendencies of which others appeared to be accusing him and, indeed, of which he appeared to be accusing himself. The patient agreed, tentatively, that this view was more accurate than the one presented by the stranger in the department store. He did not feel he had consciously done anything terrible nor that any actions performed while he was in control of his behavior had ever resembled the crimes he worried he might have committed while "asleep." The patient was slowly able to accept his therapist's recommendations. Although he might disagree with the therapist about what had happened in the department store, the socially acceptable and, in the end, most comfortable recourse for him would be to ignore such insults, although he might continue to worry about their meaning. He accepted the fact that confronting strangers in the way he had contemplated might create embarrassing situations for him.

At the conclusion of that session, the patient continued to insist that the therapist was wrong in not "believing" his account of the actions of the accuser, but he acknowledged: "What you say about me not being as bad as he said I was seems to make sense. So I can see your point about not doing or saying things that would get me into trouble, like hitting him or calling the cops."

Note that the patient and therapist agreed to disagree about the "facts." The therapist's decision to conduct the interview in this manner demonstrated respect and allowed the patient to participate while confronting the presumed distortion. In turn, the patient was able to consider more appropriate behaviors. Had the therapist insisted on his position (i.e., "the accuser's words were a hallucination"), he and the patient would have become locked in a struggle. The patient was not ready to consider the delusional nature of his perceptions. By saying what he did, the therapist presented a rational view of the events and coping strategies, while implicitly recognizing that, over time, the part of the patient that questioned his delusional beliefs would gradually be able to identify with the therapist and his views.

Case C: A Common Route of Avoidance

A 35-year-old woman was readmitted to the hospital after having lived for the previous three years on the streets of New York City. She had been briefly hospitalized two years previously because of paranoid delusions and deteriorated health. This time, she was hospitalized following the efforts of a community crisis team, which picked her up in a confused, debilitated, and battered condition. The patient requested transfer from a city hospital to the private institution where she had been treated several years before. That prior treatment had included two years on a long-term unit for schizophrenic patients. When she arrived, she told the doctor with whom she had worked in the past that she was frightened, that her life had been horrible over the past three years since she had seen him, and that she wished now to participate in treatment and would accept referral to a halfway house and day program, a plan that had been suggested several years before but turned down by the patient because it conflicted with her principles.

The patient believed that she was the subject of a mind-control experiment performed by the CIA and that her one mission in life was to expose this corruption and to bring her tormentors to justice. She was hampered, she maintained, by the fact that in her view this plot involved everyone whom she met.

In her prior hospital treatment, the patient had attempted to enlist her therapist and other staff in her struggle, to have them support and champion her cause. When she returned to the hospital on this occasion, she again renewed her plea, asking that the therapist make special efforts to help her. This included her demand that staff call the CIA to insist that they release information on her.

She was admitted to a general inpatient unit, populated by men and women primarily in their third and fourth decades of life. Most of them suffered from schizophrenia or other serious psychiatric illnesses. Despite this fact, this patient stood out amongst the group as clearly bearing the ravages of chronic illness and a hard life on the streets of New York. She was socially withdrawn, anxious, dressed bizarrely with excessive layers of clothing, and walked about the unit with furtiveness and mistrust that was disturbing to others. In addition to her belief in the mind-control conspiracy, the patient also had come to believe that she had a religious mission in life and reported frequent visual hallucinations of the body of Christ, which had appeared to her while she was praying in church.

Her physical condition improved during the three weeks she was in the hospital. Although she became less overtly disorganized and anxious, it was clear that the minimal demands for socialization, maintenance of personal hygiene, and participation in some therapeutic activities produced anxiety and insecurity. She was confronted with how severe her impairment in role functioning was. Tasks that were difficult for her were more easily accomplished by other people, in particular tasks related to relationship-building. We do not know how consciously she perceived these difficulties. It was perhaps for this reason that, despite her early evidence of commitment to seeking a different life for herself, the patient left the hospital and when last heard from had returned to her life on the streets, seeking refuge in churches and shelters for the homeless.

Each of these patients share common responses: denial; intermittent compliance with treatment; a conviction about a certain way of viewing their experience that is at odds with how we understand their symptoms and what is happening to them; and feelings of despair and futility. And yet, each of these individuals presents a very different story. Their involvement in or withdrawal from treatment follows patterns related to, but not wholly determined by, either their character or the nature and severity of the illness from which they suffer. We seek to understand what can account for their symptoms and, in particular, how their attitudes about their symptoms dispose them towards treatment.

We speculate, although we do not know, that there may be physiological factors that produce such symptoms as denial and the conviction that one's perceptions are accurate and that others are mistaken. We do not as yet have a model for understanding such denial as a consequence of organic factors, but we may discover that this disturbance is at least instrumental to the development of schizophrenia. Do these patients prefer to believe in their view of themselves, or are they utterly con- vinced of that view as a consequence of the workings of their own perceptive apparatus?[e] Being utterly convinced of one's view of the world may be a consequence of the way in which the mind evaluates what it experiences. Yet, we may consider that these patients maintain their delusional views because to do otherwise would require them to acknowledge their experience of the world to be a disordered or unreli- able one.

Perhaps this explains why, in the second example, the patient who had previously been able to acknowledge hallucinations later resisted that assertion. His original endorsement of his 'hallucinations" may have been partial or tentative. He may have remained skeptical yet hopeful, the hope fueled by the knowledge that his treatment had been associated with improved functioning and a pronounced reduction in the frequency of his hallucinations. Had he been harboring a hope that those experi- ences would stop as a result of the hard effort he had put into his treatment? His disappointment in the unanticipated recurrence of his hallucinations in the absence of any apparent, external precipitating event may have been enough to bring about the denial and contentious- ness that marked the beginning of that session. This state nonetheless yielded to the clinician's assertion that the patient was a good and worthwhile person who still, despite difficulties, could manage to cope with his life and secure happiness for himself.

This is not to say that the patient was helped simply by the therapist's asserting, "You are a good fellow." Rather, the intervention took place, necessarily, as a series of steps. First, the therapist defined the boundaries of what he could and could not do regarding the patient's experience of an event happening outside the office. The therapist made clear his inability to "prove" to the patient that the event he felt had occurred (the reference to "Son of Sam") did not occur. However, based on all the therapist knew, he was convinced that the event did not happen as reported, and he communicated this to the patient—though he acknowl- edged that he lacked the ability to convince the patient of this point of view. Second, there is an area wherein the therapist had direct experience of the patient: that is, in the office, in their treatment sessions. From his direct observation and experience, the therapist could indeed draw accurate conclusions about the patient: "Since I wasn't there, I can't, with absolute certainly, say that no one said those words. However, given everything that I know both about you and how the rest of the world operates, I'm 99 percent sure that no one other than yourself accused you."

Third, when these conclusions (such as that the patient is not evil) refuted or were in conflict with the patient's view of himself or others, the therapist could then, with authority, challenge the patient's assumptions. To facilitate the patient's ability to listen to this alternative point of view, it was helpful to first identify with the patient the adaptive aspect of his perceptions: "I could certainly understand your wish to place the blame outside yourself. If I thought I might have committed terrible crimes, I could imagine that feeling others were blaming me might even be a kind of relief."

The patient's denial may have been a result of some feature of his underlying disorder or a psychological mechanism that attempts to shut out painful realities; but in neither case can we simply assault misperceptions. The patient who holds a distorted view of himself and others is suffering a deep sense of isolation and struggling to maintain self-esteem. We also assume (and in time find) the "denying" patient in some way aware of his distortion. To assume otherwise is to take the unwarranted position that the patient is capable of destroying reality! The exercise of denial implies the individual's recurring confrontation with the stress of truth.

The evidence that delusional convictions can be supported by the need to protect self-esteem, or maintain a particular view of the self, is represented in the clinical observation that some patients, like the first two described here, can reconsider their delusional views and admit that they may not be accurate when psychological concerns related to the patient's necessity to maintain these delusions are addressed.

In the first case, the patient's overwhelming sense of rage and helplessness, both at not being able to function and because of her persecution, was empathically appreciated by the therapist. Thereafter came an understanding of how the patient characteristically tended to blame herself, thus turning the rage inward. Note that the understanding, to this point, was independent of the patient's delusional system. It was the stuff of everyday life that concerned her and with which we must empathize; but it is the stuff that, for her, became the medium in which the delusional system incubated. The need to punish oneself is troubling but, in contrast to the experience of being pursued by government agents, not extraordinary. By translating the bizarre into the usual, we connect the patient with the rest of us, and ourselves with the patient.

From this example we can see how, in order to help the schizophrenic individual, the clinician must have a good understanding of the patient's ideas about herself and the world—that is, the patient's subjective experience. We cannot create meaningful goals until we understand what the patient desires and how she perceives her difficulties. And we must learn how to make use of the patient's perspective in formulating a treatment strategy.

BUILDING THE TREATMENT ALLIANCE

A treatment alliance should be based on an agreement between the patient and the clinician concerning the goals and means of treatment. This does not mean that patient and clinician agree fully about all aspects of the treatment or about all of the goals. There is, however, no basis for meaningful work if there is no common ground or no common goal. This task first requires exploration of the patient's view of self, illness, and treatment and explication by the clinician of his or her observations, conceptual framework, treatment proposals, and expectations. Both of these tasks require a good understanding of the nature of the illness and how it affects the individual. We wish here to review the conceptual model of schizophrenia with which we work and which we ultimately seek to present to the patient.

The relevance of explaining our thinking to the patient is not generally appreciated; nor is the task easy. In particular, because of the complexity and subtlety inherent in the treatments, it is important for clinicians to translate into comprehensible analogies or to reduce to essentials the principles and modes of action of treatments. This is especially critical in work with innately mistrustful patients, who tend to attribute malevolent intentions to the environment, particularly when they are confused or threatened. Further, the likelihood that most delusional patients cannot be persuaded to renounce or abandon their misperceptions makes it incumbent on any clinician to learn innovative techniques to make our knowledge and methods available and, where possible, acceptable to the schizophrenic patient.

Making what we do and how we do it visible to the patient is an important early step. For example, a patient who was given to magical thinking, especially related to fantasies of merger with his therapist (a common phenomenon in work with schizophrenic patients, representing a wished-for union with another, that may be partly erotic as well as dependent, reflecting helplessness and a need for strength, angry, jealous, and consumptive, and usually highly dereistic), expressed the belief that previous therapists had been able to read his mind. The therapist, alerted by this statement, made an observation, careful to detail the constituent data of his conclusion:

Dr.: Because I see you fidgeting in your chair, and note how much you are sweating—on a rather cool day—and can hear your voice sounding higher than usual, I conclude that you are anxious; about what I do not know, but if I am right, perhaps we can explore why this might be so.

This intervention exemplifies the principle of careful, patient, detailed explication, which is crucial to the method we present. Although not presenting a complicated physiological or psychological model here, the clinician is sharing with the patient details that illuminate the means by which the clinician makes conclusions, how he or she goes about the job. The very persistence and equanimity required for and communicated by this style are often helpful in reducing a schizophrenic patient's anxiety and mistrust.

Many clinicians have difficulty formulating a model of schizophrenia that both adheres to what is known about the illness and allows for communication with patients and families. In part, this is a consequence of the welter of theories in the schizophrenia literature. In part, it is due to the heterogeneity of schizophrenic syndromes. Schizophrenia is not a uniform disorder; nor is outcome easily predictable. Too frequently the strains in the treatment alliance with the patient or family are a result of the clinician's assumption of an attitude of certainty (about prognosis, severity of course, etc.) where no certainty exists. In attempts to be frank, to help prepare families for often-predictable stresses and disappointments, clinicians (unfortunately) seem to the families to scatter hopes, to obscure uniqueness, and to suggest a kind of knowledge and authority we do not possess. We should resolve, at the outset, to abjure false certainties and present the science we have as clearly as we may, acknowledging its limitations and our own.

It is important to begin with a discussion of our understanding of the nature of the illness with which these patients struggle, to define what serious and significant problems they must face as well to delimit the boundaries of the illness and the boundaries of our information. We will proceed with the task we initiated above, which is to discern among the symptoms of the disorder those that may be primary to the illness and those which may, in whole or in part, reflect the patient's efforts to adapt to his or her condition.

We have noted that the common current distinction between positive and negative symptoms, or positive and negative syndromes, in schizophrenia is in itself confusing and limiting. It has arisen, in part, from nineteenth-century phenomenological descriptions of schizophrenia (which were heavily influenced by the assumption that schizophrenia was etiologically related to "other dementias")—ideas that, although challenged by Bleuler and others, continue to persuade some in the field, and color clinical depictions of the disorder (consider the persistence of the image of "irreversible, progressive deterioration" many still associate with schizophrenia, despite evidence that this picture is not accurate for most schizophrenic patients) (21).

The reasons for the prevailing conceptual bias regarding schizophrenia are complex and unclear. Although Jackson (6) first proposed the notion of "positive" and "negative" syndromes, the roots of this model lie even further in the past. The works of Kraepelin and Bleuler (22–23) have each contributed to these developments. Kraepelin, in particular, linked schizophrenia to the dementias and rigidly to a disease model that did not describe a role for psychological adaptive functioning in the production of "symptoms." Bleuler's nosologic contributions have inadvertently focused attention on the most noticeable symptoms of the disorder, as they have dominated clinical descriptions of the illness. We must now direct our attention back to other, subtler aspects of the schizophrenia illness process, including the disturbances in ego functioning also addressed by Bleuler.

In doing so, the conceptual limitations of the neo-Kraepelinian perspective on negative symptoms are immediately evident. While we must acknowledge the role of brain pathology, the complexities of the psychological presentation of the individual with schizophrenia are also apparent. Nevertheless, writers such as Brenner (24), while making valuable contributions to our understanding of the cognitive psychology of schizophrenia, virtually ignore the importance of the individual's sense of self, experience of the illness or treatment, and other psychological, psychodynamic variables. It is disturbing that this bias (especially the notion that negative symptoms are simply expressions of neurologic deficits) affects so much of the field's current theoretical framework. It is even more troubling that this attitude contributes to a therapeutic ennui, with clinicians and families feeling helpless and discouraged when confronting the chronic, debilitating symptoms of this disorder.

We contend that the positive/negative dichotomy has contributed to a stagnation in clinical research and treatment of schizophrenia. The theory is often associated with the presumption that "negative" symptoms are uniformly symptoms of a neurologic "deficit" state (resurrecting the assumptions of the nineteenth-century model of dementia praecox). By compressing a varied and variable disorder into two artificially neat "syndromes," the basis for the heterogeneity of schizophrenia is lost.

In particular, the idea that the patient's psychological reaction and adaption to the disorder plays a role in the production of the syndrome is not considered. Coping, improved adaptation, self-understanding, and self-acceptance are extraneous to these descriptions, as is the likelihood that these patient characteristics might influence outcome. Patients and families, when presented with the "positive/negative" or "flagrant symptom/deficit symptom" model, could well be expected to experience discouragement and resignation that may preclude more effective adaptation.

We have a way of thinking about the disorder that, while consistent with what is known, does not needlessly discourage us nor our patients and their families. This model includes ways of breaking down often confusing symptomatic pictures into categories that help us to see which symptoms may be treated appropriately with medical interventions or rehabilitative interventions as well as which treatment will best address the profound disturbances in self-esteem and the burden of despair with which these individuals struggle.

A MODEL FOR
UNDERSTANDING SCHIZOPHRENIC SYMPTOMATOLOGY

In Table 1.1, we propose a categorization of the most significant symptoms of schizophrenia. We will discuss the meaning of the specific categories, but one can see immediately that our approach recognizes the complexity of schizophrenia and the likelihood that a number of different processes are at work. We specifically oppose the lumping of schizophrenic symptoms into either positive or negative groups alone; and our method reflects our theoretical bias, thus differentiating this system from the undiscriminating "laundry list" in DSM III-R.

Under section I, we describe what we currently understand to be the physiological substrate of schizophrenia. We label these "primary" disturbances because currently available literature indicates that these symptoms seem most closely related to the principal underlying physiological disturbance. In support of this argument, we would like to briefly explore current knowledge regarding the physiological components of this disorder. This discussion is based on a reading of an eclectic body of literature, some of which is referenced in our bibliography. In particular, we find support for our views in a recent paper written by Dr. Daniel Weinberger (25). He has reviewed a great deal of literature as well as his own experience in studying schizophrenic individuals and proposed a conceptual organization of the disorder that may account for its confusing presentation. What we offer here is an integration of our thinking, his work, and the work of other theoreticians and scientists.

Most readers will be familiar with the basic concepts regarding the neurophysiology of schizophrenia; to those who are not, we strongly recommend a review of this topic. There is an excellent overview in *Psychiatry*, edited by Michels and Cavenar (26), and a thorough examination of the research literature by Noll and Davis in *Schizophrenia and Affective Disorders*, edited by Rifkin (27). Both texts are highly useful and clear. Professionals who find these references too medically oriented are recommended to Andreasen's summary of recent advances in the field (28).

Researchers have long believed that many core schizophrenic symptoms were based on a dopamine-excess condition, principally because of the purported site of action of neuroleptics, as post-synaptic dopamine-

Table 1.1

I. "Primary" Disturbances in Schizophrenia (Physiological Substrate)
   A. Limbic Dysfunction
      (Mesolimbic Pathways)
      1. Perceptual Disturbances
         a. Hallucinations
         b. Illusions, ideas of reference (see below)
         c. Déjà vu experiences, "Epiphanies," *Anwesenheit*
      2. Suspiciousness, paranoia
         a. Idea of reference, overvalued ideas (consisting of distorted attribution of meaning)
      3. Anxiety, agitation
         a. Disturbances in self-object differentiation ("ego boundaries")
         b. Depersonalization, derealization
         c. Agitation, excitement
      4. Irritability
         a. Hostility, aggressiveness (also "disinhibited" behaviors)
      5. Other affective experiences, including grandiosity, elation, etc.
   B. Subcortical, Cortical Dysfunction
      (Subcortical Nuclei, Prefrontal Cortex, Mesocortical Pathways)
      1. Cognitive Impairment in:
         a. Problem assessment, analysis, planning
         b. Stimulus discrimination (frontal lobe)
         c. Retrieval of stored patterns of response to stress (thalamic dysfunction)
      2. Consequent disturbances in integrative capacities and in instrumental role functioning
   C. Uncertain, but probably Organic Etiology
      1. Amotivation, apathy, avolition (see below)
      2. Restricted affect, narrow ideation (see below)
      3. Neuroleptic-responsive affective symptoms (Hirsch et al.) [40]
   D. Thought disorder (? 2° to prefrontal cortical disorder)
II. Secondary Disturbances, with Physiological Basis
   A. Depression, and Other Mood Disturbances
      1. Major Depression (frequently misdiagnosed)
      2. Subaffective Syndromes
   B. Iatrogenic Symptoms
      1. Parkinsonian Syndrome: Psychomotor retardation; poverty of content of thought
      2. Medication toxicity resulting in cognitive impairment
   C. Disinhibited affects, behavior
III. Psychological Responses to Illness
   A. Efforts to Achieve Safety and Decrease Stress
      1. Common behaviors: social withdrawal, denial of painful realities

Table 1.1 (continued)

about illness, cognitive avoidance, persistence in unrealistic plans, delusions, idiosyncratic solutions
  2. Goals of these behaviors: decreasing anxiety or confusion associated with social interactions; aiding in self-object differentiation; avoiding experiences that confront the patient with impairment in psychological continuity and clarity; increase sense of autonomy and control (however unrealistic); defense against acknowledgement of loss; defending self against perceived threats from the environment.
  B. Maladaptive or Dysfunctional Patterns
    1. Resentment or Grandiosity
      a. Predominant anger, resentment, oppositionality; undermining efforts at helping
      b. Unrealistic view of control
    2. Delusional Conviction or Denial
      a. Efforts to explain experience, under influence of abnormal mental states (especially physiologically induced suspiciousness)
      b. Resistance to self-examination because of narcissistic injury
      c. Maladaptive consequences denied or ignored
    3. Demoralization and Withdrawal
      a. Not having "model" that suggests ways to help self, improve self-esteem, and exert meaningful control (internal locus of control)
      b. Social and emotional withdrawal, both adaptive (decreases stress) and maladaptive (dysfunctional)
      c. Excessive self-reproach
IV. Symptoms of Uncertain or Mixed Etiology
  A. Amotivation, Avolition, Apathy
  B. Restricted Affect, Narrow Ideation, Anhedonia, Decreased Curiosity, Decreased Sense of Purpose
  C. Lack of Insight
    1. ? Cognitive component

receptor blockers. Recent literature (29–30) has pointed out the limitations inherent in the theory. Dopamine activity may be related to the flagrant symptoms of schizophrenia (hallucinations, delusions), but these may alternatively be associated with serotonergic neuron hyperactivity. It is noted that there are two classes of dopamine receptors, with the D_2 receptor apparently being most closely associated with neuroleptic activity. Whether blockade of the D_2 receptor in fact explains antipsychotic activity is uncertain, though most investigators feel this is so. Noradrenergic neuron metabolism may be correlated with anxiety states and thus implicated in the genesis of schizophrenic symptomatology. The rele-

Figure 1.1

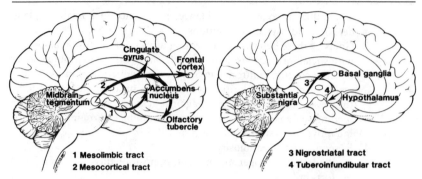

1 Mesolimbic tract
2 Mesocortical tract
3 Nigrostriatal tract
4 Tuberoinfundibular tract

Source: E. Richelson, "Schizophrenia: Treatment," in *Psychiatry,* ed. R. Michels and J. O. Cavenar, Jr., vol. 1 (New York: Basic Books, 1987), 15. Reprinted by permission of J. B. Lippincott Co. and the author.

vance and clinical or phenomenological significance of anatomical abnormalities, such as ventricular enlargement and decreased cerebral mass found in some schizophrenic populations, is also uncertain, although this data has been presumptively linked to the "deficit" theories of schizophrenic cognitive disturbance. Whether the symptoms, which most investigators now label "negative symptoms," are due to cholinergic deficiency states or other physiologic disturbances has also been debated.

Weinberger's model postulates that the primary, or inciting, lesion in schizophrenic individuals is a disturbance in the functioning of dopaminergic neurons in the prefontal cortex (see Figure 1.1). In fact, the localization of an "inciting lesion" is not crucial to our model. Whether this hypothesis is later substantiated, as Weinberger has set it forth, the elements essential to our discussion have to do with the proposed neurophysiological and phenomenological distinctions between classes of symptoms. These distinctions can be made whether or not the anatomic relationships discussed by Weinberger are true. Our interest is in differentiating the kinds of symptoms experienced by schizophrenic patients.

The prefrontal and subcortical regions of the brain have been associated with abnormal function in schizophrenic patients (13, 31). The abnormality is particularly apparent when schizophrenic patients are asking to do psychological tests (e.g., the Wisconsin Card Sort) requiring integrative, organizational cognitive functions. These latter are mental operations that help the individual determine how to approach mental tasks efficiently, analyzing tasks, prioritizing, and utilizing experiential information. This specific cognitive abnormality is correlated with decreased activity in the dorso-lateral prefrontal cortex (DLPFC), when brain-imaging studies (PET scans) are done during test-taking.

Studies done on rats (32) suggest that the DLPFC is significant because it may exert a tonic modulatory effect on subcortical catecholamine systems (i.e., nerve pathways using the neurotransmitters norepinephrine, epinephrine, dopamine, and so forth). As shown by a large body of research, the subcortical region of the brain, is vitally important to cognitive functioning (33–34). Disturbances such as those postulated here impair the individual's capacity to organize or process stimuli from the environment; to make use of learned patterns of thinking or behavior in coping with stress or challenging tasks; to evaluate and respond to the subtleties and complexities of social interactions, which require extensive use of stored, instinctive coping strategies.

Abnormalities in these anatomic pathways may, implicitly, vary in severity among schizophrenic patients. This may account in part for heterogeneous presentations. In addition, variable degrees of impairment also provide an explanation for the effect of stress on symptoms. The impairment represents a diathesis, so that certain stresses (psychological and physiological) may cause variable degrees of disturbance and different consequences. This variability may also account for differences in age of onset of schizophrenia, a topic about which Weinberger presents a stimulating hypothesis; however, that discussion is beyond the scope of our current task.

The cortical disturbance in the prefrontal cortex, often referred to as a syndrome of "hypofrontality," and the subcortical dysfunction, which may be a consequence of this disturbance, have other ramifications. As Weinberger describes in his paper, these regional dopamine deficiency states may stimulate excessive, compensatory activity in the midbrain, a critical regulatory center (see Figure 1.2). Decreased activity in the mesocortical pathways (involving the DLPFC and subcortical regions) signals the midbrain to produce more dopamine, according to Weinberger's hypothesis. But the mesocortical pathways are damaged or dysfunctional, and cannot utilize the dopamine neurotransmitter or, perhaps, deliver it where it is needed. The increased levels of dopamine may "spill over" into the mesolimbic system, which is a nerve pathway leading from the midbrain to brain structures involved in the integration and

Figure 1.2

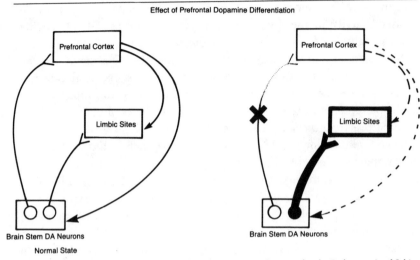

Effect of Prefrontal Dopamine Differentiation

Source: D. R. Weinberger, "Implications of Normal Brain Development for the Pathogenesis of Schizophrenia," *Archives of General Psychiatry* 44 (July 1987): 665. Reprinted by permission.

modulation of emotional experience and perception (i.e., the limbic system).

We know that individuals with disturbances in the limbic system (e.g., epileptics who have seizures that affect this area exclusively) experience perceptual disturbances (hallucinations), anxiety, confusion, paranoid states (feeling watched, threatened) and other phenomena (35–36). Drugs that overstimulate this region can produce psychosis. The inappropriate and incidental (or secondary) stimulation of these pathways may thus account for the flagrant or "positive" symptoms of schizophrenia. Neuroleptics, by "blocking" dopamine activity in the mesolimbic system, decrease these distressing symptoms. Ironically, these medications may worsen the deficit in the mesocortical pathways, perhaps accounting for the findings of cognitive impairment in some schizophrenic patients treated with high dose neuroleptic regimens, impairment that remits when medication doses are lowered and the patients become less "Parkinsonian" (37–38).

This theory, incorporating Weinberger's seminal contribution, offers the possibility of constructing a hierarchy of symptoms, such as we have outlined in Table 1.1. The disturbances in the limbic system may be correlated with those symptoms that are most neuroleptic-responsive

Table 1.2
"Negative" Symptoms

   I. Due to Subcortical or Prefrontal Cortex Dysfunction
  II. Expressions of Psychological Response to Core Illness
 III. Symptoms of Unclear or Mixed Etiology
 IV. Iatrogenic
  V. Misdiagnosed Symptoms of Superimposed Depression

---

and that have been called "positive" symptoms by others, as noted under section I.A. Most importantly, this theory allows us to make a crucial distinction between those other manifestations of the disorder, often described as "negative" symptoms, identifying those that are directly, or secondarily, a consequence of disturbances in the prefrontal cortex or subcortical region (involving the mesocortical pathways) and those that may be due to other causes. Indeed, Weinberger's hypothesis points to the essential error in grouping all so-called "negative" symptoms together.

The disorders caused by abnormalities in mesocortical pathways lead to marked impairments in cognitive functioning (14) and thus to decreased "instrumental role functioning" (performance in tasks, interpersonal situations). These disturbances can account for much of what has been called the "negative" symptom syndrome, but not all. Phenomena such as social withdrawal, amotivation, and lack of interest in treatment are complex behaviors, which must represent more than the results of discrete cognitive disruptions. We wish to distinguish, amongst those symptoms which have been variously considered part of the "negative" symptom syndrome, those that are clearly a direct or proximate consequence of the prefrontal or subcortical disturbances noted above, and those which may have other causes. In Table 1.2, we have delineated these as follows: symptoms due to subcortical or prefrontal cortex dysfunction; symptoms that represent psychological responses to the disorder (including, in many patients, social withdrawal); symptoms having an unclear or "mixed" etiology, perhaps representing interactions of physiological and psychological processes (including the syndrome of amotivation, avolition, and apathy); "negative" symptoms that are, in fact, iatrogenic, due to neuroleptic administration in many cases ("Parkinsonism"; psychomotor retardation; poverty of content of thought); and those symptoms that are due to the often overlooked coincidence of a depressive syndrome superimposed on an acute or chronic schizo-phrenic illness (39). This analysis of "negative" symptoms is reflected in the structure of Table 1.1. Each of these categories can be found under a heading that most closely reflects our thinking about etiology.

It is important to note that we are not denying the existence of the symptoms that some investigators have studied as part of the "negative symptom syndromes"; rather, we are questioning the validity and utility of that conceptual grouping of symptoms. The analysis we have pre-sented above appears to us to be concordant with the available research data. It has the further advantage of clarifying what has been an obscure situation. Treatment and treatment research have been limited by the assumption that the negative symptom syndrome has a unified etiology and that all aspects of the "syndrome" might be expected to respond to the same, though as yet unavailable, treatment.

In a recent review, Hirsch (40) describes how many of what are commonly considered "negative symptoms" may be neuroleptic-respon-sive when they appear as part of the prodrome to decompensation, or recurrence of an acute psychotic episode. Indeed, Docherty et al. (41) presented a schema, with experimental support, suggesting that the early phases of relapse were marked by psychological (and physiological?) overload or "overextension," which could produce symptoms such as withdrawal, narrowed attention and ideation, alienation, "feeling over-stimulated," anxiety, and irritability, progressing to more overt symp-toms or psychosis. These behaviors may represent attempts by the indi-vidual to "compensate" for what is happening psychologically (e.g., avoidance or restriction of distressing stimuli, thoughts, and social con-tacts; obsessional thoughts and behaviors as responses to anxiety). This "compensation" is not necessarily willful, for it may be mediated by cognitive processes influenced by the physiological disturbance. Never-theless, these psychological states may be partly controllable through the patient's active effort.

These phenomena point to the complex nature of symptoms that result from an interaction of psychology and physiology. Social with-drawal or narrowed ideation are provoked by a physiologic disturbance and, as Hirsch points out, can improve if the physiologic disturbance is treated. But these phenomena are behaviors, or cognitive patterns, that the individual may be able to recognize and influence. They may be adaptive if they reduce anxiety or stress; or maladaptive if they increase dejection, demoralization, anxiety or ineffective coping. They may be approached, then, in the same way that cognitive maladaptations are in the treatment of depression.

In the treatment of the schizophrenic individual, it is important to realize that the patient's efforts to cope can be helpful in recovery. It is equally important for the patient to acknowledge this. A conviction of helplessness supports paranoid or delusional interpretations of events and contributes to demoralization, which will surely worsen the course of the illness and preclude collaboration and more effective adaptation.

We do not intend to outline here a rationale for the role of cognitive therapy in the treatment of acute schizophrenia. By this discussion, we hope to convince the reader of the validity of our assertion: that physiological responses to the physiological disturbances in schizophrenia exist and are important in the conceptualization of the disorder and its treatment. The social withdrawal that appears in the acute prodrome of schizophrenic decompensation is a psychological, behavioral response to "unseen" disturbances. Similarly, social withdrawal in chronic schizophrenia is an adaptation to that state and to the physiological and psychological events at work within the individual.

Items II and III in Table 1.2 (and corresponding sections in Table 1.1) represent those areas of the symptomatic presentation of chronic schizophrenia where the subtle interaction of physiological disturbance (and its sequelae) and psychological response is most active. Certain behaviors and cognitive patterns seem to us more clearly adaptive (and/or maladaptive) than others: These are listed in section III of Table 1.1. Behaviors such as avolition, amotivation, and apathy appear to have a strong physiologic component and perhaps an undiscovered organic etiology. But it is also possible that they can be influenced through the active effort of the patient—that they represent psychological reactions that can be altered. These latter behaviors are noted in section I of Table 1.1 and again in section IV, reflecting our high index of suspicion regarding the important role of organic factors in the production of these particular symptoms.

Also in section I of Table 1.1, we note that the thought disorder, which is quite prevalent (though not uniform) in chronic schizophrenic patients, has a primarily organic, or physiological, etiology. Researchers (15–16) point out that this syndrome is more properly considered a disorder of speech production. Schizophrenic individuals are impaired in their capacity to organize speech as well as in other aspects of linguistic activity. It seems, intuitively, that this disturbance is linked to the disorders in the mesolimbic pathways in schizophrenia, but this remains to be elucidated. One important corollary of linguistic research in schizophrenia, however, is that while speech production is often quite impaired, speech comprehension is not equivalently limited. Comprehension of conversational speech by schizophrenic patients is not infrequently unimpaired, despite the presence of a "thought disorder," although the attribution of meaning to what has been said is frequently subject to delusional distortion.

Of particular importance with respect to the focus of this book is the material contained in section III of Table 1.1 (we will pass over section II, which is self-explanatory; these issues have in any case previously been addressed). Here we outline the conceptual core of this book in the assertion that certain aspects of schizophrenic symptomatology represent "psychological" responses to the illness itself and further that these responses may be altered.

We term these "psychological" reactions because they have identifiable cognitive and psychodynamic significance and, importantly, because they are responsive to interpersonal therapies and to the action of the patient's own psychological development and will. The mind, in a sense, demands these responses—which can be both adaptive (by decreasing stress or anxiety) and maladaptive—that satisfy internal psychological priorities. These priorities, as we shall endeavor to illustrate, grow from the central experiences of mistrust, inefficacy, desperation and loss, which typify the schizophrenic person's experience.

With our, albeit rudimentary, knowledge of the cognitive and psychological disturbances visited upon schizophrenic patients, we may appreciate how demanding and disappointing is their everyday life. In addition to disturbed perceptions, such as hallucinations, which are most often frightening or confusing (although many patients report gratifying and reassuring hallucinations that themselves pose unique challenges to the clinician), these patients frequently have ideas or convictions that are refuted or labelled as "crazy" by family and others. The disheartening consequences of such inevitable alienation, the frustrations associated with being unable to convince others of one's beliefs, in addition to the other disturbing manifestations of the illness, combine to undermine self-esteem in the schizophrenic individual and serve to bolster maladaptive cognitive and behavioral responses.

Because of the subtle cognitive impairments experienced by most (if not all) schizophrenic patients, as well as the fundamental disturbance in trust, interpersonal relations are commonly felt to be extremely stressful. The demands that such interactions place on us all—for vulnerability, empathy, reflection, and spontaneity—challenge or threaten the schizophrenic individual's existing adaptive functions. The schizophrenic persons's access to learned patterns of social coping is limited by the prefrontal and subcortical deficits delineated previously. We must often carry on an effort at understanding without the patient's active assistance, for frequently the patient is either uncertain as to the nature of his or her difficulty in relationships or mistrustful of revealing what he or she knows. In interactions with our patients, we may observe their responses to social demands and wonder: What does this encounter evoke and require? How am I being experienced?

We can describe behaviors that reflect this quandary and the patient's efforts to cope with stress. Most apparent is social withdrawal, a central feature of schizophrenia. This behavior may have complex origins, as we shall discuss at later points in our argument, but it can first be seen as a simple maneuver to decrease the stress associated with social interactions. Often, withdrawal is complicated by feelings of demoralization and futility, by resentment and a wish to punish others through self-negation, or by grandiose delusions of omnipotence and control. These latter represent, in part, psychological reactions to the illness that reinforce the stress-reducing behavior of withdrawal. If we seek to change this pattern because of its deleterious consequences to self-esteem and social functioning, we must bear in mind that this withdrawal serves at least one important purpose.

The patient's search for an explanation of his state of mind confronts him with threatening questions. Few patients are able to acknowledge they have symptoms that distort their thinking. That these patients so often manifest denial of their condition may be due to obscure physiological factors that affect judgement as well as cognition. It is also true that denial is a ubiquitous and predictable psychological response to the mental states we have described. Therefore, it is not remarkable that we confront denial in attempting to establish a treatment alliance with the chronic schizophrenic individual. When our patients do develop the capacity for acknowledgment of their condition and a commitment to seeking and accepting help, it is testimony to their endurance and courage. For those not yet able to meet the psychological demands of such acknowledgment, denial serves as a barrier (although always a permeable one) to the intolerable.

A closely related phenomenon is one we have dubbed "cognitive avoidance," by which we mean the effort to obscure or frustrate meaning, to block inquiry, to refuse to take seriously the significance of one's behaviors and statements. While most schizophrenic patients demonstrate some degree of thought disorder (which may be rooted in a physiological disturbance), many patients strive to make themselves obscure. What we refer to goes beyond straightforward denial or simple avoidance: It represents the willingness of some patients to use their communication difficulties as a screen, to appear more debilitated than they are. The aim may be to avoid the stress of scrutiny or the threat of change that understanding and help might offer. Such patients may also be obliquely expressing resentment about their condition and unconsciously acting out self-punitive impulses.

Like denial, persistence in unrealistic plans may represent an unconscious wish not to acknowledge the disturbing realities of a situation marked by dyscontrol and shame. The intensity of these patients' assertions and their durability in the face of logic and concern often inspire frustration in others. A degree of grandiosity often colors this persistence, as well as the fantasy that the individual can control events, people, or his or her own psychotic symptoms, as in the following illustration:

A young man was hospitalized three times within two years on an inpatient unit. Despite clear evidence of symptomatic recurrence on discontinuation of his medication, he insisted that this time he would be able to stop his neuroleptic with impunity. When challenged with the bald facts of his history, he would triumphantly assert that he now understood why he had become ill. He would then offer as explanation a reminiscence about an interaction with his family that he had allowed to get the better of him, occasionally invoke his marijuana use (even if temporally dissociated), and maintain that he could tell the difference between "real" thoughts and psychotic ones, thus ascribing his readmission to the consequences of fatigue, misunderstanding, or the maliciousness of his parents. He stated once, when particularly pressed, that he could make himself have psychotic thoughts, that these were entirely voluntary, and that they could be stopped at will. If he had not stopped them in the past, it was because he was angry or tired or sad.

Delusions represent a challenging and confusing problem in the assessment of schizophrenic symptomatology. They are ubiquitous, frustrating to clinicians, and polymath in their psychological functions. These phenomena surely have a basis in the physiological disturbance that typifies this disorder, but they are also complex phenomena that require cognitive elaboration, defense, and support with logic and rationalization and that, as we have previously seen, can change. Delusions, in our view, are an elaboration of primary mental events, such as illusions and misperceptions, into a framework that rationalizes these events to the schizophrenic individual. Because this process of elaboration implicates the action of unconscious psychological and cognitive forces, the delusion also informs us about the individual's subjective experience of his or her illness. The delusion is an effort at creating coherence, at defending the self from the disturbing implications of disordered mental events, and a depiction of the inner psychological state of the schizophrenic individual.

In writing his lucid and moving case history of his patient, whom he called Aimée, after the heroine of the patient's tragic novel, Jacques Lacan said:

> Organic psychiatrists tend to regard a delusional system as the intellectual elaboration of organically-determined phenomena. Its structure, according to them, is of little importance. We cannot accept this formulation. We believe that the primitive phenomena discussed above (oneiroid state, incomplete perceptions, misinterpretations, illusions of memory) cannot explain how a delusional system can become established or account for its particular organization. In our view the crucial factor lies in the personality of the subject, and this allows us to regard the development of the psychosis as a process disorder. (42)

In his argument, Lacan links two assumptions that are relevant to our conceptualization of delusions: first, that organic psychiatrists regard delusions as the elaboration of organically determined phenomena; and second, that those same psychiatrists view the structure of the delusions as unimportant. We agree with the idea that delusions are elaborations of primary phenomena; but we also assert, along with Lacan, that the structure of the delusion is relevant and meaningful and that it is unique in each patient because each schizophrenic patient's personality is unique. It is the personality, the unconscious mental life together with the individual's characteristic cognitive patterns, that lends specificity to the delusional constructions.

The delusion, like denial or grandiosity, can protect the individual from stress, help him avoid threatening experiences, and fend off, to a degree, the narcissistic injury associated with the illness. This latter function may help to explain why delusions are persistent even when patients are otherwise symptomatically improved. Relinquishing the delusion would occasion a crisis in the individual's self-perception. As with any psychological defense, the delusion will not change as long as a significant motive (e.g., protection from narcissistic injury) remains. We can see from our biological model that delusions cannot be expected to respond to neuroleptics. The primary mental events (illusions, hallucinations, a mental state of suspiciousness, or irritability, etc.) that underlie the delusion may be decreased in frequency or intensity along with other mesolimbic phenomena; but the delusion represents integrated, global cerebral activity, which is reinforced in memory and becomes a deeply embedded component of the individual's self-view. We can "eradicate" delusions only by over-medicating our patients to the point where they cannot think; or we can communicate to our patients that it is unhealthy or unacceptable to hold delusional views—and can then be assured that we will hear nothing further of them.

Delusions may serve other functions as well, including (as we have noted) functions that actually support more effective functioning. For example:

A 29-year-old male schizophrenic was told by his halfway house counsellor that if he continued to stay in bed rather than go to work, he would have to leave. The patient then developed the delusion that he was being drugged and that he needed to resist. To do so required him to "be up and about and productive." Shortly thereafter, he resumed working.

These psychological responses meet certain needs, some of which we have listed in Table 1.1, section III. A.2. These psychological factors are a window into the subjective experience of the schizophrenic patient. Our ability to understand that experience will greatly determine the success of our treatment alliance.

Many of these psychological goals have been discussed above: the effort to decrease stress, threat or anxiety, whether in the form of social interactions; confrontations with experiences that might cause injury to self-esteem; or conflict brought about by paranoid interpretations of motives or events. We also note some concepts that we will elaborate in the next chapter: the need to stabilize one's sense of self; to experience a sense of separateness from others; to see oneself as effective and capable of controlling oneself and one's environment as opposed to feeling helpless, controlled (perhaps by delusional forces), and ineffective; and the need to cope with the intense experience of various forms of loss—of abilities, of hopes, of a sense of continuity with a "past self," of relationships, jobs, and other social structures.

In Table 1.1, we also list (section III.B) three important patterns of behavior that might be described as syndromal since they are frequently observed to be characteristic responses in schizophrenic patients (although any given patient may demonstrate aspects of each or some of these categories). These categories are useful in helping us organize our thinking about symptoms and behaviors that are traditionally seen as disorganized, purposeless, maladaptive, or dysfunctional.

We note, however, that these behaviors, when studied closely, can often be seen to have important functions and sometimes to assist the patient in meeting social demands or support other useful adaptations.

Our discussion should make clear the potential for the development of frustration and resentment in schizophrenic patients. This anger may be obvious, appearing in the form of an outright hostile stance (perhaps reinforced by feelings of mistrust, misperception, or misinterpretation of motive). This hostility itself may direct patients toward a more delusional view of self and environment, in that the delusion may offer a means to avoid conscious acknowledgment of pain, disappointment, and loss and may support unrealistic feelings of power and control, which are gratifying despite their lack of substance. Anger directed at caregivers may spill over into attacks on others of whom patients are envious, who may be seen as the authors of their torment (through a delusion of persecution), or whose expectations may be threatening. Concurrently patients may act out a tragedy of self-denial and self-punishment because of unconscious anger and blame they direct at themselves. Their hostility may exacerbate symptoms and most assuredly will preclude effective recovery.

The connection between unconscious anger and anger directed at others may also be expressed more subtly in patients who may seem superficially compliant and placid, but who manifest their anger through private disregard for the help offered them, through a kind of quiet rebellion of conscience, in which schizophrenic individuals see themselves as prisoners in a corrupt world where they must be careful not to reveal their sacred disavowal of the notion that they are ill. Words, intentions may be attacked in secret, as in this case of a schizophrenic young man:

> The patient was well-liked on the ward, and seen as dutiful, eager to please, and "devoted" to his therapist. In one session, the patient complained that he had trouble remembering, or taking in, what his therapist said. When asked to describe what happened as he listened to his therapist, he spoke of the words "not getting through." Exploration by the therapist yielded the patient's acknowledgment that he liked the sessions for the opportunity to talk himself and have his therapist listen; but when the therapist spoke, the patient, although outwardly pleasant and attentive, would silently think "bullshit, bullshit, . . ." and repeat this as long as his therapist spoke. He acknowledged that his behavior was partly related to longstanding resentment about feeling ignored by his parents, but that it was largely a consequence of his fear that his therapist might have contradictory thoughts or introduce ideas that would threaten his view of himself. That self-view, he revealed, was tenuously constructed on the optimistic premise that nothing was wrong with him and that the disturbing psychotic episode from which he had recently recovered was really misinterpreted by his family and the unit staff.

Many patients, of course, are less resentful than this; if they resist help, they do so in less flagrant ways. One common manifestation of subtle resentment is an unrealistic view of control over one's symptoms.

Patients, commonly in discussing their medications, will assert that they can prevent themselves from becoming "psychotic" if they choose. This statement is supported by their rendering of what recently occurred or had occurred on previous occasions when they became dysfunctional. Patients usually describe these episodes as having been associated with a state of awareness: "I knew what was happening" or "I could see that I wasn't making sense." Sometimes they will impute a psychological motive to their failure to take control: "I was angry at my parents," "I was depressed, I didn't feel like doing anything," or "I wanted to get out of where I was living." Many of these explanations seem implausible, if not frankly irrational. Sometimes, patients will propose idiosyncratic or bizarre rationales that are colored by their delusional preoccupations but that share the theme of lapsed control that can be reasserted.

This unrealistic view of control is damaging in several respects. It is clearly motivated by the wish to avoid injury to self-esteem, but it often leads to noncompliance. Further, it is an unreasonable position that implicitly and unfairly assigns blame to the patient, blame for not having acted to prevent the psychotic disruption. Patients may be willing to accept this assignment of responsibility in return for avoiding the acknowledgment of their impairment and their limitations in managing it. Clinicians may view this as simply dysfunctional or as an irritating obstacle to the treatment alliance. It does also, however, consciously or unconsciously, resonate with the emotional experience of self-blaming, self-revulsion, and despair that suffuses the schizophrenic individual's psyche. This shame is a crucial aspect of patients' distress, about which they have great difficulty talking and which, further, they do not allow themselves to see.

That phenomenon of denial, as well as the closely associated patterns of delusional conviction about oneself or others, is yet another maladaptive psychological response to the illness experience, and the next point in Table 1.1, section III.B.2. Our understanding of delusions fuses a physiological and psychological perspective: Delusions originate in disturbed perceptions and represent a psychological process that aims at organizing disordered experiences, while simultaneously responding to the emotional demands of the psyche. Most particularly, delusions are an effort to arrive at an explanation of experience that protects patients from the threat posed by their feelings of loss, anger, and self-blame. Denial, as it is commonly manifested in schizophrenic patients, may also have a physiological basis, but this is as yet an unsubstantiated notion. Whatever the etiology of these phenomena, they are usually not resolved by medications and must be respected as redoubtable features of the patient's psychological constitution.

This pattern of defensive behavior is pervasive in schizophrenic patients—and so intense in many that we cannot fail to be impressed by the severity of the threat to the self, against which these mechanisms are engaged. The resistance to self-examination not only bedevils the clinician in his or her efforts to promote a treatment alliance, but in effect prescribes behaviors for the patient that lead to damaging and self-defeating consequences, which are themselves ignored or denied. Consider the following:

> A young man who had a several-year history of recurrent psychotic decompensations associated with noncompliance (and rapid recrudescence of symptoms after medication withdrawal) insisted that he was "fine" and planned to resume work as a tennis professional after leaving the hospital. He maintained that his symptoms were lies fabricated by his family because they did not approve of his lifestyle. As a consequence of his illness, exacerbated by his denial and noncompliance, the patient had not worked in several years and played tennis irregularly. Although it was not clear whether with treatment he could function in this role, the patient had clearly damaged himself by his persistent avoidance of treatment. When ill, he could not, and would not, practice tennis. His physical condition and his reflexes had deteriorated to the point where he was not able to play competitively. He complained that medications impaired his ability to play; but his denial and refusal of treatment had plainly racked his physical and emotional health.

Because this problem of defensiveness and resistance to self-examination is so intimately associated with the work of treatment alliance formation, it will be a major focus of our discussion over the next several chapters.

We come now to the third of our maladaptive paradigms, that of demoralization (see Table 1.1, section III.B.3). Much of what we have presented speaks to this theme in the mental life of our patients. The trauma and conflict that inspire discouragement or despair are readily understandable. But there are specific aspects of the condition and, unfortunately, of many treatments that predispose to demoralization, and it is to these that we must direct our analysis. We must also look to what we know about demoralization, as it has been studied and described in other settings.

Fear communication theory (43–44), which has recently been an important component of public health planning in relation to the AIDS epidemic, is drawn from studies of some populations' responses to presentation of vital and disturbing health information. Research has been done on the most effective methods of educating the public about the dangers of cigarette smoking or other behaviors associated with health risk. The conclusions of these investigations have a commonsensical character: They state that, with regard to any potentially dangerous behavior, there is a critical amount of information that must be presented in order to promote change in at least a significant proportion of the population. There is also, however, a point at which such a presentation, by virtue of being too intense, inflammatory, or doom-ridden, becomes overwhelming and actually discourages change. If, in the process of telling people about the dangers of smoking, you exaggerate the health consequences, even in the interest of healthful persuasion, people are likely either to ignore the argument (considering it shrill and unrealistic) or resign themselves to smoking if they conclude that their bodies are already irrevocably damaged. If in warning people about the risk of AIDS, you alarm them so much that they feel that they and everyone else are doomed to get the disease eventually, regardless of precautions, then those persons will not take appropriate measures to protect their health.

What is essential for effective participation in a health program and for collaboration with health professionals is, researchers say, an appropriate but not excessive degree of concern about oneself and a conviction that reasonable measures that will protect or promote health are possible. The individual must feel that it is within his or her power to effect change and that the goals are comprehensible, attainable, and desirable. Few of us would adhere to a thoroughly bland and colorless diet, for instance, regardless of our concern about cholesterol and fat.

These issues overlap another area of research concerned with patient attitudes that affect recovery from illness as well as acceptance of and compliance with medical treatments. Investigators have noted that an experience of control is crucial to recovery from illness and a good predictor of compliance (45–48). One study looked at people recovering from a heart attack. Individuals were studied in the ICU shortly after admission and rated with respect to their attitudes about what had happened to them. Predictably, patients who denied they were at all seriously ill and who left the hospital abruptly or did not return for follow-up had the poorest outcome. They could not consciously accept the idea that they were vulnerable and ill, and their health, not simply their compliance, suffered. Surprisingly, patients who frankly admitted they were ill, who fretted and were cautious, afraid to stress themselves, reluctant to push themselves back into life, also did poorly. They were more compliant in the sense that they passively submitted to treatments. But they were not active collaborators in their treatments and pursued an overly conservative and dependent style of adaptation. Their health suffered, too. The patients who had the best outcome, in all respects, were those who accepted their vulnerability, admitted they were ill, but were convinced that they would recover. They were determined to become healthy and active again and saw that they could reasonably enact changes in their habits and lifestyles that would produce meaningful health benefits. These patients, of course, were the best collaborators in treatment and had what we might call the best treatment alliance with their physicians.

Theorists refer to this conviction (that one has a role to play in one's own recovery and that individual actions can result in significant changes that can be described and appear attainable) as an internal locus of control. Rotter (49) developed a locus of control scale to study the extent to which individuals perceive the events following their behavior as resulting from their own efforts or as externally controlled. According to Rotter, a belief in an internal locus of control means that the person perceives an event to be "contingent upon his own behavior or his own relatively permanent characteristics" (p. 1). In contrast, attributing the same events to fate or malevolent others would reflect an external locus of control. The concept has also been studied with regard to health habits and is easily applicable to our population: The idea that one has a role to play in one's own recovery and that individual actions can result in significant change allows for the best treatment alliance. We see that patients with an internal locus of control enjoy a better prognosis and course of illness than those who do not. Indeed, individuals who do not believe they can exert meaningful control over their illnesses are prone not only to poor compliance and poor prognoses, as in the cardiac studies, but to the emotional states of depression and hopelessness.

Schizophrenic individuals suffer from an illness that assaults the very faculty through which we reason and perceive. The mind's active efforts are required to cope with serious illness, as we have seen; but in the schizophrenic patient the capacity to objectively regard the illness as an illness is impaired. What the person experiences and feels to be true has often already been distorted by the illness process itself. Having an internal locus of control is dependent on the individual's ability to circumscribe the illness, to see it as a part of him- or herself, but not the whole. It is necessary to objectify the illness, to see its limits and effects, and to imagine oneself coping with, remediating, and surmounting them. Schizophrenia is a condition that is limited in effect, though that effect is broad. Its particular quality, however, is that it involves an intimate part of the experience of the self, that the illness, in a sense, stands between the individual and his or her perception of self, of others, and indeed of the illness process.

Though there are aspects of mental life untouched by the illness experience, the disruption in functioning leads to an overwhelming degree of frustration and to a sense of having been severely traumatized. The essential character of the schizophrenic condition, including its chronicity, predisposes the individual to a state of demoralization. The adaptive ego functions that might be called into service in coping with serious illness are confounded, though not eliminated, by the illness process. Withdrawal, that is to say, isolation and alienation, and the associated phenomena of amotivation, apathy, and anhedonia are partly a manifestation of this demoralized condition. Indeed, much of what has been described as the "negative symptom syndrome" is attributable to demoralization and its sequelae. Schizophrenic individuals do not in most cases possess an accurate locus of control with respect to their illness (other than a delusional concept of control). In addition, their condition is chronic, debilitating, and associated with frequent disturbing mental events. The helplessness that schizophrenic patients feel, consciously or unconsciously, is as comprehensible as it is clearly damaging to their capacity to manage the symptoms of the illness.

We have noted that in presenting a treatment model and plan to a patient, clinicians should emphasize the seriousness of the condition, but not present so much information and in such a way that we contribute to whatever feeling already exists in patients that they have no role in their recovery or that meaningful change cannot occur. Yet, inadvertently, this is precisely what schizophrenic patients experience in many treatment settings. Treatment plans are presented with an emphasis on illness and debility and often with abrupt confrontations, such as: "Don't you see that your thinking is crazy—no one agrees with you," or "You have a serious illness, a brain imbalance . . ." On hearing this, patients are effectively, and expectedly, overwhelmed, if they have not been already—where do you begin building a life if you begin with the idea that your brain is diseased?

Preserved mental functioning, talents, and assets are not routinely presented along with the confrontations about dysfunction or debility. This is a good reason for extensive evaluation, including personality and cognitive testing. Those assets that are noted are not typically linked to potential in relationships or work. Recovery is not emphasized. If we knew that schizophrenic patients could not recover, we should of course be frank. But is our historical view of schizophrenia, of the "natural history" of the disorder, tantamount to knowledge, on which we can base a firm prognosis? Recent work, such as the Vermont Longitudinal Study by Harding et al. (21), seriously challenges the assumptions of previous studies, which, for the most part, were carried on in an era prior to refinement in diagnostic and research practices and before the intervention of the few available modern treatments (pharmacologic and rehabilitative). It seems to us that sober realism tempered with hope and support is the least our patients are due.

The point of this argument is, in part, that the cause of some of the maladaptation in chronic schizophrenic patients is the method through which their treatment and its goals are presented. We as clinicians have contributed to the distorted defensive postures of some schizophrenic patients by overwhelming them in our communications of our impressions and plans and by failing to provide the patients with a model for recovery that also incorporates the idea that they could manage or control some aspects of their illness.

For many reasons, patients do not feel they are being presented with treatment options for which they have responsibility and over which they have some control or choice. This is obviously not possible with dangerous patients, but many schizophrenic individuals are treated this way whether or not they are seriously a threat to themselves or others.

Their desires and opinions are more often dismissed or criticized than worked with, and their role in treatment is viewed by both parties as largely passive—accepting prescribed modalities. Because of their tendency to grandiosity and denial, patients' comments and goals or plans may be viewed by clinicians with exasperation and seen as but a treatment obstacle. In consequence, a genuine treatment alliance is not possible, and potentially dysfunctional alliances (passive, resentful, etc.) more likely. Clinicians must learn how better to work with schizophrenic patients' difficult behavior in order to develop collaboration.

Importantly, schizophrenic individuals must be helped to understand, as far as they are able, how the illness affects perception and thinking as well as what it does not affect. That there is preservation of normative ego functioning should be emphasized, so that patients can consider how to use their minds to understand themselves. The illness process can be demystified: Hallucinations can be viewed as an "anxiety" or "stress" response that can be met with various coping strategies, both psychological and pharmacological. Psychological maladaptation can be described and understood, and strategies developed for alternative methods of coping. Functional deficits can be approached through models of adaptive social functioning.

It is vitally important that psychological maladaptation not be confused with the illness process. Yet this tendency is quite common. In our view, this is a primary reason for the failure of many treatment alliances with schizophrenic patients. This conceptual error exaggerates the scope of the illness, contributes to the patients' experience of dyscontrol, helplessness and demoralization, and precludes the development of more effective psychological adaptation.

This issue cannot be more clear than in our approach to understanding the social and emotional withdrawal, the associated anhedonia and disinterest, and the often-associated denial, delusionality, and idiosyncratic relatedness, which are the hallmarks of the schizophrenic clinical "syndrome." We must unhesitatingly pursue psychological antecedents to these various behaviors, see meaning in their form and function, and assume that the schizophrenic individual has both some awareness of and some innate capacity to cope with them. That there are "biological" antecedents we also readily acknowledge. In turning our attention to psychological factors, we are placing our trust in the individual's resources of mind and spirit and seeking to draw what available potential we may from our patient. Even in the face of such a serious disturbance in mental functioning, inherent adaptive capacities may be identified and supported.

One specific psychological paradigm that contributes greatly to the experience of defeat, futility, and the self-abusive alienation from potential help is that of excessive self-reproach. We have alluded to this phenomenon earlier in the chapter, but it is worthwhile to underscore it because of its prevalence and maladaptive potential. This state represents the consequence of the patient's failure to satisfy the expectations that he or she associates with an "idealized self" and that are demanded by his superego. The individual experiences, predominantly unconsciously, intense disapproval of him- or herself. Some patients will report such feelings as part of their conscious experience, represented by comments such as "I am to blame for my illness," or they will identify with frequently repeated criticisms of their behavior by agreeing that they are simply lazy or arrogant. Patients themselves will often avoid understanding why they may appear "lazy" or "arrogant" and will not reflect on their confusion, uncertainty, or perceived need to defend themselves through haughtiness or derogation. They accept a superficial assessment of character functioning, perhaps because they have difficulty comprehending psychological motivation or, more probably, because their dynamic conflict about self-acceptance is played out in their self-abusive willingness to accept a distorted characterization. This unconscious self-reproach can, of course, be expressed in more patently self-damaging behaviors.

Finally, in Table 1.1, section IV, we note those aspects of the schizophrenic syndrome (along with others we have not listed) for which we have no clear etiological formulation. Amotivation and so forth have been associated with demoralization and may stand as prototypes for behaviors that have mixed etiology and are a "final common pathway" of symptomatic expression. Others may have more clearly organic or psychological etiology. This category, but a small part of what we do not understand about schizophrenia, symbolizes the necessity for a flexible and readily curious approach by the clinician.

At the beginning of this chapter, we proposed to outline a conceptual model of schizophrenia that is clinically useful, rational, and conducive to a sound treatment alliance. We have presented a model that divides schizophrenic phenomenology into five principal categories, which can be abstracted and reviewed with patients and their families:

1. *Mesolimbic Disturbances* are a manifestation of abnormal brain function. It is most important to emphasize that the patient experiences the consequent mental events as real. They constitute distorted perceptions (hallucinations, etc.) or mental states (e.g., irritability, suspiciousness). Although the cause is some disturbance in neurological functioning, these problems can be worsened by stress and can be likened to states of extreme anxiety.

2. *Subcortical, Prefrontal Abnormalities* may be hard to describe, but they can be likened to learning disabilities (cognitive impairments that limit the individual's effectiveness), while not implying necessary loss of intellect. These are subtle and serious problems, and, because of our limited knowledge, they are usually the most difficult to treat. Patients are not conscious of these problems and merely experience frustration and ineffectiveness about tasks. Families can be helped to empathize with this aspect of the disorder and to understand how problems here can provoke worsening of other symptoms.

3. *Secondary Physiological Disturbances,* such as depression or iatrogenic Parkinsonism, can also be described and treatments recommended. Assessing treatment efficacy requires informed collaboration among clinical staff, patient, family, and others in the patient's immediate environment.

4. *Psychological Responses* are crucial to an understanding of the patient and are inherently part of any interpersonal modality, including family work. It is here that empathy can be especially facilitated and here as well that the treatment alliance is placed in context.

5. *Symptoms of Uncertain Etiology* represent the mass of what we do not know about the disorder and provide a useful basis for discussing the limitations of our treatments but also the potential within the individual patient for meaningful recovery.

This model is comprehensible, although the amount of information is, from the perspective of our patients and their families, unavoidably overwhelming. The advantage of this model, in addition to its verisimilitude, is its clarity. Although many problems and complications are addressed, implicitly, at each step, there is a framework for understanding how a problem may be helped. The possibility of improved adaptation, and, indeed, of recovery of useful functioning is rationally supported. We can reliably link this model of schizophrenia to a plan of treatment and to the maintenance of hope.

The issue of the "negative symptom syndrome" has not been laid to rest by our discussion. But we hope that we have enlivened the debate and suggested fresh investigative approaches. Most importantly the presentation to this point should have provided the clinician with insights into the illness process, the psychological events which develop in an effort to cope with that process, and the subjective experience of the schizophrenic individual. It is this emphasis on the internal experience of the individual who is ill that is crucial to our method and will form the basis for further discussion of the technique of treatment alliance formation.

2

Understanding the Subjective Experience of the Person with Schizophrenia

Psychological responses reflect an individual's unique experience as well as the skills and limitations of his or her innate mental capacities. These responses are products of an organ that operates according to natural laws, depends on physiological functions, and organizes its activity with discernable and predictable patterns. When an individual, whether schizophrenic or not, meets a challenge, he or she utilizes past experience to deploy behaviors and make decisions. If that past experience does not provide useful strategies or if, in the near-instantaneous processing of memories and imagined options, debilitating associations impair effective responses, the person falters. Our accumulated reflections on our efforts to manage our lives contribute to our self-image, which in turn helps or hinders our progress. Clearly, for schizophrenic individuals, there is no meaningful, other than conceptual, distinction between biological and psychological perspectives of their experience, and no more important issue than that of their experience of themselves in the world.

The discussion in this chapter is organized according to the outline in Table 2.1. Our inquiry into the schizophrenic individual's subjective experience (1–7) begins with a theme that has been emphasized in the last chapter: If patients and clinicians are to establish a useful treatment alliance, it is essential that clinicians seek an understanding of patients' views of themselves including how they understand their symptoms; their "explanations" of events, internal and external, which others see to be the product of their illness; and their view of others' complicity, ignorance, or other responses to what has happened to them. This is done in a spirit of empathy, with the immediate goal of comprehending how patients experience their treatment, so that clinicians may, where reasonable, adapt their approach to the patients. Using this outline to

Table 2.1
The Subjective Experience of the Schizophrenic Person

    I. Literal, Stated Understanding of:
      A. Symptoms
      B. Illness Process
      C. Role of Others in Relation to Illness
      D. Treatment Process
   II. Subjective Experience: Themes
      A. Patient's Interaction with the Environment
        1. Attitudes toward relatedness
        2. Manifest communications
      B. Quality of Patient's Experience
        1. Self-object differentiation
        2. Sustaining experiences
        3. Psychological experience of continuity and clarity
      C. Concerns
        1. Autonomy and control
        2. Loss
        3. Safety
  III. Priorities, Flexibility, Demands
      A. Hierarchy of Priorities
        1. Conflicts among priorities
      B. Flexibility and Limitations
        1. Availability to treatment, to requirements of environments, *to change*
        2. What patient can and can't do at this time
      C. Demands Patient Makes on Environment
        1. Can treatment setting and caregivers meet the patient's expectations, and with what consequences?
        2. Feasibility of treatment alliance

obtain information that will simply be presented in the form of a confrontation, to convince the patients of the irrationality of their views, or to pressure them into acknowledgment of their illness is a misuse of the concept of treatment alliance and will be unproductive.

Section I of Table 2.1 directs the clinician to these primary themes, which are, appropriately, the focus of our initial contacts with the patient. While reviewing symptoms, performing mental status exams, and organizing the history of the patient's illness, we also assess the patient's psychological response to the illness, both his understanding of what is happening to him and his attempts to cope. How did he construe the onset of auditory hallucinations? Has he worked out a mechanism to explain why he hears voices or a rationale supporting his conviction that he is being persecuted? Has he found any maneuvers to decrease his anxiety? Such questions will not only inform our approach to the patient but will inestimably promote our rapport with him by showing respect for his views, even where those views conflict with ours.

The impact of this inquiry on the ambience of the treatment cannot be overestimated. In chapter 4, we present a detailed account of an initial interview with a schizophrenic man, where the clinician's exploration of the patient's subjective experience yields insights of evident and crucial importance to his treatment. The patient's view of "what has happened" was bizarre, so it is not surprising that prior treatment efforts encountered poor compliance. More importantly, the patient's humanity, his struggle with pain and isolation, had been obscured by the disjunction between the competing perspectives of his illness. The interviewer's patience and curiosity intrigued the patient and fostered conditional but significant trust. As a consequence, a richer appreciation of the patient's personality became possible.

The role of others in relation to "illness" is a theme that reminds us that in work with schizophrenic individuals:

1. No one is presumed innocent, and
2. Simple reassurance is not effective.

Since most people and, most importantly, family and friends, find it difficult to endorse the schizophrenic person's views, daily life confronts her with contradiction and disagreement. The patient must then explain, to herself, why others dispute her ideas, why they do not help her in the way she wants, or why they insist on her taking medications when she is not persuaded of the medicine's effectiveness. These conflicts are commonly resolved through delusional devices. No family member nor clinician or other caregiver can be assumed to be excluded from involvement in delusional systems. Indeed, the more important the person's approval, the more likely that his or her actions will be incorporated in the patient's delusional construction of experience.

Reassurance, statements asserting one's ignorance of persecutory plots, and so forth can be of little use, considering the forces supporting delusions. The patient must arrive at a construction of her experience that protects her from the injury of self-esteem associated with thinking that she is ill and that satisfies her wish for control or safety. To the extent that her delusional system fosters these ends, there is an intensity to these distorted perceptions that convinces the patient of their "truthfulness." Reassurance may be offered, as in the following example, but must be linked to an awareness and often a statement to the patient of our understanding of the incompleteness of this effort:

> A young schizophrenic woman told a staff member on an inpatient unit of her concern that the CIA had planted minute microphones in her eyeglasses. The staff member, in a well-meaning gesture, suggested that the patient could go to an eyeglass store, purchase new frames, and watch them put the frames together. The patient said she would think about doing just that.
>
> Later, the staff member was offended to learn that the patient had told her doctor that she suspected the staff member of having taken her glasses during the night in order to give them to the CIA so that the microphone could be installed.

We can only speculate as to why the staff member was included in the delusional system in this way. Perhaps the directness of the staff member's suggestion reminded the patient of how disturbingly devious was her own experience of people and events. The patient may as well have been angry that the staff member, like her family and her doctor, would not offer to write to the CIA on her behalf, about which the patient had repeatedly importuned her caregivers. That the staff member was offended, however, is an indication of that person's misunderstanding of the patient's subjective experience. The staff member might have added, after offering the advice about new eyeglass frames, the statement:

> "But I understand that this suggestion may not be helpful to you, for you may not trust my motives. I suppose you could come up with reasons why my advice would not be helpful. I am sure others have given you such advice, but it has apparently not solved your problem. In fact, the only "solution" I can see is based on my understanding that your belief is a symptom of the mistrust that is a result of your illness. But I also know that we disagree about whether you are ill."[a]

This response might not have altered the patient's reception of the staff member's statements or precluded the staff member's inclusion in the patient's delusion. It would, however, have given the patient pause to reflect on past experience and its implications for this and other current relationships, and it would have lent consistency to the staff member's interactions with that patient. Furthermore, in making this statement, the staff member would have been protecting him- or herself from disappointment or anger on hearing the patient's response. Understanding the model of the patient's psychology would allow the staff member to understand the patient's distortions and consider other interventions.

This vignette also illustrates how the totality of the patient's subjective experience, including but not limited to delusional interpretations of events, affects the treatment process. The patient described here manifested a pattern of tireless pleas to caregivers and others to help her uncover the plot against her happiness and her safety. It was important for clinicians working with her to appreciate the significance of this behavior, for it meant that, at this time, her participation in treatment was always considered in light of her conscious, ultimate aim: the unmasking of her CIA persecutors. She agreed to treatments, she said, because by being a "good" patient—that is, by being compliant and agreeable—she thought she might have a better chance of obtaining her clinicians' support in her dogged crusade. Although we imagine her unconscious motivation to be complex, her avowed attitude toward her treatment informs our understanding of her responses to treatment interventions.

Assessment of these components of subjective experience can and should be part of our initial evaluation of schizophrenic patients. Learning about the patient's perspective requires time and the development of some trust, but this perspective is more readily accessible than most clinicians assume. An understanding of the patient's conscious experience of the treatment process, in particular, is a crucial step, and a prelude to the evaluation of more complex psychological themes.

In Table 2.1, section II, we list three further aspects of the patient's subjective experience: (1) the patient's interaction with the environment, (2) qualities of the patient's experience, and (3) central concerns of the patient. The items listed beneath these three headings represent aspects of behavior or of psychological functioning that can serve as foci for our detailed inquiry into the patient's subjective experience. They are indicative of clinical themes that recur with regularity in, and are relatively unique to, schizophrenic individuals. Since they are not typically considered in nosologic or descriptive accounts of schizophrenia, these aspects of the schizophrenic person's experience are often overlooked or poorly understood. They should not, however, be interpreted as an exhaustive view of the individual's psychological life.

PATIENTS' INTERACTIONS WITH THE ENVIRONMENT

Like everyone else, schizophrenic individuals must cope with the insistent stresses of the environment. The environment is represented principally by people, with whom they do or do not wish to interact, as well as by the physical environment, made up of objects, spaces, and events. It is important to be open and flexible in observing how schizophrenic individuals experience that environment and how they adapt to it. We will be interested in how patients respond to people and what behaviors are associated with socialization. In some patients, it may be equally important to observe how they relate to pets or other animate or inanimate objects that may be psychologically significant. We suggest that the clinician pay particular attention to two areas: (1) attitudes toward relatedness and (2) the manifest communications of the patient. We will discuss these at length below.

Attitudes Toward Relatedness

By relatedness, we refer to the many and often peculiar ways in which schizophrenic individuals think about and relate to their environment. Relatedness takes on a variety of forms and is evidently influenced by abnormal perceptions, affects, and delusional ideation. The schizophrenic person may treat people with whom he has contact as if they are impostors, agents of some hostile force, who may pose dangers to him. Or, he may treat people as if they have no unique characteristics and are robots programmed by some central force with which he does battle. Less pathological examples include experiencing people as unvaryingly critical of his aspirations, such as his wish to be a professional athlete or a religious advocate. Such a patient might complain that all doctors or mental health professionals are united in an effort to obstruct him. He might believe that he has received a direct message from God in which he has understood the meaning of existence and been told he must convert others. Anyone disagreeing with his point of view, especially those who try to tell him he has an illness, are seen as unbelievers whose efforts represent the temptations of the devil. Since their aim is to distract him from his God-given task, they must be resisted.

The manner in which a patient pursues relationships and his attitude toward them is clearly a reflection of his subjective experience. We can learn about his psychological life by observing, and inquiring about, the behavioral patterns associated with relatedness. These have a significant impact on the ways in which he interacts with people in treatment situations as well as in everyday contacts. The patient who believes himself a prophet may have difficulty with informal interactions because his religious convictions intrude. Consequently, he may find people want to avoid him because they find interactions with him uncomfortable and unrewarding, which results, in turn, in the patient's isolation.

Schizophrenic individuals may desire more interactions but be dissuaded by psychological consequences. For example, the patient who believes he is a prophet may derive comfort from social interactions but deny himself pleasure because of the perceived primacy of his spiritual responsibilities. This fervor may be dictated by unconscious psychological priorities. To others he will appear dogmatic, intrusive, and opinionated. To himself, he says he is fulfilling his mission; should he be scorned in his view, he will accept this as suffering in service of the Lord.

There are many schizophrenic patients whose wish for relatedness is difficult to discern since it is satisfied through subtle, idiosyncratic means. Consider the regressed patient, who, because he refuses to bathe, is assigned a staff member to assist him with his personal hygiene. Such behavior may be seen as a consequence of severe cognitive disturbance or apathy and avolition. The patient may, however, be capable of these tasks but avoid them for secondary gain. Interacting with a staff member in this limited manner may provide the patient with the only safe interpersonal contact he can tolerate. In that sense, not bathing is his medium of negotiating contact with the world. At the same time, poor hygiene generally assures that most people will keep their distance, which may satisfy the patient's need to regulate stressful interactions.

Such considerations must be entertained in assessing the behavior of any schizophrenic individual lest we write off some patients, erroneously assuming that they are utterly indifferent to human contact. Furthermore, imagining that the human need for intimacy resides in even the most withdrawn patients allows for potentially creative and rewarding treatment interventions with persons who might otherwise seem hopeless and unengageable. Such efforts increase the possibility of empathy. They are equally important with patients whose level of disturbance is less severe but who may have significant difficulty in social functioning.

Clarifying the patient's pattern of relating to a significant figure (or figures) in his life is often critical in developing an understanding of what priorities he holds and what typifies his psychological life. We will illustrate this point by briefly describing some aspects of a psychotherapy that one of the authors undertook with a severely disturbed young schizophrenic man, focusing particularly on his relationship with his father.

> Sergio, a 19-year-old Italian male, had been summoned to the United States by his father, who had emigrated the previous year. The understanding within the family was that the father would establish himself in Boston and then would send for his son. Their combined incomes would be used to buy passage for the young man's mother and sister, who remained in Italy.

> After several months of working long hours in a pizza parlor and living an extremely frugal existence, the son discovered that his father was spending their savings on a girlfriend. It was at this point that the son began hearing the devil's voice, and he was admitted to the hospital where he stayed for four months. The father described his son as having been quite close to his mother and, apart from her, he had not socialized much while living in Italy. The father also felt that, as a child, the patient had been afraid of him.

> Shortly after admission to the hospital, the patient cut his wrist, dripping his blood on *Time* magazine's cover of the just-slain President Kennedy. Though the patient at that time spoke little English, he was heard to mutter over and over, "My father. Dead." He believed that he was the son of the slain president, that the devil was responsible for the assassination, and that Lee Oswald was a disguise the devil had used. In later versions, Oswald was

described as one of two human forms the devil took, the patient's biological father being the other.

During his first two years of treatment, the patient furiously insisted that the assassination had made him an orphan and that he wished to dedicate his life to the pursuit of his father's murderer. Frequently during these tirades, the voice of the devil (who was described in a way that suggested his father) would become more and more intense and threaten him. In the third year, Sergio began to discuss his sense of sorrow at being orphaned and, concomitantly, he gradually gave up his wish to avenge his "father's" death. On several occasions, he indicated displeasure at JFK's having left him and once announced that being a President's son had its limitations. After months of mourning, he no longer heard the devil's voice and, for the first time, acknowledged the identity of his biological father and his disappointment with him. Until this point, the patient had refused to meet with his father, initially voicing fear of being in a room with the devil and later falling into sullen silence whenever the issue of his father's visiting was raised. Now he expressed a wish to see his father. The patient spoke with him about his disappointment and how furious he was with him for having misused their funds. On several occasions during these discussions with his father, the patient experienced the return of his belief that he was JFK's son and that the man he was addressing was not his father but rather his father's murderer, Lee Oswald. At such times the family session would end and the patient would then review the experience with his therapist. Gradually, he was able to confront his father without feeling he was turning into someone else. When this occurred, he announced to his therapist, "I'm not an orphan after all. I do have a father. But now, when I have nice thoughts toward him, I think of my mother, get angry, and worry about the devil's voice returning."

The patient's relationship with his father included his actual relationship with his biological father, consisting of experience and expectation; his delusional images of his father, constituted from distorted and intense perceptions, organized into a bizarre but meaningful framework; and his adaptation to these perceptions in both interpersonal and intrapsychic terms. Sergio's relationship to his father, or, more accurately, his various relationships with his father, can be grouped into three phases. During the first two years, the patient angrily declared himself to be fatherless, centered his life on avenging his "father's" death, and personified his biological father as the devil. Clearly, by both aggressively denying his father's actual identity and representing him as evil incarnate, Sergio was, in a psychological sense, indicating his intense involvement with his father. The quality of his "actual" relationship was poor in that it was totally denied. He provided himself with an idealized, though slain, father substitute (JFK), while maintaining an angry and fearful representation of his father as the devil. Sergio converted his helplessness into action by vowing to avenge his father's death and, in this way, retained an intense, hostile involvement with his actual father. Note that he retained an appreciation of his biological father's authority over him by making him a figure of tremendous power, the devil. The patient was trying to maintain internal homeostasis by concealing from himself his rage toward his own father and providing himself the bittersweet comfort of having been fathered by a good and powerful, albeit slain, individual. His delusion allowed him to organize his existence around a specific task: avenging his murdered father. The delusion also allowed Sergio an explanation for events that were frightening and frustratingly uncontrollable, thus insulating him from the sadness and helplessness that he later experienced and expressed through his mourning.

When, during his third year of treatment, Sergio acknowledged the "loss" of his fantasized, idealized father, he took the essential first step toward facing his tangled relationship with this actual father. Decreasing his aggressive stance toward the assassin was a further indication of his wish for rapprochement. It's as if he were saying, "There's more that I need for myself than the cold comfort of retaliation."

This change in the character of his relationship to his father (both the delusional image and the real) paralleled his acknowledgement of loss in relation to the illness that had damaged him. The delusional father (JFK) was constructed to explain the distorted events he began to experience; we have described this process as an unconscious psychological response to the overwhelming condition of psychosis. The fantasy of the delusional father at the same time contained the conflicted and also unconscious elements of his relationship with his real father. As Sergio became less mistrustful, as his illness lessened in severity, the psychological requirement for the delusion also lessened. He then began, even unconsciously, to confront the evidence of his illness, of what had happened to him, in his everyday life. He mourned not only the loss of an idealized father but unconsciously also the loss of an idealized self. He then had to cope with the realities of his limitations.

This young man's progress through his illness illustrates several points. In reality, his mourning, his improvement in communication and relatedness, and the change in his delusions paralleled not only gradual improvement in his illness but his increased capacity for trust in his therapist. The therapist's capacity to explore and understand Sergio's experience of his father was crucial to these changes. Equally important was the therapist's determination to learn why Sergio had formed this particular delusion.

As Sergio's acute psychotic disturbance improved, so did his capacity for social interaction. He could take more risks and trust more safely. He developed an increased tolerance for vulnerability, which made possible his touching expressions of sadness. That tolerance of vulnerability was composed of lessened anxiety and mistrust, a reduction in psychotic stimuli, and the experiences derived from his relationship with his therapist.

The delusional relationship to JFK was not the only idiosyncratic relationship observed during that treatment. The therapeutic relationship itself was "idiosyncratic" in that the therapist explored the delusion and did not attempt to argue it away or discourage the patient from discussing it. In fact, they spent a great deal of time talking about Sergio's delusion. If the therapist attempted to discuss matters more psychologically familiar (such as to broach the matter of his illness or hospitalization), the patient would become silent. His delusion was the medium for contact, the way in which Sergio could tolerate looking at and talking about his experience. As Sergio's psychological necessities and priorities changed, he more directly elaborated the themes that the therapist had understood (from his assessment of the nature of the delusion and of Sergio's relatedness) to have always been present.

We see here several crucial aspects of relatedness: (1) the patient's predisposition to imbue objects with bizarre interpretations of identity or motives; (2) his tendency to avoid any consideration of particular qualities of the object (even misperceptions) in favor of categorizing objects according to predetermined, internal standards; (3) the observer's difficulty in discerning the patient's often intense interest in the object because of the subtle or unusual ways in which he manifested his interests; and (4) the importance of understanding past attachments in order to make sense of current relationships.

Whenever the clinician becomes aware of a pattern of relatedness, he needs to assess the patient's flexibility for considering other bases for interaction. The clinician tests this by inviting the patient to consider alternatives to the position he currently holds. Consider a patient who related that all of his former doctors were part of a conspiracy with his mother. Accordingly, he refused to "incriminate" himself with his new doctor and avoided discussion of his past. Nevertheless, he and his therapist had lively discussions about baseball and found they supported the same team. Their interactions were warm and friendly until the therapist brought up a "psychiatric" issue, whereupon the patient became coolly hostile. Similar patterns were evident with other clinicians. The therapist posed the following questions: Is the patient able to consider that his caregivers might not be in league with his mother? Is there anything in his own experience of the therapist or others that runs counter to his belief? What of the intimacy he has shared with them, an intimacy that seems to belie the adversarial position?

The patient's responses will tell us how rigidly and sterotypically he views his relationships and how readily he may consider a particular individual different from others. This consideration is important because the patient's willingness to suspend his prejudices, however transiently, is often the first step toward a position of trust. The patient can be helped in this process by the clinician's indicating to the patient those instances when his actions suggest he is not fully committed to his position of mistrust. However, many patients are not available to reflective discussions of this sort, in particular those who are too threatened by being made aware of their difficulties. Such was the case in the experience of a woman described below:

> A woman in her mid-thirties, who was an inpatient with a ten-year history of progressively worsening schizophrenic symptoms, angrily derided staff and other patients in group and community meetings. She vehemently accused others of "acting stupid," saying "I don't like it one bit." Although a college graduate, the patient maintained that "a high school education is enough."

As a consequence of her illness, the patient manifested a severe thought disorder. She was, in addition, quite delusional. Relatedness, as well as the performance of more organized social and occupational tasks, was greatly disturbed. That others were "acting stupid" was the patient's explanation for why others appeared not to be able to understand her. A high school education was "enough" because she had lost a great deal of her intellectual ability—though she remembered disparate facts, mused about mathematics and ciphers, and had a good (though seldom seen) sense of humor. When asked about her goals in life, she affected a disinterested pose: "Who needs work? I'm fine; I don't need anything else."

The patient displayed a unique, though constricted, form of relatedness. A few staff members were allowed to spend time with her, the interactions consisting principally of her digressions on idiosyncratic philosophical themes, which, though disorganized, consistently spelled out her cynical, isolated view of the world's incompetence, deceit, and needless pursuit of knowledge and achievement. She treated the staff members as if they were students at her lecture. Her reliance on these interactions was indicated by her predictable irritability and withdrawal when those "trusted" staff members were not available.

Such patients pose striking challenges for caregivers. But the discovery of this woman's unique demands for relatedness and the staff's adaptation to them allowed her to be more involved in the unit community. These didactic interactions might be promoted in order to increase the patient's tolerance for social interactions. Eventually, efforts might be made to direct the patient's attention to useful activities, like riding public transportation, while engaging her by accepting her need to be instructional and arrogant.

The vignettes presented here illustrate the principle that patterns of relatedness and attitudes about interactions with the environment inform clinicians about the schizophrenic individual's psychological experience. This information, in turn, helps us to understand the patient's limitations and potential and can often suggest strategies for planning a treatment. Most often, understanding these issues will help clinicians appreciate how difficult it is for the schizophrenic individual to tolerate change, challenge, or self-awareness and will dictate a patient approach to the fashioning of treatment interventions.

Manifest Communication

When evaluating schizophrenic patients, we continually come up against their ambivalence about receiving help, their defensiveness, their often arcane perspective, and their disturbed communication. It behooves the clinician to carefully consider all of the patient's behavior and other communications with regard to its potential contribution to our insight about his or her psychological state. All that the patient says or does can be seen as a manifestation, or a manifest communication, of psychological needs. In this way, appreciation of the meaning of obscure or severely disturbed behaviors can yield a fuller understanding of the patient's subjective experience.

Clinicians ordinarily find little difficulty in inferring the significance of familiar behaviors, such as friendly invitations to caregivers, cooperation in treatment plans, or helpfulness. We used the term "manifest," however, rather than "apparent" or "outward," to underscore our experience in assessing the complex intentions of schizophrenic individuals' actions. That communications are manifest does mean that they can be appreciated by an observer; it means that speculation about motives or psychological principles requires inference from this data. The use of the term "manifest communications" should further alert the clinician to the difference between a behavior's apparent purpose and what it actually accomplishes or indicates. This distinction is critical in work with schizophrenic persons because of the complexity of their psychological responses to the illness, in particular, as well as the critical effect of the illness on communication and behavior. Curiosity and suspicion of easy formulations are the greatest aids to clinicians involved in this aspect of evaluation.

The following vignette illustrates how certain behaviors can have other than apparent significance:

> A schizophrenic man in his late thirties had been ill for all of his
> adult life. He had difficulty being with other people, often becom-
> ing anxious and coughing, sometimes so hard that he would vomit.

His functional abilities were quite limited. Prior to his admission to the hospital, he had lived at home, inactive, for three years.

During his first week on the unit, the patient was withdrawn and confused. Later he participated in meetings and attended some basic activities, though he remained isolated and demonstrated limited capacities for independent functioning. His manner was always deferential. He sometimes coyly pleaded with the nursing staff to give him more cigarettes (they had been restricted because he otherwise smoked three or four packs a day) but was never disagreeable. He seemed wounded, friendless, but approachable. The staff thought of him fondly, despite his poor hygiene and severe thinking disturbance, and some felt he had become a unit "mascot." In a staff meeting, the unit chief pointed out that this 35-year-old man was being treated like a child. He raised the question of whether, behind their "kindness," the staff was expressing their anger at him by refusing to acknowledge any level of mature development.

In a family session, the patient became agitated when his mother was effusively complimentary about his having had a haircut. He mumbled to himself and turned away from her. When the social worker–therapist inquired about his reaction, he bitterly complained: "The staff won't let me have my cigarettes; they treat me like a child, like I'm stupid or something ... they smile at me because they're making fun of me, and I have to smile back to get more cigarettes."

The patient's complaints about the staff were in part a displacement of his anger at his mother's patronizing attitude. He doubtlessly felt some warmth from and for the staff, but his concomitant resentment could not have been discerned from his statements and gestures on the unit. His behavior had been apparently cooperative. But the manifest communication of his behavior could have been seen to have been, in fact, more complicated and painful.

Although delusional and seriously disturbed, he was not demented. He observed his environment and his place in it and knew that he was different, that he did not have the responsibility and independence of most men his age. But though he might see that his behavior was self-debasing, he acted thus as a consequence of complicated needs. His cigarettes helped, he felt, to decrease his constant, disabling anxiety. He was not able to sit and converse with others, so the manipulative interactions around his cigarette smoking provided some of the few opportunities he had to engage people, to have them smile with him for any reason. His behavior made him appear pitiable, reducing others' expectations of him, their expectations, and his own, making him feel threatened (like the patient who said "a high school education is enough").

The patient's interactive patterns were reinforced by his achievement of a kind of homeostasis, although at a cost of which he was periodically aware. The manifest communication of his behavior was: "I am disabled; expect little of me, but stay involved: don't desert me, but don't make me look at what hurts me about myself." His apparently cooperative, playful attitude communicated, in fact, a great deal more, once the observer looked closely. The key to understanding his behavior was the patient's lack of contentment despite occasional displays of amiability. To understand the patient's experience, we must look at behaviors in situ, not isolate them.

This assessment provides us with an appreciation of this man's poignant inner life. His subjective experience is now more readily imaginable: his isolation, disappointment, self-blame, and self-revulsion, as well as his need for people. Our analysis suggests a simple schema for evaluating the components of these behaviors that communicate to us the schizophrenic individual's subjective experience:

1. Physiological factors, for example, primary states of anxiety, aggression, or stress, lead to secondary compensatory behaviors. Often, especially if the adaptation is effective, only the latter will be apparent.
2. The patient's relationship to the environment, his or her need for human contact or wish to avoid it, fashions the behaviors we observe as manifest communications of his or her subjective experience.
3. Intrapsychic concerns, directly or indirectly related to self-image and self-esteem, such as the wish to decrease others' expectations, also have an impact on the behaviors clinicians must evaluate.

These three rudimentary distinctions can provide clinicians with a basis for organizing their evaluation of these behaviors. The significance of a given "communication" can generally be understood within the framework of one of these categories, thereby allowing for greater insight into actions and words that may seem meaningless.

A delusion is a manifest communication, expressed in words. Denial similarly informs us about the patient's psychological responses to his or her illness. When we speak about manifest communications, however, we most often refer to behaviors, such as those described above. Other examples include:

- apparently off-putting behavior that actually functions as a way of keeping people involved, though in a controllable way
- an unwillingness to make him- or herself clear, as a manifestation of the patient's fear of being understood
- physical, repulsive actions, such as aggressive behavior, inattention to hygiene, noncompliance with rules or expectations, or surliness, which are often expressions of the patient's experience of feeling threatened or out of control
- efforts to control others through manipulation, insistence on discussing prescribed topics (such as religious delusions), or demanding that others join in specific tasks, such as uncovering a persecutory plot.

As noted before, these behaviors are multiply determined. We must acknowledge the contribution made by disturbances in ego functioning, while considering whether such conduct may exist in order to accomplish particular goals. The behaviors described in the preceding paragraph distance others or create a feeling of futility, discouraging efforts to remain involved with the schizophrenic individual. The patient may unconsciously maintain such behaviors because increased interaction might be intolerable. It is important to consider the possibility that the patient is making an active effort to keep people away and to control her environment. This activity is often a consequence of the patient's fantasies about others, as in the fantasy that they are attempting to influence or control him, which stimulates efforts to protect himself. The increased stress from interpersonal interactions can thus be seen to arise from the schizophrenic individual's need to assess whether there are hidden intents behind others' actions. A common concern is that other people will attempt to convince her that she is ill. Treatment then can be effectively directed at examining those attitudes about other people that concern the patient. These interventions may well reduce anxiety and in effect help the patient to acquire adaptive behaviors.

The place to begin the investigation is not at the level of the patient's belief that the clinician is interested in convincing her of her illness but rather why the clinician has this desire. The patient may then reveal her belief that the clinician is envious of the patient's freedom, angry at the patient's stubbornness, unable to function unless he or she is in a superior position (I am well; you are sick), and so on. Over time, then, the patient is given an opportunity to compare this a priori view of the clinician with her ongoing, actual experience of that caregiver.

An additional component of the schizophrenic individual's effort to distance and control others is her resentment toward people holding expectations of her. Patients resent the expectation that they find ways to cope with their disturbances, sometimes favoring the magical expectation that someone or something will radically change their life, that all will be as it was "before." This dynamic is evident in those patients who, as a requirement for interaction, insist that the other person join them in their idiosyncratic endeavors, such as personal crusades. We can see that patients' insistence on involvement solely on their terms represents their fear that participating in treatment, for example, would require acknowledging their difficulties. Consider, for example, the following:

> A 23-year-old schizophrenic man had become reclusive following an unsuccessful attempt at a sexual relationship. By the time of admission to the hospital, he was refusing to go out of the house. He informed his therapist that he would like him to collaborate with him in "purifying the world of the sins of the body." The patient refused to discuss any other matters, most particularly anything to do with difficulties he might be experiencing. He proclaimed that only when the purification effort was successfully completed would he resume association with others.

Our goal is a more thorough understanding of patients' unique ways of viewing their environment, as well as the efforts they make to adapt to and modify that environment in order to meet their internal, psychological needs. By observing what they think about people, how they treat them, whether or not they show an interest in interactions and on what basis, we learn what people mean to them within the context of their own psychological worlds. We also derive some understanding of their difficulties with relationships and their limitations in interacting with others.

The following brief vignette illustrates some aspects of one schizophrenic individual's efforts to appear disinterested while remaining related on her terms. Only when absolutely necessary did she reveal her need for the therapist.

Despite the fact that her therapist had given the patient a written schedule of their appointment times, the therapist always had to seek the patient out when it came time for her session. The patient stared blankly at the therapist when she reminded the patient that the schedule was posted on her wall. However, the patient eagerly accompanied the therapist to her office, where she would throw herself on the couch, facing away from the therapist. She was attentive to what the therapist said, registering agreement or disagreement by nodding her head and uncertainty by shrugging her shoulders. She never left a session early, and when the therapist would announce that she would miss a session, the patient communicated, through discussion with a nursing staff member, her wish for a "make-up session."

The patient's sullenness was balanced by evidence of her interest in her relationship with the therapist. Her ambivalence communicated her desire for understanding and intimacy, as well as her commitment to controlling her relationships and concealing that desire. Awareness of this paradigm guided the clinician in predicting the patient's tolerance of a given intervention and suggested interventions for improving the patient's self-esteem and broadening her social skills. It would have been unwise, for instance, to challenge the patient about her "feigned" disinterest, for she used that stance to protect her self-esteem and to feel more in control: It is likely that "exposure" of her dependency would have been humiliating and might also have frightened the patient if she had delusions of being controlled by others. Social rehabilitation interventions thus focused on providing the patient with experiences wherein she felt "in charge," supervising others, perhaps, while attempting to increase her tolerance of vulnerability through modeling of interactions between, say, managers and employees in a work setting. For a long period of time, the therapist would simply schedule a make-up session whenever possible. She would do this matter of factly and, gradually, mention that it was important to maintain continuity. Still later, she would comment on the patient's request, saying "I'm glad I was able to make up the time, especially since you had requested it." Only much later could the therapist explore with the patient why she had to conceal her desires.

This perspective on the patient's interpersonal and social presentation increases our understanding of the patient. The techniques described above will also foster the treatment alliance and increase the specificity of our clinical interventions.

THE QUALITY OF THE PATIENT'S SUBJECTIVE EXPERIENCE

Qualitative assessments of the patient's psychological experience focus on describing internal states rather than on determining the significance of behaviors as we have just done above. However, information about these issues can certainly be inferred from the schizophrenic person's actions; as we have delineated above, there are numerous routes to an understanding of the patient's subjective experience. We mean here to describe such states as having difficulty experiencing oneself as physically or psychologically separate from others; sustaining one's hope, happiness, or will to live, through use of certain fantasies, myths, or other cognitive devices; and disturbances in one's sense of temporal or physical continuity, of self, or of others.

Self-Other Differentiation

Most people do not have difficulty in experiencing themselves as separate from other people. In normative psychological experiences, people can retain a sense of individuality while also being able to "identify with" other people—that is, see similarities between themselves and others or empathize with someone else. For schizophrenic individuals, this sense of self-integrity is not necessarily immediate or reliable, for they often describe feeling as if there is no boundary between themselves and others (8–9).

As described by schizophrenic individuals, the experience of the self's losing a sense of integrity suggests at least two mechanisms. The first is analogous to the reports of depersonalization or derealization by people who have experienced extreme states of anxiety. Depersonalization and derealization are often seen in individuals with severe character disorders during states of stress or anxiety but can also be experienced by psychologically healthy individuals during periods of extreme stress or organic mental disturbance. It is possible that the schizophrenic person experiences such states even more frequently, if not at times continuously, such that his or her sense of being separate and unique is consequently impaired.

Concern over self-object boundaries may also result from the schizophrenic person's experience of intrusive thoughts, thought withdrawal, delusions of being controlled, or other similar mental disturbances. Patients often report feeling as if their thoughts are not their own or have been taken away or as if their actions are controlled by outside forces. The accumulation of these events understandably undermines a sense of self and self-competence. Aside from developing delusional explanations for these experiences, the schizophrenic individual must contend with the profound demoralization and anxiety that attend these psychotic phenomena.

The disturbance in self-object boundary can then be seen to have two components: physiological factors that produce abnormal mental states and a psychological representation of the self as permeable, or uncontrolled, stemming from the experience of those abnormal events.

In general, patients seek to resolve this distressing state by increasing their sense of wholeness. They accomplish this in a variety of ways. Social isolation may decrease stress and so reduce disturbing experiences of anxiety and associated depersonalization; isolation also allows patients the psychological experience of privacy, which may be difficult to achieve given their recurrent feelings of being watched, of having thoughts imposed on them, and of numbing amotivation that arises, confusingly, from no thought or event. Rigid categorization of people, stereotyping, and treating all persons as if they shared common motives and psychology or are a common foe are also means of increasing a sense of differentiation between the patient and all others. Aggression is particularly useful because it implicitly defines people (aggressors versus victims or objects of hostility) and creates distance through fear and resentment.

Some patients exhibit ambivalence toward resolving problems of self-object differentiation. They may fantasize about "merging" (10) with another object (person, in most cases), becoming one with someone else and thus resolving the problem of isolation, threat, and inefficacy. The other person is frequently seen as capable of helping the patient cope, of gratifying his or her wish for successful intimacy. The other person is seen as untroubled by the patient's concerns and is thus also an object of envy. Patients may seek fulfillment of that wish in annihilation of themselves, with the underlying fantasy that they will then find comfort in a greater oneness with the object of their wish for merger. Wishes for merger can also reflect a patient's yearning for broader obliteration, symbolized as a desire for the end of the world. The merger could be fantasized as a perfected union, even marriage, between the persons.

Yet many patients fear this fantasy of merger, including some who also actively entertain the wish for it. The expression of this ambivalence is graphically illustrated in the following vignette:

> A chronic schizophrenic patient became so enamored of the film *The Invasion of the Body Snatchers* that she purchased it as soon as it came out on cassette. For her, the plot of the film, in which extraterrestrial invaders "take over" people in such a way that the invaders and the earthlings become merged, was most significant.
>
> After viewing the cassette for several days the patient obeyed her compulsion to destroy it. She reported that she could not understand how she had ever enjoyed the film since it now appeared to her as the "scariest movie I have ever seen."

The fear of loss of self-object differentiation may be expressed as an intense wish to isolate oneself to preserve a sense of separateness. The threat of loss of self may be directed at others, as in schizophrenic individuals' depiction of people as controllers or invaders seeking to overwhelm them and eradicate their individuality. This fear of being overwhelmed may lead to efforts to distance others and forms another component of such behaviors as we have discussed previously.

Patients also manifest difficulties with self-object boundaries in their failure to clarify their interests, goals, or limitations. These efforts might be understood as expressing a wish to resist defining themselves, for to do so would implicitly reinforce their separateness by identifying what makes them different from other people. Such separateness could represent a threat to their wish for merger with a stronger, comforting object, signaling the loss of the fantasied resolution to their predicament. Patients' wishes to eliminate themselves in favor of merger may be stronger than their fears of the consequences of self-annihilation. The following example illustrates this point.

A schizophrenic patient believed that he could obtain safety through submerging himself in a higher power, "Korax." To gain Korax's protection, he was required to cut himself off from all prior connections, renounce his present self, and devote himself completely. In this context, the patient became actively suicidal, informing his family, "Either way I may die, but this way I am more powerful."

Other patients might attempt to coerce another person, perhaps a therapist, into collaborating in a way that separated the two of them from the rest of the environment, this "special" relationship being similar to a fantasized merger. In hospital settings as well as in other treatment environments, such behavior often excites resentment and envy in other patients and staff members. In part, this results from shared, instinctive envy at seeing exclusive relationships. It is also frequently a response to the patient's subtle hostility toward others, which further serves to isolate the patient and the patient's chosen object, as in the example below:

In one case, a hospital staff member felt so drawn into the struggles and suffering of a young schizophrenic man that she arranged to meet with him in the community after the patient's discharge despite her ethical concerns. The patient initially seemed glad of the attention, but felt disappointed that his psychiatrist still seemed aloof, refusing, for instance, to visit him at home. Eventually, he became angry and resentful and reported suicidal thoughts, necessitating rehospitalization, at which time he insisted that his hospital psychiatrist resume treating him.

The schizophrenic person's difficulty with defining self-boundaries, even when stemming from a physiological disturbance, comes to assume an important role in the patient's psychological life because it offers a fantasied resolution to stressful experience and rekindles unconscious wishes for an end to the isolation that is a central aspect of his or her psychic life.

Understanding the patient's experience of self-object differentiation greatly enhances the clinician's awareness of how the patient interprets aspects of the treatment situation. Change itself may be frightening, representing the threat of further loss of control. Advice, efforts to educate, insights may all be felt to be foreign intrusions. At times, the mere presence of the clinician may activate the patient's concerns about self-object differentiation. If these concerns are prominent in a given patient, specific treatment interventions may be indicated. In the patient who has intense fear of others and a wish to maintain a sense of separateness, efforts may be made both verbally and physically to reinforce to that patient his or her sense of integrity. Consider the following:

> A schizophrenic patient who shared a room with a fellow patient kept moving his roommate's name from the door while failing to put up a sign with his name on it. He believed that there could only be "one soul" in the room and, whoever that was, that "soul" would take over the other. The staff helped him find a temporary solution by suggesting that three signs could be put up: His roommate's name, his name, and one directly under his stating that he was not his roommate. The patient accepted this with one modification—that the negation precede his name. Thus, the signs read:

> 1. John Jones
> 2. Not John Jones
>   but Steven Smith.

> Several weeks later the patient removed the "Not John Jones" part, remarking he could not understand why he had felt that necessary.

Such clarifications may even extend to reinforcement of a sense of physical integrity, because some patients describe feeling so unreal that they cannot distinguish parts of their body from other objects close to them in the environment. Such a patient could be helped by becoming engaged in exercises that would promote awareness of his or her body and a sense of control over bodily movement and functioning. For example, a patient who felt his arms were not part of his body was helped through playing pool to appreciate that the force of his arms applied to the cue stick determined where the ball went.

A patient who feared the influence of others' thoughts might be approached by hospital staff members with a routinized introduction in which the staff member acknowledged the patient's anxiety about the interaction and reassured the patient that he or she could terminate the discussion at any point. Fear of merger can also be helped by insisting on one's separateness from the patient. One catatonic patient, when he began to speak, announced that the thing that had made him feel most safe about his therapist was overhearing him tell a colleague that he was going away for the weekend. For the first time, the patient felt the therapist was not interested in merging with him. This and similar interventions might be specifically oriented towards problems with self-object differentiation while at the same time addressing other concerns.

Sustaining Experiences or Expectations

A second important aspect of the inner experience of the schizophrenic individual is an appreciation of which aspects of his life he conceives of as psychologically sustaining. All of us characteristically think of certain categories, such as life goals and important relationships, as being important to our mental well-being. We recognize that ongoing pleasant interactions and events help us cope with the stresses and uncertainties in our lives. The schizophrenic individual often has a paucity of experiences that would be considered sustaining by ordinary standards. Certainly, the situation of the individual who experiences frequent perceptual disturbances, uncomfortable states of anxiety, cognitive disruption and multiple difficulties with relationships and effective social functioning is one of limited opportunities for gratifying experiences. At the same time, it becomes extremely important for him or her to find some aspects of experience that are sustaining in order to tolerate the difficulties inherent in that experience.

For some schizophrenic individuals, effective social adaptation, when it is possible, allows for satisfying interpersonal experiences that contribute to self-esteem. For many patients whose difficulties limit involvement in work or intimate relationships fantasy may function as their psychological sustenance, especially in the development of compensatory idiosyncratic behaviors or thoughts. In our experience, this is not an infrequent cause for patients' refusing to take antipsychotic medication. A 43-year-old schizophrenic woman, for instance, who was profoundly upset by her childlessness, believed herself when delusional to be the "old woman in the shoe," surrounded by imaginary children. She steadfastly refused treatments that had in the past "taken my children away."

Some individuals find major gratification through maintaining contact with people, and yet the way they go about it makes their object-seeking difficult to recognize. An example might be the patient who takes pleasure in disappointing people who attempt to help him. For someone whose sense of pleasure is restricted and who experiences intense resentment about that limitation, the perverse pleasure of frustrating the helpful efforts of others may become a critical motivation for survival. Other patients may be unable to consciously acknowledge a wish for interaction with others because of conflicts about intimacy. For some, to express a desire for intimacy would overtly challenge their need to see themselves as self-sufficient. Still others may behave helplessly or obnoxiously, in ways that require others to spend time with them, even if that time is often colored by antagonism. In all these examples, the sustaining experience is the interaction which is conducted along lines that simultaneously afford the patient a sense of safety while gratifying his or her particular desires.

It is often hard to obtain a statement about sustaining experiences from schizophrenic individuals because they may feel that those experiences cannot be shared without risk of losing them. They may fear that others will try to take away anything that is identified as pleasing. Some patients are so threatened by their ill-understood and capricious unconscious, whose effects they may attribute to an external source, that they may vaguely experience part of themselves as dangerous and so not wish to assert what is important to them. The patient who must believe in her perfection will experience any yearning for greater fulfillment as inimical. Such a patient also needs to deny, even to herself, that there are things that are important to her. It is as if she will betray herself if she speaks. "It wanted something. It had to be taught that there is nothing I cannot provide for myself. Otherwise I would not be the daughter of Zeus."

The ability to identify sustaining aspects of the patient's experience allows the clinician to begin to fashion the treatment in a way that takes advantage of that information. In the case of the patient who sustains himself by frustrating treatment interventions, the treatment would have to begin with an effort to modify this situation. Ongoing inquiry and interaction would be required to attempt to help the patient find some way in which other aspects of his experience could become sustaining so that the wish to sabotage helpfulness would assume a less central role.

Often the clue to resolving situations like this comes from the methods the patient employs to effect sabotage. For example, a young male schizophrenic repeatedly frustrated staff members' efforts to communicate with him by talking over them and reciting verses from the Bible. The patient was therefore encouraged to start a Bible class for other patients. The class would begin with his delivering a formal reading and would be followed by a discussion. Although the patient had difficulty with the exercise, he gradually demonstrated increased tolerance for others' views about the readings. He simultaneously developed a source of self-esteem and tolerance for some social vulnerability.

For the patient for whom social interaction is important but who cannot acknowledge that need, the clinician could structure activities allowing indirect or compulsory socialization, being careful not to force upon the patient the awareness that this is important to him or her. The patient could be encouraged first to observe activities that did not require his participation. Depending on the patient's tolerance of socialization, a job could be devised that closely matched his abilities and limitations: delivering books or mail to other patients in the hospital; answering a telephone; working as a receptionist. Compulsory activities would be an alternative for the resolutely withdrawn patient. Contact with staff members could initially be prescribed. The rationale for the interactions would be clearly stated in terms reflecting only the staff's interests: "We must meet with you to obtain information necessary for our work." This might relieve the patient's unconscious fear that his interest in such contacts would be uncovered. The aim of the treatment interventions would be specific: increasing the patient's ability to tolerate socialization while helping him to understand and cope with his anxieties or other psychological reactions to those experiences.

A list of sustaining experiences might well read as a catalog of human desire. Developing a compendium of such items is thus an unapproachable task. In work with schizophrenia persons, however, crucial issues do recur in our assessment of what is important to and motivates them. These issues, not surprisingly, are related to themes such as sense of self-integrity and self-esteem; psychological continuity; and safety, avoidance of loss, and preservation of autonomy. These are the aspects of the patient's subjective experience we treat here; they are of central psychological importance.

PSYCHOLOGICAL CONTINUITY AND CLARITY

We described earlier the schizophrenic individual's experience of profound, repeated, and often persistent perceptual and cognitive disruption. These difficulties create a psychological experience of discontinuity. The physiological basis for this state may be ameliorated by medications, but there may remain significant disturbance in the qualitative psychological experience. It behooves the clinician to make a careful assessment of the patient's psychological experience of continuity and clarity (11) because this aspect of mental functioning has significant import when the clinician attempts to assess the patient's handling of treatment interventions.

Most schizophrenic patients experience treatment interventions (including interviews, presentations of the treatment plan, and some tasks) as a significant challenge to their cognitive functioning. In this respect, care must be taken to determine, without insulting patients, that they have been able to attend to the task at hand, that they are able to concentrate on what is expected of them, and that the particular task does not exceed their present abilities. Sensitivity to patients' states of anxiety, as well as to their potential frustration or discouragement, is an important attribute of the empathic clinician. By the same token, it is also apparent from the research literature that, although schizophrenic individuals have difficulties with some aspects of cognitive performance, these problems are not global or uniform. A schizophrenic patient who was dubbed "Joey Slowey" by his fellow patients because of his slowness of thinking was noted one day to be arguing with a TV sports announcer's comments about a baseball player's past performance. An alert staff member noted this and engaged him in discussion about the merits of this particular player. From this chance event, Joey was found to possess an encyclopedic knowledge of baseball records going back decades, as well as a keen appreciation of the current game and its strategies. He soon became recognized as an authority in this area and held court during and after games.

Clinical experience informs us that we cannot assume that a patient who is gravely impaired in some respects does not possess areas of competence (12–14). This very state of affairs, however, illustrates one aspect of discontinuity: the disparity in cognitive and other psychological functioning within the same individual. What is more, schizophrenic patients are often perplexed and frustrated by their limitations, not infrequently becoming self-critical and imagining that they are lazy, stupid, or demented.

Individuals with schizophrenia often report experiences that indicate distorted perceptions of identity. A patient may not recognize that the staff member who is holding out a cup to her is the same person whom she had just asked for water. This may represent more than a deficit in memory function. A patient who says in a family meeting, "These aren't my parents, they're impostors," has experienced a dramatic and disturbing disruption in his ability to identify objects and a sense of continuity of those objects over time. Similar phenomena have been described in the neurological literature, including persons who are unable to recognize faces, despite having intact memories (for the well-known case of "the man who mistook his wife for a hat," see Oliver Sacks's book by this title). This discontinuity can also affect complex cognitive and emotional experiences. Motivation, desire, commitment, and persistence, all of which have a temporal dimension, may be elusive because of psychological discontinuity, as the following illustrates:

A woman in her thirties had suffered a severe and prolonged psychotic episode three years before. Although partially recovered, she continued to have ideas of reference and occasional auditory hallucinations. Her psychotic symptoms reiterated her delusion that her ex-husband, who was a police officer and of Italian descent, had contracted with the Mafia to have her killed or driven to suicide by mental torment.

Whenever she became involved in activities, she would predictably become anxious (because she was afraid she had lost her intellectual abilities and because tasks were often difficult) and would soon report hearing taunts prompting her to suicide. She would then become discouraged and withdrawn and cease working.

When describing these experiences, the patient would say, "When I hear those voices, its just like I'm back in that hell three years ago. I can't function, I forget where I am, what I'm doing, and I just want to die." Feeling, like Sisyphus, repeatedly defeated, thrown back, she was unable to muster desire for more effective adaptations, was amotivated, and convinced of her inability to work persistently towards meaningful goals.

Like all individuals, schizophrenic persons have psychological mechanisms that can repress awareness of painful, confusing, conflictual aspects of their life (14–16). As one would expect, much in the schizophrenic person's mental life is subject to defensive elimination from consciousness. These operations also contribute to the patient's ignorance of internal consistency.

Some patients, particularly those who have long been ill, seek through fantasy to eradicate empty years. They avoid awareness of suffering, as well the sense of loss due to the passing of opportunities. They often act as if no time has passed at all, as in the case of the man described below.

A man who was in a professional school in his early twenties developed symptoms of his first acute psychotic episode. He was able to return to professional school only briefly and then had to leave school and return home. Over the ensuing ten years, he had lived at home without working, tied to the fantasy that he was still working actively toward his professional degree and that opportunities were imminent. When he was in his thirties, this patient spoke about his experience of professional school as if it were but a few months ago and asserted that he would be able to take up his career at any time as soon as he could work out some formal issues regarding applications for more schooling.

This man, who had suffered for a number of years and could acknowledge the emptiness of that time had sought hope (through a sustaining fantasy) and relief from despair. His unconscious provided a kind of hope through his delusional treatment of time, but the consequences for his life and his treatment were debilitating. Coping with the symptoms of his illness and scaling down his expectations were not at issue, given his insistence on returning to work he could in fact not reasonably resume.

Other individuals act as if time were not moving or as if their lives were unending. They maintain they have no need to change, to compensate, to revise goals, or to think about the future. They await something that will change them, relieve them of the responsibility of accepting and coping with their illness and circumstances.

One such patient, who was verbal and intelligent but functionally impaired, spent several years in a hospital setting, maintaining all the while that he had no need to engage in therapeutic work, rehabilitative efforts, or activities that would promote his independence and autonomy. He planned to return home and live with his family but said he would wait until his family relented in their insistence that he not return home. Faced with resolute noncompliance, the staff transferred him to a state hospital, from which his family eventually extricated him.

Many schizophrenic individuals also experience discontinuity with their former habits and abilities, despairing about regaining any aspects of that past self. They find themselves unable to reclaim coping skills, frustrated by difficulty accomplishing once-simple tasks, and feeling so different about themselves and their goals that they believe they have been irrevocably changed, become different persons. This is what happened to a young woman in her twenties.

This young woman had been a superior student in high school and was active in extracurricular activities. At that time, she was full of hope and promise and planned a career in photography. She had trouble in college, first manifest as social awkwardness and some difficulty carrying through school assignments. She nevertheless completed all but one semester of college, but just prior to her final exams in her senior year, she experienced her first psychotic episode. She endured six years of severe and persistent paranoid psychotic symptoms and several hospitalizations.

When, in her twenties, she was encouraged to reminisce about her past, she showed pictures of herself receiving awards during that halcyon high school period. She spoke poignantly about that person as if she were dead, as if there were no connection between who she was now and that person ten years before. Not only did she feel she had lost a great deal, but she denied retaining any of her past qualities. It appeared that acknowledging the persistence of prior traits, abilities, ideals, or values in herself would indicate that she really had changed. This absolute disconnectedness allowed her to maintain that her current state of mind was temporary and not real.

She attributed her cognitive disturbances to brain experiments performed by the CIA. Her single-minded goal was to determine some way to put an end to this experiment so as to be able to return to the state of mind she possessed at the end of high school, to return to that point when she could still imagine dreams and goals and the possibility of survival. She wanted only to discover her punishers so as to recover all that had been taken from her. Her past self was like some perfectly preserved relic, frozen but ready to spring back to life.

This disconnectedness was severely maladaptive because it contributed to her refusal to engage in treatment. She resisted recognizing her residual abilities, which she could otherwise have put to good use, for to recognize them meant acceptance and compromise for her. She clearly needed help in several areas: to mourn her loss of prior functioning; to contain the anxiety that would be brought about by efforts at adaptation (which would inevitably remind her of her past accomplishments); and to reestablish links with whatever skills remained and to build on these.

How could this be done while her manifest goal was stopping the brain experiments? The patient had first to be persuaded that other activities might be of use to her. When the staff planned a rehabilitation or resocialization program, the patient would be interested in work only if it helped her achieve her single-minded goal. Her stubbornness was also felt to be a resistance to assuming responsibilities at which she might fail. The staff chose to focus on a highly learned and relatively preserved skill and interest, photography. The activity that came closest to that was a volunteer position in the hospital's radiology department. Although her work would be largely physical (transporting patients, etc.), she would be able to observe the functioning of the department and its equipment. The staff presented the rationale, but the patient was encouraged to think it over herself and determine if she could find any reason why this work might appeal to her. The patient agreed to take the job, saying that her interest in mind-control experiments led her to want to learn more about neuroradiology techniques.

Appreciating a patient's unique psychological experience allows for greater empathy with the patient's instinctive coping efforts. Some treatments need to be modified because of specific disturbances in the clarity of mental experience—that is, in conditions wherein perceptions are regularly distorted and marked impairment in basic cognitive functions, including orientation and attention, is noted. These patients also manifest the phenomenon of discontinuity because of the marked disruption of mental life. Patients who have difficulties with cognitive clarity may benefit from environmental support that emphasizes consistency and some degree of routine and structure but also opportunities for activity, challenge, and newness tempered by staff support. It would be a mistake to assume that patients with cognitive difficulty need only an environment that is stable and routinized. Such individuals, like anyone else, also benefit from meeting and mastering new experiences. They require help in greeting these new experiences and in devising compensatory strategies to cope with them. Therapeutic staff who have an understanding of the psychological experience of such patients may be better able to suggest creative strategies for coping with new circumstances, as they did in the example described below.

An inpatient in a hospital that had a rather labyrinthine structure continually found herself getting lost as she tried to find her way from one activity to another. She had considerable difficulty orienting herself because she was unable to remember significant landmarks along the way. The occupational therapist accompanied her from the unit to the occupational therapy department. They then discussed making a map to enable her to get to various places. The patient chose first to learn the route to her therapist's office, which was a considerable distance from the unit. Rather than sit in the activities department and construct the map from memory, a concept which would have maximally stressed the patient and characteristically led her to withdraw and/or to turn over the entire task to the activities person, the therapist decided to walk the patient through the experience. They began on the unit and, in the course of going from there to the therapist's office, noted along the way all structures that were familiar to the patient. They then went back to the activities department and constructed a map utilizing the information gained from their walk together.

Treatment of cognitive disturbances may be eased by linking the patient's present experience to previous ones and implicitly addressing underlying discontinuities. For example, a staff member working with a schizophrenic individual, such as the woman described above, might approach her and say, "We are going to go for a walk today as we discussed two days ago in our last treatment planning meeting. Our plan was to walk into town and do some research on bus routes. That's something you said was important to you at your last treatment planning meeting." The important issue in the staff member's communication to the patient is the supportive emphasis on what the patient had expressed as her desires, interests, and goals, an emphasis that encourages a sense of continuity and, it is hoped, increases the patient's sense of competence. It also decreases her tendency to experience others as making decisions for her because of her difficulty in maintaining an awareness of the continuity of her own interest.

Patients can be helped to see that recovering aspects of a past self is not as threatening as they fear and may be crucial to their current survival. The tendency of such patients to eradicate time, to act as if there is no need for them to address their difficulties in the here-and-now, to maintain that their only hope is a complete return to their premorbid state must be presented with the bleak consequences of that stance. A patient whose psychological disposition indicates disinterest in any outcome other than one that removes all of the real difficulties his or her illness imposes is not prepared to engage in a useful therapeutic alliance. Such an attitude is an ultimatum that all must be put right and indicates that the patient abdicates responsibility for coping with reality. This attitude, though often superficially optimistic, is infused with hopelessness, anger, and despair. Clinicians must evoke awareness of that demoralization and help the patient to a more tractable position. Confrontation about this issue will predictably lead to expression of deep sadness and resentment, as the following illustrates.

A once quite successful actress, who had spent the majority of her last ten years unemployed and in and out of hospitals, infuriated the treatment staff by insisting that the only thing she needed to do for herself was to call her agent (who no longer returned her calls). She insisted that when the right part came along, he would arrange an audition for her. She also insisted that, given this opportunity, she would then make the most of it. "When I get the part," she would say, "the rest of my life will fall into place." Until that time, she was content to spend her days on the couch in the day room vociferously protesting any efforts to get her to move.

The patient's therapist began to point out various residual talents hinted at in her present behavior, such as the fact that she had good vocal presence even though her remarks were generally curt and off-putting, and that her persuasive abilities were considerable, even when complaining of how unjust people were in demanding things of her. But he also pointed out to her how she was allowing these skills to stagnate. He predicted that her social skills would continue to deteriorate unless she decided to accept help.

The patient was troubled by this line of argument and began to refuse her sessions. She seemed to cling to the sofa even more desperately. She also became more withdrawn, stifling her complaints about the staff, as if repressing all evidence of her vocal and interpersonal skills. It was as though for her to acknowledge these remaining talents was also to acknowledge her infirmity and her difficulty using these skills as effectively as before. She was fortunate in that her cognitive skills were relatively preserved, so that she was able to find work, after hospital discharge, though in a clerical position and not the theater. She was often noncompliant with her treatment and resentful toward those helping her.

Nevertheless, she and her therapist persisted in exploring her sadness and resentment and her experience of discontinuity with her past self. It was more than a year before she was again able to express herself with the vitality she had displayed in the hospital. At first, this vitality was seen in her outbursts of anger and derision. Gradually, she could be seen to possess more emotional depth, and, concomitantly, her life and treatment became more stable.

Experiencing discontinuity with one's past self is not wholly arbitrary nor imaginary. In many instances, schizophrenic patients do lose skills, relationships, careers, and some dreams. The therapeutic goal, whether in supportive psychotherapy, rehabilitative interventions, or other modalities, is to help the patient identify parts of his or her current self (skills, relationships, potentials) that are links to the past, while also helping the patient to forge links to a feasible and desirable future.

CONCERNS

The third area to which we direct our attention in gathering data on the patient's subjective experience is one we have designated "concerns." By this we mean emotional issues that are of overriding importance to most schizophrenic individuals. The three we have listed here are not exclusive, but in our judgment, they are nearly ubiquitous features of schizophrenic patients' psychological lives. These themes overlap with one another and with aspects of the subjective experience that we have discussed above.

Autonomy

Autonomy is a concept that connotes such varied ideas as independence, control, integrity of the self (that is, wholeness or oneness), and responsibility. Intact self-object differentiation and a capacity for intimacy without fear of merger are psychological functions characteristic of autonomous individuals. For schizophrenic patients, this issue presents great difficulty. For them, independence is both held as a goal and resisted because of its frightening implications. Intimacy is highly conflictual insofar as it requires management of interpersonal relatedness at a sustained, intense level that many schizophrenic patients find threatening and overwhelming. The sense of identity or wholeness of the self, which is closely related to the concept of self-object differentiation, is also impaired, perhaps primarily because of physiological dysfunction but also as a consequence of their unique psychological experience.

In our discussion of self-object differentiation, we made the observation that schizophrenic individuals are ambivalently disposed as to whether they prefer a state of individuality or merger with another person or object. Schizophrenic patients' struggle with autonomy is over whether and how to pursue it, how to delimit the boundaries of the self, where to insist on their authority, and where to rely on the hope that another's actions, another self may provide them with support and safety. Many schizophrenic individuals opt for a state of relative isolation because closeness to people is fraught with stress and uncertainty and the need to exercise disturbed interpersonal skills. For many patients, however, that isolation is a renunciation of a fantasied union with another person that would provide them with security and relief from stress. Movement toward autonomy is a conflictual compromise between the desired ends of self-integrity and the contrasting goal of closeness. Both goals carry risks and are associated with unique stresses. Often the patient, such as the one described below, oscillates for a considerable period of time between polar opposites, as if protesting any possibility of integrating these two positions.

A young woman described oneiroid (dreamlike) states wherein she "retreated" to a private "planet," a world without violence. She related her fantasy that one day she would go there forever, because people were too cruel.

Alternatively, the patient described a delusion that entailed a much more public and active image of herself. She believed she could predict the future and felt an urge to communicate her premonitions about tragedies, natural and political, to governments and the media. She had, in fact, on a number of occasions reported her premonitions to authorities, on one occasion prompting a call back from a police agency, which frightened her.

Her public "self" was assertive and impatient. When she discussed her wishes, she related high expectations and a strong desire for love, intimacy, and commitment. These discussions would be predictably followed by a period of withdrawal, marked by bitter reminiscences about past lovers who had hurt her and then descriptions of her private world of peace.

Although the patient referred to her withdrawal as a voluntary "retreat," the staff working with her saw this as a response to anxiety, intense sadness, and resentment. The oneiroid state was a physiological consequence of the stress of relatedness and desire. Her prediction of an ultimate retreat was linked to her recurrent and serious suicidal ideation.

Control—Its Relation to Autonomy

It is apparent that in addition to autonomy, the schizophrenic individual is concerned with issues related to control, such as the control of boundaries of the self, of objects in the environment, or his or her mood. The schizophrenic person's interest in autonomy reflects a wish for control.

This arises out of his or her frustration, awareness of limitations, and the unresponsiveness of objects in what is to this individual an insufficient environment.

Some patients manifest a fantasy of control in which they imagine, like the young woman in the preceding vignette, they can control their symptoms, that psychotic states are in whole or in part volitional. This patient had fantasized that she could retreat from her problems to a private world. Such beliefs are maladaptive in that they usually cause patients to argue against reasonable treatment interventions, as is seen most frequently in persons who decline medication and relate the fantasy that they can control the appearance of their hallucinations. When hallucinations do appear, they explain that for some reason they "do not choose" to control them now. They avoid the need to acknowledge that they have an illness with which they must cope.

When we challenge such fantasies of control, or denial or delusions, it is important that we also inform patients about our expectations for their collaboration and how we see them being able to assert meaningful, realistic control over their symptoms. Patients can learn to identify prodromal symptoms of decompensation and to use medication appropriately to avoid relapses. Cognitive and behavioral interventions directed at decreasing social isolation or stress can help to treat sadness and anxiety, whether these occur as part of an illness recurrence or as the psychological reaction to that illness. Insight, self-understanding, and familiarity with characteristic coping patterns can assist schizophrenic patients in achieving a healthier adaptation to their condition.

Control in Relationships

Social stresses, the demands of interactions with people, also stimulate a wish for control. Various behaviors, adaptations, result from the schizophrenic individual's efforts to cope with these demands. A fear of the consequences of closeness often drives the patient toward isolation, which is relatively less stressful because there are fewer stimuli and less demand for performance that may be unrewarding. Yet such isolation is not consoling. The loneliness and inability to be involved in gratifying activities, including interactions with others, and the lack of assistance and support of others are damaging.

The schizophrenic person may then seek a way to obtain the values of relationships without feeling threatened. To accomplish this she may seek a relationship in which she is in control of what the other thinks and feels. From the patient's perspective, any object may possibly undermine her self-esteem by threatening her view of herself. Objects may be made safe only when subjugated. This control may be enacted through engrossment in fantasy or by manipulation of the relationship.

When working with schizophrenic patients, many clinicians discover that they feel restrained and deskilled. This may result from the schizophrenic individual's subtle attempts to undermine the effectiveness of the clinician's psychological reasoning, objectiveness, and attention to external standards. The treatment contract may be challenged. The patient may attempt to convince the clinician that real help will occur outside the treatment framework, through a "special" relationship. By enlisting the clinician in special work, such as uncovering the perpetrations of a persecutor, the patient is demonstrating her wish for control over the clinician's thoughts. The patient may often be persuasive, offering the person helping her the fantasy that she, the patient, can be cured if only someone will trust and listen to her. She may blatantly ignore the clinician's presence, treat the clinician as an incompetent, or threaten the clinician with unleashed aggression to create distance when necessary. The patient may become preoccupied with fantasies of merger such that the clinician directs his or her efforts to getting extricated from an entangled dyad rather than attending to the patient's symptoms or debility; or more subtly, the patient may refuse to acknowledge the therapist's actual qualities through idealization.

The patient may try to straight-jacket the clinician by restricting him or her with regard to the kinds of questions and areas of inquiry that may be initiated. The clinician may find that he or she is able to engage the patient only within a limited range, that the patient allows only certain kinds of inquiry. One patient, upon meeting her therapist for the first time, announced, "Your job is to take care of my body fluids—see to it that I'm fed and watered. The only thing you are to talk to me about, apart from my health, is how you can protect me from my enemies."

A more blatant example of control occurs when the patient tries to undermine the meaning of the clinician's words and understanding. Many patients state that they object to the clinician's reaching independent conclusions. That is, the patient questions the clinician's right to use insight, judgment, and reasoning to evaluate the patient's situation. Such a patient might say, "Those were not my words. You can't say that because I didn't say it," or "Don't put words in my mouth. You're trying to put thoughts into my head." The net effect of these efforts is to leave the clinician feeling incapable of using his or her own reason to understand the patient or to help the patient see him- or herself. The patient's efforts are aimed at maintaining isolation and safety because words that impute insight or awareness of painful circumstances are felt as a threat.

The form of control most difficult to manage involves the patient's attempt to engage someone in the special relationship, described above, that excludes others and promises a unique and privileged status. Through an element of seductiveness, the schizophrenic individual may limit the clinician's activity by prescribing the conditions under which the relationship must take place: The patient may insist that their relationship remain secret (and, therefore, not shared with other treaters, in turn preventing the clinician from obtaining valuable information from colleagues and depriving them of what he or she knows); the clinician, or other might be proscribed from raising concerns that have to do with the patient's "illness" or directing attention to life problems. The prescription is typically for the object, be it a clinician or other, to abandon interest in treatment or attention to the patient's disabilities. There is, further, an effort to cause the clinician or other to see the patient's symptoms as less pathological and most strongly to identify with the patient's expressed wish for freedom from treatment, supervision, or other restrictions.

Summarizing the Autonomy/Control Dilemma

Coupled with the desire for control is the patient's simultaneous wish for autonomy. Autonomy may be desired because it is socially acceptable to be independent and self-sufficient, and there may also be an innate wish for competence and effectiveness that can only be associated with autonomy. However, independence is frightening and in some respects unrewarding. Autonomy may be associated with isolation. The pain in looking forward to a life seemingly filled with challenges to self-esteem and disappointment is a daunting prospect. The schizophrenic person often yearns for partnership with another so that life can become less painful, less lonely, and more bearable.

Yet this need for contact is conflictual because of the anxiety and frustration experienced in interpersonal relatedness. Nevertheless, that intimate contact is desired because, if it can be controlled and managed, it promises a degree of support and safety that the patient cannot otherwise experience. The patient will attempt to balance this need for a relationship with his fear of its consequences through maneuvers that titrate intimacy according to his tolerance and reassure him that the partner in the relationship is not uncontrollable, not threatening overwhelming involvement nor sudden rejection and abandonment. Correspondingly, the clinician often experiences anxiety about loss of control when working with such patients. The intense, unconscious demands on the clinician provoke sometimes startling countertransference events. For example:

> A psychiatrist in training found it difficult to speak with his supervisor about his work with a young schizophrenic patient. The young doctor explained, "He [the patient] and I have such a special thing going; it's hard to explain to anyone else." Several months later, the therapist, while waiting for the elevator in his apartment building, had the distinct fantasy, accompanied by a feeling of anxiety and anger, that the patient (who was in fact on a locked unit twenty miles away) had followed him home, run up to his apartment, and would get out of the elevator just as the therapist entered it. At that point, the doctor began to discuss his interaction with the patient, beginning with his belief (as exemplified by the story), that the patient was taking over his life. The therapist's reaction was to want to stop treating the patient.

Loss

The theme of autonomy is closely related to experiences or anticipation of loss (17). The illness process itself robs the individual of a degree of autonomous mental experience. Furthermore, the intense ambivalence associated with trust and relatedness presents the patient with alternatives implying different but constant loss: If the schizophrenic person opts for vulnerability by trusting another and allowing for intimacy, he or she relinquishes some control. As noted, some patients who fantasize about tyrannical control over others would experience such a loss as extremely threatening. Alternatively, choosing to remain aloof or withdrawn necessitates loss of support and understanding, impoverishment of emotional life. These are not always conscious "choices" and may be dictated by physiological or unconscious factors, but the experience of loss is abiding and real, as was the case for the woman described below:

> A 46-year-old female schizophrenic entered treatment with the belief that she was a distant relative of "the old woman in the shoe." She claimed to have twenty-nine children, and in the initial interview, the therapist was prohibited from sitting in many different chairs, lest he inadvertently "crush" one of the children, all of whom were tiny and invisible to anyone but the patient. Within the first eighteen months of treatment, twenty-eight children "died"— through accident or illness. The patient's mood remained bland. Two years later, amidst much work and change, including exploration of the psychological significance of her last remaining "child" (and the underlying issue of this patient's actual childlessness), the child was "killed" in a car accident the patient insisted was her fault. She then became depressed, but allowed clinicians to support her, and was able to be more vulnerable and genuine.

The loss of functional capacities is a common and devastating feature of schizophrenia. Past skills or personal qualities as well as mood and outlook may be dramatically altered. Patients may in fact have lost relationships, supports, and jobs, as well as opportunities. Perhaps most importantly, they have lost a self-image that was associated with those goals and skills.

One patient, a previously successful artist, felt that, as punishment for her accomplishments, her talents were "stripped" from her and that now she was not fit to draw anything more than stick figures. She would become angry at the occupational therapist's urging her to draw, declaring, "That person is no more!"

For many patients, this profound loss produces utter discouragement and a tendency to see past capabilities as unavailable. This attitude precludes recruitment of useful aspects of potential ego functioning since those aspects of themselves are viewed as dead or distant. The anxiety that a schizophrenic patient experiences in social situations might be helped by his or her ability to recall a sense of competence from earlier social experiences, but very frequently that capacity is compromised by the profound sense of helplessness that is associated with the sense of loss of the old self.

In clinical experience, this sense of loss is particularly acute with respect to loss of time, of opportunities, and of relationships. Many patients, however, are not able to consciously acknowledge the nature of their loss. Typically, they experience loss as something that has happened to them as a result of outside forces. The schizophrenic patient who has lost friendships or a career will delusionally maintain that these things have been taken away. A patient who perceives herself to be the subject of persecution may claim that the losses she has experienced are only a result of her persecutor's efforts to turn friends against her, convince employers to kick her out of a job, and so on. The psychological forces favoring these delusional interpretations are evident: The loss is more tolerable if denied or distorted. The delusions in turn have two intriguing characteristics:

1. The delusion suggests a potential resolution for these losses. The persecutor could stop, or be persuaded to stop, or a cure could be found for the damaging effects of mind control experiments and the like. Although the possibility of such a resolution may be remote, it offers a magical hope of restitution to the patient and often prompts him or her to enlist others in bringing about this release.

2. Unfortunately, the delusions also promote passivity. Coping is not possible. The patient experiences him- or herself as a victim and sees change as an external event, if it is possible at all. Not only does the delusion seem to preclude effective adaptation and treatment collaboration, it also furthers a disabling psychological state of helplessness, which predisposes the patient to depression, futility, and symptom exacerbation.

Consider the following:

A young man, who had been ill for several years since his last year in high school, reported the delusion that he had had electrical devices planted in his brain at the time of his first hospitalization. These devices included a computer that told him what to think and occasionally made him have disturbing sexual thoughts. These devices, he said, were implanted by psychiatrists, who were punishing him for having been rebellious toward his parents.

Although initially angry at all mental health professionals, the patient had over the years modified his views. He had come to accept the idea that he had diseased brain tissue and that this is what caused his schizophrenia, which was responsible for his aggressiveness. He now believed that the computer in his brain was steadily, carefully "zapping" the diseased parts of his brain, killing the schizophrenic parts. He believed that ultimately he would be cured and that then the computer could safely be removed.

Though a likeable young man, he was characteristically resistant to participation in treatment programs, unmotivated for rehabilitative work, listless, and without goals for his future. Though often superficially compliant, he typically avoided productive work at home, becoming progressively more reclusive, then irritable, and finally paranoid and disorganized by the time he inevitably required rehospitalization.

His treatment was eventually furthered when clinicians, taking into account his psychological experience, suggested that participating in an activity program would promote healthier mental functioning. The patient came to believe that new brain tissue might grow as a result of his work, and this delusion helped him to increase his consistency and motivation at work.

The defense against acknowledgment is such a ubiquitous feature of schizophrenia that it may be a source of discouragement for clinicians. In this regard it is important to recall that this denial is in part a product of unconscious conflict and thus a consequence of the patient's psychic distress. Loss in its polymath forms is vigorously defended against, as are memories of past selves or dreams that threaten to reveal the burdens of the present.

This defense can take many forms. Patients may destroy pictures of themselves, deny their name, alter their dress, posture, body habits (by gaining or losing significant amounts of weight), mutilate themselves, and so forth. One patient, when shown his high school yearbook picture from a year ago asked, "Do I look like him?"

If one looks back at the person one was some years ago, one remembers old interests, values, and abilities and reflects on how and why they have changed over time. That process of change would be seen as a result of experience, reflection, decision, growth. There may still be a sense of loss, perhaps a loss of innocence or newness, but the nature and process of the change can ordinarily be understood. This experience of continuity is directly subverted by the illness experience in schizophrenic persons and represents yet another perspective on the dimension of their loss.

Safety

We may begin to look at the issue of safety by reviewing what it is that makes schizophrenic persons feel unsafe: disturbances in self-object differentiation; stress associated with interpersonal relatedness (due to cognitive and emotional demands); threat to self-esteem by anyone who may challenge the patients' (often delusional) view of themselves and/or their illness; delusions of being controlled by others; states of paranoia, including fears of bodily, spiritual, or mental harm; intense, disruptive states of anxiety, producing discontinuity; fears of helplessness; and interminable emptiness. The concern for safety represents the patient's wish to control these phenomena or somehow to create a haven secure against these threats.

We have observed many behaviors whose principal aim appears to be the maintenance of a feeling of safety (18). Some are particularly relevant to the situation of the treatment alliance. In most instances, the most threatening aspect of a therapeutic encounter is the clinician's capacity to observe, reflect, and pose questions to the patient, a process that inevitably forces the patient to confront one or another facet of his or her liabilities or defenses against acknowledging them.

Some patients must control all inquiry: Every time her doctor began to speak, one patient placed her hands firmly over her ears. After some months of this, she brought in a framed picture of herself, threw it on the therapist's desk, and, pointing to the cracked frame, declared, "Can't you see the glue isn't holding? It's because people are trying to look at the picture, and I can't always stop them." The patient explained that, whenever anyone came into her room, she would turn the picture face down but that she wasn't "fast enough sometimes." The therapist suggested there was a parallel between the picture and the patient. The patient felt other people's looking was destructive to the frame and that the therapist's words were somehow dangerous to her. "Perhaps," the therapist suggested, "you're afraid if you take your arms away from your ears, you'll crack. But," he added, "I take your showing me the picture as a sign that you want me to know something about you."

Another patient, who participated complacently in his activity program at the day hospital, was routinely pleasant until his case manager attempted to discuss treatment goals with him. He would then predictably become belligerent and accuse her of trying to seduce or castrate him. Although apparently willing to coexist peacefully and indefinitely in the day program, he intensely resisted any efforts to bring him to consider change, his future, or even the notion of fuller recovery from his severe psychotic disorder.

Patients differ in the degree to which they exclude parts of their life from inclusion in the treatment process. The degree of symptomatology bears little relationship to the breadth of scrutiny deemed permissible. This is important since too often prognosis is based simply on the intensity of pathology rather than on the limitations the patient places upon what can and cannot be explored. One patient tolerated her relationship with her therapist and their work together exceedingly well, except when asked about her sexual life. At those times, the patient would feel "possessed" by the spirit of her dead grandmother, become verbally and physically abusive, and appeared to hallucinate. Though quite delusional, the patient allowed broad exploration of her life and behavior and benefitted from treatment. A second patient was always stiffly polite with his therapist, punctual for meetings, and never manifested loud, dramatic, or unmanageable symptomatology. However, he constantly insisted that his life was nobody's business but his own, that he had every right to live it as unconventionally as he wanted. This translated into his refusal to review his maladaptive behaviors, despite the fact that, at 37, he had spent nearly half of his adult life in hospitals.

In their desperate efforts to establish an atmosphere of safety, patients may be forced to exclude most forms of intimacy, with a resulting impoverishment in their social experiences (19). A patient who could not tolerate any acknowledgment of her illness could maintain relationships with people only under strict circumstances. She would insist that one and all take an "oath" stating their belief that her troubles were the result of mistreatment by her doctors. Her conversations with her few intimates were limited to repeated harangues about the injustices done to her.

Such a rigid posture dramatically limits the range and effectiveness of the individual's experience with others (20, 21). In a global sense, the motive for such rigidification is the patient's perception that such drastic measures are required for a sense of safety. As we have already discussed, these measures also meet other needs, such as improvement or resolution of difficulties with self-object differentiation, resolving concerns about autonomy and control, and perhaps more psychological continuity.

A patient in a day hospital who experienced thinking as "unsafe" was encouraged in patient government meetings to formulate position papers or unique perspectives on topics that differentiated his thinking from others. These experiences were then reviewed with the patient and emphasis placed on pointing out the uniqueness of the patient's thinking and how it differed from others' as well as on how the patient may have been able to influence other people's thinking and reviewing with him how this process ordinarily happens. In this way, the clinician emphasized the patient's autonomy, control over his thinking, and his uniqueness as well as providing a model for the patient about how people can be influenced by others' thoughts without that being a malignant or damaging process.

The issue of safety returns us to the concepts that began our discussion of the subjective experience because it reminds us that there are powerful reasons for any schizophrenic individual's adopting the coping mechanisms he or she now manifests to the clinician. Behaviors and thoughts represent multimodal attempts to cope with the schizophrenic experience. Among all the aspects of that subjective experience, safety and the wish to avoid feeling overwhelmed or threatened or experiencing a fragmentation of one's sense of self remain major concerns that modify the patient's ability to cope and, especially, to engage in a treatment alliance (22).

Aspects of the patients' subjective experiences, such as concerns about control, loss, and safety, may be manifest in their behavior and thinking, or they may be inferred through careful clinical observation. In either case, we are ultimately interested in the internal psychological priorities that motivate the patient. One patient may manifest concern about safety by saying overtly, "I don't trust people here. People are trying to hurt me." Another patient might not discuss feeling unsafe for fear that by acknowledging his concern he would compromise the efficacy of his efforts to protect himself. That patient may nonetheless exhibit behaviors from which we can infer a concern about safety, as in the case for a patient who avoids discussing anger in family therapy sessions. This patient may deny that anger exists, despite reports of fighting in the home. Therapeutic exploration of the relationships in the home might be a threat to his efforts to fight for his place there.

Inference about aspects of the subjective experience can assist the strengthening of the treatment alliance. By deciphering the meaning of obtuse behaviors, and being prepared with our understanding of the critical psychological issues concerning the schizophrenic patient, we may act to facilitate the patient's adaptation, whether or not he or she participates with insight. When we perceive that a patient feels unsafe, for example and have an idea about what threatens him or her, we can structure our interactions so as to increase a feeling of competence and security. This was done for the man in the following example:

A 31-year-old schizophrenic patient appeared to defend himself against any affective experience of loss. He developed a ritual of tearing the obituary column out of the newspaper as soon as it was delivered to the unit, proclaiming he did this "to protect the patients from the lying, Jewish press." This behavior was one manifestation of an intricate delusional system in which no one "really died" but, instead, false reports of their deaths were circulated by Jews as part of their plan to take over the world. Thus, it was felt helpful to engage the patient in some benign activity in which loss might occur as part of the daily routine, but in a manner sufficiently nonthreatening so that, over time, the patient could begin to examine it.

Since he had expressed an interest in botany, he was encouraged to work in the garden. The first approach emphasized activity without discussion. That is, the patient would prune branches, cut away dead leaves, and so on, and no comment would be made. Gradually, the activities therapist began to comment about what the patient was doing, always staying at the concrete level of the gardening activity, saying, for example, "I noticed you cut away those dead leaves." Over time, in his individual therapy, the patient began to discuss the cycle of life and death as evidenced in the garden and, from there, to explore the themes of death and loss in looking at other people and their experiences.

In this case, the nature of the gardening activity had to be clearly described to the patient in advance. What was not initially discussed was the relationship between this intervention and internal psychological concerns that the clinician saw to be relevant to the patient's recovery. This strategy is analogous to the withholding of an interpretation in psychotherapy until the patient is able to hear it and use it productively.

The categories we have described represent common themes that have been apparent to us in our work with chronic schizophrenic patients. That is not to say that they are unvaryingly present or that all patients will be adequately served simply by attending to these themes. Rather, they provide a starting point and a structure through which the clinician can order his or her work. The clinician must actively explore schizophrenic patients' experiences of themselves and, in that process, generate hypotheses that reflect a tentative understanding of those patients. Such hypotheses lead to ideas about treatment interventions, the results of which would help to inform the clinician as to whether or not his or her hypotheses were accurate. The more the clinician is exposed to and aware of the kinds of psychological responses that characterize the schizophrenic patients' adaptation to their illness, the more likely that his or her treatment interventions will be relevant to that given patient.

PRIORITIES AND FLEXIBILITY

Finally, we come to our last perspective on the subjective experience of the schizophrenic individual. In Table 2.1, section III, we direct the clinician's attention to issues that reflect the integration of patients' psychological reactions to their illness. Until this point, it may have been possible to consider the themes, concerns, and categories of the subjective experience in isolation. This clearly does not mirror the psychological life of the patient. Coincident and even conflicting concerns can occupy schizophrenic persons and cause complex compensatory behaviors to arise.

We have alluded to the ambivalent nature of the patient's mental life, particularly with regard to important issues such as loss, autonomy and self-esteem. The idea that the patient possesses an implicit hierarchy of priorities, which determines to what degree and how a given psychological concern is handled, is an abstraction of a common-sense principle.

It conceptualizes a question we naturally begin to ask: How do schizophrenic individuals experience all of these aspects of the subjective experience as these aspects interact within themselves? When considering the patient's characteristic management of a given issue, such as self-object differentiation, we must wonder how important this matter is to him or her, compared to concerns about safety. How does that issue influence self-view and world-view? How does it alter the confirmation of his or her delusions? When do some psychological priorities conflict with others, and how does the patient resolve them?

Given the complex demands on the patient's psyche, how effectively does he or she render these conflicts settled? Can we imagine that, because of intensely conflicting priorities, the patient is hemmed in, restrained, in his or her ability to effect satisfactory relatedness or gainful functioning? We can then conceptualize the patient's flexibility, which is a measure of how beset by rigid demands is the patient's ego.

A patient who must struggle to meet too many priorities that conflict too much is less able to consider change. Because these issues affect character functioning and relatedness, this state may be said to affect the patient's availability to treatment. Can the patient tolerate the idea of change or accept inquiry and/or intimacy?

The patient's availability can be assessed on a number of different levels. One could assess the schizophrenic patient's willingness and ability to participate in a psychosocial treatment paradigm. One might consider the patient's ability to be involved in a medication trial. From all the relevant clinical data, including the assessment of subjective experience, the treatment team or a given clinician can construct an assessment of the patient's ability to participate directly in a given task.

Constructing a hierarchy of priorities helps us understand how the patient goes about resolving the requirements imposed on him by his illness. The subjective experience informs us about the origin of priorities. The patient's behavior, thinking, and modes of adaptation tell us about how he seeks to resolve those priorities. This awareness of the patient's efforts to balance his competing needs allows for more empathic and creative treatment planning. This approach creates in the clinician a sensitivity to the patient's experience, to how the patient will receive a particular treatment intervention and contribute to the clinician's assessment of how to promote the treatment alliance and how best to revise the treatment plan.

The consideration we have given to the subjective experience in this phase of our clinical assessment allows us to make judgments and predictions about two important areas of our work with patients. As we have discussed, we learn first about what patients can and cannot do at this time, and second, what patients request or demand of us. In the latter instance, we are evaluating what messages patients give to the environment, how they communicate their tolerance for and interest in relatedness or other aspects of social functioning. The patient who insists that no one mention or discuss with him that he has an illness, refuses to participate in psychosocial treatments, or avoids taking medications poses different challenges than the patient who is compliant in some respects but who believes that her illness is a just punishment from God. Such a patient might insist that the clinician agree there is no justification for any attempts at promoting her recovery and demand that the clinician collaborate in her remaining chronically disfunctional, below her potential. Both such patients manifest different forms of maladaptation that impose different requirements on the environment.

Treatment planning takes into account these patient-authored demands by clinicians' first understanding the priorities that these demands reflect. This aspect of our experience of the patient is often the most intense and difficult part of our work. Before we begin to explore the patient's subjective experience, we are in many cases acutely aware of the patient's effect on us. Our countertransference to the schizophrenic patient is in this way extremely informative, especially regarding critical aspects of the patient's psychological functioning. Those priorities that are most important are usually, if not always, manifest in the demands the patient makes of us. For this reason, the priorities associated with this critical aspect of the patient's behavior are most important for us to address in the treatment plan. Appreciation of this clinical issue thus provides us with some guidelines about what to address first or most urgently. It is likely, also, that these priorities will require the most tact and creativity in presenting a treatment plan that does not overwhelm the patients; that does not stress them beyond their capacities; that begins where they are able to begin.

3

From Understanding to Action:
The Alliance and
the Treatment Program

Our goal in emphasizing the nature of the treatment alliance with schizophrenic patients is to bring about the patients' increased collaboration in and commitment to treatment and thus promote their effective coping with their illness (1–6). These aims are reflected in the first section of Table 3.1, which outlines the goals of treatment. Particular attention is given to the attitudes communicated to patients and to the understanding patients derive from the work. In this sense, these treatment goals are particular to our interest in the treatment alliance and its place in the implementation of any therapeutic modality.

A recurrent theme is our emphasis on collaboration rather than compliance, a theme that distinguishes our treatment approach from those that do not actively consider the patient's complicated role in accepting and effectively using help. Most importantly, we acknowledge that the patient's active participation is a prerequisite to the treatment process. Without such collaboration, the patient will be at best passively compliant. A patient who merely consents to be in a treatment setting cannot effectively cope with his or her illness. We prefer to see compliance as a natural consequence of understanding and collaboration rather than a goal in itself.

When reviewing the psychological consequences of the schizophrenic illness process, we have noted the dominance of patients' experience of diminished self-esteem (7–8). Many realities impinge upon patients' experience of efficacy and satisfaction. They are unavoidably confronted with evidence of often-denied or controverted vulnerabilities. Self-acceptance requires acknowledgment of those vulnerabilities and of an image of the self representing some diminished capacities; it also requires intense experiences of loss and discontinuity. In order to accept participa-

Table 3.1

I. Goals of Treatment
   A. Increased Collaboration (versus "Compliance")
   B. Increased Self-Esteem
   C. Understanding and Management of Symptoms
   D. Coping with Psychological Responses to Illness
   E. Developing Effective Cognitive and Behavioral Responses
II. Treatment Frame
   A. Establishing the Clinician's "Presence"
     1. Separateness, Uniqueness, Limitations, Fallibility, Empathy, and Hope
   B. Presenting Model of the Illness
     1. Construct Acceptable to Patient; Timing
   C. Treatment Tasks
   D. Patient's Goals and Treatment Goals
III. Treatment Alliance Techniques
   A. General Principles
     1. Reexploration of Subjective Experience
     2. Reinforcement of Treatment Frame; Limitations
     3. Tone
   B. The Parallel Dialogue
   C. The "Resigned" Patient
   D. Countertransference

tion in rehabilitation, medication administration, or other treatments, the patient must be able to tolerate some acknowledgement of a need for help and of the limitations that this implies. The following example illustrates this issue.

A 28-year-old woman, with a twelve-year history of chronic schizophrenia, told her psychiatrist, in his office, that someone was listening to her through the walls of her bedroom. She also said that she had heard people discussing her on the street outside her home.

She had begun to complain of feelings of mistrustfulness some three weeks before. She had continued to attend her day program, but would not eat lunch in the hospital cafeteria because "people there laugh about me when I walk in." She had agreed to an increase in her neuroleptic, which served to decrease the intensity of these experiences. However, her improvement led to her to stop the medication after one week.

The patient had previously been able to discuss her psychotic symptoms with the psychiatrist and the rationale for medication use, while still maintaining that "these things that happened to me may be true; I think I can tell the difference between hallucinations and real events." Her strongest reason to doubt the reality of her symptoms proved to be her religiosity. As it developed in her treatment, the most ego-dystonic aspect of her delusions was the fear that she might be or become possessed by the devil. The psychiatrist helped the patient to contrast this irrational fear with the multiple evidences of her kindness, scrupulosity, and adherence to her religious beliefs.

In the weeks and months prior to this decompensation, the patient had been frustrated by her lack of progress and particularly by her difficulty in working (she had withdrawn from two volunteer jobs arranged by her day program). She found social demands quite stressful and became easily discouraged if her responsibilities or performance did not meet her own high expectations. She complained bitterly that family and day program staff did not "support" her when she discussed ambitious plans for full-time work or school.

On the day she presented her paranoid concern about eavesdropping, the patient was uncharacteristically insistent that her psychiatrist accept these symptoms as true. When he demurred, she stormed out of his office saying, "You don't support me either! No one does!"

The psychiatrist wondered if she would be safe and contacted her supervised residence. Later that night, the patient called. She had been unable to sleep and related terrifying experiences: feeling paralysed; vivid visual hallucinations; a sensation like the top of her head being lifted off; premonitory dread; and the fear that her body was being taken over by the devil. In contrast to her attitude in her earlier session, the patient allowed her psychiatrist to empathize with her fear and confusion without insisting on his acceptance of these experiences as evidence of demonic possession.

She asked the psychiatrist if anything might help her sleep. He noted that these symptoms could be due to anxiety, as he understood these phenomena. They discussed increasing her neuroleptic and adding a minor tranquilizer for sedation. The psychiatrist reminded the patient of her previous successful efforts in titrating medication to control her acute symptoms.

This interaction was made possible by the patient's allowing herself to be vulnerable, letting her psychiatrist help her in the way he could—although that required her acknowledging that she was not managing well enough on her own. The patient might still wonder about the "reality" of her symptoms, but she trusted her psychiatrist's capacity to help her.

That trust in turn was built on the treatment alliance, with its model of the patient as a good and spiritually correct person and the implied model of the illness and treatment presented fairly and openly, without embellishment or exaggeration. Because the psychiatrist stood consistently for a compassionate and reasoned view of her and her illness, the patient was able to return for help when that proved necessary.

Our formulation of a working treatment alliance proceeds toward this goal and offers strategies for achieving it. We will recapitulate these points, but to some extent they suffuse all of what we say. Understanding the patient's difficulty in tolerating self-awareness underlies our conceptualization of the disorder and its manifestations. This understanding is a cornerstone of our thoughtful treatment of delusions and our view of their importance to the schizophrenic individual. It is also reflected in our recognizing how frequently schizophrenic persons are critical of themselves. They blame themselves unfairly for their illness, for relapses and failures, and especially for failing to satisfy their own or their families' expectations. They also suffer from their inability to formulate realistic expectations or be satisfied with them, since such formulations often imply tempering grandiose demands. In these issues are contained the sources of patients' sadness and demoralization.

The goals of our work, as listed in Table 3.1, may even seem self-evident, given the discussion in the preceding two chapters. Increased collaboration and improved self-esteem have been the clarion motifs of this presentation. In section I.C, "Understanding and Management of Symptoms," we present an issue derived from principles set forth earlier in the book. We have proposed that the conceptual model of schizophrenia we outlined in chapter 1 can be and should be presented to the patient when and to the degree he or she is able to use the information productively. We can sometimes depend on the patient's curiosity to help us know how much to say. The creative and empathic introduction of this material is nevertheless crucial. Although it may be stressful for the patient, a rational understanding of his or her illness can help to resolve self-blame, confusion, and irrational fears about the future. This knowledge is far from being a panacea, but it is an asset if it can be accepted.

We also recommend the patient's active inclusion in treatment decision-making and particularly in the selection of treatment options. This can be a troublesome issue because it requires the clinician to tolerate relinquishing some of his or her authority. More importantly, it demands discretion and judgment in determining both how to make opportunities for the patient's participation available and when the clinician's authority must be appropriately asserted. These issues are exemplied in the following:

> A patient was discussing her treatment goals in a patient-staff treatment planning meeting. In addition to goals of reducing suicidality, coping with her delusional interpretations of events, and family stresses, the patient brought up her difficulty tolerating aggression in others. This had caused her considerable difficulty in the past, in particular in work settings. When running a cash register, she would frequently become anxious and disorganized in response to irritated and critical customers.
>
> The patient wondered about joining an activity that would allow her to role-play and learn techniques for coping with and using assertiveness. Her therapeutic activities coordinator was noticeably uncomfortable when this was mentioned. The coordinator noted that the patient had been reticent in challenging herself in other activities and had generally worked below her potential. For this reason, the coordinator said the patient would probably find the role-playing activity too stressful, particularly because that activity required tolerance of observation and criticism by other patients and staff. The coordinator ended by saying, "I just don't want you to try something and fail at it."[a]
>
> The staff discussed this interaction at a later meeting and decided to allow the patient to choose whether or not she would join

the role-playing activity after receiving recommendations from the activity coordinator. It was felt that the patient was capable of assessing the coordinator's advice and then freely deciding. If she "failed" at the activity, it would be uncritically viewed as a learning experience.

The activity coordinator was urged to collect her impressions of the patient and present them in the context of her expert assessment, including recommendations based on the activity coordinator's experience. In this way, the patient was given a consultation but retained, appropriately, the right to take on a challenge. No serious harm would have eventuated from her "failing," and "failure" itself was not certain, though very possible. The patient elected to follow the coordinator's advice and delayed enrollment in that activity for a few weeks.

Physicians certainly retain a crucial authority over the accurate uses of medications. But within this domain, there are many occasions where choices among reasonable alternatives can be made in consultation with the patient. The simple exercise of prerogative can meaningfully support a patient's self-esteem. When a specific treatment is indicated, the rationale for this decision should be plainly presented. These are common-sense principles that are nevertheless neglected due to the mistaken assumption that the patient is utterly apathetic or unable to comprehend what we wish to present. Though disturbances in communication and relatedness may be present, regarding the patient as an unconcerned, unthinking entity is hopelessly detrimental to the treatment alliance.

The act of explaining implicitly introduces and later maintains a model for comprehending illness and subjective experience apart from the patient's autochthonous view. We have referred to this process as demystifying both illness and treatment because the clinician's model presents reason and clarity that the patient may over time review and accept. At best, the clinician's understanding of the patient is organized, hopeful, realistic, and free from unreasonable expectations, harsh judgments, or guilt. The patient may reconcile himself to that model over time because it instills in him a feeling of control (an internal locus of control) more satisfying and effective than his illusions of mastery. Due to limitations imposed by his illness and his psychological response to it, each patient differs in his relative capacity to accept help and information. This means that treatment plans will necessarily be individualized and require creativity even in the method of their presentation.

Indeed, one of our most important tasks is to enlighten patients regarding the existence in them of psychological reactions to an illness they may or may not acknowledge—reactions that are usually not consciously understood but that do determine a great deal of the patient's affective life and behaviors and thus are a not inconsiderable source of frustration and uncertainty. Schizophrenic patients, like other people, are often unaware of self-defeating patterns or of the practical price they pay for avoiding conflict or confrontation in an area of vulnerability. Exaggerated fears of mental incompetence and mystification over the causes of impairments in relatedness are among the common antecedents of such maladaptive responses as social withdrawal and avoidance of challenges in the service of avoiding confrontation with cognitive limitations.

Clinicians can use an educative paradigm, talking about schizophrenia and the common psychological responses to the disorder, or they can rely on traditional modalities, such as supportive psychotherapy, milieu therapy, and rehabilitative treatments, to inculcate principles and convey pragmatic recommendations. All interpersonal therapeutic modalities offer opportunities for reflection on the cognitive and behavioral patterns that manifest the patient's psychological adaptation.

The five goals noted in Table 3.1, section I, encompass the breadth of change that is the desired outcome of any successful treatment. Although we have chosen to focus on the treatment alliance, it is clear that a well-functioning, maintained treatment alliance will be accompanied by positive psychological and behavioral change. Indeed, these goals may be seen as general treatment goals themselves. We realize, however, that work with schizophrenic individuals is often not reducible to the concerns we present. Attention to environmental conditions, to physical and psychological complications, and to severe or debilitating symptoms may predominate treatment planning. In such cases, the goals specific to the treatment alliance will, in our view, still be critical but as one facet of an integrated, complicated task.

THE TREATMENT FRAME

When clinicians identify concerns about the treatment alliance with a given patient, they must then organize their efforts to achieve the goals we have outlined above. The remainder of this chapter will suggest a plan to effect the principles we have set forth. We will orient our presentation largely from the perspective of the individual clinician working to establish a treatment alliance with a schizophrenic individual. This outline is appropriate to any treatment modality and useful regardless of the clinician's discipline. The plan can also be part of a multidisciplinary treatment effort, for what we learn about the patient's subjective experience and other psychological concerns will be relevant and adaptable to the work of all members of a treatment team. The reader can follow the discussion using the outline in Table 3.1, sections II and III.

In any treatment setting, we begin by defining what the treatment is and what it is not, the roles or expectations of both clinician and patient, and the goals of the work. In psychoanalytic writing, this is often referred to as the process of setting the treatment "frame." Although many times, through habitual oversight or ignorance, this crucial exercise is neglected, its theoretical and practical importance is well-established. Selzer (9) has emphasized the importance of a treatment contract—essentially the process we are describing here—in work with borderline patients. The role of the treatment frame in work with schizophrenic individuals is no less central nor less critical with respect to outcome. Patients who are mistrustful and often misperceive others' actions require a clear and consistent structure within which their treatment may occur.

Even at the beginning of their relationship, the clinician is often forced by the patient's behavior or importuning to define for both of them what responses are and are not possible. In initial contacts with schizophrenic patients, many clinicians have had experiences in which they are prematurely asked for their "diagnostic impressions." Or they are made to feel that if they proceed with their work, they will lose the patient's trust and goodwill because, for example, the patient has stated that she is not ill but is being treated unfairly. Not uncommonly, the patient urges the clinician to defend or champion her or his cause in opposition to others who have been punitive and prejudiced. As we have discussed previously, the psychological motives for these behaviors are complex, but no less complex is the predicament in which well-meaning clinicians can soon find themselves.

Our approach to the beginning of the treatment is based on principles we delineated in chapter 2. We must first take care not to commit ourselves to promises or conceptual positions in the early phases of our work. When a patient barrages us with demands, we must insist on our right—like the patient's—to take time to reflect before making decisions or agreeing to a point of view. This is especially important when we discuss the patient's "diagnosis." How frequently the patient states, provocatively or defiantly, "I suppose you think I'm crazy, too." The appropriate response, in the early part of treatments, is for the clinician to recount what he has been told about the patient, while confronting the patient's insistence that he must know about her before he has experienced her. This latter point will likely lead into a discussion of the patient's experience of the clinician as "just like all the others," having the same thoughts as prior clinicians, and therefore not unique or individual (for an excellent example of such an interaction, see chapter 4). It is also fair for the clinician to tell the patient that he respects the sources of information about the patient, but that he will reserve the right to make his own conclusions after he has come to know the patient better. It is also important for the clinician to note when some of the patient's assertions, particularly delusions, seem implausible, while adding that it is not possible for the clinician to prove or disprove them. The clinician can amplify on his criteria for plausibility based on his experience of the world as a place where, for example, people are not whimsically singled out for unremitting and fantastic torture by intelligence agencies or supernatural forces. The clinician's impressions do not preclude the reality of the patient's, but are the basis for the clinician's own subjective experience. By presenting them, the clinician emphasizes his separateness. The clinician also begins to let the patient know how his analyses and opinions are formed. Whenever possible, it is best to defer extended discussion of this issue until the treatment alliance has been better established.

The reason for this cautious deference to the patient's paranoia is simple: Patients are threatened by the prospect of scrutiny and change. They are consequently mistrustful on several accounts, and not merely because of their perceptual suspicion. Patients may unconsciously look for a reason not to listen to what will unavoidably be hard lessons in self-understanding. The therapeutic alliance must be more firmly based so that patients' premature dismissal of clinicians can be avoided. In particular, time and careful work can allow the patients to integrate perceptions of clinicians' honesty, integrity, consistency, and compassion. Then patients may be better able to listen. Our guiding principle is our respect for patients' limitations and our resolve not to expect patients to do more than they can do at a given time.

What we propose is in fact nothing more than being frank with patients. Our first impressions are often based on unproven assumptions. We may be able to diagnose a thought disorder, excitement, active hallucinations (but not their cause), or a mistrustful, guarded stance. We can explore the unreasonableness or maladaptive implications of some of the patient's beliefs or statements. But we cannot know the patient is delusional without proof! Obviously, certain views are implausible. It is enough to note our curiosity, confusion, or incredulity and, when appropriate, to point out what we see and search for plausible explanations. In this, we can sometimes enlist the patient's capacity to reason and be reasonable. If we are, on the contrary, prematurely dogmatic or authoritarian, we risk acting not on principle or theory, but on the anger and resentment, the countertransference, evoked in us by the difficult, devaluing, and paranoid patient.

It is more meaningful to point out the active intrusion of symptoms of the illness than to debate the significance of past events. Some patients prefer anchoring their attention and the clinician's in a review of the past rather than confronting harsh, present challenges. It is also more relevant to describe how a patient uses delusional concerns or the past to avoid acknowledging the truth about current difficulties. For example, schizophrenic patients who confront cognitive limitations subtly affecting social performance or aspects of work skills will avoid situations that so stress these limitations, while maintaining that their inactivity or withdrawal has some other cause, typically one we see to be delusional or at least irrational. Such explanations include assertions of mind control; of past brain damage from medications; supernaturally ordained restrictions on activity; or lack of interest in any other than the patients' focused concerns, which, typically, they cannot pursue without being free of treatment, especially medications. Although it is a long-term goal, it is inherently therapeutic to help such patients see the psychological function of their delusion, for example, and to explore alternative means of coping with their problem. This kind of work is not possible, however, if the discussion becomes mired in a pointless attempt to win patients' disavowal of their beliefs.

Once the clinician has established a firmer base for the therapeutic alliance, it is also possible to begin pointing out behaviors and cognitions that have occurred in meetings with the patient, events that both parties have witnessed, and to use these as data on which to base diagnosis and treatment recommendations. Common experiences are better sources of information and can lead to a discussion of trust and differing perception, which is essential for the progress of the treatment alliance. Suggestions for treatment plans arising from these observations are less likely to be experienced as prejudicial.

It is essential that, in looking for evidence of 'symptoms' in the present interaction with the patient, we broaden our view of schizophrenia in a manner consistent with the model we presented in chapter 1. If we persist in "diagnosing" schizophrenia by considering delusions, hallucinations, and thought disorder the most important symptoms, our approach to the patient will be similarly skewed. The search for symptoms in the here and now must follow the thrust of our model, wherein the patient's principal concerns are seen as:

1. Perceptual, attentional, and mood disturbances
2. Mistrustfulness
3. Cognitive limitations
4. Psychological maladaptations and low self-esteem

In our day-to-day interactions with the patient, in any treatment modality or setting, we can find evidence for disturbances in each of these four areas. Patients who meet DSM III-R criteria for schizophrenia will have disturbances in these areas; the reverse is also true. But in organizing our thinking in this way, we focus our concern and have a useful way of focusing our treatment interventions. We can discuss some of these impairments without having to directly address the patient's delusional views—for these must be dealt with patiently and over time. Patients can begin work on problems in these areas while still grappling with their uncertainty over why this has happened to them or what it means to them. Importantly, we can help to combat their demoralization by showing them that work can go on despite delusional or irrational concerns.

ESTABLISHING THE THERAPIST'S "PRESENCE"

These various issues implicitly differentiate the clinician's perspective from the patient's. While this distinction may be assumed, it is not safe to assume that the patient accepts or appreciates it. As we noted in discussing the nature of the patient's subjective experience in chapter 2, the schizophrenic individual may not experience the clinician as a separate person. He or she may entertain fantasies of merger with the clinician or have expectations about the clinician's role that represent unconscious projections. When we speak of establishing the clinician's "presence" (10–11), we refer to the complicated task of defining the clinician's role and responsibilities in light of the schizophrenic patient's typical concerns. This is, of course, a crucial part of the treatment frame.

The clinician must assert his or her uniqueness and separateness without conveying disregard for the psychological basis of the patient's tendency to treat the clinician as not separate, not unique, or subordinate. We must remember the profoundly troubling disturbances in self-object differentiation that may lead the patient to assume the clinician can read his or her mind, that the patient's thoughts are created or controlled by the clinician, or that the relationship with the clinician must be spurned in order to alleviate anxiety consequent to intimacy. When patients attempt to blur the clinician's uniqueness ("You're like all the other nurses"), our response must be dictated by our understanding of the potential perceptual disturbances accounting for these phenomena, as well as their defensive function: If the patient need not consider the clinician's uniqueness, he or she is required to do less work in integrating the clinician's varied behaviors and statements. The patient also characteristically devalues whatever change-provoking observations the clinician then makes.

Disturbance in self-object differentiation (12), as well as experiencing lack of control and concern about safety, often leads to defensive efforts to control the clinician by extorting promises, seducing the clinician into a "special" alliance or deviation from standard practice, or contemptuously demeaning the clinician's capacities. These psychological mechanisms of defense, or adaptation, frequently complicate the clinician's efforts to establish a treatment frame. All can be dealt with, in part, by the clinician's careful delineation of his or her role, understanding of the nature of the patient's difficulties, and proposals for their work.

How does the clinician define him or herself as separate and unique? First, we must note when patients make assertions that imply the opposite. A patient's statement "You're just like all the rest" (see chapter 4, as noted previously, for an extended discussion of this theme) is an obscuring of uniqueness. When patients maintain that clinicians can read their thoughts, there is an implicit blurring of separateness (which may be the consequence of abnormal perceptions). More subtle are the circumstances when patients are inordinately passive, inviting clinicians to take control, make decisions, or organize priorities for them. In these cases, there has been a de facto loss of separateness that, when recognized, must be confronted by all parties. The clinician must resolve to distinguish between genuine, empathic, professional help and making choices or setting priorities, tasks for which the individual must in all events, barring predictable danger to self or others, assume responsibility. In the cases of a characterization stereotype, a clinician may respond by pointing out in the first instance how he or she is different, since we are all in some respects unique. The clinician can then help the patient to see that obscuring uniqueness leads to a "deadening" of experience and difficulty predicting the behavior of individuals, who do not respond uniformly to most challenges and stimuli. In the case of accusations of mind-reading or mind-controlling capacities, repeated denials will be of limited avail. Rather, over time, the patient may come to instinctively appreciate the differences in thinking processes, between himself and the clinician, if the clinician takes care to elucidate how he thinks. This task is also aided when the clinician takes opportunities to point out how the patient's reasoning differs from his or her own, as in the following situation:

> When a patient in the hospital complained about a staff member who had made what the patient interpreted to be a condescending gesture, the clinician, who was a nurse, said the following:
> "I see why you thought that, but I looked at it differently. When I see someone gesture like that [a wave of the hand], I think that person is trying to be playful and friendly, and in my experience,

that's usually true. Besides, I know that staff member, and she often acts like that, but she's never condescending—though I realize we may view her differently. Also, rather than being condescending, I think, from what you told me about your conversation with her just before, that she was worried you were angry with her and was trying to get through to you, to let you know that she wasn't put off by your irritation with her."

This approach also requires frankness if it is to be successful, which means our acknowledging the fact that we *do* get angry at patients and sometimes express this in our behavior. This candor also commands our eschewing defensiveness when reviewing with the patient the behavior of colleagues, a process that is applicable when treatment takes place in a hospital, day-hospital, or rehabilitative program setting. Consider this situation:

A schizophrenic man, in his mid-thirties, was angry at a day-hospital staff member whom he accused of being arrogant and condescending. Another staff member reviewed the relationship of the patient with the "arrogant" clinician, and remarked:

"You know, C [the "arrogant" clinician] and you have the same problem. You're both sensitive to rejection, and you both pull away to protect yourselves when you feel hurt. I've talked with C, who feels you don't respect her, that you don't think she can help you. I know that when C feels that way, she rarely shows it. Instead she is removed, even aloof. But inside, she's quite disappointed that the two of you have not found a way to work together."

Although the patient and "arrogant" clinician continued to have difficulty, the patient learned a great deal about his own character from this process.

Throughout the course of treatment, clinicians must present themselves as limited (in the sense of being human and imperfect), fallible, and vulnerable. Schizophrenic individuals have understandable difficulty with empathy and will be hostile in an environment where the clinicians present themselves as authorities, unapproachable, and "different" from patients and where fallibility or humanness are not actively acknowledged. At the same time, clinicians must also comfortably assert their expertise and, where relevant, their objectivity. Patients certainly wish to believe they are in competent hands. Competency will not be communicated through unnecessary authority or force. Is not the imprudent or pointless use of such authority rather the work of insecurity and incertitude? Our sure understanding of the disorder, our ideas about how we can help, and our frank acknowledgement of what we do not know or cannot surely help constitute the framework of our expertise.

The acknowledgment of the fundamental role of the schizophrenic patient's psychological adaptation to his or her illness implicitly defines any clinician's role as that of a consultant. The treatment cannot work until the patient is an active participant. The crucial first step of the treatment, which is the establishment of the treatment alliance, is the very process of eliciting interest, conviction, and hope. The clinician is not responsible for the patient's improvement and cannot think so. The patient is responsible; the clinician provides knowledge, observational skills, and a plan.

It is, in this sense, dangerous to want the patient to become well, to base professional esteem on obtaining a desired response from a given patient. Clinicians must focus on technique, the refinement of knowledge and experience, and on the steady application of the treatment model. Of course clinicians would soon despair if their efforts did not generally meet with success. It must be enough for us to know that, in general, our principles and methods are valid and valuable. It is not countertherapeutic to hope for a given patient's recovery. But we must often press on, faithful to our conceptualization of the disorder and our work, while the patient resists or avoids or passively complies with the treatment.

The rationale for this admonition is threefold. First, work with these individuals is intense, provocative, and complicated. If our spirits and esteem depend on the patient's apparent improvement, we will soon become dispirited, demoralized, and ineffective. Second, schizophrenic persons' psychological state is complicated by intense self-blame and deeply unconscious anger. They view caring and helpful intentions ambivalently and both desire and resist intimacy. The patients' perception that clinicians want their improvement, indeed need it for their own self-esteem, offers an unfortunate medium in which patients may act out anger and envy as well as self-destructiveness in demoralizing or alienating a potential caregiver. Third, clinicians' dependence on a patients' clinical improvement puts their objectivity at risk. Treatment decisions, even unconscious decisions about what or what not to say, may then be influenced by countertransference rather than theory and experience. In such circumstances, it is quite common to see clinicians acting out their own frustration and resentment through use of clouded, even prejudiced treatment rationales.

As clinicians, we must have in mind the model of the consultant, regardless of each of our disciplines, and accept the fact of the patient's ultimate control and responsibility (13). In so doing, we concentrate on what we understand about the patient's behavior or symptoms and communicate that understanding together with a plan for coping with the problems presented. When the patient does not utilize what we offer, we resort to our techniques of understanding the patient's resistance to treatment. We explore the patient's subjective experience, consider the psychological functions of denial, and assess the patient's psychological adaptation and how it might be influenced by his or her participation in the treatment intervention. It is crucial, above all, to remember that psychologically motivated denial, resistance, and unconscious anger stem from low self-esteem and fear of the humiliation or disappointment that might follow efforts at change.

The only antidotes to unrealistic expectations are education and self-examination. Clinicians must expect the slow rate of change of the schizophrenic patient. But they should also feel that they understand why, and why their efforts may be helpful even without immediate and observable alterations in symptoms or psychological adaptation. If a clinician repeatedly struggles with expectations for work that are ultimately self-defeating and limiting, it is perhaps appropriate for the clinician to reflect why this is so.

Part of our presence as clinicians is expressed in the highly individual ways in which we communicate empathy and hope. Indeed, our personal commitment to endure our schizophrenic patients' despair, doubt, and rage is the most important communication of hope. Although, at present, we can offer no cures and must frankly acknowledge the real and persistent difficulties with which our patients struggle, perhaps throughout their lives, understanding and compassion may create a bond that can support schizophrenic individuals in their struggles with suffering and frustration. That we also offer a plan for coping that challenges demoralization is added reason for hope that schizophrenic persons may develop greater self-understanding, self-acceptance, and improved adaptation to their illness.

PRESENTING THE MODEL OF THE ILLNESS

As we discussed in chapters 1 and 2, it is inherently difficult for the schizophrenic person to appreciate the disturbances in his perception and thinking. Correspondingly, it may take him quite some time to accept the fact he is ill (if he ever fully does). He may not want to hear a description of his illness or a delineation of the symptoms that reflect the disorder's influence on his psychological state. Nevertheless, when and to the degree the patient is able, education about the model we outlined in chapter 1 is a central element in setting our treatment frame.

This task is central precisely because it defines our function and the theory that informs our plans. Furthermore, insofar as the model is logical and consistent (while not complete), it generates predictions and assessments that support its reasonableness. Although this does not insure the patient's acceptance, such reliability can appeal to the schizophrenic individual who is awash in feelings of discomfort, uncertainty, and futility. For example:

> A man in his late twenties reported incessant wordless "chattering" in his head for the past year. It was distracting, discouraging, and associated with tension and irritability. The patient believed this noise was caused by "transmissions" from an unspecified device controlled by confederates of an apparently well-to-do man whom he had seen at a distance on a plane, but who, the patient imagined, resented him for having had envious thoughts and for being attracted to the man's wife. The patient also manifested, but did not acknowledge, significant cognitive and behavioral impairments, including difficulty assessing affect in others; trouble when trying to prioritize tasks; difficulty assimilating new information; facial grimacing; and social withdrawal.
>
> The patient initially did not accept neuroleptic medications. He was quite mistrustful, even hostile, saying he wanted to stop the

perpetrators of his torment and did not think his psychiatrist could be of any help, yet he continued to attend sessions.

The psychiatrist recommended a neuroleptic regimen, and explained his rationale. The patient showed interest in the neurological issues, so the psychiatrist drew some explanatory figures. They reviewed how the medications would work according to the theory (concentrating on the mechanisms responsible for producing anxiety and hallucinations). The psychiatrist emphasized that he understood that the patient might be convinced of the reality of his perception of the "chattering" (i.e., that it came from an external source) and described in psychological terms why this would be so.

The psychiatrist concluded by saying:

"You maintain that the 'chattering' is caused by transmissions. The trouble is, you don't know how or why this is happening, and there is no apparent way, you tell me, for you to stop it. This causes you frustration and discouragement.

"I believe, for the reasons I have stated, that your experiences are symptoms of this illness, as I've described. If I am correct, the medication I'm prescribing will help, although gradually. The anxiety, tension, and hallucinations will get better over the course of a few weeks; if we can find the right dose and if the medicine works—and it does most of the time. It may not remove all your symptoms, but it should make those that remain more tolerable. *My plan* suggests that you will feel better soon. The plan offers you a way to do something that will produce results; you tell me that otherwise you're helpless. I hope you'll consider this treatment plan, because I think you'll be less frustrated if you see that you can have some control over these experiences."

After some further clarification of side effects, response characteristics, and prognosis, the patient agreed to take the medication, although he said, "I don't quite buy the idea that this is an illness, but I figure maybe the medication will help decrease my sensitivity to the transmissions."

It is necessary to think about when to present the model of the illness. Timing has important implications for the treatment alliance. If presented too soon or with too much urgency, the model may be perceived as threatening, which can lead to a rupture of the treatment alliance. Yet some allusion to the clinician's rationale and theoretical approach is necessary early in the treatment: if a clinician is offering someone treatment, it is presumably because that person has a mental illness. As we stated above, the clinician's uniqueness is an important part of the treatment frame; the clinician cannot abandon his or her practice or theoretical approach even if it is with the intention of rescuing a failing treatment alliance. We begin with some statement of how we do our work, how we evaluate and recommend. We agree to respect the schizophrenic individual's viewpoint and differences and indeed affirm our interest in his or her ideas and subjective experience of self, illness, and treatment. With this approach, we hope to reach an agreement for patient and clinician to work and learn together.

Although we cannot standardize this intervention, we can recommend that the clinician begin with an overview of his or her understanding of the illness model and ask if the patient is interested in more detail, particularly as it is relevant to the clinician's treatment modality. The patient's curiosity may then be a guide. In the presentation, the clinician should make liberal reference to the patient's model—that is, to the patient's subjective experience of his illness, which often includes delusional elements. Commonalities and differences may be described, as well as implications for treatment. This last guideline assumes that before presenting the model to the patient, the clinician will have made a diagnostic evaluation and explored the patient's subjective experience.

If there is diagnostic uncertainty, but enough certitude to begin some treatment, this uncertainty may be appended to the discussion of the model as outlined near the end of chapter 1. To recapitulate, the illness' primary and secondary manifestations can generally be presented using these categories:

1. Perceptual, attentional, and mood disturbances
2. Mistrustfulness
3. Cognitive limitations
4. Psychological adaption to illness and low self-esteem

The delineation of symptoms may then lead into a discussion of how these various problems may be addressed through specific treatment modalities.

TREATMENT TASKS

Although this chapter cannot encompass a multidisciplinary treatment manual, we will briefly describe the principal mental health treatment modalities and what specific aspects of schizophrenia each may address. In setting the treatment frame, the clinician must know what each treatment modality may accomplish and how it will do so. This understanding should be imparted to the patient in some detail as part of the process of clarification and demystification on which our plan for the treatment alliance is based.

Psychotherapy

The practice of psychotherapy has endured an uncertain and, recently, much maligned reputation in the treatment of schizophrenia (14–17). The surrounding controversy is too complicated to address here, but we do note our conviction that psychotherapy has not enjoyed general success or support because there has not yet been a plausible psychological model of schizophrenia or of the role of psychotherapy in treating the disorder. We present a model that clearly suggests a role for a kind of psychotherapy. We hope in later works to amplify on the themes we will outline here. Most generally, the tasks of psychotherapy for the schizophrenic individual include: reviewing and clarifying the patient's subjective experience; understanding the dynamics of self-esteem, self-acceptance, and experience of his or her illness; and, importantly, achieving an increased understanding of the patient's psychological responses to the illness, while guiding the patient to better adaptive functioning. We list below several conceptual categories that organize our psychotherapeutic work with schizophrenic patients:

Information

The first role of the psychotherapist is to provide information, in a considerate and thoughtful fashion, regarding the scientific knowledge about schizophrenia that may be pertinent to the patient. This task may be shared by other mental health professionals in a multidisciplinary treatment setting. As discussed above, this information might include scientific evidence and theories (noted to be theories, rather than facts) regarding the production of symptoms; the actions of medication; the nature of cognitive disturbances in schizophrenia; and strategies for coping with symptoms. We tend to emphasize the importance of cognitive and behavioral strategies (such as structuring daytime activities, setting achievable goals, experiencing success and praise) that combat demoralization and social withdrawal and to base these recommendations on research in rehabilitative psychiatry. It is also important to outline rationally, using available data, the risks and prognosis for schizophrenic patients and to reassure them that mental incompetence is not an inevitable outcome, while being frank about the limitations of treatment and our limited capacity to predict outcome.

The amount of information each individual can tolerate varies. A given patient may need time, improved self-esteem, greater trust, and a stronger treatment alliance to accept the facts and theories we present them. We have found that this exercise can be attempted even early in the work, and that the patient will typically indicate intolerance by becoming angry or withdrawing. In this case, we pause and try to discuss the material later, particularly at a juncture when the information would be valuable to the patient. It may be opportune to discuss symptom generation and cognitive coping strategies at a time when the patient is experiencing a mild recrudescence of symptoms. In this context, the information might provide the patient with useful means to reassert some control over his or her thinking and thus reduce anxiety. We have found that such a discussion does not alienate patients, unless the presentation is made thoughtlessly, in service of the clinician's anxiety, insecurity, or frustration, as in the case of a clinician who remarked to schizophrenic patients manifesting denial of their illness, "Don't you realize you're crazy, that you have a brain disease? Doesn't that worry you?" Our understanding of schizophrenic individuals' psychological reaction to their illness would lead us to consider such an intervention fruitless and potentially abusive.

Exploring Subjective Experience

We have taken some pains to emphasize the importance of this task in the establishment of the treatment alliance: it is furthermore essential to the conduct of psychotherapy (18–19). In dealing with delusional patients, this task is central. It requires, in addition to data-gathering about the patient's experience of the illness and of treatment, astute efforts to establish a dialogue, wherein the patient's and psychotherapist's views are evaluated. We will discuss this process in detail below, when we refer to the "parallel dialogue." These themes can then be available for psychotherapeutic work.

Support

The psychological experience of the schizophrenic person—the feelings of vulnerability, lack of control, and futility, in particular—generates defenses and a narrowing of awareness, which handicap cognitive and behavioral adaptation. The psychotherapist must function, in part, as an auxiliary ego (2), helping the patient to construct alternative coping strategies and using the patient's priorities to do so. In this process, the therapist does not assume that he or she knows better than the patient how to make choices, resolve conflicts, or make judgments. The therapist does acknowledge the patient's relative limitations, at this time; these may be psychological (i.e., the narrowing of "perspective" that is a consequence of unresolved conflict within the psyche) or cognitive (uncertainty caused by intense anxiety or ambivalence that is primarily physiologically mediated; or prefrontal subcortical cognitive impairments as described in chapter 1). The therapist's task in this aspect of the work is to fashion alternative coping strategies that the patient may then elect to use; the matter of choice and setting priorities is appropriately left to the patient.

Two specific ego functions are commonly modeled by psychotherapists working with chronic schizophrenic patients: a sense of psychological coherence and continuity over time and the task of deciphering the emotional content of interactions or the psychological motivations of others. The first of these is accomplished, often unconsciously, as a consequence of the therapist's innate capacity to reason, remember, and organize his or her experience of the world. These psychological functions can be impaired in some schizophrenic persons, as we elaborated in chapter 2. The therapist can consciously address this problem, if he or she perceives it to be significant, by taking opportunities, especially when a patient is anxious, disorganized, or mistrustful, to recall past conversations and remind the patient of feelings or convictions the patient has previously espoused. The psychotherapist in a sense contains a coherent and continuous (though incomplete) image of the patient; the act of remembering aids the patient in experiencing a desired but elusive continuity with his or her past.

The latter of these ego functions is one that can also be modeled, though the task is complex and cannot be treated thoroughly here. As we noted above, this aspect of the work is far from the therapist's telling the patient what to do or what to think. The therapist assists the patient in clarifying distortions, noting patterns in the way the patient responds to certain people or events; presenting the patient with alternative ways of looking at an interaction; and suggesting different cognitive or behavioral responses, which may depend on a different assessment of the situational challenge in the environment. So far in this book, we have given a number of examples of this kind of modeling that illustrate the principles noted here, as does the following vignette:

A 29-year-old woman who was diagnosed as suffering from chronic schizophrenia was transferred from an inpatient unit to a long-term, residential treatment facility because of severe and persistent paranoia, suicidal ideation, and impairments in social and other role functioning. Despite these difficulties, the patient had the capacity to engage and interest others, was personable, even charming when not mistrustful, and had made a good many friends among staff and other patients on the inpatient unit.

A week after her transfer, she called a staff member from the inpatient unit to say that she felt unsafe at the new treatment facility. She believed the staff there wanted to punish her and "drive me crazy" because they knew that she had filed suit against a psychiatrist who had treated her when she was a teenager. (The patient had in fact complained to the State Medical Review Board about alleged abuse by a former therapist, complaints that were plausible and being duly investigated). The patient felt the staff at the residential facility were connected to this former therapist. She accused the inpatient unit staff member and the other staff members there of deliberately sending her to a place where she would be tortured. Despite reassurance, she insisted that the inpatient staff were angry at her because of her suicidality and her inability, or refusal, to get better for them.

The staff member first reminded the patient of how she had felt when she first came to the inpatient unit. Together, they recalled many incidents in which the patient experienced the same kind of mistrust and hostility toward the inpatient staff that she now felt for the staff at the new treatment setting.

They then reviewed how the patient had gradually changed her view of the inpatient staff. Specific encounters were remembered. The patient was encouraged to try again, as she had so successfully before, to take risks, to give people around her a chance to know her.

The staff member then explored the patient's awareness of her own behavior at the new facility. The patient grudgingly admitted that she had been withdrawn and irritable. She recounted several incidents since her arrival that convinced her of the new staff's malevolence. The inpatient staff member noted that the patient's impressions could not be disproved, especially since the staff member had not been there to witness the incidents. The patient was given alternative constructions of the events, however, which were presented as hypotheses. The patient was then given ideas about how to test these hypotheses: for example, that she could approach one person at the facility, who, she was convinced, hated her, and discuss their recent interaction. The patient's capacity to tolerate such vulnerability was reviewed in the context of past similar efforts that both remembered. Suggestions were made about how to evaluate the other person's possible responses.

The phone call ended with the staff member continuing to remind the patient of her ability to work through obstacles with people, as she had in the past, and the patient remaining ambivalent and mistrustful. Nevertheless, a few months later, the inpatient staff member received a large decorated thank-you note from the patient, announcing that she had settled in at the residential program.

Dynamic Psychotherapy

Those involved in psychodynamically oriented work with the chronic schizophrenic person must consider that the physiology and psychology of the disorder is too complex for precise identification of exact causes of symptom exacerbation. While it is important to explore theories about psychological stressors, room must be left for an unavoidable lack of certitude.

The task of the psychotherapist is to help the schizophrenic person achieve the broadest, richest possible understanding of his or her psyche. The tasks we have outlined above are oriented toward this goal. So, too, is dynamic psychotherapy, which can be a part of what might be seen as an educative, though not didactic, exercise. Dynamic psychotherapy is distinguished by its attention to transference and its persistent effort to explore motivation and elucidate the mechanisms of psychological defenses.

Transference is certainly important, though often not studied, in work with schizophrenic individuals. In a sense, the "subjective experience" of the schizophrenic patient is related but not limited to the concept of transference. How the patient "sees" or "hears" the therapist is important to the treatment alliance and to therapy. Exploration of the subjective experience and of the transference will yield important information about dynamic themes, particularly as they relate to issues of trust, self-esteem, superego pressures or expectations, and dispositions toward intimacy and vulnerability.

Additionally, as we have noted before, one of the goals of treatment is to increase the patient's understanding of his or her psychological responses to the illness process, which means understanding, among other things, his or her unconscious and psychological mechanisms of defense. As we described in detail in chapter 2, the rage, despair, and confusion associated with the schizophrenic illness demand coping strategies that are often maladaptive. To be able to look at and revise those maladaptive strategies, the schizophrenic individual must be confronted with the affects and thoughts that motivate him or her. New strategies must take into account the patient's concerns in order to be effective and desirable. Finding more adaptive ways to experience a sense of control than maladative withdrawal or control through fantasy will be helpful where mere confrontation about disturbed behavior will not.

We can consider, though without proof, that this kind of dynamic work may not be appropriate for some patients. Those individuals who respond more readily to cognitive and behavioral tecniques may also find dynamic therapy too threatening to self-esteem. This kind of exploration is helpful when maladaptive behaviors and cognitions interfere with the progress of recovery and in a way that suggests that the patient must be helped to confront intolerable internal affects or conflicts in order to permit change. But the patient's limits of tolerance for self-knowledge will determine whether he or she persists in this part of treatment.

Rehabilitative Strategies

The specific tasks of rehabilitative clinicians (20–22) require a thoughtful integration of psychological understanding, including the principles used by psychotherapists as described above, and knowledge about social skills learning, behavioral techniques, and motivational strategies. The rehabilitation therapist must identify impairments in instrumental role functioning and then discern their causes. We have seen that schizophrenic persons have impairments in cognitive functioning (especially subtle prefrontal, frontal, and subcortical disturbances) that may produce such problems as impersistence, difficulty initiating tasks, or trouble working independently with directions. These same cognitive disturbances may also explain the schizophrenic person's struggles with interpersonal relatedness.

We have also described, however, the role played by the individual's psychological reaction and adaptation to the illness. The rehabilitation therapist must take these concerns into account when devising interventions and must have as clear an understanding of the patient's psychological determinants as the psychotherapist and other treatment team members. One cannot treat task avoidance or social withdrawal without a "psychological diagnosis." This step is crucial to treatment planning as well as to the treatment alliance.

Rehabilitation interventions provide patients with opportunities to experience competence and improved self-esteem. From the perspective of cognitive treatment theory, this is vitally important to recovery. What rehabilitation therapists must not do, in our view, is see themselves as simply teachers. The schizophrenic individual's inability to carry out a task is due to a web of factors, including cognitive impairments (which are not altered by teaching), experiential deficits (for which teaching may be appropriate), and psychological adaptations that may impair performance. By providing the schizophrenic patient with work or interactional paradigms, we give them opportunities to discover improved skills for coping with their impairments, though we cannot often teach those skills (because they involve preconscious subcortical processes). These paradigms such as involvement in a work-like setting as part of treatment, are part of an ongoing evaluative process, which teaches the clinical team about the schizophrenic person's cognitive and psychological qualities. Rehabilitation interventions can be better devised when these various perspectives are integrated.

Nursing Interventions

Like rehabilitative paradigms, nursing activities, which at this time are most often limited to inpatient settings, provide opportunities for observation of a patient's cognitive and interpersonal functioning. Nursing staff on a psychiatric unit have a special role that is a consequence of the incidental intimacy that exists between them and their patients. They may study the cognition and behavior of patients in a natural social paradigm (albeit not natural in the sense the inpatient unit is a unique community), but only if they understand the psychology of schizophrenia. This requires an appreciation of the effects of physiologic disturbances as well as the psychological concerns and adaptive strategies characteristic of the schizophrenic individual.

Not only do nursing staff have a particular perspective, but they have opportunities to help patients adapt by modeling interpersonal or cognitive coping strategies. This task falls between the psychotherapist's role in elucidating the patient's conscious, cognitive appreciation of his or her psychology, and the rehabilitation therapist's focus on specific social or work skills. Relationships, as we have noted, are vexing and complicated for the schizophrenic individual, and they are only partly and often not practically dealt with in either psychotherapy or rehabilitation therapy. Nursing can involve a unique adjunctive role, assisting patients in practicing relatedness.

This practice need not, indeed best not, occur formally. Nursing staff have the advantage of intimacy and immediacy. Using what they know about the patient's psychology, nursing staff can "model" in either of the following ways:

1. They can respond to anger, mistrust, or other dispositions in pa-

tients by careful reflection on events, impressions, and patients' distortions. Nursing staff can detail how they understood or reason about an event, presenting this as an alternative model to patients (not trying to convince the patients of "the truth" but offering another way of understanding that may be more consistent and useful and providing more direction regarding interpersonal coping strategies). Further discussions about an event (e.g., an argument with another staff member) could include review of different behaviors, responses, that might have worked better.

2. When a patient demonstrates persistent maladaptive patterns, such as intrusiveness, social withdrawal, or bizarre behavior, a plan can be organized that will:

a. help the patient understand why he or she acts in certain way;
b. provide opportunities for more useful, esteem-building functioning;
c. reinforce or discourage certain behaviors through a behavioristic paradigm emphasizing positive reinforcement of such a plan.

The following vignette outlines the formulation of such a plan.

A 25-year-old woman was hospitalized for worsening of paranoid symptoms that had been present, with varying severity, for approximately four years. While actively hallucinating and delusional on admission, she took great care with her appearance and was flirtatious with male staff members and patients. She had also been suicidal prior to admission, but these feelings had abruptly submerged.

The patient had a history of self-abusive sexual liaisons—often with violent men—prior to admission. On the unit, she was sexually provocative, frequently touching various men, talking about her "need for sex," and on several occasions was found in some male patients' rooms.

Her poise, her polished appearance, and her affectation of a kind of haughty denial of illness or vulnerability were quite disturbing. Nursing staff felt protective of her, especially with regard to her potential for sexual behavior that could be humiliating and self-destructive, and were frequently angry with her because of her arrogant demeanor and her indifference to their concerns.

A plan was devised to help patients and staff cope with these problems and to model different interactions. When the patient was found to be sexually inappropriate or intrusive, nursing staff would take her aside and read from a prepared outline on which the reader would amplify. The outline was used to insure consistency, to reinforce the interventions through repetition, and to help staff cope with their tendency to get irritated with her. The intervention was also a mild "negative" reinforcement in that it was difficult for the patient to hear. When discussed by the nursing staff member, using the outline, the intervention would typically sound like this:

"We are concerned about your behavior because of the possibility that you will humiliate yourself—you have told us what happened when you were at home and acted like this—or be hurt by verbal or even physical rejection—some people, as you've found in the past, don't like your advances.

"We think that this behavior comes from feelings of low self-esteem. You have told us how sad you were before you came here and that you were also suicidal. We think that you feel sexual attractiveness is your only asset—so much so, that you must force sexual intimacy because you feel bad about yourself.

"We're not trying to control your sex life. You're an adult and free to do what you choose. But if you want to continue in treatment here, control of your sexual impulses is part of the treatment we prescribe, because we are convinced this is an important self-esteem issue.

"We also prescribe other activities that we think you can accomplish and that will help your self-esteem. Let's hope you don't give up on what is certain to be a slow, frustrating, but potentially rewarding course."

Of course, the nursing staff member also implicitly models through his or her character. People learn in part through their experiences of others. The behavior of nursing staff members, their relative tolerance, openness, and benevolence or impatience, disdain, and criticism, have a qualitative effect on the patients with whom they work, and on the milieu on the treatment unit. Rather than seeking ourselves simply as natural models, however, we may strive to share our thinking, our emotional experience, while providing more in the form of integrating psychological constructions, as in the following vignette:

A 35-year-old man who had been ill for several years and who was also quite bright had begun a successful career as an architect before the onset of his schizophrenic disorder. He was hospitalized most recently for an exacerbation of his symptoms. One of his principal difficulties was his persistent noncompliance with medications.

He approached a nursing staff member to have a talk. They spoke for about twenty minutes, when the nurse had to leave. At this time the patient, who had been attentive and open during the discussion, said, "What you've told me—I've heard it all before. It's nothing new."

The nursing staff member responded instinctively, saying, "You know, that makes me feel like shit, that after talking with you for twenty minutes, you just say 'I've heard it before.'" They sat in silence for a moment, after which the patient smirked, although it was not a gleeful smile. He appeared anxious, the nurse thought, because the smile was so awkward, so out of place.

"I also think," the nurse went on, "that you said that because you are too proud to admit I may have helped you or that just talking is helpful even if the things we say aren't new; and that's sad, because we all need help to learn, to have someone share our troubles. I do it everyday with other staff and with my friends and family. I hope you can let people help you and not push them away, as you just tried to push me away, because otherwise you'll be very alone."

Later that day, the patient, who had said nothing further after the nurse's statement, came up to her and said tentatively, "I apologize for what I said earlier." He stood there, unable to say more. The nursing staff member thanked him, apologized as well for her earlier heated tone, and made arrangements to talk with him when she was next on duty.

This mixture of directness, openness, and reflection, which makes use of what we know about the patient and about psychological principles, is in our view extremely valuable and appropriate. The model easily conforms to the kind of work practiced by nursing staff and to the circumstances of their practice. The only caution we would add is to note that this model can be abused if it is simply an excuse to tell patients that they are offensive and thus gratify our offended sensibilities. Without compassion and understanding, mere frankness will be of little benefit.

We would note that the developing practice of case management, sometimes performed in the community by nursing professionals, shares many of the features of nursing practice as we have described it. The same combination of directness and insight in modeling interpersonal relatedness may be an important component of case managers' work, in addition to their supportive, practical interventions.

Family Therapy

The literature amply documents the importance of the family system in our understanding and treatment of the schizophrenic individual (26–27). Research into the role of expressed emotion in families of schizophrenic persons has led to interventions the efficacy of which has been documented. It is likely that high levels of expressed emotion are stressful because they represent an interpersonal situational demand that (1) taxes subtle cognitive functions involving subcortical neural activity, as described in chapter 1; (2) reinforces schizophrenic persons' low self-esteem by communicating criticism for behaviors not entirely in their control or for failure to meet their families' expectations; and (3) challenges certain adaptive behaviors, such as social withdrawal, denial, or fantasies of control.

In the language of our model, expressed emotion confronts aspects of the core physiologic disturbance as it affects cognitive functioning, as well as conflicting with the patient's efforts at psychological adaptation.

We encourage family therapists to integrate their clinical and treatment models with the model we present in chapter 1, as we have done here with respect to the expressed emotion paradigm. We present further thoughts on family treatment concepts in chapter 8, where a clinical example is also provided. It is our conviction that the concepts presented here can facilitate most family treatment interventions.

Our model has particular relevance to the psychoeducational component of family work (28–32). Some family therapists favor a model of schizophrenia that utilizes the dualistic conceptualization we criticized in chapter 1. Many specifically refer to negative symptoms as deficits in neurological functioning and describe no role for the psychological responses we have characterized. As we noted in chapter 1, we feel that this understanding of the disorder is unacceptably reductionistic and needlessly pessimistic. We suggest, also in chapter 1, that the model there can be presented to families. In our experience, understanding it has facilitated their efforts to cope with the schizophrenic family member. We have noted a significant reduction in blaming and angry or guilty responses to provocative symptoms and improved coping behaviors in family as a consequence of instruction in our model of the disorder. Much of the discussion oriented to helping clinicians' understand their reactions to schizophrenic patients can be translated to help families understand their psychological responses. In this way, the psychoeducational work can assist in elucidating psychodynamic themes for use in insight-oriented family therapies.

Other Modalities

It is, we hope, apparent that any treatment modality may be augmented by consideration of the principles outlined in these three chapters. Even the practice of psychopharmacology (23–25) must, in our view, adopt a broader perspective if it is to be done thoughtfully. It is no simple matter to decide whether a symptom is a product of disturbed physiology or a manifestation of psychological adaptation (good or ill). Nor can we be presumptive in assessing the implications of a treatment response. It is necessary to understand and use psychological principles because our knowledge of physiology is limited and because pharmacotherapeutics is itself a blunt instrument. Moreover, we can see that any mind, including that of a schizophrenic person, has innate capacities available to psychological treatments. Until science permits us to prune inappropriate synapses and regulate the appearance and sensitivity of specific membrane receptors, we must use interpersonal, experiential treatment, the very conditions that contribute to the development of each individual's anatomy, physiology, and, thus, psychology.

We close this section on the treatment frame by noting the importance of defining and elaborating the patient's goals for the treatment. As we have discussed, these may be quite different from those of the clinician or treatment team. Nevertheless, the treatment alliance should not proceed unless these discrepancies and conflicts are first acknowledged. It is difficult enough to pursue a treatment where the patient understands the process very differently from the clinician, as in the vignette of the young man who thought neuroleptics might decrease his mental sensitivity to the occult transmissions that caused "chattering" in his head. It is more difficult still to imagine that the clinician and a patient are working in concert only to find that the patient's later treatment avoidance is due to unknown and unresolved differences between the clinician and the patient's conceptualization of the treatment's purpose.

Exploring and acknowledging such differences allow the clinician to make better prognoses, anticipate crises, and better understand the patient's participation and response. The knowledge of the patient's subjective experience may also lead to creative strategies to deal with delusions, as we have discussed. Identifying and talking about the patient's treatment goals are specific aspects of our inquiry into his or her psychological view. Insofar as this exercise also communicates respect, interest, and a collaborative, non-authoritarian stance on the part of the clinician, it further recommends itself as an essential step in beginning the treatment alliance.

As we pursue the various measures described here in connection with setting the treatment frame, we will implicitly communicate our views on the treatment goals. By discussing our limitations with the patient, we will define in part what we think we can and cannot accomplish. Presenting our model, our conceptualization of patients' symptoms and their struggles, we make reference to what is disturbed and what may change. Describing specific treatments, their tasks, and how they may work, we cannot avoid introducing our thoughts about where the treatment is headed. Therefore, although a formal statement about treatment goals is useful, the process of beginning the treatment alliance by setting the treatment frame reinforces the clinician's unique and specific view of his or her capacity to help.

It is also important to construct, to whatever extent possible, treatment goals that are meaningful to the patient. We may see that a given patient would do best working, for example, as an assistant in a medical laboratory; but if his dream is to become a physician and medical researcher, our goals are useless. When conflicts such as these arise, we must step back and consider other approaches and other goals that will enlist the patient's motivational capacity, however trammelled it is.

When we present treatment goals it also helps to indicate how these goals will assist the patient in developing self-esteem and confidence in specific skills. The discussions about goals are not perfunctory exchanges; they are part of the process of forming the treatment alliance. This part of the work can and must communicate our appreciation of the patient's anticipatory anxiety, fear of humiliation, and avoidance of achievement that will lead to further feared demands, as well as the importance of setting and achieving goals in order to avoid isolation and discouragement.

TREATMENT ALLIANCE TECHNIQUES

We wish to close this chapter with comments on the conduct of our interaction with schizophrenic patients in the process of forming a treatment alliance. In doing so, we emphasize the primacy of the alliance in the treatment experience. Repeated evaluation of the status of the treatment contract and the patient's understanding of and respect for the treatment frame as well as comparison of the patient's psychological model with that of the clinician are critical and basic techniques in practice. They are as much a part of the work with schizophrenic individuals as repeated formal mental status and traditional diagnostic evaluation.

In particular, reexploration of the subjective experience provides an invaluable tool to our understanding. In the manner described in chapter 2, questioning the patient about his or her psychological perspective is qualitatively, and often practically, useful, as in the following example:

> A schizophrenic man in his late twenties was being treated as an outpatient for a recent exacerbation of his symptoms of mistrustfulness and persistent auditory hallucinations. His neuroleptic had recently been changed because of his complaints of extrapyramidal side effects. The patient's father had called, relating his concern about the patient's irritability and hostile threats toward others.

The father also noted his uncertainty about the patient's compliance with the prescribed neuroleptic regimen.

In the session, the clinician asked the patient how he currently felt about the medication and whether he thought it would help. The patient said, "I don't think it is helping. And, anyway, I'm not so sure it will help. . . . I mean I'm pretty convinced that this thing [i.e., the hallucinations] is external. I wish I could believe it was internal, 'cause it's be a lot easier. . . . I'd be calmer if I knew it was internal. As it is, I get pretty frustrated . . . infuriated . . . thinking that somebody's trying to control my mind."

The clinician explored the issue further, attempting to discover how ambivalent, if at all consciously, the patient was regarding the etiology of his mental experience. It was apparent that the patient was consciously convinced that he was not ill and that whatever uncertainty resided in his mind, it was not at that time available, being, presumably, deeply repressed (either because it would not be easier to think he was ill, as the patient suggested, or because the experience of his symptoms was so intensely convincing that he felt doubts to be spurious).

Although it was possible that the medication was not effective, it was more likely, given the tone of his subjective experience, that the patient was not taking the medication as prescribed. The clinician informed the patient's family of his concerns, and of his impression that the patient would probably require hospitalization in the near future.

The patient in fact argued with his parents that night, became hostile and withdrawn, and was admitted to the hospital the next day. The patient's father remarked that the argument leading to admission felt strange to him, as if the patient was forcing his family's hand, making them hospitalize him because he could not consciously accept his need for help.

In light of the patient's saying that it would be "easier" if he believed he were ill, the clinician told the patient's father it was not hard to imagine that the patient might have an unconscious wish to find help. His own efforts to understand and manage his mental experience had been futile and frustrating. He had stated in the past that the model of his illness and treatment as presented by his clinician, were sensible and suggested hope and a means of coping—though he added that despite these advantages he was unable to accept the model then.

This patient's frustration with his own inefficacy and confusion may offer a beginning for a fruitful treatment alliance, although the characteristics of the patient's denial also suggest that it may take some time for him to acknowledge his wish for treatment, even in part. Nevertheless, reexploration of his subjective experience gave a clear picture of his attitude about treatment, allowed the clinician to counsel the family about the inevitability of hospitalization, and made clear that further education and exhortation would be inconsequential at that time.

Equally necessary is the periodic, unavoidable task of reinforcement of the treatment frame. This is often done in concert with exploration of the subjective experience and involves assessing the schizophrenic individual's expectations of the clinician. Unrealistic demands and resentment of the clinician's limitations are often symptoms of anxiety about the risk inherent in treatment. Depending on the schizophrenic persons' specific subjective experience, she may anticipate failure, criticism, or even betrayal if she commits herself to the proposed work.

A schizophrenic woman in her mid-thirties was hospitalized principally because of a history of repeated suicide gestures and attempts. She had made progress in her treatment, which had helped her confront her necessary choice between death and the risks of accepting that she was ill and needed help.

Nevertheless, she continued to have episodic bouts of paranoid ideation and maintained, in her words, "on the back burner," a delusion regarding her persecution by a malevolent organization. She frequently questioned others' motives and worried that her treatment itself was a hoax, to be followed eventually by betrayal and destruction.

She had developed a habit of asking her psychotherapist and some nursing staff about statements made in individual discussions. She would, for example, approach her psychotherapist outside sessions inquiringly and, at times, accusingly, saying, "What did you mean when you said . . . ?"

As she approached the time for her discharge, her psychotherapist noted an increase in these extracurricular questionings. He said to her, "You know, I can't possibly answer all the questions you have. Nor can other people. When you're an outpatient you won't have opportunities to check out your impressions. You have to be able to tolerate some uncertainty or this treatment plan will fall apart."

The patient was quiet on hearing this. Later that day, she confronted her psychotherapist in the hall, saying, "What's wrong about my asking you questions? You're telling me you can't help me."

He responded, "It's not that your questioning is wrong; I was simply pointing out the fact that I have limits. I'm talking to you now, but I can't be available to you, like this, all the time. I believe I can be of help to you, since we've worked together up until now. But I can only do so much to reassure you, and I don't think I can ever reassure you about all your doubts."

In her next session, they went on to discuss how her preoccupation with what people "meant" by their statements not only occurred due to her ongoing suspiciousness but might also have reflected her heightened anxiety related to discharge. She was quite afraid that she would never be able to work again, that her despair and suicidality would again become unmanageable, and that she would be friendless, isolated as she had been for the past several years. These fears were present despite her many achievements during her hospital stay. Her trepidation about life outside the hospital was painful to discuss because it often led to her awareness of persistent feelings of skepticism and hopelessness. In some respects, she agreed, her rumination about incidental statements made by staff served as an unconsciously motivated distraction from thinking about her discharge plans. Reinforcing the treatment frame, which included noting the clinician's limitations, then served to facilitate a discussion of the patient's affective experience and to focus both patient's and clinician's attention on the difficult tasks at hand.

It may be said that, generally, perturbations in the treatment frame or attempts at such represent a resistance to or avoidance of some difficult aspect of the work, as illustrated above. Requests or demands for more or something other than what the clinician had offered implicitly indicate that the schizophrenic patient has expectations of the clinician that go beyond their understanding about what the treatment process can offer. As such, those incidents that require a restatement of the treatment contract should be explored for they will typically reveal psychological concerns of direct consequence to the treatment alliance.

Finally, with respect to general technical principles in conducting interactions with schizophrenic patients, we come to the matter of the tone of the clinician's communications and its importance to the furthering of the treatment alliance. We speak not of specific interventions but of an attitude and philosophy that at their best suffuse all the clinician's work. In a sense, this book is meant to demonstrate that tone.

It is most important in our work with schizophrenic patients that we illustrate our conviction that they can attain meaningful autonomy and to provide them with opportunities to exercise this basic component of self-esteem in a healthy fashion. As we have noted before, in most mental health treatment settings, patients are treated as if they were unable to make decisions, even when they possess the ability to do so without risk to their or others' safety. There are some treatment decisions and many life decisions in which the schizophrenic person must make choices and not be told what to do. Even those patients who are seriously disabled will benefit whenever their ability to decide, and thus to define their individuality, is reasonably supported.

In general, we wish to exemplify an attitude of tolerance and understanding that does not yield to imprecise thinking or a dilution of our professional roles. Self-respect and rational hopefulness can be modeled by clinicians. The clinician always serves as a model for the observing ego that is often under siege in the schizophrenic individual. In this we emphasize the value of rational assessment and reflection in understanding the psychology of ourselves and others.

As noted at the beginning of this chapter, we see the patient as an active participant in the treatment process and not merely passively compliant. While acknowledging the schizophrenic patient's many difficulties in contemplating change, ranging from anxiety to bitter resentment, we identify in them the capacity for improved adaptation, the possibility that change can occur, though perhaps slowly. In helping them, we point out the destructive role of unrealistic expectations that contribute to their self-condemnation. This process requires a rational examination of plans, goals, and the unrealistic fantasies that serve to defend against an at times oppressive reality.

THE PARALLEL DIALOGUE

It is difficult to maintain a balanced tone when working with mistrustful, delusional schizophrenic patients. Particularly difficult are those patients who persist in consciously endorsing a distorted view of people and events, especially insofar as they relate to their illness and other objects of treatment. As exemplified by several vignettes in this text, clinical work can go on with such patients but only when the distortions and differences are understood and when some basis for continued collaboration has been established—even if it is only the patient's curiosity about what we think. The clinician must be prepared to tolerate the tension inherent in this kind of work.

What we mean by a "parallel dialogue" is a modification of technique necessitated by continually interpreting events in and around treatment through two frames of reference: that is, the clinician's and the patient's ways of viewing events. The dialogue is "parallel" because the clinician must make frequent reference to the patient's way of interpreting events (as she understands it) in contrast to her own. Several specific measures are indicated.

First, the clinician must not focus on gaining the patient's agreement about the literal or consensual "truth" of events. Treatment will not progress if we try to make a delusional patient admit he is ill, produce a confession, or prove the falsity of a delusion. Truth is in all events always partly subjective.

Second, the clinician must direct the treatment toward mutual goals that will help the patient to feel effective and to experience improved self-esteem. These kinds of goals are more likely to win the patient's support, in the face of the patient's delusionality and denial, and are thus important in serving a tenuous treatment alliance. The clinician must also try to identify ego-dystonic aspects of the patient's delusional views: What is it about the patient's explanation of events that is unsatisfactory, that causes the patient discomfort or anxiety? Identifying themes such as loneliness, fatigue over a protracted, isolated struggle, and shame or frustration about observed ineffectiveness or failure can be an important first step in establishing a treatment alliance. Such concerns can be used in deciding what kinds of treatment goals may be useful to the patient. This process might be said to be one of finding what about the patient's psychological adaptation (including his understanding of what is happening) to his illness is ego-dystonic; for the schizophrenic individual is more likely to accept help, at least initially, with a problem that produces distress.

Third, we should attempt to help the schizophrenic person see his illness clearly—to see, that is, what symptoms are a result of the illness and what constitutes his psychological responses to that illness. In psychotherapy, we must help him to understand the psychological motives for maladaptive behaviors. After describing the various features of his illness and his efforts to cope with it, we try to help him understand the interaction of these aspects of his mentation. In other modalities, we try to help him understand why he has difficulty with certain interpersonal and cognitive functions. Finally, we must offer alternative means of coping, suggesting supportive interventions and assisting the patient in discovering what kind of different adaptation he can achieve. This general model of treatment should be presented to the patient, particularly in the context of the "parallel dialogue." Although the patient may continue to resist the assumptions and implications of treatment, this outline offers a concrete explanation of the treatment phases (with all modalities) that partially address the mistrustfulness such schizophrenic persons manifest. Presenting this model also helps in that delusional patients are more irritable and intractable in settings characterized by ambiguity of purpose.

Fourth, we believe that the schizophrenic individual's delusionality and denial is at least in part exacerbated by his difficulty imagining that he can or will change and his belief that coping with the illness is futile and worthless. Accordingly, in work with patients whose severe view of self and illness requires a parallel dialogue, we must repeatedly describe the gains that may be possible through using the treatment, including the predictability and practicality of our model. We must also clarify our realistic expectations about the course of the schizophrenic person's illness and potential recovery to a position of independence and self-esteem while coping with his symptoms. Important components of the psychology of recovery are addressing unrealistic expectations and supporting patients when they avoid change or challenge because of the fear that improvement will occasion eventual expectations they cannot possibly fulfill, whether they imagine such renewed expectations will be self-generated or represented in others.

Conducting a parallel dialogue means remembering that the patient may be interpreting the clinician's words or actions in a distorted way and that delusional expectations influence perception and reasoning. This kind of work implies regularly having to contrast the clinician's point of view with one consistent with the subjective experience articulated by the patient: "I believe that what happened was a coincidence; whereas you are convinced that this was arranged by the people persecuting you." Such contrasts allow for further clarification by the patient and serve to identify the clinician as a reliable repository of the patient's experience, a condition that may enhance trust.

Many of the clinical vignettes presented in these first three chapters have contained elements of a parallel dialogue and exemplify these principles. The clinical examples in chapters 5, 6, and 7, will also elucidate these themes. The tone of these various interactions with patients demonstrates restraint and respect for the patient's deeply held delusional convictions and their psychological function. The restraint is particularly manifest in the clinicians' patient expectation of slow and subtle change.

The parallel nature of the clinical experience also requires the clinician to pursue the schizophrenic patient's subjective experience through repeated inquiry. Patients with intense delusionality are mistrustful of revealing their true dispositions, especially about their treatment. Planning on various interventions can often go awry when this concern is not addressed. For instance:

A schizophrenic man in his twenties had been hospitalized for delusional ideation. Although initially quite resistant to taking medications, going to activities, or seeing a therapist, he eventually cooperated when it was clear that he would otherwise be committed to treatment by the court. Nevertheless, his participation in treatment was unenthusiastic.

Discharge plans were readied by the patient's treatment team. Because of his social isolation and cognitive impairments the team recommended referral to a residential treatment facility in a farm setting. The patient said little about the plan, which was presented to him as a "firm recommendation." He said he would go there after he left the hospital, and his family tentatively agreed to the plan, for they were surprised at the patient's acquiescence.

The patient was discharged home and was to go to the residential program the next day. Once home, however, the patient refused to go anywhere. The patient's family was frustrated and helpless because they would not simply throw him into the street, despite their concern.

When later speaking to his outpatient therapist, who inquired about the patient's feeling about treatment and the residential program, the patient said:

"I don't think I'm ill. I've had problems, but I don't need these medications. I heard what they told me in the hospital—but I feel I've been persecuted by the FBI, and I know that won't stop if I live somewhere else. Going to work is pointless because *they* [the FBI] will screw it up for me. I have to stay home and pursue the truth."

It is apparent that this patient would not then or in the near future voluntarily assent to the treatment plan prepared for him. Eventually, his therapist was able to initiate a treatment alliance with him by focusing on the patient's feelings of frustration and acute discomfort due to his anxiety and hallucinations. (Anxiety and hallucinations were the ego-dystonic features of his condition; his ineffectiveness in stopping the persecution and the associated frustration and discouragement were the ego-dystonic aspects of his psychological adaptation.) He slowly began to accept treatment, including medications, as his therapist helped him understand the treatment and illness model, described what medication and other interventions could and could not do, and suggested how together they might work on the other problems he faced—despite his continuing conviction that what he perceived to be the causes of his problems were not due to an illness.

THE RESIGNED PATIENT

Some of the techniques described above can be useful in dealing with "resigned," or withdrawn and apparently hopeless, patients. Indeed, many such schizophrenic persons are also delusional and believe their problems have a concrete, external origin. But before thinking about what to do with patients who appear resigned to an isolated, amotivated life, we must understand the various reasons for patients' manifesting this syndrome.

We noted in chapter 1 that symptoms such as amotivation, disinterest, and resignation arise from unclear etiologies. We do not know and have no way of documenting whether a given schizophrenic individual's symptoms of amotivation are due to disturbances in frontal lobe functioning (the most likely anatomic correlate) or to what we refer to as psychological causes. Although the substrate of psychology is the brain, we presume that psychological disturbances are those that may change in response to experience and conscious mental effort (reflection, insight, imagining alternative coping strategies). Since we do not have evidence that a given schizophrenic patient's resigned attitude has an organic etiology, we must work to discover and change maladaptive psychological mechanisms that may also produce or intensify such symptoms. We should keep in mind the putative role of frontal lobe disturbances, and so not badger patients or insinuate where we do not have psychological clues or evidence. Nevertheless, to give up on such patients, ascribing their withdrawal to unproven organic causes, is to abandon human beings who may be caught in a trap of psychological self-deceit and inhibition.

What might be the factors underlying the psychological state of a resigned schizophrenic patient? The following list though probably not exhaustive, indicates those factors:

1. Secondary Major Depressive Illness or other Affective Disorders;
2. Iatrogenic Syndrome—due to over-medication and drug-induced Parkinsonism;
3. Discouragement, Demoralization;
4. Anger, Resentment, Wish to Control—by defeating others' efforts to help;
5. Delusionality—perception of risk if interest is shown, or certitude regarding eventual destruction or betrayal;
6. Putative Frontal Lobe Syndrome.

Obviously, we must first evaluate the patient for evidence of an affective disorder or iatrongenic Parkinsonism, as we discussed in chapter 1. There is as yet no treatment for frontal lobe disturbances, although we must consider their potential contribution. The other factors represent forms of psychological adaptation that may be of some limited benefit to the patient but are associated with disabling consequences. In particular, social withdrawal may have a deleterious effect on cognitive and emotional life. These behaviors not uncommonly expiate unconscious wishes for self-punishment.

Once clinicians imagine that psychological factors may be pertinent, they must proceed as we have described before: by first exploring the patient's subjective experience. The process may be difficult with resigned patients, who commonly deflect curiosity through apparent indifference, muteness, obstinacy, or passive compliance. They are typically frustrating and can inspire in clinicians questions about their mental orientation, competence, or relatedness.

It may be useful to confront patients about a demeanor that is apparently placid or docile in the face of their desperate situation. Thus one might say, "You seem not to care what happens to you, you let others make decisions for you—yet it's hard for me to imagine you are in fact so indifferent." When one can elicit evidence supporting a psychological motivation for the patient's resignation, many other interventions become possible. The clinician might say, for example, "It is apparent that you have felt little genuine control over your life [perhaps "little control over your mental experience"] and that as a consequence you have expressed your sadness and anger by controlling those who wish to help you, alternately encouraging them to assist you and then dashing their expectations." Interventions such as the latter are more elaborate, require more information, and are appropriate for a patient whose resignation is otherwise resistant to engagement. In exploring these issues, it is important that we not act on our countertransference by making merely critical comments. Confrontational interventions must be thoughtful, and constructed so as to be acceptable to the part of the patient that wishes to change, to the part of the patient's observing ego that is aware that her resigned disposition is damaging to her.

In order to engage the resigned patient in a treatment alliance, one must discern and then elaborate the schizophrenic person's psychological motivation for this unique behavioral and cognitive adaptation. It is useful to consider certain paradigms, such as those we listed above, although such a list can never be exhaustive. Certainly, anger plays an important unconscious role in the development of a resigned attitude in many schizophrenic patients. As we discussed in chapter 2, the many frustrations of schizophrenic persons' external and internal life, their sense of isolation, alienation, and mistrust, contribute to their resentment, envy, and self-disdain. These psychological stresses can be expressed in a demoralized state, as well as by efforts to control or defeat others, either family or mental health practitioners. There are also patients with acute delusional concerns, who fear intimacy, who are convinced that destruction may come at any moment, or who fear raising their expectations because of certain consequent betrayal. For some, it may even be dangerous to speak, to let the simplest wish be known. The two vignettes below illustrate these phenomena.

A man in his early twenties had a history of schizophrenia for several years. He was hospitalized for evaluation because of social disfunction, disinterest, apparent hopelessness, and treatment avoidance. His neuroleptics were first decreased because he had evident iatrongenic Parkinsonism and did not otherwise require such high doses.

Despite some enlivening of his affect, he remained bland and unmotivated. He was compliant, but required nearly constant attention and direction. It was apparent he had some cognitive disturbances, but his task performance was puzzlingly inconsistent. He was playful and friendly with other patients, but nearly mute when talking to clinicians.

When reviewing the patient's life at home, the treatment team learned that the patient's mother was caring but also overweening. She insisted on doing his laundry, making his meals, running to get things for him. She had spent her life as a caretaker, first for her mother, then for her son. When asked what would happen if the patient became more independent, she said, "I don't know if I could tolerate that."

The remainder of the patient's treatment in the hospital consisted of engaging him in rehabilitative programs, which enhanced his self-esteem and taught him skills; family work around issues related to autonomy; and the patient's psychotherapy, in which his experience of his illness, and his relationship to his parents, were explored.

His therapist learned that "behind" the patient's apparent indifference and resignation, he was in fact quite demanding and haughty at times. He considered many activities to be beneath him and scorned much of his treatment. It was clear that this arrogance was defensive, however, in that the patient was also able to discuss his failed expectations, his sadness and sense of loss, and his intense ambivalence about his relationship with his mother. A part of him was comforted by her solicitude; a part of him was ashamed of his dependency. He also worried about how he would survive after she died. This last theme became the first firm basis for his treatment alliance.

A schizophrenic man in his late twenties presented to the hospital after a serious episode of genital self-mutilation. He said he felt he must hurt himself because "voices" told him to. He further stated that he had been reincarnated and that in his past lives he had been sinful. He was convinced that he would be destroyed for his past transgressions, that there was no hope for him, that no one could help; he was simply waiting for the end.

When staff members offered help, he was uninterested. When asked questions, he often would not respond. Although there was equivocal evidence of psychomotor retardation, he did not manifest a major depressive syndrome.

Through exploration of his subjective experience of his illness—which he felt was a divine punishment, not a medical entity—the treatment team learned that the patient was actually quite angry and afraid to let that show. He was convinced that if he "transgressed" in this manner, it would hasten his destruction. Although a part of him was resigned to the inevitability of an early death, a part of him was struggling to maintain a tenuous equilibrium. In the interim, the treatment team observed many instances of his behaviors that expressed unconscious resentment, envy, and self-dislike.

The latter of these two patients was in a desperate condition. His constellation of psychological adaptations was quite worrisome and suggested a prolonged course of treatment before the patient might be at reduced risk of further self-mutilation or suicide (which he had attempted several times). The treatment alliance would take time to evolve and might begin with the clinician's exploiting his conflicting attitudes about the eventuality of imminent death (i.e., that he was helpless, although he might delay death by containing his anger). This conflict might be seen as a consequence of unconscious ambivalence about his wish to survive, to accept his illness, and to cope with it.

The initial phase of the treatment alliance, however, might be based on so slim a notion as his uncertainty about the amount of time left to him. If that destruction were to occur in the distant future, he might agree that coping with the present would be useful. Otherwise, he would be like the protagonist in Henry James's *The Beast in the Jungle*, awaiting a calamity that had already occurred within. From there, the treatment alliance would require finding some basis through which to address his functional impairments. Activities that could support self-esteem would help him to tolerate confrontation with interpersonal or task paradigms that were difficult, as would some conceptual understanding of why these impairments existed and how he might learn to manage them.

COUNTERTRANSFERENCE

Throughout these three chapters, we have made liberal reference to clinicians' countertransference and its relationship to work with schizophrenic patients. This subject has been effectively treated in the literature (33–36), and our recognition of its importance is much indebted to the work of others. We conclude this chapter with this topic because we wish to leave the reader with a reminder as to the importance of critical self-examination, objectivity, and reflection in the treatment of chronic schizophrenic individuals.

The schizophrenic person engenders intense reactions in others, including family and mental health practitioners. This may be due in part to the punitive nature of patients' transference as well as to the presence of disinhibited behaviors that provoke disturbing unconscious reactions in observers. In addition, the typically passive and/or hostile attitude of these persons, their help-rejecting stance, and the intractability of some of their symptoms—which exposes the limitations of our scientific knowledge and treatments—cause clinicians to feel frustrated or ineffectual. Being deprived of gratification from or praise and thanks for their work may lead clinicians to unconsciously blame patients for their professional dissatisfaction. Finally, the characteristics of the disorder may disquiet some clinicians, provoking reflection on their understanding of the mind and its too obvious vulnerability.

Most disturbing are countertransference responses associated with unconscious guilt. Clinicians may be guilty about the anger or fear, the wish to avoid or get away from patients that can occur in this work. These feelings are often a consequence of patients' efforts to discourage others. Perhaps because of our frustration, we often feel that we should do more, that we are not generous enough, that we are guilty for not wishing to give more. In periods of quiet reflection, we may say to ourselves that if we were better at our work, if we understood more, then we could help. Subtly, unconsciously, we blame ourselves for our inability to make patients well, to "get through" to those who make us feel that they would respond if we said the right thing, made the right step, went a bit further for them. Ironically, we often feel we have hurt schizophrenic individuals through being human, because we have limitations, make mistakes, respond thoughtlessly, or fail to comprehend.

We must be generous to work with chronic schizophrenic individuals. We must also be tolerant of ourselves. We should strive to learn and improve, but also to acknowlege our limitations to our patients and ourselves. The schizophrenic person experiences great need and often a great emptiness; that individual might well take all that we could give. The tension, the struggle, for the compassionate clinician, is in the need to recognize and experience the humanness and suffering of the schizophrenic person, while adhering to the principles and structure of our work.

4

The Man with a Bug in His Brain:
An Initial Interview

This chapter presents and discusses an initial interview in the assessment of a chronic schizophrenic individual for the purpose of understanding his subjective experience so that a treatment partnership can be formed.

Peter was interveiwed by an attending psychiatrist as part of a course on how to form an alliance with a so-called "hard to reach patient." The interviewees, all inpatients, were selected by the treatment team because of their difficulty in making contact. The patient chosen for this particular session was described by both his therapist and head nurse as someone who "refused to participate." Indeed, the staff felt at such a loss that they were considering transferring him to a state hospital. The nurse said, "It's not that he doesn't talk. In fact, he talks a lot, almost too much. But it's such crazy talk that there's no way in." The patient's therapist said that the patient's chronicity was the most disturbing factor, exemplified by his repeated use of the same apparently meaningless "hollow phrases." The therapist complained that when he tried to get the patient to change subjects, the patient would bombard the therapist with "weird stories about being bugged." The patient's formal diagnosis was chronic schizophrenia.

THE INTERVIEW

The patient, in his mid-thirties was of average height, somewhat stocky in build, and dressed in ill-fitting, plaid shorts and a Hawaiian shirt that hung out of his pants. Generally, he had an amiable look, though occasionally he eyed the interviewer warily. At other times, he stared off into space. Periodically, he tapped his left foot vigorously and seemed unaware of his behavior. Early in the interview, he avoided the interviewer's gaze. As the interview progressed, he fixed increasingly on the interviewer, and, by the end of the session, the interviewer had the feeling that the patient wanted to sit in his lap.

Each patient has a unique voice, an individual set of images and stories (including delusions) that reveal his or her experience. The patient discussed below tells about his humiliation, pain, and concerns about power in a story about being bugged. The interviewer starts with a serious attempt to understand this story as a message about the patient's psychological experience and uses this to demonstrate that the patient has a model of himself and his problems that can be used by the two of them to begin a treatment alliance.

As we have described in previous chapters, the interviewer is interested in assessing the patient's subjective experience, the manner of his relatedness, what he is communicating to others about himself, and how he is attempting to adapt. Since the staff viewed the patient as inaccessible, the clinician was also interested in helping them discover areas that might allow for contact with the patient.

The interview will be interrupted periodically to explain the interviewer's choice of comments.

Laying the Groundwork: Establishing Contact

Dr.: Well, it was good of you to come in. I don't know what your understanding is of this meeting.

P: Well, part of it is research of the staff and different clinics of the hospital, and part of it is practice for you. Part of it is practice for me, part of it is practice so that you can give certain recommendations to my doctor, Dr. Smith, about my condition. That might help. Therapeutic advice, anyway, that might stimulate something where different drugs are used, or different methods, or different psychological abeyance.

Dr.: An abeyance?

P: I think I might have used the wrong term.

Dr.: I don't know. It might be the right term. I'm just unfamiliar with what you're talking about there.

Interventions

The First Intervention: Letting the Patient Know the Therapist Wants to Understand

The interviewer notes the patient's odd use of the word "abeyance" and draws attention to it, wishing to clarify how the patient is using the word. More importantly, he wishes to inform the patient that the interviewer places importance on the patient's choice of words and ways of thinking about himself. The interviewer also wishes to avoid the risk of ignoring what is confusing to him about what the individual is saying. Acting as if he had understood the patient's statements when he has not would mean treating the patient's communications as unimportant and, therefore, not worth clarifying. The interviewer is informing the patient about his role as the provider of data, a role that will eventually permit the patient, with the interviewer's help, to better understand himself. Patients who have difficulty with self-object differentiation may assume that other people know their thoughts without their having to explicate them. For this reason, it is important that the interviewer say that he cannot read the patient's mind. The interviewer communicates this by indicating that he does not automatically understand what the patient is saying.

When he makes clear he has no special access to the patient's idiosyncratic use of the term "abeyance," the interviewer draws attention to the fact that he is separate from the patient. Even though at this point we do not have evidence that the patient has problems with boundaries, it is a possibility that would be important to consider early on. The interviewer chooses to ask about the use of that one word because it is the quickest and probably least threatening way to communicate all of the above. The interviewer could have made a general observation about the patient's elliptical, loose speech, but the patient would probably hear this as a criticism, which would halt the process at the beginning.

A Second Intervention: Anchoring the Interview in the Patient-Interviewer Interaction

Dr.: I don't know. It might be the right term. I'm just unfamiliar with what you're talking about there.

P: Just your advice and seeking different advice from another doctor in layman's terms is beneficial to me because I've had a lot of doctors look at me. And I felt extremely well while I was here. I had a problem with voices. They have completely gone away. I've had problems where I, you know, where I was flying, and I had cues in me, but the cues got all messed up 'cause people were spinning me on the roads and a lot of people were making love to me, you know, they were really fucking me up good! I came in here because I was all messed up and I wanted to straighten myself out with placements so I get myself on the right trail again.

Dr.: I'm particularly interested in one thing that you said—that a lot of doctors have looked at you.

The patient has just presented the clinician with an overwhelming amount of data. As will be seen in what follows, the clinician intervenes by anchoring the discussion in the patient-interviewer relationship in an effort to slow the patient down and thus reduce his potential for confusion. Anchoring the interview in their interaction allows for greater clarity because patient and interviewer are then reflecting together on a shared event, their relationship.

It is likely that the patient's anxiety is largely a function of his anxiety about the interaction. To the extent that this is true, supportive attention to the interaction would be helpful in reducing the patient's anxiety and might promote greater clarity in the interview.

The clinician's comment also introduces the general subject of how the patient relates to doctors and, in particular, this doctor who is now sitting with him. The clinician's comment anticipates a sequence in which he will confront the patient's tendency to categorize him as identical to all other doctors, who are interested in him only as a clinical specimen. Such confrontation (of how the patient lumps all doctors together) is part of the exploration of the patient's ability to differentiate among individuals.

P: A lot of them have, you know, a lot of them just said, "Okay, the medicine's the answer." No therapeutic counselling or anything like that. They just felt that if they gave me medicine it'd take care of the voices and that I'd be 100 percent better.

The patient's response to the clinician's intervention confirms he is angry at physicians who "look at him" without trying to understand him. At this point, the patient seems to be categorizing this interviewer with all the other doctors.

The Third Intervention: Working on Differentiation and Discussing the Interaction

P: [continuing his statement] That's not the whole answer. The whole answer is that I've got many problems on my mind, and some of them—you wouldn't believe what some of them are. Heavy problems and, and, and, what happens is they build up to an overload where I get these voices. I can hardly talk. I'm ready to blurt out stuff, cues, and everything else. Everything's comin' out of me. You know? It seems like somebody toyed with my mind when I was young and they really screwed me up.

The patient's comment "You wouldn't believe [some of my problems]" confirms the hypothesis that he mistrusts his doctor. This speech also offers us a look at his subjective experience: He feels himself hardly able to talk and is threatened by the possibility that everything inside him is going to come out.

Subjective Experience

Central Issues

Up to this point, the patient has been describing the actions of others on him; now, he tells us about his inner experiences. He suggests that his way of coping is faulty in that he feels he may not be able to contain himself. He indicates he is experiencing difficulty with his sense of control over himself: "Everything is coming out of me."

When he refers to the voices as "they build up to an overload," he is hinting that there is a mechanism within him that produces them, suggesting that he has thought about the origin of the voices. The interviewer notes this statement because it suggests that the patient has constructed a theory about his experience in order to understand what's happening to him and, by implication, that he is interested in thinking about mental processes. The patient may be willing to elaborate his view of himself if the clinician supports him in this task.

The clinician's principal aim in much of the interview will be to explore the patient's "self-construction," his theory about himself. By suggesting amendments to or modifications of that self-construction, the clinician hopes to be able to determine the degree of flexibility the patient has with regard to considering alternative views about himself. The extent to which the patient is able to consider other ways of looking at himself is an important indicator of his availability for treatment.

Self-Other Differentiation

At this point in the interview, self-other differentiation is a key issue under investigation. The interviewer confronts the patient's attempt to categorize the clinician (as someone who "would not believe" him) to see if the patient can differentiate the actual clinician from the patient's a priori expectations of him. This intervention evaluates whether the patient can recognize "you are not who I thought you were." The patient's failure to distinguish the other person from the patient's projections onto him would make meaningful interactions problematic.

At the same time, the clinician must be aware that the patient's attempt to categorize the interviewer according to his a priori assumptions may be his attempt to deal with the anxiety engendered by being in contact with a stranger. If the patient is expected to abandon these categories in favor of active exploration of who the individual interviewer actually is, the interviewer will have to help the patient find other ways to cope with his anxiety.

Dr.: One thing that I'm wondering about now as we're talking is this idea that I wouldn't really believe you. Why is that? Why do you think I wouldn't believe you?

The interviewer here repeats his focus on the interaction as the central event. He uses whatever material the patient offers to underscore the point. Had the patient said, "I think you would believe me," the interviewer could have focused on this issue by saying, "Given what you have told me has happened to you in the past, why would you believe me at this point?" Focusing on the interaction provides a way to clarify the preconceptions the patient brings to the interaction as well as to determine whether the patient alters his view of the interviewer as the interaction unfolds.

P: I don't know. I don't know what your affiliation is. I'm a John Bircher, and you know our position is that you take all the pressure you can take and you don't budge an inch. If they put pressure on, you're not supposed to buckle.

Vulnerability in the Interaction

By indicating his interest in the interviewer's "affiliation," the patient shows curiosity about the interviewer, a sign that the patient may be motivated to look at the interaction. In referring to the John Birch Society, the patient reveals his predilection to see himself and others in extreme terms. Consistent with his ideal, he wishes to be impervious to pressure and implies that anything other than this stoic position is a sign of weakness. In wondering where the interviewer stands, he is trying to determine the interviewer's attitude towards vulnerability. Does the clinician see it as a sign of weakness or as something tolerable and understandable? This is an important question to the patient because he has said he feels he's about to blurt everything out, to lose control. Since doing so would mean he has failed to achieve his ideal, he might be concerned about how the interviewer judges him. The patient does not appear to be aware of conflicts within himself concerning how well he can tolerate his own vulnerability, but he is concerned about the interviewer's response to his vulnerability and whether the interviewer, like a "John Bircher," will pressure him into breaking in order to humiliate him. At this point, the clinician might be forming a hypothesis that the patient is unconsciously wondering if the interviewer would accept him even though he cannot accept himself.

What the patient himself consciously desires is not clear at this stage. The patient may desire to be humiliated or feel deserving of humiliation, while at the same time, a part of him may wish for acceptance.

Returning to the issue of self-other differentiation and assumptions about the interviewer in the interaction, the doctor persists:

Dr.: Did you think you answered my question about why you thought I wouldn't believe you?

P: Well, when I first started talking to Dr. Green, he wouldn't believe anything that I was saying to him. He thought I was hallucinating or dreaming it up. Actually, I went through it.

Dr.: What would that have to do with me?

Note here the clinician's repeated focus on the central importance of the interaction, as well as his communicating his expectation that the patient can respond to an inquiry about their relationship. Additionally, the interviewer is insisting that he will not treat the patient as if he were incapable of thinking.

> P: I guess I just took the negative attitude just for a second, you know, without really testing you out, or anything like that.

The patient acknowledges his expectation that he will be misunderstood. The interviewer considers this might be a way the patient tries to maintain a self-object boundary. That is, he is separate insofar as he, as the misunderstood person, is distinct from the person who misunderstands him. A corollary would be that being understood might be dangerous because it could be equated in the patient's mind with merger, understanding being seen as equivalent to sameness.

> Dr.: But I wonder. . . . That's a good point you're making. I wonder if you tend to generalize————
> P: [interrupts] I might.
> Dr.: . . . and don't really treat me as if I'm separate from other people?
> P: That might have been the case, but I'm being very honest with you. I don't know what you want to know from me. I can go back to when the illness started and everything . . .

Assessing the Patient's Ability to Participate in the Exploration: Manifestations of Defensiveness

The patient here indicates that the interviewer's direction in the interview is making him nervous. Perhaps he is confused about the interviewer's psychological inferences. Whatever the cause, the patient attempts to reduce his anxiety by returning to something familiar—that is, a recitation of his history and symptoms. This would suggest that his return to the familiar may be a reaction to the interviewer's attempts to expand their inquiry into unfamiliar areas.

The interviewer's attempts to increase the patient's awareness of himself might make the patient curious as well as anxious. To the extent that awareness seems threatening (since he feels both limited in his capacity to understand himself and threatened by self-exposure), his becoming curious would itself pose a threat. His recitation of all-too-familiar symptoms could be the patient's effort to resist any inquiry directed at new areas of information. At this point, the interviewer would be interested to know if the patient can tolerate further exploration into self-awareness despite his attendant anxiety.

In the interviewer's next intervention, given below, he notes the patient's conflicting self-images as a knowing versus a not-knowing person. The interviewer assumes that the patient can understand what is being asked of him, but is in conflict about acknowledging the sentient part of himself. The interviewer's intervention is framed so as to confront the patient with his responsibility for maintaining awareness of that knowledgeable part of himself and to resist the patient's temptation to retreat from it or act as if it doesn't exist. The interviewer selected this particular intervention because the patient's prior behavior in the interview suggested his own dissatisfaction with types of inquiry that were not appreciative of his ability to understand himself. In addition, the patient's reference to a John Birch sort of stoicism suggested that a confrontational stance would be efficacious (since it would give the patient a chance to be "tough") as a first effort at eliciting the patient's recognition that there is a "knowing" part of him.

Dr.: But why do you now act as if you don't understand what's going on? I'm trying to find out something about your attitude toward me and I've been very clear, I thought, so far. I asked very specific questions———
  P: [interrupts] I like you.

In interrupting the interviewer, the patient suggests he is anxious about what the interviewer is saying. The gratuitous offering of affection might be an effort to conceal his anger at both the interviewer's intrusivenss and demand that the patient do something (look at why he acts as if he can't understand), which he experiences as threatening. On the other hand, he is able to allow some expression of vulnerability—that is, of his feelings of interest and affection for the interviewer. Perhaps he is in conflict about his feelings about the interviewer, expressed through his blurting out, "I like you," despite his also being angry with him.

The interviewer continues to confront the conflict within the patient:

Dr.: . . . and you say, "I don't know what you want to know," when in fact there's no reason for you not to know, since I've asked very direct questions. Haven't I?

P: Yeah.

When the patient agrees without argument, the interviewer repeats his focus on the interaction, but expands this to include his experience of other doctors.

Dr.: Okay. Now, let's go back to something I asked you a few minutes ago: what it meant to you that a lot of doctors have "looked at you"? To my ear, that sounded like an odd phrase. It didn't seem like anything was going on between you and the doctor.

P: Well, when I first got sick, I saw a doctor by the name of Smith. He did a lot of counseling. It was all therapeutic. I was on Thorazine. I didn't feel good 'cause I had the voices, but he said it was more or less job counseling and other things. He didn't tend to attack the voices, but the problem was the voices and the cues. The drugs I'm on now, I don't know, they balance my mind where I can sleep. I'm not one where I sleep a lot, but that's because of boredom not depression.

Dr.: Are you dealing with my question? Do you remember what the question was?

The patient, in these comments, directs anger toward others, specifically doctors who have worked with him in the past. Notably, the interviewer is spared any criticism. The fact that the patient is repeatedly expressing anger at doctors who have not helped him makes the interviewer wonder whether the patient is angry about the immediate interaction but afraid to express his anger directly.

The patient's anxieties about expressing aggression directly may lead him to displace it onto others, drift away from focusing on the interaction, and, instead, talk about extraneous or historical events. In order to assess the patient's capacity to modulate and express affect directly, the interviewer tries to direct the patient back to the interaction. But the patient may have difficulty with this task because he may be frightened that a focus on the interaction will lead to an eruption of intense affect, either in himself or in the interviewer.

Dr.: Do you remember what the question was?

  P: No, I don't.

Dr.: The question was: What does it mean that a lot of doctors have looked at you?

  P: Okay, what that means is that a lot of doctors have tried to psychoanalyze me and they've come up with conclusions that I'm in a space world, or that I'm not telling the truth, or that I'm making up a lot of stories. That uh, uh, those things didn't happen and, and, and my problem with the voices . . . they couldn't solve my problem with the voices.

When the patient states that he doesn't remember the interviewer's question, the interviewer wonders whether this is true and what might be responsible for the patient's memory loss. Is he too distracted to remember or has he forgotten the question because it is threatening? But the interviewer chooses to take the patient's statement of not remembering at face value, for several reasons. It is early in the interview, and the patient has not demonstrated a clear pattern of memory loss. Moreover, should the interviewer attempt an exploration of what constitutes the patient's difficulty with his memory, such an exploration might touch on themes of aggression (such as his wish to forget threatening questions or his anger at the interviewer for askng disturbing questions), and, at this early point in the interview, the alliance may not be strong enough to tolerate an examination of aggression directed toward the interviewer. On the other hand, the risk of the interviewer's accepting the patient's statement at face value is that the patient might conclude from this that the interviewer is afraid to confront (and therefore unable to contain) the patient's aggression.

The patient's response indicates that he feels despair about himself and hopelessness about being understood. He says that other doctors have seen him as being in a "space world" and unreachable or felt that he was a "liar" and beyond the reach of effective help.

It appears that the patient is anxious partly because of the vulnerability implied in his answers as well as because the interviewer has persisted in drawing the patient out with regard to his feelings, especially his feelings about treatment. The patient implies that doctors incorrectly see him as unreachable or a liar because of their unwillingness to acknowledge their own failure: "They couldn't solve my problem with the voices."

The Patient's Theory

This last statement is important because it reveals a theory the patient has about why people do certain things to him. When listening to patients discuss their delusional perceptions, clinicians often neglect to find out what patients think has brought on the event. Exploring this issue is crucial since it tells us about the patients' attitude regarding people who interact with them—in this instance, the people who are trying to help him. The idea that the doctors thought of him as a liar or as unreachable because they were frustrated in their attempts to make his voices go away is the first theory that he has presented.

Understanding the patient's theory of his experience is crucial to planning treatment interventions. For example, the patient may feel that previous doctors had disregarded him because they wished to withhold the appropriate treatment for malicious and/or envious reasons. Such understanding would need to be incorporated in any proposed treatment interventions: The staff, aware of the likelihood that the patient would see their efforts as malevolent, could anticipate the patient's rejection of their ministrations and would have a context in which to understand his behavior. Instead of seeing him as negativistic, they could appreciate that, from his perspective, he was trying to protect himself. Further, they might articulate their understanding by saying something like, "We wish to give you medicine because we feel it will help you be less anxious. However, we are aware you may believe that our intent is simply to drug you."

In this sequence, the patient also demonstrates his willingness to reveal his anger at doctors. In describing the errors of other doctors, the patient may be attempting to build an alliance with the interviewer as an idealized object. An alliance based on an idealizing transference would be acceptable as a starting point because it may be the safest and most workable transference the patient can tolerate at the outset.

The interviewer continues to examine the possible implications of the patient's statement that "a lot of people have looked at me."

Dr.: Let me be more specific. If I say that a lot of people have looked at me, I mean that people have been doing things to me, but that nothing much is going on between myself and anyone else.

The interviewer is suggesting that the patient has difficulty in stating that he feels that people, specifically doctors, look at him in a dehumanizing and critical way. This is a hypothetical construction that the patient may endorse, elaborate on, or disagree with. In addition, by presenting this statement in terms that suggest what the interviewer would feel if he were in the patient's place, he is implicitly evaluating the patient's capacity to empathize with the interviewer. That is, even if the patient did not (or could not) agree with the interviewer, does he have the capacity to appreciate how the clinician might come to feel that way?

The interviewer's intervention suggests that the patient's statement (that people have "looked at him") means that he feels abused and disregarded and that he is (appropriately) angry about that fact. The clinician's idea that aggression or resentment may underlie the patient's statement endorses the patient's right to express aggression.

The content of the interviewer's intervention underscores his expectation that the patient be an active participant in the interview process: What the interviewer implies is "That's how I see it. How do you see it?" This is especially important given the interviewer's intervention ("If I say———, I mean that ———"). The interviewer's talking about how he sees things runs the danger that the patient may agree in order to conceal his true feelings, but the risk is justified as long as the interviewer carefully continues to rely on the patient's responses for confirmation or negation of his hypotheses.

> P: Oh, I see the analyzation. I've had a lot of doctors where they worked two-way feedback and everything else, but every time I got to the real problem of the voices, they said they didn't understand the voices. They didn't know what caused them! They said it was a chemical misbalance in my mind.

The patient indicates his belief that, to cover up their ignorance of the true etiology of his voices, the doctors told him they were brought on by a chemical "misbalance." He might have simply indicated that he and the doctors had a difference of opinion—that he understood his voices one way and they another. His view that they conceal their ignorance through chemical mumbo-jumbo may indicate his anger at and suspiciousness of doctors. It may also be a way of keeping open his involvement with them. Since they have not understood him, he may yet be able to convince them, an attitude that may imply an ambivalent wish to maintain a connection with them.

Dr.: Let me stop you there and see if we can't make sense out of something. If a lot of doctors, when you got to the voices, said they didn't understand, in a way that you felt meant they dismissed you, then I wonder if you came in today thinking that I would not believe you? Perhaps you feel that when the doctors say they don't understand you, what they really mean is they don't believe you, and neither would I?

Presenting the Patient's Themes: The Patient Can Be Understood

The interviewer here offers a suggestion as to how the patient might be experiencing the interview. He is aware that the patient is confused about his internal experience and may not experience a sense of connectedness between his feelings and behaviors or between his past and his present. The interviewer's formulation implicitly connects the patient's past with his present—that is, his attitude towards the current interviewer can be seen as influenced by his prior experiences with doctors. The interviewer indicates that what the patient says about himself is valuable not only for the immediate understanding it provides but also because it may predict how he might behave with other clinicians in the future, and it may indicate the psychological motivation underlying that behavior as well.

P: They believe me. There is a lot of people with problems with voices, especially in the psychiatric hospitals. There's a lot of problems with it. They just don't understand the nature and what causes them and I talked to Dr. Smith and I went into great detail about pressure, anxiety . . .

The most interesting thing about the patient's response is his unwillingness to agree with the interviewer's statement that he (the patient) felt the doctors didn't believe him. The interviewer has presented a point of view entirely consistent with the patient's presentation, but he avoids endorsing what the interviewer has said. Acknowledging that the interviewer understands him may threaten the patient, for reasons that are as yet unclear. The patient in effect denies himself the opportunity of being understood, even though that is something he has previously said he yearns for. By indicating to the interviewer that his assumption is incorrect (the doctors really do believe him), he has grouped the interviewer with all the other doctors who have not understood him. This represents a dismissal of the interviewer, perhaps as a response to his anxiety or irritation with the interviewer's more intimate understanding of him.

In the next exchange, the interviewer persists in focusing the patient on the immediate concern, which is the patient's expectations of whether or not the interviewer would believe him. This exchange confirms the interviewer's hypothesis that the patient believed that the interviewer would treat him as other clinicians had.

Dr.: But those are all suggestions as to causes, guesses.

P: They're guesses because I get the voices really bad when I do have a lot of pressure and anxiety.

Dr.: But I'm still confused as to why you thought———

P: [interrupts] That's nerves.

Dr.: . . . I wouldn't belive you. You see, I can't get off that yet because until I understand that, I don't know how we can talk together.

P: Okay. I felt like it was just a thing where a lot of doctors have told me that. I figured you'd be just another doctor that's gonna go along with the pattern of twelve to fifteen doctors.

Dr.: I'm not happy with the idea that you would judge me so quickly. Can you understand that?

P: Yeah. I can understand that.

The interviewer closes this portion of the exchange with the suggestion that a central proposition of the work is that each be open to the unexpected in the other. At the same time, the interviewer must be mindful that the patient's tendency to generalize may represent a (maladaptive) attempt to deal with the threatening nature of involvement with another person. Nevertheless, the interviewer's assertion that he and the patient cannot talk meaningfully until the issue of the patient's expectations is understood reinforces to the patient how important it is to the interviewer that he understand the patient's subjective experience.

Dr.: And, it's not at all clear to me whether, at this moment, you are giving me a chance, in terms of whether I will belive you or not. I don't know what you think about that. Do you think it's possible that I might believe you?

P: Okay. I know you're coming in with an open mind.

Dr.: But that's not what you said ten minutes ago. You said, "I know you're not going to believe me." So, have you changed your mind about that since we started to talk?

P: Just talking has changed my mind.

When the interviewer says, "I don't know what you think about that," he is asking the patient if he can step back from the expectations and prejudices that he may have held when he began the interview and "think about" what may be, for him a new idea. That is, the interviewer is asking the patient to utilize his neutral, observing capacities to think about the interviewer, not in terms of his previous assumptions, but in terms of the context of what has actually transpired between them in the last few minutes. The interviewer's question reminds the patient that the interviewer values the patient's contributions to their work as a thinking, observing collaborator. In addition, it asserts that the interviewer is not omniscient, that he does not know what the patient is thinking. When the interviewer asks, "Have you changed your mind about that since we started to talk?" he is underscoring his assumption that the patient can change his mind, that he can take in new information.

Having made progress toward his early goals (assessment of self-object differentiation, presenting a model of therapeutic partnership), the interviewer next pursues those areas of subjective experience the patient has indicated he is willing to talk about. From those, the interviewer will attempt to expand the inquiry into other areas.

Building the Model

Further Exploration of Subjective Experience

Dr.: Okay, then, since these voices seem very important to you, tell me something about them.

P: They're vicious, they're accusatory. They never tell me to do anything though.

Dr.: Are they your voices?

P: I've been told by doctors that said they are my voices.

Dr.: No, no, I'm interested in only what you think—what you believe.

P: I would say they're my voices.

The interviewer reinforces the idea that the patient is the final authority about his experience. The emphasis on the way the patient understands himself, rather than relying on what other people think about him, has, as a second goal, reinforcing self-object differentiation.

Dr.: You believe that? Then, why do you say you "get" voices. If they're your voices, they belong to you. You don't "get" them.

 P: Let's make a differentiation right now. There's a difference between a thought and a voice.

The interviewer insists on clarifying the patient's experience of the origin of the voices. In so doing, the interviewer may privately think that the patient's inconsistent presentation (of whether the voices come from within or without) reflects his conflict about what the voices represent. The interviewer notes this and will look for further confirmation in the patient's discourse. At the same time, in this comment, the interviewer indicates his willingness to hear the patient describe these voices as something occurring outside of him rather than attempting to convince the patient that the voices represent his own thoughts. The interviewer thereby gives the patient permission to describe his experience as he understands it. In response, interestingly, the patient, for the first time, introduces a thought of his own rather than simply reacting to some inquiry of the interviewer. He says, "Let's make a differentiation right now." His spontaneous clarification represents early evidence of collaboration.

Dr.: Are they your voices?

 P: They're my voices, but right now I'm only getting thoughts.

Dr.: But when you get the voices, are they your voices?

 P: They are my voices.

Dr.: Then why do you say you "get" them? If they are yours, you must have them all the time.

 P: Probably subconsciously.

Dr.: Are you saying that you believe that you harbor within yourself accusations toward you?

 P: Yeah.

Dr.: That's your idea?

 P: Yeah.

Dr.: Then why do you call your own accusations "voices?"

 P: That's not true. The voice tells you that you're Himmler's son and you know you're not Himmler's son 'cause you already checked it out with the West German Embassy.

Dr.: But you just told me a minute ago that these voices are really your voices.

P: They're my voices.

Dr.: They belong to you? They come from you?

P: They weren't created by me.

Dr.: Uh, I didn't understand that.

Through this exchange the patient discusses his internal world with seeming ease. This may be a consequence of the interviewer's repeated emphasis on the patient's ability to make himself clear.

Autonomy and Control

At the beginning of this exchange the patient partially endorses the statement that his voices are related to "subconscious accusations," but he remains undecided about their definitive origin. He later states that the voices do not come from him and were not created by him. His uncertainty is important with respect to his experience of the locus of control. Is he or is he not the master of his own fate? The patient can partly accept the idea that the voices are an expression of his inner feelings of self-blame (he is his own persecutor). On the other hand, he sees the voices as having been imposed on him by some outside force. The patient is also uncertain about whether he has the capacity to control the voices. This indicates to the interviewer the importance of continuing to ask the patient about who is really running the show.

Dr.: I didn't understand that.

P: The voices were created by people saying stuff and putting cues in me.

Dr.: Are you saying that at this point these voices are yours, but they didn't originate with you?

P: They didn't originate with me.

Dr.: How does that work? Explain that to me.

P: Well, sometimes when I get the voices———

Dr.: [interrupts] Now, you're saying you "get" them again.

P: Okay, when I have them.

Dr.: When you talk to yourself?

P: No, not when I talk to myself. It's like I was lifted to a point where I boil over or pressure or something like that. My anxiety and nerves get bad and it triggers a bell. The voices just start coming. I can hear them from outside.

The patient has begun to relate his understanding of the processes at work within him. His last statement is significant for several reasons. He begins by using a simile to describe what has occurred in his mind: "It's like I was lifted." This represents his effort to clarify his experience as well as to begin to construct a model of that experience. His statement "It's like" suggests distance or uncertainty on his part, presumably indicating his unwillingness to fully endorse this position (of being lifted), although it may also reflect his difficulty in putting his experience into words.

As he describes this experience, the patient uses terms that depict him as passive. He is "lifted" and then he "boils over" and the voices just start coming.

Many patients do not immediately identify ways in which treaters can be of help to them. Our patient says he feels "pressure, anxiety, and nerves." The patient who can speak of feeling anxious about what is happening to him- or herself (whether we agree with this view of the experience or not) is describing a reaction all of us have had in relation to a sense of danger, whether it be real or imagined. The same can be said of this patient's speaking of "pressure and nerves."[a]

Developing the Patient's Model

Dr.: Now, just a minute. I think this is terribly important, and I want to understand this with you, and you went too fast for me.
P: Okay.
Dr.: You have an idea that there's pressure inside you. I can't get to the next step from the pressure inside you to voices outside. Make that bridge for me. What is it that happens?

The interviewer reinforces his commitment to seeing the patient as an educator, someone who must teach the interviewer about his way of experiencing himself and the world. The interviewer acknowledges his own limitations by the statement "I [alone] can't get to the next step." By asking the patient to "make that bridge for me," he insists that the patient provide the connection. This encourages the patient to make sense of himself to the interviewer and repeats the interviewer's conviction that the patient has the capacity to make sense of himself as well as the capacity to communicate that sense to the interviewer.

P: It's sort of like you say something to yourself. I like a certain girl, or something like that. I say that girl's name.

Dr.: Like what girl's name?

P: I could be lying in bed without no voices and if I say a girl's name, 'cause the girl might be famous or she might know somebody who's famous, or something like that, it'll trigger off a voice.

Dr.: Now what's the connection? I don't understand that. I can say a girl's name while I'm lying in bed and I don't hear any external voice. What's the mechanism inside you that makes your saying the name cause the girl's name to sound like it's coming from outside of you? I don't get the connection there.

P: I think it's just pressure.

Dr.: I don't understand how that works.

P: I don't understand how it works either. It's just the way it is. I had a car accident and I'm not so sure. It could be a bug in my brain.

The patient begins this segment in a conversational idiom, speaking with ease and familiarity, acting as if the interviewer is capable of understanding what he is trying to communicate. The patient's manner of speaking indicates his interest and absorption in communicating his experience. This represents a change in the interview because it suggests that the patient has at least temporarily accepted the paradigm that the interviewer has been presenting: We are meeting to try to make sense of your life.

When the interviewer shortly thereafter asks the patient, "What's the mechanism?" he is using a concrete term that draws upon the patient's own earlier mechanistic description of his mental life. The more familiar the terminology is to the patient, the less likely he is to become confused or to feel that an alien model is being imposed on him. It is not crucial at this point that the patient's elaborations be final or correct. What is important is the capacity of the therapist to communicate his interest in developing with the patient a model of his inner experience.

The interviewer focuses on elucidating those areas of the patient's mental life where the patient appears able to tolerate the interviewer's participation. When the patient then states, "I don't understand how it works either," he is identifying that he too feels uncertain and lacks control in a crucial area of his life. He implies that his understanding of himself is not fixed and, therefore, that he may be able to consider alternate hypotheses from those he has already offered. Further, identifying an area in which the patient does not feel in control presents the interviewer with another topic to collaborate on.

The patient's last comment in this segment introduces a hypothesis about what has happened to his mental life. He may have been bugged.

The patient has identified some issues that concern him. What the patient identifies as dysphoric can serve as the starting point in the formation of the treatment alliance. The temptation on the part of the clinician is often to begin by focusing attention on what the clinician defines as the disorder. While keeping in mind what we understand the problem to be, we must begin the treatment alliance around those issues where the patient is in conflict with himself and where he, therefore, may be interested in pursuing the issue further.

Dr.: What do you mean, a bug in your brain?
P: I had a car accident in 1977 . . .
Dr.: Yeah.
P: . . . you know, and I was driving on the road and somebody cut me off. I started to speed up behind them to find out who it was. I had two beers in me and as we were going around a turn they opened up their door and threw something out the door from a bucket and it went all over the road. I tried to get out of the way and I went right into a telephone pole. I put my head right through a windshield right up here where the gash is. And then the policeman in the car says, "Watch out Bill, how many beers you had?" I said, "Two" and said "I'm alright," and he says, "Okay, you watch out. They might put a bug in your brain." And I went to the hospital and this Dr. Steel started talking about bugs and he said, "You should have a bug in your brain."
Dr.: What does that mean, "You should have a bug in your brain"?
P: He's a powerful man and all this other stuff. I don't know what it is. It could be just a regular tap, you know, where a bug picks up brain senses and thoughts and the brain translates it and microphones it out to the outside.

Dr.: Let me see if I understand it so far. This is a theory that I'm about
to present————

P: [interrupts] Well, it's my experience that the guy said he's gonna
put a bug in my brain.

The patient has begun to describe an accident, which he identifies as
the starting point of his persecution. It all began on the road. The
interviewer does not focus on the obvious irrationality of his claims nor
challenge the patient's idiosyncratic logic. Rather, the interviewer's questions are geared to further the patient's explanation and exploration of
himself.

In suspending his own sense of reality in favor of taking in the
patient's account of these events, the interviewer can then appreciate the
logic of the patient's subsequent constructions. If we can imagine what
it would be like to believe that an electronic device had been implanted
in our brain, then much of what would follow would approximate what
our patient has to say about his experience.

We may speculate about the degree to which the patient doubts his
own story, but the patient makes very clear that, at this point in the
narration (or, perhaps in the relationship), he is adamant that his construction is not simply a hypothesis, but rather his "experience." He
corrects the interviewer when the interviewer attempts to describe his
statements as a theory by saying, "It's my experience that the guy said
he's going to put a bug in my brain."

The Interviewer's Reactions

Empathizing with the patient's experience of himself (which in no way
implies agreeing with it) requires a considerable cognitive and emotional
effort on the part of the interviewer because, as is evident here, the
patient's experience may be one that can be frightening and perplexing
to us. The patient's recitation is his attempt to make sense of and/or
exert control over his experience. The incident just described is marked
by naked aggression, danger, injured narcissism, and fear, as well as
curiosity and benevolence, the latter represented by the policeman who
offers him friendly advice and a warning. There is also the ambivalent
figure of the doctor as powerful, potentially helpful, and certainly dangerous.

In listening to him, the interviewer silently notes those themes (aggression, danger, fear, benevolence, and so forth) as areas that he will attempt to explore further later. The clearer both patient and clinician become regarding the patient's central concerns (including the extremely important issue that they agree on what is central), the greater the likelihood that they will arrive at a working agreement. The nature of what is agreed upon must be acceptable to both parties. For example, the clinician cannot agree to work with the patient on his literally having been bugged, since he does not believe that. He could, however, agree to collaborate on helping the patient feel less intruded upon and exposed.

When we refer to encouraging the patient to elaborate his version of what he feels is true, we mean that such a version represents his best reconstruction at the moment. The patient's presentation of his or her internal contradictions, ambivalences, and self-doubts alerts the clinician to the patient's internal conflicts about his story. It is precisely at that point where the clinician can join the struggle.

As the interview progresses, whether we are becoming familiar with the patient can be tested by our constructing imaginary situations for ourselves and seeing if we are able to imagine what his behavior would be. Once we have reached that level of understanding, we can begin to retranslate the concrete information he is presenting into a more metaphorical statement that does justice to what he is saying and also makes sense to us. This process generally implies a leap of several levels of abstraction from what the patient has said without violating the spirit of his statements.

Thus, in the above segment of narrative, we would know that "somebody cut me off" means he felt prevented from doing something he wanted to do at that time. When he tried to clarify the nature of the obstruction and "started to speed up behind them to find out what it was" and so on, he experienced even greater difficulty, which suggests that he lacks the means to get on with his life on his own.

The figure of the policeman, who warns him of the danger but is unable or unwilling to provide further protection, may represent a real or, more likely, wished-for protective figure. His subsequent giving up on such assistance ever happening suggests he is pessimistic about receiving help. On the other hand, the policeman may represent an intrapsychic event—that is, his inability to heed his own (the policeman's) inner warning signals about impending doom.

Based on what we know thus far, his inner sruggle appears to center
on issues of power (real or imagined) symbolized by the immensely
powerful and controlling doctor. Note, too, that the patient is capable
of observing that what he is reporting is bizarre. He strives to correct
that impression by presenting himself as if he were in the mainstream.
For example, he refers to the bug as possibly "just . . . a regular tap,"
trying to cloak these exotic events in normalcy. This early evidence of
his wish to present himself as normal is something else the clincian
makes note of and may call upon later to enhance collaboration.

P: It's an experience.
Dr.: Okay, but I want to offer a theory.
P: You want people to hear the bugging?
Dr.: I want to present your theory as I understand it. It would be a
theory, based on certain real experiences of yours, but this is the
theory, the explanation, that I understand you offering me. Okay?
I want to be sure I understand it.
P: Okay.
Dr.: Like all of us, you live with a certain degree of tension. However,
unlike most of us, the consequence of the tension within your head
may cause you to respond differently than most people. A pressure
builds up in your head, and the pressure that builds up in your
head can occur for a variety of reasons. So far you're in agreement
with me? This is what you've been saying? [Patient nods.] At some
point, there is a triggering mechanism, which, if the pressure exceeds a certain amount, the bug that has been placed in your brain,
activates. It's like throwing a switch, and the switch is thrown
when the pressure exceeds a certain limit, which one could perhaps
even measure. At the point at which the switch is thrown, the bug
is activated, throwing voices outside. The second part of the theory
has to do with the implantation of the bug. That is, at some earlier
point, people tampered with your brain. Now you are walking
around with a bug in your brain and the only control that you
have would be to diminish the pressure, because the pressure has
to exceed a certain amount in order to throw the switch to activate
the bug. Do I understand you?

In his extended comment, the interviewer takes the raw data of the
patient's experience and provides a more integrated construction than

that which the patient articulated. The model of the interaction is that of two scientists who are examining a phenomenon of nature and attempting to elucidate its features. The value of this effort lies partly in helping the patient structure his experience and consider the consequences of what he believes, an effort that, in being organizing, may therefore be anxiety reducing. At the same time, by establishing a structure to clarify the connections among various parts of the patient's subjective experience, the interviewer forces more scrutiny of the details of that experience. In particular, the interviewer's reconstruction allows them both to examine in greater detail critical aspects of the theory the patient has presented, generating more information about the forces at work within him, in particular, the "pressures" that influence him.

The manner in which the interviewer constructs this theory highlights the interviewer's appreciation that the patient's subjective experience represents his effort to cope with difficult and disorganizing events.

Resistance to Accepting Help as an Issue in Alliance Formation

An important aim of this interview is to develop information about the patient's resistance to being helped. The interviewer comes to this interchange with the knowledge that many, if not most, schizophrenic individuals feel threatened by psychological exploration as well as by exposure to psychiatric treatment. We have already been told that this patient has been described as "treatment resistant," which suggests to the interviewer that he may see mental health professionals as dangerous and fight their efforts to help him. The patient provides support for this hypothesis in the way in which he describes his interactions with previous doctors and through his statement that it was a doctor who put a bug in his brain. His theory of what has occured does not allow for psychiatric treatment, since he has attributed his troubles to the presence of a bug in his brain, not to a psychiatric condition.

The interviewer's presentation of the theory allows for further joint scrutiny of the patient's understanding of himself and prepares for a process in which the patient has the responsibility to identify how he can be helped and, in particular, how the interviewer may be of help to him. By forcing the issue with respect to the patient's unwillingness to see himself as troubled or ill, the interviewer plans to determine how he may be able to engage the patient most effectively.

The Alliance

Using the Patient's Model to Think About an Alliance

The treatment alliance can best be founded on a collaborative process in which patient and interviewer experience sharing and empathy. The world our patient describes is short on these qualities. The interviewer wants to present to the patient a view of himself that underscores his struggles, his pain, and the sadness underlying his conflict over aggression. In his statement above, this interviewer focuses on those details of the patient's experience that have the best chance of forming a solid groundwork for their treatment alliance. Beginning with "like all of us . . . ," he reinforces the common human aspects of the patient's experience. At the same time, the interviewer alludes to the idiosyncratic nature of the patient's experience when he says "unlike most of us . . ."

Then the interviewer describes how he thinks the patient understands himself. The interviewer believes the patient's self-construction represents his effort to adapt to and makes sense of a variety of disturbing experiences. The interviewer is also laying out, for later examination, the cost to the patient of these adaptive efforts. The cost lies in the degree to which the patient does not experience himself as having control over what happens to him and in his vulnerability and aloneness. The interviewer anticipates that further work could help the patient construct a new understanding of himself that would be more adaptive and that would permit a greater sense of control, more tolerance of interactions with others, less isolation, and more hope.

At a few points, the interviewer takes care to gain the patient's endorsement, which will be useful later when they return to the significance of this theory. He does this by saying, "So far you're in agreement with me?" and later, "Do I understand you?"

While very concrete and mechanistic, the theory has the advantage of suggesting points of potential control. When the interviewer says, "which one could even measure perhaps," he suggests to the patient that they can engage in a more precise and critical examination of the patient's mental life. In the process, the interviewer indirectly states that the patient is not helpless in the face of his experience and that areas of control can be identified. He suggests that there are practical ways to look at the patient's experience with the promise of finding better adaptations.

This process (of finding better adaptations) is prefigured when the interviewer says, "The only control that you have would be to diminish the pressure." The interviewer's clarification of the patient's theory, while endorsing the patient's experience of an environment where forces beyond his control act upon him, suggests ways in which the patient may be able to control his experience more effectively. This is where treatment can help. At the same time, it hints at a later stage when the patient may be helped to acknowledge that there are, indeed, aspects of his condition, including his illness, he cannot control.

The patient responds:

P: Yeah. It's sort of like a release mechanism, where in other words you don't die mentally. When the pressure builds up to a point it won't kill you 'cause the bug will activate something when it's released.

The patient's response to the interviewer's presentation of his theory endorses its reasonableness to him as well as its importance. When the patient says that the pressure might build up to a point where it could kill him if it were not released, he is revealing how threatening his own mental processes are to him and the degree to which he lives in a state of terror—a significant admission of vulnerability.

Below, the interviewer follows this acknowledgment with a comment that represents a logical conclusion derived from the patient's presentation of himself; that is, why is the patient seeing a psychiatrist instead of a surgeon? After all, there must be some explanation for why he even bothers to talk to a psychiatrist. He could, for instance, choose to say nothing. This line of inquiry asks the patient to clarify the reasoning behind his behavior; specifically, it encourages the patient to present his rationale for seeking psychiatric treatment despite presenting his dilemma in neurosurgical terms. Since the patient has just declared his terror and confusion, the interviewer knows that the patient feels frustrated, helpless, and alone and, therefore, on some level, recognizes that psychiatric help may be of benefit. But the interviewer wishes the patient to tell him in what terms their collaboration may take place. Rather than telling the patient what he will help him with, the interviewer asks the patient to tell him how he can help him. At the same time, the interviewer is staying within the bounds of the patient's logic and communicating to the patient that the interviewer appreciates his logic, without necessarily agreeing with the underlying premises. By staying within the framework of the patient's own story, patient and therapist may be able to identify a paradigm for their interaction, avoiding, thereby, some of the resistance coincident with most treatment alliances.

P: . . . the bug will activate something when it's released.

Dr.: Yes. Now the thing I don't understand, however, is why you're seeing a psychiatrist?

P: I should be seeing somebody in the operating room.

Dr.: Exactly!

P: To get the god damn bug the hell out of me! I don't want the bug in my brain. I know damn well, the surgeon, you know, he was talking to my father, he said, "Well, I don't want a bug in him." And then I got out of the hospital and you know, after walking out of the hospital with my father with blood all over me, my father says to me, 'Is that you I hear?"

The patient begins the segment with a statement, the tone of which is angrier than that of anything he has said previously. This suggests that, in response to the interviewer's acceptance of him, the patient is able to be more open about what has happened to him. At the same time, the patient assumes too readily that the interviewer is endorsing his view of himself as true, as if to say, "Finally someone believes me!" His lack of suspicion about what the interviewer believes suggests something of his fragility as well as his tremendous need to be understood, a need so intense and so frustrated that it fairly bubbles out of him in response to the interviewer's effort at understanding.

The patient's introduction of his father is significant for what it suggests about his internal struggles around power and understanding. The father is presented as a compassionate but ineffectual figure. He stands by helplessly while his bloodied son is abused. The image of the father is of a diminished and demeaned person, perhaps reflecting a feeling that people who are not powerful are valueless. He devalues the image of his father and demeans the people who empathize with him, perhaps because he equates empathy with being powerless and unimportant. This also suggests that the patient may view efforts to empathize with him as being of little value if they are not associated with the power to change his circumstances.

An important corollary to this image is that the father may represent some aspect of the patient's own experience—that is, his own devalued view of his empathic capacities. The themes of devalued empathy and admired power would be important aspects to explore in the interview and later on in ongoing treatment.

Dr.: Yes. Yes. But I'm confused. You came to this hospital voluntarily?

P: Yeah.

Dr.: Okay. If I were you, my temptation would be to leave no stone unturned until I found someone, an expert on brain matters, who could remove this bug.

P: There might be one in my heart too, 'cause I had a heart attack in Seattle, and I felt something like a timer or something like that was put in. I felt my chest went out, my head went back like this [jerks his head back], and I went unconscious. Just before I went unconscious I felt some real tapping. There could be bugs all around.

Dr.: I think you're avoiding the implication of what I'm saying, which is why are you seeing a psychiatrist rather than a neurosurgeon? Perhaps you should also see a heart surgeon, but one step at a time.

The interviewer focuses on the question again in order to try to determine which experiences are dysphoric for the patient. Those areas that the patient acknowledges as conflictual are the ones where the clinician has a possible entry: "Since you are in pain [confusion, uncertainty, etc.] about X, I can help you to decide what you want regarding X. However, to do that, first we will need to understand much more about X."

What the interviewer has not thus far suggested, but which is crucially important to the patient's understanding of himself, is that he is in conflict about and/or unsure of the validity of some of his perceptions. This doubt or inner struggle is experienced affectively as dysphoria.

The interviewer's pressing home the apparent conflict in the patient's behavior—that despite his belief about being bugged he is seeing a psychiatrist rather a surgeon—helps the patient identify that the contradiction is a consequence of conflict and uncertainty regarding what he thinks is true.

The Interviewer's Response to the Patient's Challenge: Can You Take It?

The patient responds to the interviewer's returning to what he believes to be the patient's predicament by suggesting that his problem is more serious and pervasive than has yet been understood. Not only does he have a bug in his brain, but there is a timer in his heart that may, at any moment, cause him to have a heart attack. This communicates to the interviewer how frightened the patient is about his moment to moment existence. At the same time, his allusion to a heart bug is a response to the interviewer's request that the patient explain why he has not tried harder to improve his condition.

The interviewer asks how the patient views the process of getting help. The patient responds as if to say, "It's futile to try. 'They' not only have my mind, they are all over, and they have control of my very existence, and that's why I haven't tried to do anything about it." This represents a warning to the interviewer that the patient feels exploration may be dangerous to him and perhaps to the interviewer as well. The patient warns the interviewer that getting involved with him could be an ordeal. In effect, the patient is saying to the interviewer, "Are you sure you're prepared to join me in such a frightening endeavor?" or "Can you take it?" The interviewer addresses this by saying that when one faces an overwhelming situation, one deals with it "one step at a time." The interviewer responds to the patient's implicit warning in a way that he hopes will communicate that further understanding is neither futile nor dangerous. Further, he indicates that the way for him to understand the patient is by dealing with his experiences in a steady, systematic fashion. Implicitly, he tells the patient that this process will take a long time.

This forms a crucial prelude to the further discussion of the patient's experience:

P: I don't know who, you see, I know my uncle John had a bug in his brain. He said, "I'm gonna give you the power." Now, whether these animals, these people are really animals . . .

Dr.: Are you about to explain why you haven't contacted a neurosurgeon?

P: Every time I tried, they've denied me and said it wasn't a bug in my head.

Dr.: Who have you seen?

P: Dr. Steel. I went to see Dr. Steel.

Dr.: Who is Dr. Steel?

P: He's the doctor who put it in.

Dr.: You went to see the doctor who bugged you in the first place, to help you?

P: To take it out.

Dr.: That's the first thing you've said to me that makes no sense whatever. Let's go back a step. Now I'm wondering whether you don't need to see a psychiatrist. There's something odd about what you just said. If I felt that someone had implanted a bug in me, that person would be the last soul on earth I'd ask to take it out! How can you trust such a person? Do you see that makes no sense?

P: Yeah, but the way the thing is set up, you have to put enough heat on the man to take it out.

Dr.: You mean, you believe that only the person that inserted the bug can remove it?

P: No.

Dr.: Well, then why are you seeing him?

P: I don't know who to see. I told . . .

The interviewer's thrust in this exchange is to clarify the patient's reasons for talking to a psychiatrist rather than to a surgeon and then, as the patient reveals that he has talked to people about getting the bug out, to understand why the patient would go about it in the way that he has. Several issues are presented and developed simultaneously in this line of questioning. Most concretely, the interviewer is attempting to elucidate the patient's understanding of his motives and behavior and, in the process, to learn how the patient experiences his efforts to help himself. Does he see himself as someone who has the power to change his circumstances? How overwhelmingly powerful are the people who are persecuting him? Does he think they can be made to change their course of action by "putting heat on them," as he suggests? Would he endorse the idea that he might be able to effect a change in his circumstances if he could gain enough powerful allies to force the enemy to alter their behavior? And does he see the fallacies in his sense of reality?

Potential Allies

As just discussed, the interviewer collects data about the patient's attitude toward potential allies, who include the interviewer and other people involved in the patient's treatment. This information is useful for predicting the transference issues that the patient might develop toward those helping him. For instance, would the patient devalue helpers who are not overtly powerful? Would the patient dismiss efforts to help him that are not directly aimed at helping him have more power to challenge his persecutors? Is he uninterested in understanding himself if that understanding is not associated with the attainment of greater strength or forcefulness?

At the same time, the interviewer is pursuing this line of questioning with a crucial hypothesis in mind: namely, that the patient's struggle to have the bug taken out represents his internal struggle to understand and control the disturbing events that have occurred. The patient has made it clear that no one has joined him in fighting his persecutors. On the contrary, he has not been believed, and he feels alone in his battle.

There may be a part of the patient that wishes to find allies and still hopes for a resolution to his problems through forcing the persecutors to stop. On the other hand, there is also a part of the patient that takes note of the disapproval and disbelief of those around him. At this point, he appears extremely resistant to acknowledging that these events (the persecutors, the bugging, etc.) are manifestations of inner conflict. His resistance is represented by his adamant view of himself as persecuted and his conviction that the only resolution is to make those responsible for the implant remove the bug. Associated with that view is a feeling of hopelessness and helplessness because, up to this point, his efforts to convince others to help him have been unsuccessful.

The Patient's Conflict in Relationship to Alliance Formation

The interviewer has evidence that the patient is uncertain about whether he is a victim whose salvation depends on his tormentors. His doubt is most apparent in the fact that the patient is talking to a psychiatrist (rather than his tormentors) about his difficulties. The radical position that his only resolution is by changing the mind of the persecuting doctor or his cohorts is inherently frustrating because it cannot be effected. The interviewer hopes to help the patient see that he already partially understands this. This acceptance would require the patient to face the fact that he is the source of his difficulties and that his belief system is a distortion.

The focus is on providing the patient with an alternative way of looking at things and, therefore, a reason to consider changing his (defensive) adaptation. Hope is intimately related to the concept of alternatives: If the patient can see other solutions to his predicament, he is then able to exercise choice. The alternatives may be ones he is aware of but feels have been beyond his grasp. The task of the interviewer or the treatment staff would be to help the patient see that these are not beyond his grasp and that, indeed, some alternatives are potentially more rewarding than the resolution he consciously endorses. For example, if the patient can understand that he can acknowledge his helplessness directly, he may no longer find it necessary to believe he is being persecuted (as a way of justifying his sense of futility).

Dr.: I just want to find out why you would go back and see the person who inserted the bug in your head? That would seem to me like playing right into the enemy's hand.

P: Yeah. I know what you're saying. I know what you're saying. It was a stupid move on my part.

Dr.: Maybe it's stupid, but, in my experience, people are not stupid. They're always after something. It's as if you want this to go on.

P: No I don't. I want it out.

Interpreting the Wishes Behind the Conflict as Understandable

The interviewer has just made a crucial intervention—namely, interpreting the patient's behavior. The interviewer has advanced the hypothesis that the patient "wants this to go on" (because the patient believes an alternative view would be too threatening to him). In making this interpretation, the therapist also indirectly tells the patient that he possesses the power to influence his circumstances. Suggesting that the patient's attitude (of wanting this to go on) has something to do with the malevolent process continuing implies that if the patient changed his attitude, he might alter the process.

Dr.: Do you understand why I would think you would want it to go on? By seeing Dr. Steel, you act as if you want to play right into their hands. Do you understand that? Can you follow that reasoning?

P: See, the whole thing is, I'm a John Bircher . . .

Dr.: Can you follow that reasoning? Now you're going off on a track. It's hard for you to talk with me and stay on the track. Have you noticed that?

P: I know. It's stupid reasoning.

Dr.: You keep on saying, "It's stupid reasoning," and I'm saying, "There's method to your madness." You're acting like a guy who wants to stay bugged, even though you say, "I want to get this thing out." . . . Why did you see Dr. Steel?

P: I saw Dr. Steel because I wanted to find out definitely, 'cause I saw him put something in my head and I wanted to find out . . .

Dr.: Why would you trust him, of all people?

P: I want to make trouble for him, actually.

The interviewer has confronted the patient about his contradictory behavior regarding removing the bug. The patient now indicates that he conducted his efforts without any real expectation of success. He did not expect the doctor to remove the bug but rather wished to "make trouble" for the doctor. He is describing an essentially futile position in which his expression of anger cannot change the one thing that matters—his being bugged. If the patient can acknowledge the futility and sadness implicit in his expresion of impotent rage, he might be able to look at the maladaptive nature of his activites and, therefore, begin to consider other alternatives.

Dr.: Let's try to get something straight here in terms of our priorities. What's the most important thing for you?

P: To get the bug out.

Dr.: All right. What kind of reasonable plan can you make now, perhaps with my help, to do something about that? What kind of thought do you have about that?

The interviewer is sensitive to the threatening nature of directly proposing any suggestions for how the patient might understand himself differently or affect his circumstances. With that in mind, the interviewer

cautiously makes a potentially facilitating suggestion. He first alludes to
a collaboration in creating a "reasonable plan . . . perhaps with my
help," a comment that reinforces the interviewer's willingness and availability to join with the patient.

P: Okay, take an x-ray of my mind. It's inside the gauze. He put
something inside the gauze and . . .

Dr.: Is it a metallic substance? Is it heavy metal? Is it going to show up
on an x-ray?

P: I'm not sure. I'm not sure what it was.

Dr.: Well, have you had any x-rays of your mind?

P: I've had . . . I've had no, no x-rays of my mind.

Using the Patient's Logic to Confront Him with His Sadness

Dr.: How long has this been going on?

P: Seven years.

Dr.: Seven years? Do you understand that the more we talk, the more I
begin to doubt whether you ever want to have any definitive information about this bug? Could it be that you want to keep this bug
inside you?

P: No I don't.

Dr.: First you tell me that you————

P: [interrupts] I'm not 100 percent sure there is a bug in me. He said
he was gonna put a bug inside of me and I heard voices as soon as
I walked out of the hospital door . . .

The interviewer pursues a process that will be repeated throughout
the remainder of the interview. He stays within the frame of the patient's
own experience, using terms that stick closely to those the patient uses
to describe himself. For example, in pursing the question of the patient's
motivation about removing the bug, the interviewer's questions derive
from the patient's suggestion of taking an x-ray. Thus, the interviewer
asks about the radio-opaque qualities of the bug. By consistently utilizing the patient's own frame of reference, the interviewer hopes to extend
the patient's thinking to the point that he will discover the contradictions
and ambiguities in his own beliefs. When confronted with those, the
patient may be able to acknowledge his uncertainty and become more
open to other options that offer greater security or more effective adaption.

At the close of this exchange, the patient acknowledges that he is not certain that there is a "bug" in his brain. Moreover, the patient next describes events that may be closer to the actual experience he had at the time of the accident in his description of hearing voices as he left the hospital.

Dr.: Twenty minutes ago I presented a theory to you, which I said was your theory, as I understood it. You agreed with me. Let me diagram it here, just to be sure that we agree. Let's see [interviewer goes to blackboard and begins to draw a graph], we'll call this "voice" down here, okay? This is the voice and we'll call this 'stress" over here, okay?

P: Okay.

Dr.: Now, as I understand you, what you're saying is that everything to this side of the line means that there is no voice. At this point of stress [points to graph], and at this point of stress, and at this point of stress, there are no voices. At a certain point, from this here on, as the stress occurs, the voices start appearing. Right? More stress, more voices. . . . By the way, do you think that's true? Once you get a certain level of stress, the voices start. Does more stress produce more voices, or is there no relationship?

P: It's a heavier voice with more stress.

Dr.: Same number of voices, but the voice is more insistent?

P: The voices are heavier and louder.

Dr.: Louder. Okay, so we'll also say that these voices are not only present or absent, but that they get louder. With more stress, the voice gets louder? Is that it? [adds this information to graph]

P: Yeah.

Dr.: Okay. And this point here [indicates point on graph], the point at which, right here, the point at which the stress occurs and is sufficient to bring out the voice, is the point at which a switch is thrown which releases the bug [marks it on graph]. That's your theory, is that right?

P: Right.

The interviewer steps back from his successful confrontation, and constructs a graph that illustrates the patient's experience (see Figure 4.1). The graph helps the patient concretely visualize the connections between the various statements he has made in a way that allows for

Figure 4.1

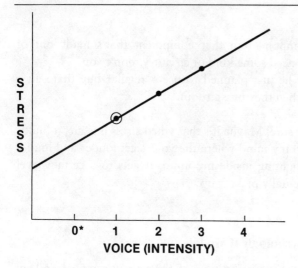

⊙ = point at which switch is thrown, releasing bug.

0 * = does not mean the absence of voice, simply that the intensity is not sufficient to be heard. (The asterisked information represents the revision based on additional information supplied by the patient.)

greater elaboration and clarification. The process is collaborative. The interviewer involves the patient in modifying and clarifying the diagram. This collaboration is a paradigm for the treatment alliance, and it includes the recognition that understanding is not absolute but rather an ongoing process that is enriched by further exploration. There are elements of playfulness and creativity in their designing the graph together, important attributes for many different kinds of treatment paradigms.

Dr.: Now you're telling me in the last minute or two, that this model may not work. It may not be true.

P: I'm not sure exactly. He said he was gonna put a bug in my brain and he had something in his hand and he put something inside the gauze. What he put inside the gauze, I don't know. I don't know, I'm not a doctor. It could have been styrofoam or something weird or . . .

Dr.: Do you know anything about electronics?

P: No.

Dr.: Nothing about electronics? Do you have a stereo? Do you have a TV?

P: Yeah, I have a TV.

Dr.: Is there any component in that equipment that's made out of styrofoam? You need some kind of circuitry, don't you?

P: It could be that he just planned to use a regular bug that's in a lampshade, or when they bug a room.

Dr.: What do they look like?

P: I don't know for sure. Maybe it's that when stress hits me, it builds up the tension in my mind where the voices get louder and louder because of the fighting inside my mind. It gets to a certain level where the bug actually picks it up.

Moving Toward a Psychological Model

The interviewer pursues a clarification of the patient's model and, in doing so, helps the patient see that he can use his ordinary, everyday experiences and knowledge to explore the validity of his own thinking. The interviewer portrays the patient as having the capacity to understand himself and suggests that the patient may not have made adequate use of all of his skills and talents to understand himself. For example, the patient can employ his knowledge of electronics (based on the home equipment he possesses) in trying to think about what may have happened to him.

This process brings the patient to the acknowledgment that his voices get louder "because of the fighting inside my mind." His acknowledgement of the relevance of his mental life to the production of his symptoms is crucial. He will repeat it later, when he speaks of subconscious events influencing his thinking. The interviewer's aim is to enhance the patient's appreciation of those psychological forces within him, as well as his capacity to look at and understand them.

Dr.: That's this model [points to graph]. Now you're making one modification that's an interesting one. You're suggesting, if I understand you, that these voices, in fact, go on all the time. It's simply that you don't hear them until the stress throws the switch that activates the bug. Is that right? In fact, it may be that the voices are going on right now, but you can't hear them? [revises graph according to new information]

P: Right!

Dr.: Now that's a very confusing model to me for the following reason: I would then have to understand what's responsible for the voice or voices in the first place, since now you're suggesting that the voices may be going on all the time.

P: Is there a constant interaction in the human mind . . .?

Dr.: Between?

P: You know, a human mind never shuts off—it's always thinking.

Dr.: Yes, that would be your thoughts though.

P: That's how I would think it is. No matter if you're speaking about one thing, your mind could, your subconscious could, be thinking something else.

Dr.: But that's all within you then? Let me be explicit about what the confusion is for me. Originally, when I first heard your theory, I heard you say that your mind was perfectly alright and that, following this accident, something was inserted in your brain which carries within it the voices, so that if one took the bug out, the voices would be gone. Now, as we talk further, it turns out that the bug may be simply a kind of microphone, an amplifier if you will, and that the voices are going on all the time in you——

P: [interrupts] But I would never hear them if I didn't have the bug.

Dr.: My question to you now is what are those original voices in the first place? You wouldn't hear them without——

P: [interrupts] I would say they're my subconscious.

Dr.: So, in this new theory, then, all of us have these voices?

P: All of us.

Dr.: Right. And that the only difference between you and the next guy is that you happen to be unfortunate enough to have a bug which amplifies the voices that all of us have. So, for example, if I had this bug, I would be hearing my voices?

P: You would be able to hear your voices.

Dr.: Yes, I would be able to.

P: It's sort of like, you see, the whole thing with the bug is it takes the pressure away.

Dr.: What do you mean?

P: You know, you call somebody an SOB and you can hear it outside.

Dr.: Alright, but let's go back———

P: [interrupts] People can hear it and it takes the pressure—it takes the pressure to a certain point where you won't die mentally, if there's such a thing as dying mentally.

Dr.: I'm not following this last point.

P: I've had a lot of people follow me on the road and they've been white, but they're real thin and their faces are all chocolate like they're all black, withdrawn, you know. Somebody either has done something to their mind that's killed their system—their, some part of their normal body system, you know that normally—I think they're dead in the head—that their mind is dead, 'cause they have no life.

Dr.: Then why do you pretend not to know whether people can die from mental things? You've come to your own conclusion about that. You're quite convinced one can.

P: I think one can.

Dr.: In fact, if I understand you, your terror is that this may be happening to you.

P: I think I'm dead.

Dr.: Already dead?

P: Already dead.

Dr.: But if you are already dead, what's the relevance of all this? What can anyone do to you anymore? The popular notion of being dead—the popular notion—and this may be incorrect, the popular notion is once you're dead, nothing more can happen to you. Is that a view you subscribe to?

P: That's a view I subscribe to.

Dr.: But then, if you believe that, once dead, nothing more can happen to you, and you believe that you're dead, then what are you worried about?

P: I still don't like my thoughts 'cause———

Dr.: [interrupts] But nobody can harm you anymore.

P: Nobody can harm me.

Dr.: What's the danger?

P: It's hard to say.

Dr.: It seems to me there is something unclear about your logic.

P: I'm not sure I'm dead. I could be sick, and not dead.

Dr.: It's possible that you're sick?

P: 'Cause I don't know how to handle myself, how to take out cues and things like that.

Dr.: There are three possibilities that occur to me immediately. One is that you believe you're sick. Another is that you believe you're dead; not sick, but dead, and that you're worrying about nothing, since when you're dead, you're supposed to be safe. There is a third possibility—that even though you believe you're dead, being dead doesn't give you any protection. There is hell for people after they're dead too. That's a third possibility.

P: Yeah. I don't understand. I know I'm probably dead, but I don't understand the second or third one. You know, there's time when things change in my mind, you know, or something will come up that somebody put a cue in me, and the cue will stay in me.

Dr.: Let me go back now to this earlier question that confused me. On the one hand, it seems to me, you are presenting yourself as if you are the victim of some weird, bizarre, and rather unique experience. A bug has been placed in your brain, and the experience is so unusual that there are very few people who could understand you, and you would be feeling quite alone. In that sense, this bug in your brain isolates you from the world. But then, you have an additional theory, which is that all of us have these voices inside, but only a few of us have a bug that increases the volume. In that sense, you belong to the community of mankind in that all of us have these voices.

So, on the one hand, you are in a very unique group, and on the other, you belong with everyone. Right? You are with me so far?

P: Yeah. I'm with you.

Dr.: Now, what I don't understand when you have trouble getting doctors to believe you is why don't you begin your story with the similarity between yourself and other people, rather than the differences. The similarity being, "Dr. X, you have voices inside you—I have voices inside me and the difference is that I have an amplifier that makes my voices loud so I can hear them, while you lack that amplifier." . . . Do you follow me?

P: It makes sense.

Dr.: What do you think about what I said?

P: It makes sense. . . . I wish you could help me. I'm asking you to help me.

Dr.: How could I help you? What can a psychiatrist do for a person who may be dead and who has an implantation in their mind? What wc ld be my role? . . . Now you're smiling. [Patient has broken into a grin.]

P: I'd ask you to take the bug out. It's right here, it's not deep. It's right here.

Dr.: You would trust a surgical procedure to a psychiatrist?

P: All it is . . . anybody could do it. Anybody could do it. Anybody could take it out.

Dr.: How do you know that what he did requires very little talent? Are you an expert on surgical procedures? How do you know he didn't train for years to do that procedure?

P: The only thing I know is, it can't be much 'cause it's not deep 'cause the cut, the laceration, was not deep.

Dr.: But isn't it dangerous to fool around inside the head? Are there no risks?

P: It's just a bug. It's probably something like that.

Dr.: Let me go back the other way. There are two parts to your theory. One part is the bug amplifies the sound, right? But the first part of the theory is that the sound that's being amplified is your "own unconscious," in your own words. Okay? Let's say, for a moment, that your voices which, for the most part, you don't hear until the stress factor gets big enough to throw the switch to activate the bug [points to graph]—were friendly voices. If you could change the character of the things you tell yourself, if the voices were friendly, would you mind having the switch thrown?

P: Yeah.

Dr.: Why?

P: 'Cause I hate when I go in crowds of people, you know, they read your mind and say things that are . . .

Dr.: Do they read your mind, or do they just have good hearing and can hear the voice?

P: They lift up their ears and they say the same thing and it aggravates the shit out of me.

Dr.: But is it because the bug has been activated and they can hear?

P: Right.

Dr.: So that if I now understand you—this is the next modification of the theory—if I now understand you, what you're saying is that even if you had sweet, loving, caring voices within yourself, it would be awkward, embarrassing, and infuriating for you that other people would know your innermost thoughts, since they are projected outwardly. Right?

P: Yes.

Dr.: Now that makes sense. You wish to have some kind of sense of privacy.

P: I have no privacy [stated emphatically, leaning forward toward interviewer].

Dr.: Given what you've described, that's correct. Now you've explained why, no matter what the content of the voices, you don't like having them audible to the outside world. Still, I am interested in why you would have within yourself self-accusatory thoughts which then become heard by you as voices when the switch is thrown. Why do you feel that way about yourself? Why do you accuse you? Remember, that's the other part of the theory, your theory— that the voice within you is your own subconscious. Why don't you take the position that a terrible thing has happened to you, and that the last person on earth who should be critical of you is yourself? Why don't you tell yourself soothing, comforting, protective things? It's true that you would still be embarrassed in public because people would hear your inner thoughts. I understand that, but at least you could be good to yourself.

P: I'm good to myself.

Dr.: I don't hear that.

P: These are subconscious things. When I talk——

Dr.: [interrupts] Isn't that part of you? Isn't the subconscious part of you?

P: How do you change your subconscious?

Dr.: Are you interested in finding out?

P: Yeah.

Dr.: That's something that a psychiatrist might be able to help you with. That's within the province of psychiatry. With all the doctors you've seen, have you ever discussed that?

P: Yeah. I asked them, "How do you change this?" and they said they didn't know.

Dr.: You have talked to bonafide psychiatrists about how you might change your subconscious and they all said they didn't know? What's your reaction to that?

P: I thought there was no way you could change your subconscious.

Dr.: So you accepted that view?

P: So I accepted that view. I'm not a doctor.

Dr.: Well, let me put it to you this way. Psychiatrists are not surgeons and can't take the bug out. That's my statement to you today.

P: Okay.

Dr.: Psychiatrists, however, deal with the subconcious all the time. If they can't take the bug out and they can't change the subconscious, what good are they to you? [Telephone rings.]

P: That's why I keep telling everybody I'm in the hospital for peace and relaxation.

Dr.: I would think it would be terribly frustrating to be in a place where you can neither get the bug removed nor get help with the subconscious. Is this relaxing to you? A man as tormented as you are, not getting the relief you need? What is relaxing?

P: So I smoke cigarettes.

Dr.: You mean it's not relaxing here?

P: No, it's not relaxing.

Dr.: I'm right back at the beginning again, wondering what a guy with a bug in his head is doing in a psychiatric hospital? I don't get it yet. Are you here of your own free will?

P: Yeah. The only thing is I want to be able to defend myself more.

Dr.: How can you do that?

P: You know, in life that everybody, there's wars and mental wars and stuff like that and . . .

Dr.: So you want to get some way to defend yourself against . . .?

P: I want to know how to defend myself.

Dr.: Against?

P: Against other people. They're trying to put stuff in my mind. The reason why I went back to him is 'cause he's the only one who'd believe me that there's a bug in me, 'cause he put it in me. I've been told by doctors who said there's no such thing—"You don't have a bug in your head."

Dr.: But do you understand the irony of the situation? The only person who will believe you—look at the situation that you say you are in—the only person who will believe you is your arch enemy. And why will he believe you? Because he, apparently, is the only person who knows that it was done because, in your view, he did it. So you're without allies. Either no one will believe you, or the one person who does believe you has absolutely no interest in taking it out.

P: The trouble with me is I made myself so valuable. Every time I try to get the bug out it's being blocked by a telephone call or something like that. Like you just had with the telephone ringing and nobody picked it up and it stopped ringing. To me that was a cue for you to get off the subject.

Dr.: So now you're able to admit that you are of the opinion that I too may be involved in your destruction?

P: I didn't say that. It's just a warning.

Dr.: But, did I get off the subject?

P: No.

Dr.: That interests me. . . . I didn't get off the subject. How did you interpret that?

P: I interpreted that you had some backbone and you were willing to make decisions.

Dr.: So that it is possible for you to find allies? I find that a rather optimistic note for a guy as isolated and struggling as you are. But, how was I to have known that if you didn't tell me?

P: It's just that I'd seen it so many times before.

Dr.: Maybe you were afraid to let me know about that?

P: I didn't want to lose an ally.

Dr.: I can appreciate that, and I think it's very important that you are able to acknowledge your wish to have someone help you. . . . Unfortunately, our time is nearly up. We're going to have to stop in a minute. I was wondering if there was anything you wanted to ask me?

P: Okay. You want to help me. You're going up against a whole bunch of tough people.

Dr.: So you want to know if I want to help you? Is that the question? And you're saying that for me to want to help you means that I better know that the odds are bad. Let me put it to you another way. You're asking me whether I want to help you. Let me ask you whether you're willing to———

P: [interrupts] Help myself?

Dr.: . . . work with someone. Because I don't think at this point you can do it alone, but I can be wrong about that.

P: I can, I want to work . . .

Dr.: Alright. Now, the person———

P: [interrupts] You make the rules.

Dr.: No. That's what I'm about to say. I would make one rule. That whoever you work with, and apparently the therapist you're working with is Dr. Warren, be someone with whom you be as open with as you possibly can, even if that makes you feel you've put yourself in an endangered position. Okay?

P: Okay. [Patient leaves].

EXPLICATION OF INTERVIEW

What follows is an effort to organize the patient's apparently disjointed, fragmented, and bizarre story into a coherent whole, while remaining faithful to the chaos he describes. Our conclusions are not final but rather represent the evolving state of our understanding of this man. Our understanding would undergo continual revision throughout the course of working with him.

The Patient's Subjective Experience

Persecution

The patient's fundamental experience is that of persecution. In his world, even death fails to provide rest, psychiatrists fail to believe him, and his surgeon is his torturer. Worse, because no one believes him, only his enemy can save him, since he alone knows that the patient is telling the truth. The patient defines his major persecutor as someone whom he might be able to influence in the future to undo the harm he has caused. If persecutor can become savior, can the patient make other dramatic changes in the way he views himself and those around him?

Power

The theme of power preoccupies our patient. He suggests that his own power has brought about the problem: "The trouble with me is that I've made myself so valuable." Even an indirect association to power can be dangerous: Pressure is brought to bear on his mind not only if he says a girl's name who is famous but even if "she might have known someone who is famous."

The abuse of power is omnipresent. The most flagrant example is the horrible surgery to which the patient believes he was subjected. In more subtle form, the abuse of power is seen in the notion that the reason that doctors tell him that "I was dreaming" or that "I'm in a space world" is because they need to preserve their own self-esteem at his expense. He suggests this when he links "Many doctors have told me I am not telling the truth" with "They couldn't solve my problems with the voices."

Relationships

The patient sees relationships as fraught with danger, characterized by duplicity and envy, with only the remotest hope for change. An implicit theme might be that his own sexual and aggressive impulses threaten him and that therefore he must displace them onto others. Since his wishes to be powerful are frustrated, he feels helpless and envies others' power. He describes a fantasy of unleashed, disinhibited impulses when he pictures "people spinning me on the road or making love to me."

In his interaction with the interviewer, he manifests his suspiciousness by announcing, "You wouldn't believe what some of my problems are. . . . I figured you'd be just another doctor going along with the pattern." However, when confronted, he is able to recognize that "I took a negative attitude without testing you out." When he says, "I don't know what you want from me. I can go back to when the illness started and everything," we see that, with clinicians, he handles his anxiety and confusion by returning to a familiar though stereotypical exercise, reciting his "history." His use of a "canned" history might also represent his effort to conceal the pain associated with the interaction, thus isolating himself from the interviewer's potential empathy. Yet, despite this possibility, his wish for an all-protective figure emerges with the entreaty "I'd ask you to take the bug out." Perhaps it is this need that encourages him to keep trying and sustains him in his efforts.

He is able to acknowledge the interviewer's importance to him both as a hoped-for rescuer and dreaded foe, much like the surgeon. His interpretation that the interviewer's response to the phone ringing shows "backbone" might suggest he wants the interviewer to be strong because of his wish to find an adequate protector. However, his suspiciousness about the interviewer's sincerity (or his fear of his need of the interviewer) prompts him to test the clinician further, as when he asks the doctor if he fully understands the danger of the situation.

The patient has some capacity to see others (the policeman and his father) as supportive, albeit ineffectual. The policeman warns him, "You'd better watch out. They might put a bug in your brain," while his father does not want him to be bugged. However, neither male authority figure is able to prevent the assault. Indeed, the father is the first person to hear the patient's amplified voice.

The Bug Metaphor

The bug idea is a central organizing mechanism. It is a complex fantasy serving multiple functions. The patient describes it as "picking up brain senses and thoughts ... and microphoning them outside," a concrete expression of his boundary disruption. The bug links him to Dr. Steel since he is the only one who can remove the implant. The link is of a particular nature: "The thing is set up—sort of like you have to put enough heat on the man to take it out." Thus, the bug forces a sadomasochistic tie between the patient and his persecutor and also hints at underlying homosexual concerns.

The bug also provides some degree of safety, though at considerable expense: "It [the bug] reduces pressure, so you don't die mentally."

Safety

A recurring theme is his search for safety and how that quest compromises his self-esteem. He needs to find a way to stop the (bug-activating) switch from being thrown by searching for methods to decrease the pressure. He sees the hospital as a respite from this struggle: "I'm here for peace and relaxation." Ultimately, however, the struggle must go on if he is to feel safe: "I want to be able to defend myself more against other people."

Though he focuses on the danger being outside him, there is evidence that, over time, he could understand his struggle in intrapsychic terms. He hints at that when he says, "In life, everybody, there's wars and mental wars," and, more specifically, "I'm not sure there's a bug inside me," and "The voices get louder because of the fighting inside my mind." As an alternative to the bug theory, he even suggests that the pressure may be related to the fact that, "A human mind never shuts off. It's always thinking." Buried in these remarks is a potential role for a therapist. "I could be sick. I don't know how to handle myself." More explicitly, he inquires, "How do you change your subconscious?"

Loss

His experience of loss is devastating. He thinks he may have lost his life and describes a model for how this could have happened: "Somebody has done something in their mind that's killed their system—some part of their normal body system. . . . I think they're dead in the head." Perhaps even more significant is his loss of the capacity to be his own person, an event he speaks of as having taken place many years before: "It seems like somebody toyed with my mind when I was young and they really screwed me up." He also notes a loss of spirit: "I'm not one where I sleep a lot but that's because of boredom."

Autonomy and Control

His experience of autonomy and control is most poignantly expressed when he explains how, because of the "overload", he "gets" the voices, which cause him to "blurt out stuff, cues and everything else. Everything is coming out of me." On another occasion he expresses his sense of porousness when he says, "I have no privacy." He feels he is a passive container for hostile projections coming from the outside. Not only does he "get" the voices but he has no control over the pressure that builds up to activate the bug: "It's like I was lifted to a point where I boil over."

He makes a valiant effort to counter his helplessness through his identification with the John Birch Society. "You take all the pressure you can take and you don't budge an inch. If they put pressure on, you're not supposed to buckle."

Self-Object Differentiation

Although the patient experiences a considerable assault on his sense of wholeness, self-object differentiation, at least superficially, appears to be relatively intact. At the very beginning of the interview he is able to say that the interview is "an experience with advantages for each of us—it's part practice for you and it's part for me," as well as "I'm not a doctor." Perhaps the clear presence of an external foe, "the animals" responsible for the implantation, coupled with his militant posture, maintain his boundary with the outside world. However, his boundary is tenuous as the statement about lack of privacy suggests.

Assessment of Integration of Subjective Experience

This assessment illustrates that an interview with a schizophrenic individual can productively elucidate crucial aspects of his or her subjective experience. The clinician then moves on to consider the effect of the patient's subjective experience on his or her psychological life, motivation, and behavior.

Priorities

The patient is pushed and pulled by opposing priorities. In an effort to avoid persecution, he must decrease his importance, while, at the same time, he feels the need to be powerful in order to face his persecutors. He must live up to the hypermasculine ideals of the John Birch Society while struggling to find a protector. To preserve his intactness, he must try to keep everything inside himself, but, in doing so, he risks mental death. The bug (which projects his thoughts to the outside) prevents him from dying, but at the risk of being humiliated. The struggle is between power and dependency, retaining control and acknowledging his vulnerability and need for help.

Introspection

The patient shows a (limited) capacity for introspection and self-observation. For example, he is able to observe that he treats individuals in terms of categories. A case in point is his recognition that he views the interviewer as someone who would, a priori, "be exactly like the other doctors." His comment that he wants to be able to defend himself better reflects his belief that he is an endangered individual needing additional strength. Though predominantly viewing himself as the victim of external forces, he voices doubts about whether there is a bug inside him. Moreover, he acknowledges a role for inner processes in the production of voices: "The voices get louder because of the fighting inside my mind."

Relationships

In a man who sees relationships as power struggles in which the oppressor hounds the oppressed, it is difficult to speak of intimacy. Compounding his difficulty is his trouble differentiating libidinal from aggressive impulses. They are equally dangerous. The most he can hope for interpersonally is to become better able to "defend myself." But how to accomplish that when the mere mention of a girl's name can cause instant retaliation? There is the suggestion that he would like to surrender himself to someone else in the hope of being protected, but such a venture would require him to relax his guard.

The patient would prefer to keep the world at arm's length, and, better yet, to remove himself from it altogether. What bedevils him is precisely the opposite: his inability to keep the world from knowing even his most intimate thoughts.

Attitudes Toward Change

Though extremely pessimistic about effecting change, he nonetheless struggles to accomplish it. The first step is to become stronger, so as to tolerate more "without buckling." He also considers other strategies, such as finding a way to decrease the pressure so that he will not have to endure so much, convincing the surgeon to remove the implant, or finding an ally with sufficient "backbone" to join in the struggle. On occasion, he alludes to the possibility of intrapsychic change, acknowledging that he "could be sick" and indicating an interest in changing his subconscious.

Loss

Our patient constantly struggles against loss. His bodily self has been damaged by the transplant, his psychic self by the projection of his inner thoughts, and his self-esteem by the discrepancy between the triumphant figure he would like to be and the defeated figure he sees himself to be.

Assessing his subjective experience brings us to a clearer awareness of the pain the patient would experience if he recognized his vulnerability. This recognition would conflict with his expectation that he be a wholly self-determined individual. The patient's conflict with regard to acknowledging his need for help heightens our sensitivity to how he may experience the act of being helped and thus influences how we approach him in a treatment setting.

The assessment identifies some of the liabilities that he experiences—for example, his limited capacity for insight and intimacy—and portrays these as at least a partial consequence of the psychological adaptation to his illness.

From this integration, we move to a consideration of how we would construct a treatment alliance.

BASIS OF TREATMENT ALLIANCE

A treatment alliance is a pact between two people that maintains they will work together on some issue or issues for some stated purpose. The most important factor in selecting which issue or issues to focus on is that it (they) be of central concern to the patient. Next, the issue chosen must be identified by both parties in more or less the same way, and patient and clinician must be reasonably comfortable that what they have chosen to examine merits their effort.[b] There may be vast areas of disagreement on a host of other issues, but, unless they impinge on the agreed upon task, they have no immediate relevance and may or may not be taken up later in the treatment. The clinician must also feel that the nature of the task falls within the purview of his or her expertise. For example, to the patient who insisted that the solution to her problem lay in astrophysics, the clinician would say he knew nothing about that subject but would be happy to discuss with her the dilemma of being treated by a psychologist whose area of expertise was in matters psychological rather than astrophysical.

Our patient has let us know that he does not feel safe. Other problematic issues for him include his profound difficulty determining basic questions about himself, such as whether he is alive or dead and whether the enemy is inside or outside of him. In addition, he lacks a way to prevent others from knowing his innermost thoughts.

A clinician seeking to form an alliance with him would have to demonstrate that he or she understands and gives credibility to the patient's sense of being endangered. We are not saying that the clinician must claim to believe that the patient has, in fact, been bugged (a distinction we have made in previous chapters), but the clinician must indicate an appreciation that the patient feels porous.

The clinician would indicate the patient is raising concerns that are the proper province of their work. With the patient just described, the clinician might say, "The issues you have spoken to me about—your uncertainty about whether you're dead or alive, whether there is a bug inside your head—are precisely the kind of worries that mental health professionals are interested in and able to help you with." The clinician would next suggest how together they might go about the task and what the clinician's responsibilities and limitations were, as well as what would be required of the patient. Assuming, as in this case, that the patient is in the hospital, he would be informed that different clinical services would be utilized, each tackling different tasks.

Let us for a moment consider how the various members of a treatment team might form alliances with the patient: The psychotherapist would attempt an alliance in much the same manner as the interviewer did. He or she would confront the patient with his doubts about the external nature of the assault, coupled with the suggestion that internal matters (the "subconscious") are the domain of the therapist.

A rehabilitation therapist might select a task just at the threshold of the patient's functional abilities. The rehabilitation therapist would be wise not to give the patient tasks that are too easy because he would likely devalue these tasks and see them as being insufficiently challenging for a John Bircher and thus damaging to his self-esteem. By the same token, the rehabilitation therapist could introduce the task with the statement "Since you are used to fighting long and hard, I didn't want to start you with anything easy." If the patient becomes annoyed with himself for having difficulty with the task, the therapist could point out to him how harshly he judges himself, even on the basis of high standards.

The nursing staff could become allies with the patient by considering issues of privacy, acknowledging how understandable it is to want one's own privacy. Staff members could give examples from movies, books, and so on illustrating how people felt when their privacy was invaded. While acknowledging their understanding of the patient's concern about loss of privacy, the nursing staff would also insist that they were unable to hear him unless he chose to make himself audible. That is, they would be agreeing with his feeling that loss of privacy is terrible, but insisting that, from their perspective, he has not lost his privacy. In each of these modalities, the clinician would have to acknowledge that he or she is unable to change certain things about the patient's experience, while recognizing that the patient may wish for him or her to do so.

To facilitate an emerging alliance, the clinician must respect what supports the patient has already set up. Over time, these may be modified, but, at the outset, they form a crucial element of the initial alliance. In our patient, it would be essential to respect his need to be strong and "not buckle," to indicate awareness and appreciation of how hard it is to live up to such a demanding set of principles as those the patient has set out for himself.

To the extent that the clinician can appreciate the magnitude of effort the patient has made in his own behalf, (even though the specific form it has taken appears maladaptive to the therapist), he or she will be able to consider the patient as possessing a potential for contributing to his treatment. The clinician can thus imagine the patient as collaborating in the struggle to seek answers to the perplexing problems confronting the patient, recognizing that the patient has the strength to persevere in the absence of quick or easy answers.

TECHNIQUES OF
INTERVIEWING AND INTERVIEWING PRINCIPLES

Each patient tells the story of his or her experience in an individual and characteristic voice. We begin by identifying the patient's unique idiom and adjusting ourselves to it. Thus, with our patient, his telling us about his torment and humiliation through the tale of the bug shows us where we should begin. Within that frame, we seek to show him that his fundamental message has been received with seriousness and interest. The interviewer does this by making a graph depicting the patient's experience with voice transmission. The graph is a collaborative effort, the interviewer modifying the points on the graph on the basis of corrections made by the patient.

The summary that follows is offered as a guide to clinicians engaged in interviewing and assessing chronic schizophrenics.

1. Recognize that patients are the central informants about themselves, their experience of their world, and their treatment. When clinicians believe that understanding their patients depends on what the patients tell them, clinicians communicate their belief that what the patients say can, over time, be understood as something patients are not always certain about or wish to acknowledge.

Clinicians seek a picture of patients' sense of themselves. Unlike the traditional medical model of history-taking, clinicians must not rely too much on their own assumptions. They must be careful not to dismiss patients' attitudes or conclusions a priori; and they must discourage the fantasy in either the patients or themselves that everything that needs to be understood has already been understood.

2. Assist patients in elaborating their view of themselves. Communicate to patients the belief that they can tell us about themselves and reinforce those instances where patients demonstrate their desire to know and be known. (A clinician might say, for example: "Just now you allowed yourself to see that, despite the fact that you came in describing a fixed universe in which everything is determined in advance, including all aspects of your life, you're also thinking this might not be true. The thing that tipped me off to that was when you said a minute ago, 'I wonder if I can change any of this?' ") Patients are often unclear about what has happened to them and why, and they are demoralized and uncertain about what they have become and what, if anything, can be done about it.

Clinicians are not attempting to nail down the absolute definitions of who each patient is, but only to develop some understanding of the patient's self-perception at the moment. This important task involves getting patients interested in thinking about themselves, expecially about their self-construction as an evolving event. As patients attempt to clarify who they are to clinicians and to themselves, they begin to demystify their psychotic experiences.

Turning patients' attention to the task of understanding themselves implicitly fights against the demoralization and helplessness that often accompany chronic schizophrenia. In addition, by supporting patients' own efforts and helping them feel less helpless, clinicians are less likely to be seen as omniscient, omnipotent, or the object of the projections of patients' superegos (i.e., as an oppressor). The latter view is often an outgrowth of patients' struggles with feeling guilty and at fault for the illness.

3. Anchor the discussion in the here-and-now of the interview. Focusing on the patient's interaction with the interviewer has several advantages. As compared to anything the patient may say regarding his past, the interaction in the interview is the one arena where the interviewer can confront the patient with the interviewer's first-hand knowledge of what is going on in order to try to clarify differences in perception.

At the beginning of this interview, the interviewer says, "I'm interested in one thing that you said—that a lot of doctors have looked at you." This comment invites the patient to explore several issues directly and indirectly related to the current interaction. The focus is not on the past (what the previous doctors have said), but how that past history relates to the current moment. One says, in short, "So what does that [past event] have to do with us?"

The interviewer's comment opens up an exploration of the patient's overall attitudes about trust; about his perception of doctors and treatment, including both how he has felt about it in the past and its relevance to him now; and what his expectations and attitudes are toward the interview itself. In anchoring the discussion in the interaction, the interviewer also encourages relatedness and, therefore, provides an in-vivo opportunity to experience directly how the patient handles an interaction.

By concentrating on the interaction, the clinician opens a door through which the patient's reaction to the interviewer and the interview can be explored. By understanding the patient's attitude toward the interview process, the therapist can put the patient's remarks in context. If patients are mistrustful of interviewers, they will sound more hesitant and guarded, which may or may not be the way they would speak about themselves or others in another setting. The patient's attitude about the interview (and interviewer) will influence his or her presentation of many other topics. Of course, it is also true that the patient's attitude about the interviewer may also reveal the patient's picture of him- or herself in the world. In either event, clarification of the patient's expectations about and experience of the interview is a crucial step in assessing what he or she says.

These first three principles constitute a general understanding of the attitudes that the clinician wishes to convey during the course of the interview, and some broad outlines about the goals of the interview. What follows are some specific suggestions referring either to the clinician's attitude or interview technique and directions for what kind of information we need to glean from the interview in order to construct an understanding of the patient's subjective experience.

4. Communicate to patients that understanding their points of view on all matters (including their ideas about etiology) is crucial to our understanding them. This might be described as an attitude of benign curiosity on the interviewer's part. In later work with patients, it will be important to present *our* model of what is happening to or in them, but, in an assessment interview, we want to obtain as much detail and richness as possible regarding patients' understanding themselves. This process would be hindered by a premature confrontation of patients' distorted, idiosyncratic, or delusional interpretations of their symptoms or problems. In practice, this means avoiding any direct confrontation with patients regarding the etiology of their symptoms until patients have communicated their understanding of them.

An important corollary is that obtaining a clearer view of patients' positions regarding themselves and their symptoms helps detect the degree to which patients are aware that their self-constructions are inadequate with regard to their power to explain and predict experience. As the interviewer does in our example, clinicians must probe the internal consistency of patients' positions (as when the interviewer asks, "Why didn't you go to see a neurosurgeon?"). In doing so we will learn more about patients' views of themselves. If we had said, "That's crazy to think someone put a bug in your brain," we would have inhibited the patient's efforts to describe his experience.

Most patients who have delusional constructions of themselves will directly or indirectly reveal the ways in which their views of themselves fail to explain their experiences. It is this inefficacy of their self-view that provides us with a place to begin work with them. When we assist them to see that their self-view severely limits their ability to accurately anticipate their inner and outer experiences, they can then be helped to consider alternative points of view.

5. Pay close attention to the issue of object differentiation in the interview. If patients are confused about where they end and others begin, they may attempt to create physical distance or otherwise control the situation. In addition, if patients do not feel separate from clinicians, they may not be motivated to help clinicians understand them. If a patient does not distinguish a boundary between the clinician's mind and his or hers, the patient has no need to put his or her thoughts or feelings into words. Such patients may experience requests for them to articulate feelings and thoughts as taunting or humiliating, since they believe interviewers already know what they are thinking, and, therefore, their questions are insincere. Interviewers cope with this issue by confronting patients about their assumptions regarding the interviewers, forcing patients to attend to the here-and-now experience and to contribute their observations to it. This technique emphasizes the differences between patients' perceptions and those of interviewers and, therefore, their separateness. A clinician might say, "So, though from my perspective I'm asking you to tell me more because I don't understand what you've said so far, you hear my request as an effort to put you down." Interviewers should also be open about what they don't understand, primarily for the sake of authenticity, but, in the context of problems with differentiation, to reinforce a boundary.

6. Convey to the patients an interest and ability to contain their affect, particularly their rage and grief. Many schizophrenic patients have horrific fantasies about the power of (their or others') anger. This may be associated with psychotic experiences in which emotional states have been translated into physical actions with terrifying consequences, or it may reflect a degree of cognitive disinhibition in which intense affects are associated with cognitive disorganization. Nevertheless, when one simply looks at the factual circumstances of their lives, it is apparent that schizophrenic individuals have much to be angry about. In addition, the fact that they often exist in an atmosphere of suspiciousness and

mistrustfulness adds to their resentment and anger or helplessness. It is important to let patients know that interviewers can listen to that anger and help them express it verbally and safely.

Grief is most often the affect patients would experience if they faced the reality of their current situation. Indeed, rage defends against that grief. "Support" from family, friends, or clinicians may be their efforts to deny schizophrenic individuals' grief. Frequently, the patients are left to bear it alone. "I'm sure you'll get better" may, on the conscious level, be meant as a friendly, helpful comment, but it can make patients less able to express their anger. Assurances from others about the future may be heard by them as an unwillingness to listen to their anger and despair.

The primary way interviewers communicate their willingness to work with affects is by their attitude. Clinicians raise such questions as "You must be furious" or "It must seem so terrible," and, most importantly, they continue their inquiries after patients have refused to answer (often as a way of testing interviewers).

7. Resist patients' pressure to come to premature closure about who they are and what has befallen them. Allow ambiguity, contradiction, and, most importantly, ambivalence to emerge. In the preceeding interview, the patient attempted to present himself as a victim who could do nothing on his own behalf. The interviewer persisted in exploring alternatives—such as the possibility that the patient did indeed play a role in shaping the events of his life and that his behavior was not entirely consistent with his view of himself as a victim (i.e., having been bugged).

Many schizophrenic persons deal with their difficulty in organizing their experiences by insisting on a rigid, devitalized categorization of those experiences. These individuals talk about themselves and others in ways that rely on stereotypes rather than on the qualities of nuance and ambiguity that are so much a part of life. One consequence is that patients treat their understanding of themselves and of others in ways that lead to premature rejection of new areas of inquiry and to the unrealistic expectation of being able to arrive at solutions rapidly, without the tension and uncertainty that is a part of any learning process. It is important for clinicians to avoid reaching definite conclusions and treating them as immutable. Clinicians must help these individuals accept their potential for change. And patients must accept that growth is gradual and slow. The unrealistic expectations that beset most schizophrenic individuals have a great deal to do with their lack of self-acceptance, their impatience, and, often, their self-destructivenss. Helping patients to see that these attitudes are hurtful can open up the assessment interview for a more collaborative and free exchange and set the stage for a more productive treatment alliance.

8. Assess the patients' flexibility with regard to their view of themselves and others. As suggested by the preceding principle, many schizophrenic individuals are not flexible, feel they can tolerate only minimal uncertainty or ambiguity, and are wary of looking at the conflictual and contrasting nature of human experience, including their own. While it is difficult to assess how flexible patients are with respect to tolerating uncertainty and ambiguity and to considering alternative positions about themselves or others, it is nonetheless an important diagnostic task. This assessment is most readily carried out by asking patients: (a) whether they can imagine themselves differently and/or (b) whether they can empathize with the interviewer's position, when that position represents a change within the interviewer and/or is at variance with the patients' position.

In the interview treated in this chapter, the patient was able to consider the possibility that the interviewer might be different from his expectations (and, by implication, the possibility that his perception of previous psychiatrists may have been distorted). In addition, he expressd some doubt about whether he had been bugged, a crucial admission given that the idea of an electronic transplant was a central organizing mechanism for him. His willingness to consider an alternative to this idea indicates significant flexibility and is, therefore, a positive prognostic indicator.

9. Identify those things about which patients are curious. This assessment includes the degree to which the patients are interested in knowing about what has happened to them, why it's hard for them to get along with other people, what makes other people respond to them the way they do, and so forth. These issues are the ones to which patients are affectively connected and, therefore, invested in exploring. Curiosity implies that the issues involved are not so dangerous that patients cannot afford to risk wondering about them. Identifying these issues often indicates the first topics for engagement. In the interview above, the

clinician used the patient's curiosity about how the bug operated to explore whether his model adequately explained what was happening to him. The patient was able to begin to think creatively about himself and to reflect on how the views he held did not satisfactorily account for his experience. One conclusion derived from this interview would be that a treatment plan should take into account the patient's curiosity about how his mind works.

10. Use the patients' own idioms, particularly when exploring patients' understanding of their psychology, thinking, or symptoms. Using patients' particular word choices, symbols, and way of thinking helps to foster the discourse and to communicate that we respect the way in which they think about themselves. Patients are more likely to consider any suggestion we make about a new way of viewing themselves if that suggestion is expressed in phrases that are already familiar to them. However, before employing patients' idioms, it is necessary to understand the idiosyncratic meanings they give to particular words or phrases. We must be careful not to assume that we and patients are talking about the same thing, even though we use words that may seem to mean the same thing.

In the earlier example, the interviewer chose to describe the patient's mental operations in mechanistic terms—"pressures," "forces," "tolerance points," "excess loads," and so on—thinking the patient would be more receptive to that phrasing since it mirrored the way he spoke about himself. The clinician used the patient's metaphorical sense of his world as the vehicle to communicate an alternative point of view.

11. Encourage patients to remember their own prior experiences in order to better understand themselves in the here and now. In doing so, we demonstrate to them that they can understand their current selves better by linking them to previous aspects of themselves (which they may devalue or view as irrelevant or dangerous). Most importantly, helping patients appreciate how their past lives can illuminate the present underscores the value of acknowledging a historical sense of self.

Many schizophrenic individuals view time as having stopped at the point when their illness began. They experience a sense of discontinuity between the self prior to the illness and the subsequent self. This discontinuity promotes a tendency to avoid any important relationship between aspects of the past and the present self. Alternatively, there are patients who have the fantasy that things can be put exactly right again, that they will return to the precise place where they were before they began to have difficulties, that no time has been lost. It is as if the illness occurs in a time warp they will one day step out of and return to their previous selves. Not uncommonly, such patients are unwilling to recall their past.

This attitude (of murdering the past) leaves patients feeling there is nothing within them that they can call upon. Since they deny their past experiences, they must greet each situation as if they were encountering it for the first time. It's as if patients have made deals with themselves in which they agree to act as if they have no past so that they won't have to compare what they were with what they are. In eliminating their past, they have had to forget all that was effective, adaptive, and pleasurable then.

The final three items refer to tasks that are appropriate to the later stages of the assessment interview, although clinicians will certainly have these in mind in the early stages. They represent further means for gathering relevant data as well as interventions to facilitate the beginning of a treatment alliance.

12. Clarify with patients each instance in which either their pathologic views lack explanatory or predictive power or in which they are in internal conflict about these views. In the interview above, a striking example occurred when the interviewer confronted the patient with the illogic of seeing a psychiatrist if indeed he had a problem that could only be dealt with by a surgeon, unless the patient was acknowledging by his request that he viewed his problems as fundamentally psychological in origin.

The identification of an area of internal conflict within patients indicates to clinicians the issues around which they can begin to form an alliance between themselves and the health-seeking aspect of the patients. In the case of the patient just described, the clinician might begin the treatment by saying, "As we both saw in the evaluation, there is a part of you that recognizes the need for psychological help. That part, which I actively endorse and will support, will have to struggle with the rest of you that is dedicated to seeing yourself as victimized by an electronic inplant, incapable of helping yourself or profiting from psychiatric intervention."

13. Establish an empathic environment. This will be accomplished through many of the techniques already suggested. In addition, recognizing the commonality between patients' experiences and their own allows clinicians to identify with patients. In the interview just presented, the clinician might have said, "I would have been quite frightened had I felt that [the bugging] were happening to me." Or, following the patient's acknowledgement that had he been entirely comfortable with the implant idea, he would have searched for a neurosurgeon rather than a psychiatrist, the clinician might have said, "It was hard for you to admit that whatever is the matter with you isn't just the result of an evil doctor. I can appreciate how things could feel so overwhelming that you might wish that you could pin your entire bag of troubles on someone else." Therapists should articulate such sentiments only after they have recognized analogous situations within themselves. Clinicians who speak without having made that internal association first run the risk of sounding (and being) patronizing. Recalling their own similar reactions permits clinicians to better assist patients in accepting their experience. This process, however, must be distinguished from clinicians' acting on an awareness of commonality by making self-disclosing statements. Most often these actions stem from the therapists' own needs, such as seeking expiation from or closeness to patients.

When addressed to patients' needs, such comments help them experience the interviewer as understanding what they are going through. At other times, interviewers are empathizing with some buried or withheld aspect of patients' inner lives. In those instances, the interviewers' empathy anticipates and paves the way for the patients' own acknowledgements. This is especially true for those schizophrenic persons who feel quite distant from their own affective life, who may not value it, or who may be suffering states of emotional numbing.

14. Provide suggestions for how patients can develop alternative adaptations to their problems. Once we have some idea about the patients' views of themselves, understand something about the forces that cause them to behave in certain ways, and have identified how those adaptations may not work effectively for the patients, we can begin to facilitate

their engagement in treatment by making suggestions about alternative solutions. This would be the task of a treatment plan, but it would not be inappropriate in an assessment interview, which, after all, is the initial step in a treatment process. In the case under discussion, the interviewer suggested that, had the patient wished to make contact with people, he might have approached them by emphasizing his similarities rather than his differences.[c]

In the process of an assessment interview it is important to observe how the patients accept the interviewers' suggestions. Suggesting alternatives can be useful in assessing patients' flexibility. During the interview, our patient demonstrated his ability to collaborate by participating in the construction of the graph. This joint effort provided the staff who were viewing the interview with the encouraging evidence that the patient did have the capacity to collaborate.

With some patients, assessment interviews may yield useful starting points for treatment plans. Even without this, however, the process of collaboration based on careful understanding of patients' experiences begins in the assessment interview and creates both reasonable expectations and a framework for all of the treatment that follows.

5

The Case of Sharon: A Hospital Stay Involving Noncompliance, Violence, and Staff Conflict

In this chapter, we discuss the difficulties in treating schizophrenic individuals who require inpatient care because of noncompliance and potential for violence. We have taken the case of a woman named Sharon as an example. This case was noteworthy for many difficulties and failures, but we chose it to illustrate our approach to the troublesome management and therapy issues raised by violence and noncompliance. Hospitalization is a frequent solution, but hospital treatment raises issues of its own because of the complexity of the institutional and social systems it entails. How the hospitalization becomes part of the overall treatment is a challenge for both outpatient and inpatient therapists.

Sharon's noncompliance was so severe that her refusal to participate in a medication regime once in the hospital eventually resulted in a request for a court order, and at times she was an involuntary patient. As we have discussed in previous chapters, our approach to understanding this person's subjective experience centers on the themes of autonomy and control because we believe that noncompliance implies extreme concern with these themes. Similarly, violence expresses a need for control while presenting an extreme statement of autonomy from social norms. Issues of autonomy and control are therefore played out in the experiences of patient and therapist as well as the hospital staff who had to work with this woman on a daily basis.

We also take this opportunity to explore the nature of the working relationship between a hospital psychotherapist and the other members of the hospital staff or team. This relationship is always important, but especially so when the patient requires more than a brief inpatient stay and when, as in this case, the interpersonal demands made by the ill person are extravagant but compelling. In our example, Sharon was generally experienced by others, at least initially, as quite appealing. It was only with time and experience that people realized that her demands for proof of concern required complete, irrational loyalty to her paranoid delusional system. When this loyalty was absent, she felt betrayed, abandoned, and despairing, and the likelihood of violence toward others or herself increased. This sort of impossible demand often confronts the clinician working with individuals suffering from schizophrenia, and our discussion uses merely an extreme example to illustrate our approach to this problem.

BACKGROUND: SHARON'S HISTORY AND INDICATIONS FOR HOSPITALIZATION

Sharon was a 24-year-old woman admitted to the inpatient service for suicide threats and decreasing ability to care for herself. She had many paranoid ideas about family and friends and delusions of persecution by government intelligence agencies. She had a history of abortive attempts at outpatient psychotherapy directed at her recurrent suicidal ideation and severe difficulties in getting along with others. Although she was intelligent and had completed college, she was unable to keep jobs. Former therapists had thought she suffered from depression and severe personality problems, a common history for some well-educated, intelligent, and very paranoid individuals who actually suffer from schizophrenia. Like Sharon, these individuals are so invested in issues of control and autonomy that the acknowledgement of serious symptoms is extremely difficult for them. They are severely conflicted about letting another person be helpful and important to them because they dread the associated feelings of vulnerability. This leads them to deny their illness, blame family, employers, or past therapists, and hide their symptoms. For years, Sharon had feared that if people knew how fearful and paranoid she was, they would use this knowledge to hurt her. She had read some psychiatric texts, and she used this knowledge to decide what to tell the professionals she consulted in an effort to control what diagnostic label would be assigned, although she would never admit to this and perhaps did it unconsciously.

While her guardedness prevented her from receiving the most appropriate treatment at times, this was the best compromise from her perspective. Her psychological response to her illness was to deny all signs of difficulty in herself. Any admission of pathology was experienced as an extreme blow to her view of herself as intelligent and talented, a view that had been developed, with outside validation, in her childhood and adolescence. Blaming others while admitting she was "under stress" of some kind allowed Sharon some minimal contact with helping professionals, which was all that she could tolerate and still maintain a necessary feeling of safety. More interaction would have led to humiliation and increased depression.

Sharon was prone to episodes of violence to protect her self-image. She attempted suicide when she felt too demoralized by her failures to live up to her unrealistic goals. And she assaulted a therapist who had wanted to put her in a psychiatric hospital after a suicide gesture. Terrified at this perceived threat to her autonomy, Sharon instantly lost any insight into the possibility that the gesture was a cry for help. She threatened to kill the therapist, and, when the therapist picked up the phone to call an ambulance, Sharon threw a paperweight at the therapist, and fled.

When she was finally hospitalized, Sharon externalized all responsibility for her predicament to malevolent outer forces: her family and the FBI. Following a disappointment in a formerly idealized outpatient therapist, Sharon had left home and begun to travel around the country, impulsively visiting friends and relatives, but more often roaming without any plan, frequently without any money, picking up men in bars or sleeping in parks. She was molested a number of times. When she would call and ask for money, her parents attempted to convince her to return home and to treatment; they felt powerless to control her. Throughout this time, Sharon began to believe that she was actually an undercover agent recruited by the FBI against her will and initially without her knowledge and that she had been brainwashed and was now the subject of mind control procedures. She believed that, since leaving home, she had had devices implanted in her that directed her speech, behavior, and thoughts, and she thought that these devices would torture her if she attempted to resist. She also felt that psychiatrists had been a part of the FBI's plan and that they had used hypnosis to control her. These delusions seemed in part a reaction to the increasing evidence of her failure to succeed as a writer, which had been the rationalization for her odyssey. This explanation had worked up to a point, allowing her to create distance from family and therapists and to feel independent, although she had to go to considerable extremes to establish this condition (which suggests the depth of her difficulties with autonomy and dependency). This was Sharon's sustaining experience, but it was a very maladaptive one since it entailed a great deal of suffering and kept her lonely and without help.

Sharon was hospitalized when she returned home briefly and her parents saw her agitated, delusional, semi-starved condition and insisted she see her former doctor, whom Sharon allowed to admit her to a hospital.

Indications for Hospitalization

Sharon's situation exemplifies certain issues regarding hospitalization. Though she was psychotic, it was not her psychosis that led to the hospital stay; rather, it was her inability to use outpatient treatment to manage her illness and hence to manage her life safely. While she was not in immediate danger of mortal hurt to herself or others, her history indicated an inability to care for herself that might well become life-threatening if changes did not occur, changes that only treatment could offer. What brought Sharon to the hospital was her inability to form a treatment partnership in an outpatient setting because of idiosyncratic relatedness.

Thus, in our opinion, need for hospitalization is not directly dependent on the degree of psychosis present. Conditions suggesting that hospitalization should be considered include:

1. Inability to relate to clinicians in a collaborative way despite clear need for treatment (1)—that is, serious problems in forming a treatment partnership. This includes intense transference reactions that do not appear to be resolvable in outpatient treatment since they seem to require greater distance from the clinician and the availability of other objects (in the hospital) so that the patient can gain perspective and control over the reaction.

In general, if there is a solid treatment partnership, the clinician is usually willing to tolerate greater latitude and uncertainty about a patient's "disturbed" behaviors, if the individual is coming to appointments, taking medication, talking about his or her life, and so forth in a committed way.

2. Acute risk of violence.

3. Risk of self destructive behavior.

4. Risk that the patient's life situation will be destroyed if his or her behavior has the potential to irretrievably alienate family, residential treatment staff, or other persons critical to the patient's well-being without whom the patient faces loss of job or home.

5. Need for control of the patient's external life, which cannot be provided by family, day hospital, and/or halfway house, as in the case of a very withdrawn patient who needs constant support and encouragement to maintain minimal self-care and relatedness.

Thus, a person who would be considered very psychotic because of fixed delusions and somatic hallucinations about a radio in his brain, who nonetheless maintains a job and a treatment relationship and takes his medication faithfully because it allows him to "turn down the volume" on the radio, would not require hospitalization unless other factors entered the clinical picture.

Clinician's Attitudes Toward Hospitalization

The clinician's attitude toward hospitalization and how it is presented to patient and family should be informed by his or her hypotheses about the patient's understanding and experience of his or her current situation and probable reactions to the hospitalization. For example, for an individual who will feel humiliated because it is critical for him to be in control, the approach needs to include his involvement in the mechanics of the process to remind him that he is an adult making a decision and carrying it out. Another individual will need to fight the hospitalization and the clinician and family need to find a face-saving way the patient can accede to the request for hospitalization, after which the patient will be secretly relieved and grateful. Individuals with severe stimulus barrier problems may be happy to temporarily relinquish the struggle to manage ordinary existence by moving into a setting with less stress, and the hospital can be presented as a refuge or respite from challenges such as the stress of daily life, a specific trauma, or the emotional demands of family and others. Others fear being surrounded by troubled people, and the therapist should emphasize the possibilities for empathy from others in the same predicament and help the individual to see the ways in which she can maintain her autonomy even in these surroundings. For many, the hospital represents a place of regression that can be either frightening or attractive.

From the patient's point of view, hospitalization can give a message to important others, including the outpatient therapist, that something in the person's life was becoming unbearable. In this case, it is helpful for the clinician to let the patient know that he or she has heard the message, whether it pertains to family, friends, work, or some aspect of the treatment relationship. For example, one schizophrenic man who had been maintaining a stable existence for eight months following discharge from a medium length hospital stay suddenly brought beer to his dormitory, breaking a rule with which he was very familiar. This occurred as he and his therapist discussed the latter's first vacation since the patient's discharge. Despite considerable discussion and support, the patient's behavior deteriorated until hospitalization was inevitable. An important component of the therapist's presentation of the necessity of hospitalization and of the hospital staff's work with the patient was to acknowledge that the patient felt (rightly or wrongly) completely unable to function in the therapist's absence.

What the Hospitalization Means to the Outpatient Clinician

A key factor in the outpatient therapist's attitude toward the hospitalization is what it means personally to him or her, because this affects how the patient's experience is perceived by the clinician. For the therapist, hospitalization may represent the only response to a crisis, but it may also serve other functions: to adjust medication, to provide a respite from the patient's demands on the clinician, to enable the clinician to regain perspective on the treatment, to obtain consultation. Thus, depending on the setting and the clinician's wishes and needs, his or her relationship with the hospital staff will vary. The clinician may make regular visits to carry on psychotherapy or to consult with staff, or the clinician may use this time to reconsider the nature of his or her involvement with the patient from a distance, freed from certain worries. The patient may also need to reconsider his or her investment in continuing with the therapist, and it can be easier to change therapists from the safety of a hospital room. It can be very therapeutic and supportive of self-object differentiation for the schizophrenic individual to see that a therapist can recommend, without losing face, that he or she might need to be replaced in the patient's life. This also lessens the schizophrenic person's fear of being controlled by the therapist, so that just seriously considering the possibility may have a beneficial impact on the treatment partnership. The therapist's willingness to consider these options during a hospital stay are part of his or her sensitivity toward the patient's experience.

Even if hospitalization occurs for crisis management, the hospital milieu provides an excellent opportunity to understand the meaning of a regressed patient's central concerns through his or her various manifest communications, or specific behaviors. The number of people interacting with the schizophrenic individual and their ability to share their experiences and try to understand what is occurring may clarify issues that were clouded in outpatient treatment. Hence, the hospital staff can serve as consultants to the outpatient therapist. Consider the following example:

A 23-year-old man was hospitalized for an acute psychotic episode in which he was found disrobing on a busy street instead of beginning a new job he had worked hard to obtain. He had been ill for many years but had an apparently good relationship with his outpatient therapist and had been doing better over time, using his therapist's encouragement to socialize more and look for a better job. Once in the hospital, he appeared quite regressed to the staff, sitting silently for hours, apparently withdrawn and unable to relate to others, with many characteristic negative symptoms. However, discussion among staff of brief interactions with him revealed a subtle but definite pattern of provocative, passive-aggressive behaviors that were too precise and directed to be merely the side effects of social withdrawal and an amotivational syndrome. Alerted to these by staff and his own feelings of annoyance, which had seemed excessive, the patient's hospital therapist began to talk to the patient about the possibility that he was furious, not just withdrawn. The young man then revealed a wealth of sadistic fantasies that occupied him much of the time and were related to specific disappointments with important people in his life, including the disappointment of grandiose hopes in his outpatient therapist. He imagined he had been pressured by the therapist to find a better job and he was angry that he had to, as he felt, "perform."

His regression reduced the stress he felt. Once this issue was out in the open, he was able to find other ways to express this anger, so that he became less provocative and more able to participate meaningfully in his treatment, instead of needing to destroy his own chances of success to communicate (in a very idiosyncratic way) his anger at the expectations and hopes of others.

This example also demonstrates the advantages of a good alliance between the inpatient staff and inpatient therapist and between the inpatient therapist and outpatient clinician, who are thereby enabled to share information. In too many situations, competitiveness, envy, or feelings of failure interfere with this type of collaboration.

Sharon's Need for Hospitalization

In Sharon's case, hospitalization was indicated because she was unable to take good care of herself, and her very life was threatened by her disorganization and neglect. She had begun to feel that killing herself might be better than a life of control by the FBI coupled with nearly complete inhibition of her creative writing skills. Her sustaining experience was no longer sustaining. In addition, she had been unable to form a treatment partnership over the years, despite several attempts with various clinicians and her serious need for treatment. Her suspiciousness and need to control her relationships led her to be totally unable to develop a trusting therapeutic relationship. Moreover, since she denied she was ill, she was irresponsible about medication, limiting the possibility for gathering good information about her response to medications. When she felt her self-image and autonomy were threatened, she was also prone to intense and hostile and sometimes simultaneously erotic and hostile transference reactions, which could erupt into violence or other actions that completely disrupted therapy. Because her experience of psychological continuity and clarity was very poor, she quickly lost sight of episodic good experiences with professionals.

With this extreme need to control the environment and hence her treatment (a need that may be hypothesized to stem from the severity of the illness she sought to control), it was very hard for Sharon to accept hospitalization. She was willing to try it in her current situation because of the degree of physical discomfort she was beginning to experience, including malnutrition, fatigue, and the bruises she had suffered in a recent traumatic episode during her wanderings. Although Sharon was very well aware that she was entering a mental hospital, not a conventional medical setting, she did not make an issue of this; instead, she merely agreed that she was suffering and and that it would be worth getting a rest. After his initial recommendation, her doctor was careful not to talk about the hospital in a way that would "rub it in" for Sharon that she would become a psychiatric patient, although he did not misrepresent the setting.

HOSPITAL COURSE

On admission, Sharon appeared waif-like, emaciated, and very burdened by notebooks containing her "case." She was oriented, and her speech was clear and goal-directed but extremely delusional in content. On the ward, Sharon was aloof and intent on concealing any psychic distress; however, she struck out at the nurses who tried to look at her bruises, claiming that they were going to attack her. In individual therapy she took pains to be pleasant, charming, and agreeable and to present an appearance of interest in and motivation for psychotherapy. Unfortunately, this apparent motivation was primarily part of a complex defensive process to protect Sharon's self-image rather than a firm basis for a therapeutic relationship.

Individual Therapy

This need to convince her hospital therapist, Dr. B., of her goodness, health, intelligence, and desirability characterized the initial stages of her hospital therapy. Dr. B. hoped to form a treatment alliance around Sharon's acknowledged sadness about the way her life had gone, although he recognized that he would probably need to confront her help-rejecting behavior carefully. Development of some basis for collaboration would precede Sharon's willingness to admit she had an illness and symptoms needing attention.

Sharon had a different conscious agenda. To impress Dr. B., she showed him articles she had written, pictures of herself from college and high school, awards, and artwork. She begged him to keep an open mind about her diagnosis, though she had heard many times that she suffered from schizophrenia. She sought to convince him that this was incorrect, claiming that all her suffering was due to persecution by the FBI or her mistreatment by family members who did not understand her sensitive feelings. When she briefly discussed some sadness and regret about the years she wasted wandering around the country and about a life that was nonfunctional despite her intelligence and talents, Dr. B. felt encouraged. But Sharon could never sustain exploration of her depressive and suicidal feelings in this context and would revert to externalization instead. At such times, she quickly wanted Dr. B. to just "do something" about her depression, because she had "explained" it and there was nothing else she could do—certainly nothing more to talk about. Although at such times it seemed as if his failure to produce a miraculous improvement in her situation might lead Sharon to feel angry at him, she maintained a steadfastly idealized view of him (as well as of herself) during the first part of the treatment.

In the context of her resistance to full discussion of her difficulties, Sharon was also developing an erotic transference. Her attempts to impress Dr. B. were also directed toward convincing him of her loveliness and desirability. She tried to make him see her as an innocent victim, a charming girl, not the controlling, devaluing, aloof woman she appeared at other times. As will be detailed below, Sharon was condescending and obnoxious in her interactions with nursing and activities staffs, and her only contacts among the patients were with the most paranoid individuals, whom she tried to organize against the staff. It was notable that none of her complaints about her hospitalization experience were directed at Dr. B. It was later learned that she did wish that he had the power to change hospital rules and expectations, since she held fast to the conviction that he shared her view of herself as merely mistreated, not ill, and as not contributing in any way to her difficulties (as when she was verbally abusive or contentious or refused to cooperate in ward activities).

In the therapy, Sharon at times talked in a bland way of wishes to mutilate herself, the details of past suicide attempts, and the vicious revenge she felt entitled to wreak on her FBI tormenters. But Dr. B. was not supposed to comment or question her on these issues because his doing so threatened her need to present herself as blameless and not ill. At the same time, such images and hints tended to destroy the "good" image she tried to build in his mind, a form of destruction for which she refused to take responsibility. As time went on, Sharon did begin to become exasperated with Dr. B.'s refusal to join in her idealized view of the two of them. She sought to cast Dr. B. in the role of rescuer to her damsel in distress but was disappointed in his unwillingness to sustain this drama.

On the one hand, Sharon believed she was good and innocent, totally worthy and deserving of love from Dr. B. She often requested proof of his devotion by asking him to stroke her face (although he never agreed to do this). On the other hand, she gleefully detailed how she would torment the FBI agents who she felt had wronged her, including the FBI psychiatrists. However, she never accepted the implication of this behavior: that she was also capable of angry, vengeful feelings and was not simply a harmless innocent. For example, on one occasion she alternated among statements that her face was mutilated, that this was good because it justified her revenge, and that she wanted Dr. B. to caress her face.

Dr.: You would really like it if I would touch your face.

S: Yes.

Dr.: How would that help? What are your thoughts about that?

S: It would be so nice, we have such a special relationship.

Dr.: But I can't help remembering how a few minutes ago you were talking about your face as mutilated, and you seemed to want to hold on to that idea, as proof of the wrong you say has been done to you and the revenge you want. So I don't understand the shift— it's like you want me to forget something important that you just told me about your angry feelings.

S: You don't understand anything! You only think about the bad things about me, you focus on my faults! Those things are such a small part of me! You never praise me for how well I can manage, for all I've accomplished, you are always reminding me of things that don't matter!

Dr.: But it does matter, if it's a part of you, because I'm interested in everything about you, and I don't want you to feel as though there are parts of you that should be cut off and we shouldn't talk about them.

S: You don't understand at all.

The therapist tried to engage Sharon in the process of integrating the disparate parts of herself, the angry and ugly parts as well as the charming, affectionate, childlike parts, believing that this was a necessary step before she could admit the rage and wishes for revenge implicit in some of her rejections of treatment. But his plea was again rejected, and instead, Sharon began to spend part of her sessions debating whether therapy could be any use to her or not.

Countertransference

Therapists of patients like Sharon must struggle with countertransference tendencies to join them in their avoidance of painful confrontations with their angry, sad, despairing selves (2–3). When Dr. B. reminded Sharon of some of her past strengths and tried to build on these, he wondered if he was helping her with her problems in continuity or trying to sanitize the unpleasant here and now. But the effect of therapists' avoiding painful realities is to leave patients alone in the miserable present with their despair. In fact, research has suggested that therapists' ability to remain comfortable with schizophrenic patients' strong affect positively influences therapeutic outcome (4). Yet the extensive denial and projection used by people like Sharon severely tax clinicians. The attempt to tactfully help Sharon to recognize her illness, her difficult personality traits, and the ways she made it nearly impossible for anyone to help her became a wearing struggle.

In her guise of the innocent victim, Sharon was extremely controlling of interactions with her, constantly setting limits on what she would discuss. There was also the threat that she would lose control and throw things if she became enraged at what she experienced as a criticism or threat to her autonomy. In this context, Dr. B. at times felt so angered and frustrated that he wondered if in fact her critical accusations of him were correct: Was he confronting her too harshly in some of his comments? Was he really being sadistic in some of his interpretations?

This is the kind of confusion, guilt, and implicit loss of boundaries that therapists of very paranoid persons undergo, since eventually these therapists wonder if the patients are more than partially correct in their accusations. That is, therapists doubt their own ability to judge interpersonal reality, and this doubt constantly plagues such patients, who react by developing a rigid system of mistrust that provides a rule for interpreting every questionable situation: They want to hurt me. Therapists begins to suffer confusion and doubt about control issues, a confusion that parallels patients' distortions in this area: Am I being sadistically controlling out of my anxiety, or am I merely asserting my own identity in the face of control by others?

Another aspect of Sharon's boundary confusion resulted in a pull for others to share her world-view in its entirety, since she saw any dissent or questioning as life-threatening. Her preferred mode of idiosyncratic relatedness was to fuse in some way with an omnipotent, idealized object (5), and she tried to make her therapist into this, creating a pressure that added to countertransference problems.

These patients' combination of boundary confusion, pull toward an omnipotent, idealized object, and control issues results in a countertransference paradigm in which therapists must constantly be aware of what it means to be one's "own person." At times therapists may need to strongly assert their identity in what seem to be trivial ways. They may feel an overwhelming need to hold sessions in the office rather than on the ward, even when patients are not allowed to leave the ward; they may strenuously insist on ending appointments on time; or they may refuse to answer reasonable questions, feeling they are personal intrusions.

Transference

In her conscious experience, Sharon's most important goal was to enlist Dr. B's support in her battle, so that he would testify in her favor and intervene in her life by contacting the FBI on her behalf. In a similar way, she insisted that staff and other patients agree that she was being persecuted, a stance that placed everyone at a disadvantage.

Thus, while Sharon appeared to have a positive, erotic transference to Dr. B., she at the same time behaved in a hostile and masochistic way. She constantly put him in the uncomfortable position of having to tell her that he couldn't do as she insisted because her demands were so unrealistic. In effect, she was constantly asking him to tell her she was psychotic. Then she would become enraged or saddened and blame him for her depression, again failing to acknowledge, even when he pointed it out to her, how she contributed to the situaiton that was so painful to her. That is, she demanded that her therapist live in her delusional world with her, as if any compromise represented the death of her ideals or the destruction of her self-image.

Faced with such a controlling individual, a therapist can subconsciously start to feel that the interaction in a treatment is based on the question "What will she make of me?" rather than on "What is she telling me about herself?" That is, even more than usual, the therapist ends up having to use some of his or her own subjective feelings as clues to the patient's feelings and needs, since the patient is so unable to use a psychotherapeutic relationship in the usual way. The example above demonstrates this process, in which Dr. B. felt tempted to join Sharon in avoiding the painful present by reminding her of her past successes. His awareness of this wish in himself alerted him to the possibility that Sharon was actively trying to avoid looking at her present condition and situation.

In the work with a person who feels so threatened that she must be this rigid, it is helpful to step back from the therapy experience and to ask, "What is the overall pattern? What is this individual trying to achieve with me, and why? What does this tell me about her experience of herself and the world and about what she can tolerate in the way of treatment right now?"

Treatment Alliance Evaluation (see Table 2.1)

Sharon's stated understanding of her condition was almost totally delusional: She was the unwilling (though perhaps important) subject of others' malevolent acts. These others included psychiatrists. She had no realistic idea of treatment other than that it was, perhaps, a rest from her life on the streets; her goal was to use this hospital stay to gather evidence for her case against the FBI.

Sharon's first priority, maintained at risk to her life, was to preserve a strictly defined sense of personal control and autonomy in which all blame and responsibility for anything negative was placed elsewhere than on her. It was hard to see any conflict about this priority or any other priorities in opposition to this; however, the fact that she had entered the hospital voluntarily (in the legal sense—obviously, she was under pressure) and attended psychotherapy sessions might be indications that on some level she was willing to ask for help and to admit to some difficulties in herself. But the paucity of evidence for any ability to consider alternative viewpoints that would allow others to help seriously limited Sharon's flexibility in accepting treatment of any sort.

Her illness had run a chronic, deteriorating course so far, despite what appeared to be above-average constitutional and environmental endowments. The long history of relatively fixed delusions also bespoke a severe core disturbance. Whether these delusions derived directly from the core disturbance or from her adaptation to her difficulties in concentrating, problem-solving, and processing stimuli (obligatory versus functional priorities), their severity and pervasiveness were remarkable. Furthermore, she had been acting according to her delusional beliefs for some time, so that their integration into her life was complex: To give them up abruptly would have been like amputating a limb. In addition, Sharon's illness had never responded very well to medication. All of these factors limited Sharon's availability to change. They also pointed to the importance of autonomy and control issues in her life, because change seemed not only difficult but terrifying to her.

Still, the fact that Sharon was in treatment at all had to mean that she had some hope that human contact would be gratifying. The complication was that her manifest communications and attitudes toward relatedness defined such narrow rules for sustaining human contact: Either she was free of conventional constraints, roaming the countryside being abused, or she was in a hospital angrily limiting what she would talk about and insisting that everyone join in her fight against the FBI. All interactions with the potential for more richness of human contact and feeling seemed repeatedly to collapse into battles for control: Would she attend a meeting, take her medication, stay in the hospital, get up in the morning?

The explicit demand that Sharon placed on her environment was that everyone follow her rules completely. Since this was impossible, it made sense to consider whether this concealed an implicit demand from Sharon, perhaps to have an environment to fight against, perhaps in order to reinforce a set of very tenuous self-other boundaries. Perhaps the rigidity of Sharon's conditions for contact indicated the degree of threat to her sense of self and self-worth, human contact entailed.

While these demands did not leave a great deal of room for the clinician to form an alliance with Sharon, they did suggest that interventions aimed at supporting her sense of autonomy and control and at clearly outlining the boundaries between herself and others would be important steps. For example, a comment directed at Sharon's boundary problems might have been: "It's clear that I cannot convince you of anything you do not want to accept. I wish I could. Since I can't, I am unable to figure out a way to begin with you. The advantage to this is that it makes me think I can understand better what it's like to not be able to get anywhere—which seems to be a predicament you have experienced." While this remark would emphasize the boundaries between the patient and therapist, it could also tactfully offer a means to contact and the beginnings of collaboration.

Thus, our recommendation that clinicians spell out their own limitations and the limitations of the therapies they offer would be part of the basic work on the alliance with Sharon, since this should reassure her than the clinician was not about to try to take over or change her entire life, nor did he have the power to do so. Finding areas where it would not be too detrimental to the early phase of her hospital treatment if Sharon refused participation would be another way to encourage an alliance. That is, because it would be necessary for Sharon to say "no" often, staff would quickly become discouraged and frustrated if they began enthusiastically with many plans for her treatment in which they felt very invested. A discouraged and frustrated staff would not be able to respond as well when (and if) Sharon became less frightened and rigid.

Medication

Although it was not the only goal of hospitalization for Sharon, one hope was that a better medication regime could be developed so that she could manage better outside the hospital. Sharon had been given neuroleptic medication prior to hospitalization by her doctor, but this had had minimal effect on her delusions and agitation. In the hospital, continued trials of various neuroleptics were made, again with limited success.

At one point, a case conference was held in which Sharon stressed her depressive symptoms to the visiting consultant. Since she had thought of suicide for years, the possibility that she suffered from an affective disorder rather than schizophrenia took hold in the minds of the staff, with the hope that a trial of antidepressant medication would help. (This is a common development in families and clinicians in these days where new drugs for affective illness seem more plentiful than new treatments for schizophrenia.) Sharon also eagerly accepted this idea and reported marked improvement in her mood and a decrease of suicidal wishes after a tricyclic antidepressant was begun. Unfortunately, she responded within three days of the institution of the medication, rather than the period of several weeks required to reach adequate blood levels of this drug, and her changes appeared more consistent with a "flight into health" as she tried to convince hospital personnel that she was no longer suicidal and could leave the hospital soon. Her mood remained slightly improved when she was told that staff saw her as being in need of a long period of hospitalization. Eventually, the antidepressant trial ended because it seemed to have little impact and because there was considerable fear among the staff about eventually discharging Sharon from the hospital while she was taking a medication which she could easily use to kill herself.

Sharon continued on a regimen of thiothixene, which seemed to have been most helpful to her in the past, but she frequently complained that the medication interfered with her thinking and that the nurses who gave her the pills were unsympathetic and critical of her. She met regularly with her psychotherapist but tended to use this time to complain about the rest of the hospital staff while idealizing the therapist, although this idealization intermittently collapsed into rage or pouting when the therapist took no steps to rid the institution of the people Sharon felt were incompetent. In the midst of one such disappointment, Sharon ran away from the hospital to live on the streets, but eventually showed up at her father's office and allowed herself to be taken back to the ward.

That Patient's Subjective Experience of Medication

For most individuals with schizophrenia, medication symbolizes the fact of illness, reinforcing ideas about being a passive victim of a chronically out of control condition. For those who deny or minimize the idea that they have an illness, medication is a terrible narcissistic blow that seems to define them as mental patients, unless they can keep awareness of its implications separate from the action of taking it, a policy followed by Maryann in chapter 6. Side effects reinforce the feeling of being unfairly treated by fate and discourage compliance. In addition, persons with particular concerns react badly to specific side effects; for example, it is well known clinically that very paranoid invidiuals find even mild sedation excruciatingly distressing because it is so important to them to maintain their alertness.

Other reactions include mourning the loss of familiar symptoms that served a purpose in the patient's psychic life. Especially if a hallucination disappears abruptly, the drastic change may be overwhelming to someone who has lived with this for a long time. Then, with less florid psychotic symptoms, the individual is asked to deal with the demands and frustrations of everyday life, but with the history of his or her psychosis as a context and usually with personality problems or ego-function deficits that medication has not cured. This leads to greater frustration. In order to form a partnership with the patient in the area of medication treatment, the clinician must be sensitive to issues of loss and mourning as the patient's subjective experience changes in the context of medication response. However, there is some possibility that the formation of a psychotherapeutic relationship can enhance the effectiveness of medication (6).

All of these negative reactions to medication can lead to noncompliance. For some patients, it may actually seem preferable to sit quietly with familiar hallucinations than to have to face the world and compete with "normal" individuals as anxious, confused, partially skilled persons with ordinary problems. At least the problems of being overtly psychotic have a dramatic and special feel to them. As we have stressed, schizophrenic individuals need to maintain self-esteem as much as anyone else, and the choice between medication and having to face a difficult life with residual impairments or remaining ill enough to avoid some of life's responsibilities can be more difficult than we might think.

Our approach is to present medication as a partial treatment in which the patient's efforts are still very important. We try to have the individual collaborate as fully as possible in decisions about drug treatments, at the very least by providing as much informatiion as possible and giving the patient responsibility for reports on symptoms and side effects. In some cases, it is appropriate for a schizophrenic individual to control dosage or timing of administration within limits given by the physician. For example:

> One highly intelligent and talented semi-professional tennis player
> had competed nationally while finishing college despite severe

paranoid delusions that were accompanied by hallucinations. He had always refused treatment, especially antipsychotic drugs, until his behavior grew so bizarre that he would be involuntarily hospitalized. He quickly grew more calm and rational while taking medication, but it was clear that he would never continue taking it once he left the hospital. One consultant, however, spent a considerable length of time trying to understand what he disliked about the subjective experience of taking medication. The young man gave vague remarks about being sedated, then finally mentioned some physical sensations. The consultant continued to question him in detail:

C: So it slows down your reaction time, you think?
P: Yes, it interferes.
C: So does it interfere when you play tennis?
P: Yes.
C: Tell me more about that. How exactly does it interfere?
P: Well, it interferes.
C: Does it interfere all the time, or only with some strokes?
P: Some of the time.
C: Is it when you serve, for example, or whenever you hit the ball?
P: I notice it when I serve.
C: So it's when you serve. Can you tell me how it interferes?
P: Well, it's most of the time when I serve.
C: What does it do, for example, when you serve?
P: It ruins it.
C: At what point in your serve? What does it do, exactly? Does it slow down the serve, or the toss, or what?
P: Well, I can still toss the ball and bring my racket back, but when I bring my racket forward to meet the ball, it's just not as fast—just a few milliseconds off, but it ruins my serve.
C: So that's really bad.
P: Yes.
C: And what dosage does that?
P: Thirty milligrams.
C: Would twenty-five have the same effect, do you think, or twenty-seven, or twenty?

Eventually the patient decided that he might be able to bear taking 23 milligrams and agreed to try this and to try playing tennis on this dosage while in the hospital so that he could see the effects.

One of the points we wish to make through this example is the need for clinicians to be serious and patient in their inquiries and to avoid assuming that they know best or know what patients will say. Patients are accustomed to being asked briefly about side effects, but they themselves have a detailed image of the deleterious effects of the medication on specific elements of the activities that form the basis of their self-esteem and identities. They do not assume that clinicians are interested in this until clinicians have proved the contrary by lengthy and precise inquiry. In all likelihood, patients agree to try a medication in part because they feel understood, rather than coerced.

Thus, the most important aspect of the clinician's work in the treatment partnership around drug therapy is his or her attitude toward the medication and toward the patient's attitude. As always, it is necessary for clinicians to empathize with the specifics of patients' reluctance to engage in such treatment and to avoid preaching. Clinicians should be clear and explicit about why they are asking for drug compliance: life goals expressed by patients, making therapy feasible, keeping patients out of trouble or out of a hospital, reducing clinicians' anxiety about suicide in depressed but impulsive and disorganized patients. This latter rationale for a request for medication compliance can be very powerful: It lets patients know that clinicians are not in control of patients' lives because clinicians have to *ask* for compliance to manage their own feelings of worry. It is much better for clinicians to openly acknowledge their wish to control patients to prevent their death or destructiveness than to verbally present the need for medication as something simply for patients' own good, while in a contradictory way clinicians' actions express the need to control patients. The clinicians' attitude should be that the individual with schizophrenia is nontheless an individual with the right to make unhealthy choices within limits set by society and the physician's concern to save life.

Sharon's Medication Experience

Sharon illustrates a particular type of medication noncompliance, which is related to her general noncompliance and inability to form stable

treatment partnerships. When she returned to the hospital she was globally bitter, hostile, and withdrawn. She began to refuse medication and
eventually refused to eat or to take care of her personal hygiene. While
her life was not immediately at risk, hospital personnel began to think
of requesting a court order for involuntarily medicating Sharon. However, in the context of her life-long aversion to participating in treatment, taking this step felt to her therapist like getting into one more
power struggle in which Sharon would temporarily submit to control by
others more powerful than she, with her basic reluctance to form a true
treatment partnership unchanged throughout. In fact, she might be less
likely to work with staff in the future, since there was no evidence that
she was significantly more trusting or cooperative *with* medication than
without. She had been asked or forced to take medication on others'
terms many times before, without any lasting change in her attitude
toward compliance.

Knowing her long history of noncompliance and her concerns about
control, which stemmed from extremely porous self-other boundaries,
the therapist sought to find some paradigm for negotiation about medication in the hope that they could avoid having this become another
major battle. He waited to apply for a court order, simply having Sharon
weighed daily and her input and output noted for a time when she was
not in physical danger, while trying to discuss with her ways she could
participate in the development of a drug treatment plan. He saw this as
merely a continuation of her treatment, which had focussed on her
noncompliance based on her rejection of the idea that she was ill since,
she insisted, she was the victim of mind control experiments by the FBI.
Sharon was relatively unable to form a treatment partnership, at least a
stable one, because of her need to say she was not ill and to avoid real
contact with others who could help. Her therapist saw her refusal to
take medication as a desperate attempt to assert a self-other boundary
and was concerned that, if this power was forcibly removed from her,
she might reason that suicide or violence directed at others was the only
way to assert self-control and to differentiate herself from the powerful,
controlling others in her life.

Sharon and her therapist spoke about whether there was any way her
"brain could be repaired," utilizing her idea that the FBI had tampered
with her by implanting devices in her. But Sharon used the idea of
revenge against the FBI as an organizing principle, so that the idea that

she, or she and her therapist, or she and the medication, could do anything to repair the damage done to her was unacceptable. She was set on a trial to prove the FBI had harmed her, and her goal in life was therefore to gather evidence to support this contention. The idea of medication was too frightening and made her feel too powerless for her to respond to the therapist's offer. In the end, legal proceedings were necessary to convince her to take medication. The therapist told Sharon of his feelings of powerlessness and his willingness to risk her anger by going against her wishes as part of the discussion of this development.

Sharon's noncompliance rested on her failure to integrate information about her illness into her picture of herself. This, in turn, rested on her considerable problem maintaining a sense of her identity—hence her rigid rules for herself and others and for interactions, that is, her paranoid and avoidant stance. To integrate awareness that she had an illness into her self-image would apparently have represented too much of a loss, too much damage to her self-esteem and her hopes. She was unable to find in herself the flexibility to allow for a different self-image.

THE HOSPITAL THERAPIST'S RELATIONS WITH HOSPITAL STAFF

When the patient's doctor is engaged in psychotherapy in the hospital setting and when this task is differentiated from those performed by other disciplines, certain issues tend to arise simply because of the nature of the system (7–9). Most often, there are narcissistic conflicts in staff, centered on envy and its denial through devaluation. That is, because the therapist is usually a member of a profession with higher status in the hospital setting, other staff focus their envy of status attributes on the psychotherapy activity, which is a clear-cut example of something that is supposed to require a great deal of training and skill but that superficially appears easy to do—after all, it's just talk. Or, alternatively, they may devalue psychotherapy, relegating it to the realm of ivory towers and fantasy lands, while considering the work they do in dealing with the patient's concrete problems of getting up in the morning or going into town as more important. Either way, the system is usually set up so that narcissistic issues, envy, competition, idealization, and devaluation are close at hand if a patient arrives whose pathology can exploit the situation.

Sharon's Idealization of the Therapist

The situation that developed with Sharon was not uncommon. She was generally devaluing and uncooperative with nursing and activities staff and frequently refused to be civil to them. Although she was not really very cooperative in psychotherapy, the rest of the staff shared the fantasy (which represented one side of Sharon's idealized fantasy) that she was talking to her therapist and had some kind of good relationship with him. Sharon supported this fantasy with glowing reports of her wonderful sessions with Dr. B.—reports that lead to the staff's envy of that (imaginary) good relationship. Furthermore, staff saw the doctor as a powerful figure who ought to be able to control this (impossible) woman since he felt it worthwhile to spend so much time talking with her. The staff assumed that if he didn't stop her devaluation of the staff, he must be doing something wrong. It is worth adding that the kind of idealized relationship between Sharon and Dr. B. the staff imagined has its reflection in reality in the kind of special relationships schizophrenic individuals often try to set up with persons who they feel will take care of all their problems. Sharon was in fact attempting to establish this type of relationship with Dr. B., who at times restrained himself with difficulty from feeling a special closeness with her that was only partially supported by the reality of their interactions.

Another aspect of the staff's idealized fantasy about this pair reflected the feeling that Sharon was really a very powerful, controlling person. This fantasy was that, if Sharon talked to her therapist at all, he must be so influenced by her powers that he would always believe her distortions and never believe that the staff's view of her problems with them had any validity. She was seen as someone who could spoil what they actually knew to be the therapist's good ability to understand and empathize with staff reactions to a patient and with the difficulties presented by someone like Sharon.

Envy of the therapist's real or supposed ability to contain and not act on the rage generated by a patient like Sharon is also frequently a part of staff reactions. Sharon made everyone feel frustrated, helpless, and furious. Those who felt least aware of or least comfortable with their anger were most likely to also feel intense guilt, which was again dealt with by projection. In this kind of situation, the therapist sometimes overtly or covertly accuses other staff of being sadistic, and sometimes the nursing staff accuses the therapist of the crime of "overinvolvement" or countertransference that interferes with the proper therapeutic maneuvers. Usually, the fantasy about proper therapeutic maneuvers involves something punitive and controlling to "get" the patient to behave differently.

With Sharon, staff were angry and guilty as well as afraid that Sharon would report their anger to her doctor in a way that fit in with Sharon's view of herself as the righteous accuser of the evil-doers of the world. On the other hand, they also wished that she *would* spend her sessions on their anger, since they needed to have it expressed somewhere and their guilt assuaged. Discussions revealed that many staff entertained the notion that the therapist was never angry at Sharon: it was only the "bad" staff who had to try to get her out of bed in the morning and who felt such rage when she would strike out at them. This notion intensified their feelings of guilt for this anger.

The result of all these factors was a powerful need in the staff to defend against feelings of guilt aroused by understandable rage at a troublesome patient. The defense consisted of contempt for the therapist's work, idealization of the staff's work ("It's harder"), and denial of guilt about the anger. Staff members typically felt that it was the therapist's fault that Sharon considered the aides "bad objects," since the therapist should have been insisting to Sharon that she get up in the morning. If he didn't get her to do this, it meant that he failed to understand the nursing point of view and was undermining treatment.

Management of the Dilemma

This type of problem exemplifies the need for regular, open discussions among therapist and staff members. Otherwise, hospitalization and hospital rules can be used to keep the patient's difficulties with certain affects out of everyone's conscious awareness (10). The crucial element in these discussions about Sharon was Dr. B.'s sharing his feelings of frustration and anger and the fact that Sharon was not utilizing psychotherapy very well. This countered the fantasy that only the nursing and activities staff had such feelings (11), but further stimulated guilt as Dr.

B. spoke of how he tried to manage these feelings in the service of the therapy and to minimize the likelihood that he would act on his frequent wish to be rid of Sharon.

In this way, Dr. B. modeled how he used his feelings with Sharon to understand not only her subjective experience but that of the staff. This knowledge also helped him clarify what Sharon was trying to accomplish. Just as it is necessary for therapists to manage their countertransference, containing patients' unwanted affects is helpful in managing difficult patients' hospitalization.

Dr. B.'s openness created a problem for the staff. It disrupted the defenses already in place, whereby therapy was devalued but secretly idealized and envied. That is, there was the hope (which, paradoxically, forms the basis for the disappointment and the rage) that Dr. B. would make everything better. Instead, the staff had to confront their own realistic failures in treating Sharon: They were generally approaching her in a way that reflected their hatred of and hopelessness about her, by acting as if their only task with her was to "get her to do" something.

The Nursing Role

This view of the role of staff reflects a basic error in understanding schizophrenia. From this perspective, patients are assumed to be able to just "will" themselves to do something, including acting well or getting better, and if they don't, this is seen as "acting out." It also reflects a despairing feeling that if patients are ill with something as hopelessly severe as schizophrenia, all that a concerned, trained staff member can do is take care of them in a maternal way, without expecting any contribution from the patient or any role for the psychiatric nurse's skills in understanding and conceptualizing the physical and emotional demands of life. Such an attitude contrasts with our belief that some behaviors result from psychological reactions to the core disturbances and hence are amenable to change.

The role of nursing staff in the treatment of this kind of patient is far different, in our opinion, unless an informed decision for custodial care is made. Getting patients to "do something" is not the major role; rather, staff serve as auxiliary egos, models of how to deal with life and its demands and frustrations, people who know how to contain feelings and act appropriately. They realize that patients require examples of how to deal with various situations. They understand that patients are sick, but nonetheless they tell the patients the effect of their behaviors on others, including themselves, to provide data for patients. They articulate the details of patient-staff interactions so that patients are forced to look at what they are doing, what the impact of a behavior is, good or bad. Staff maintain their own view but realize that delusional patients do not see things in the same way, and that a delusional world-view dictates certain actions.

For example, a nurse might have said to Sharon, "I understand you don't trust me and you feel you must treat me like a jailer because that's what you think I'm here for, but I have a different view. I don't believe I am your jailer, and it hurts my feelings and makes me feel unappreciated when you don't trust me after all these months. I know you have your view, but I have mine too." This intervention could also have helped Sharon with self-other differentiation.

Another element in Sharon's presentation to nursing staff was her need to act as an advocate for all the paranoid, hostile patients on the ward. She did this in such a contentious way that it was very hard for staff to find the kernel of truth in complaints and respond seriously rather than defensively or by dismissing Sharon completely. This is where the therapist or clinical administrator of the ward can be helpful. It is necessary to empathize with the staff's plight, when they are feeling devalued, frustrated, and criticized. At the same time, it is important to continue to relate to the patient in a therapeutic way, identifying an ego strength in the patient that is being utilized in a maladaptive way and then offering other avenues for its expression, given an understanding of what it means to the patient.

For Sharon, organizing the patient group (or its most paranoid subgroup) felt like proof that she would eventually be able to plead her case against the FBI successfully, convincing the world that she had been wronged. Being an advocate for the downtrodden was also part of her liberal–creative writer identity. Allowing Sharon to be an advocate but limiting her activities to community meetings where she had previously arranged to be on the agenda and where she agreed to follow the usual procedural rules offered some relief to both Sharon and the staff. This compromise allowed her to advocate, but in a much more bearable fashion. Staff could even compliment her on the strength of her convictions while disagreeing with her presentation of the facts and her interpretations of them. This empathy from staff was made possible by their feeling that the ward administration did not plan to allow Sharon to attack them constantly and that empathy for their situation was available. In turn, this freed people to see her strengths, such as they were, so that they could be more creative in offering her alternative channels to express them.

THERAPEUTIC ACTIVITIES

Therapeutic activities are an important part of the rehabilitation program now offered by psychiatric hospitals. Patients are usually evaluated in terms of task, social, and occupational skills and then placed in appropriate groups, their activities progressing to more challenging ones as the individual's condition and length of hospital stay allow. These activities include discussion groups (current events, information on local community activities, assertiveness training) aimed at withdrawn patients or those who need help with social skills; sport and hobby groups to help develop leisure interests; and supervised work programs, such as putting together a hospital literary magazine or running a gift shop or snack bar. These activities include group meetings in which issues of stress management and authority relations can be discussed with vocational counselors who have observed the patient's job performance.

The Noncompliant Patient in Therapeutic Activities

Evaluation and placement of Sharon in therapeutic activities programs was very difficult for the same reasons that made it hard for nursing staff to work constructively with her. Her attitude was critical and antagonistic, and she often refused to work at anything. While her disorganization and intense concern with her delusions prevented her from effective cognitive work, she refused to openly acknowledge her own limitations in anything resembling a task. At the same time, she scorned less challenging work and viewed it as a deliberate attempt by staff to humiliate and frustrate her (which, at times, it was, though not on a conscious level). At such times, she would feel that she was losing her identity as a college educated person and that the staff had also forgotten, in a very real way, who she was.

Part of Sharon's delusion was that, in a plot to prevent her from exposing a gigantic, evil FBI project, she was being held against her will. Since she planned to leave someday and be vindicated by the Supreme Court, she was concerned to make her case while in the hospital. Unfortunately, she felt that this meant that she must refuse treatment in order to maintain her position. To act like a patient in any way would, she feared, weaken her case and argue against her basic contention that she was incarcerated in error—which did not leave much of a role for staff to work with Sharon. Such limiting of staff's usefulness, as much as the derogation of staff, is a typical problem with very paranoid patients, whose need to keep their distance from staff and to control the possibility of any mutual relationships and, especially, the development of any dependency needs on the patient's part, is particularly severe. But the staff tried to work within the bounds that Sharon first set.

They initially attempted to respect Sharon's training in literature and creative writing by assigning her to a group that published a patient newspaper, even though most patients in this group had proved the status of their task skills through earlier participation in less complex group tasks. However, the fact that staff allowed her to "skip steps" in the hierarchy of activities programs, combined with misconceptions about the nature of the illness, led to a poor outcome. Activities staff would give Sharon assignments with the feeling that she had to prove herself and then criticized her severely for her failings, since she wasn't performing at the proper level. The idea was that it was beneficial for Sharon to be confronted with her disabilities, as if it were the task of the activities therapists to disabuse her of her delusion that, while in the hospital, she was an investigative reporter collecting material on the plans of the FBI. Since this delusion was a central part of her identity and had been unresponsive to many types of treatment efforts, including medication, this plan for Sharon's self-confrontation was doomed.

Drawbacks in Confronting a Patient's Deficits

This experience illustrates one of the problems with certain types of psychosocial rehabilitation programs. Given Sharon's need for denial in order for her to maintain her autonomy, confronting her with her deficits in functioning destroyed the chances of forming a treatment alliance. Attempts to force confrontations derived from the assumptions that she would never change or get better and that she should just learn to accept her difficulties and give up all thoughts of being a writer. While such change in vocational plans might eventually have become part of Sharon's life, to impose it on her at a time when she barely accepted any need for treatment at all could only be demoralizing and enraging to her. It made her feel not so much that people were wrong in their judgment, but that they had no concern for her feelings and could not be trusted. Thus, they could not be trusted to collaborate helpfully with her if she did admit she had problems, since they had shown themselves to be so tactless. The net result was Sharon's greater feelings of despair and an upsurge of suicidal ideation.

One alternative approach might have been to allow Sharon to publish articles in which she had a specific interest—for example, articles detailing her views about the FBI. Such an approach would sidestep the control issue somewhat, especially if staff could refrain from destructive criticism. However, there are risks in approaching too directly a patient's skills when the individual is as sick as Sharon was and when there is so much denial. Sharon might have verbally responded well to such a suggestion, but probably would have discovered reasons for its not being a good idea: It might reveal what she knew to the enemy, it might weaken her defense in court, and so on. To have the opportunity to show what she could do would have touched too centrally on her delusional system and her denial, so that eventually she would have experienced this activity as a humiliating ploy to get her to reveal what she secretly knew—that she was too disorganized to write coherently.

Partial success was achieved by allowing her to meet regularly with a poetry and writing consultant who volunteered time on the unit. Ostensibly, the two met to discuss Sharon's writing projects, but the definition of their activity was broad enough so that no pressure was placed on Sharon to produce material. Instead, Sharon and Ann, the volunteer, went over articles she or Ann had read recently, or they discussed stories and poetry from books they read together. Even though the material Sharon selected for criticism was obviously related to issues of major dynamic significance for her—control, invasion, autonomy, boundaries—Ann knew to avoid any potentially interpretive work about this content. Given that Sharon was in a very beginning stage of trying to form a treatment partnership, the goal of their meetings was for Sharon to have positive experiences of sharing with other people that did not turn into situations of danger for her. It was understood that Sharon needed not examples of vocational successes, but examples of sharing an activity with another human being in a way that did not threaten her self-other differentiation problems and needs for safety and control.

Sharon felt she was engaging in these literary activities voluntarily, not as a mental patient performing an assigned task. The approach to her activities was nonconfrontational and noninterpretive: These activities did not involve a type of psychotherapy, even though the idea that rewarding human contact could be possible despite her severe psychological problems came from an understanding of Sharon's psychological life.

Using the Patient's Subjective Experience to Design a Rehabilitation Program

The approach to rehabilitative activities therapies with schizophrenic patients can be, as in Sharon's case, noninterpretive and nonpsychological, utilizing the principle of approaching a patient's talents tangentially, as it were, rather than making a direct demand for performance. To ask a patient to use a skill that was formerly part of his or her life can be supportive, but unless there is evidence that the skill is relatively intact, it can be yet another invitation to defeat and humiliation. On some level, schizophrenic individuals are aware of their limitations—that is, they are aware of the areas to avoid so that they will not feel humiliated by a public failure to function. It is crucial for clinicians to respect the signals the patients give about these limitations, even though the messages may be indirect. For example, if a patient misses therapeutic activities appointments, behaves obnoxiously so that he or she is asked to leave, or develops paranoid ideas about the task leader, it may mean that the patient has judged the task to be too difficult to risk at this time.

Approaching tasks as tasks, rather than as material to be interpreted in the activities setting, also respects the person's difficulties with boundaries. Sharon had made no agreement to discuss meaningful psychological material with Ann. Even though such material appeared in their meetings, it would have been intrusive for Ann to interpret it, for her doing so would have assumed more of a treatment partnership than existed. If the patient agrees to participate in creative arts therapies with the goal of increased self-understanding and the expectation that material to be discussed further in psychotherapy will arise, the situation is different, but it is wise not to assume that the patient agrees to these conditions of participation unless they are explicitly discussed.

VIOLENCE

Sharon's propensity for violence toward herself and others magnified the difficulties in forming a treatment partnership and underscored her concern for control and autonomy: She often "needed to be controlled." In addition, everyone who tried to work with her felt, in some way, violently controlled by her, in the sense of being put in a position where nothing seemed to help and everything seemed to make her more enraged and unavailable. Staff and therapist alike felt coerced into being something other than they were, as Sharon made it clear she viewed nurses as cruel jailers, and then, because of her behavior, they found themselves having to restrict her.

Sharon's actual violence, not just the violence of her feelings, was an ongoing issue for all the staff but most of all for the aides and nurses who had to try to engage her in daily activities as simple as making sure she got up and washed in the morning. Her tendency to strike out at them was frightening and enraging, since she took virtually no responsibility for this behavior. Knowing her history of violence with therapists and her present behavior, Dr. B. felt, uneasily, that she could suddenly strike out at him in response to some perceived failure on his part, but it was hard for him to engage her in discussion of this behavior because of her need to idealize him while she devalued everyone else. Her inability to admit to both positive and negative feelings toward him reflected Sharon's problems with cognitive integration and her fears of another kind of boundary loss, whereby she felt that she could not prevent any potential rage at him from completely spoiling her good feelings for him.

Naturally, Sharon's selective assaultiveness exacerbated staff anger and envy. It was necessary for the therapist to tell Sharon that he viewed her violence as directed at him as well as at the specific nurses she hated because they were his colleagues and because her behavior indicated that her treatment partnership with him, as part of the hospital package, must be very poor. He also had to remind her that if she continued to attack people, she would not be allowed to stay in the hospital, so that her contentions that he was so wonderful and that she wanted to keep working with him were contradicted by the behavior that would result in an end to their work. The therapist was able to see how Sharon's violence was directed at him by recognizing how violently coerced and controlled he felt with her and sometimes by noticing how violent was his wish for her to just leave him alone. He was thus able to empathize with the staff's reaction and to see how Sharon was using the rest of her day in the hospital to express a part of herself she had trouble talking about in therapy. This, in turn, led him to try to address these issues. Without his alliance with the rest of the staff, Dr. B. would have thought he had an alliance with Sharon where in fact there was none, or not much of one. This case thus demonstrates the therapist's need to maintain a treatment partnership with all staff members as well as to consider all the patient's behaviors and peoples' reactions to these as useful information.

SUMMARY

We have not covered all aspects of hospital treatment of schizophrenia in this chapter. We have, however, attempted to demonstrate how consideration of the patient's subjective experience can be used to inform potentially difficult areas of this work: when a patient is violent and noncompliant and stirs up rage and guilt in all who work with him or her. Having a psychological model of Sharon's experience of herself and her illness in mind made it possible to understand what capacity she had for forming treatment partnerships with staff. This facilitated the development of practical interventions and dictated psychotherapeutic maneuvers. We have also stressed the importance of the partnerships between outpatient therapist and inpatient staff and between inpatient therapist and inpatient staff.

Given her need to deny her illness, Sharon's marginal ability to allow another to help her limited what could be accomplished with her, despite the sustained efforts of many. She eventually returned to a somewhat nomadic existence, yet the hospital where this treatment had taken place became the geographic center of her movements.

But we can never predict what thoughtful care means to the severely resistant patient who apparently refuses our help. Sharon ultimately returned to the hospital at her own request, without pressure from others, and began to try to create for herself a life that would include the fact of her illness.

6

The Case of Maryann: Psychotherapy and Community Management, Rehabilitation, and Rehospitalization

The individual with schizophrenia who is able to live in the community needs the help of family, friends, therapist, and community agencies. The collaboration with a client in such circumstances must take into account the involvement of others in the person's life and, in particular, work with rehabilitation and other agencies, day hospitals, and residences. The patient's wishes for the therapist to take a particular role vis-à-vis these others complicate this process. The patient's need for other professionals in addition to the therapist affects the patient's feelings and hopes with regard to the therapist. While other programs are not designed to address the patient's subjective experiences of his or her daily life, the psychotherapist can do so. Yet the patient often needs support to manage the demands of rehabilitation programs if he or she is to maintain a rewarding existence and as a result, often requires the therapist's help to collaborate effectively with outside agencies.

For severely ill patients with previous hospital stays, concern about rehospitalization is always a part of outpatient treatment. Such individuals fear the disruption to their lives, the interruption to their freedom, the loss of therapists, and the visible sign of illness that the hospital comes to represent. Rehospitalization may also feel like an indication of failure. On the other hand, the hospital may well represent safety and asylum—in the best sense—from the demands of a world that is poorly designed from the standpoint of schizophrenic individuals' vulnerabilities. The hospital may also be the only way in which patients can imagine creating emotional distance from their outpatient therapists, who are usually very important figures in patients' lives. Hospitalization can interrupt this dependency. With the added pressure of an emergency situation the question of rehospitalization raises all these issues.

In this chapter, we take up the issue of rehospitalization in a recurrently suicidal patient living in the community and discuss the effects of the therapist-community relationship for this particular individual. The case we consider also exemplifies the difficulty of the alliance with the apparently help-rejecting client: that is, how the therapist fosters and tolerates a "hidden" alliance with a patient who needs a great deal of support but fears what it may cost in terms of the patient's self-image of independence. In addition, we address the development of a disruptive transference and its management in terms of the principle that, since the patient has not become a new individual when disruptive transference occurs, consistent attention to the patient's experience remains the goal. Finally, this case also shows how it often falls to the therapist to be the repository of the patient's history and of the history of the patient-therapist relationship.

OUTPATIENT PSYCHOTHERAPY AND REHOSPITALIZATION ISSUES FOR THE CHRONICALLY SUICIDAL PATIENT

One day, after having been out of the hospital for about a year, Maryann left a message cancelling a psychotherapy session for the second time that week, adding that the therapist could call her. When he did so, Maryann said that she had left her day hospital program early because she felt ill, as she had all weekend, which she spent in bed. When the therapist asked about her depression and the suicidal thoughts that she had been having lately, Maryann said that she was still having impulses and thoughts about killing herself, but that she had no plan to do so and was also telling herself that she really didn't want to die, blocking these thoughts out of her mind.

Maryann added that over the weekend she had been disturbed by a movie in which a doctor fell in love with his female patient. Since Maryann's therapist was male, the reference to the movie seemed highly significant. She said she felt alienated, disoriented, and as if she got no support from anyone. She was generally annoyed at the therapist but agreed to his suggestion that she come in earlier than her regular appointment the next day.

On Thursday, Maryann attended her day hospital program and her therapy session and said she felt better. The therapist insisted that she talk about the sessions she'd missed lately and about whether she'd felt suicidal. He also inquired about whether he could trust her to be honest about these issues, given that she had been telling him that there were many areas of her life, especially her religion, she felt she could not share with him. In an apparently sincere and related way, Maryann repeated that she thinks of suicide but knows that God does not want her to kill herself. She didn't want to die, but it was very hard for her to think of facing the rest of her life if things did not get easier.

T: Can you understand my concern about whether or not I can believe you the times when you promise you'll go to the emergency room rather than act on a suicidal thought?

M: Yes, I know you're worried when I don't tell you things—but I don't want to change, you know, I just can't change. You know, you are still a threat to me sometimes. I know you don't share my faith. It's bad for my mind for me to try to talk to you about these things.

T: So there are still a lot of areas where you really can't trust me, as if I'd try to get you to change your identity or your religious beliefs?

M: Well, yes there are. I don't want to talk about it. I've been thinking a lot about judgment day lately. You know that the Bible is very meaningful to me—I've been reading it a lot lately. I think that judgment day is coming sooner than most people think.

T: Like how soon?

M: I know most people wouldn't believe this, and sometimes I don't either, but sometimes I think it might be in two weeks. I know that you probably think that's crazy.

T: What I was wondering about was how you see all this in relation to you and your life specifically, because judgment day usually implies people being dead, and I wondered if you were feeling that you're supposed to take an active role in this—like making sure you're dead in two weeks.

M: Oh no, nothing like that. That's not the way it works.

T: But when you talk about it like this, and when I know that you don't trust me very much, I worry that you might not feel you could tell me if you were going to kill yourself. Do you think you might feel more safe in the hospital for a while? I'm still worried about whether you'd really trust me enough to tell me just how bad your suicidal impulses were getting.

M: I know what you're saying, I know what you mean. I really don't think I need to go into the hospital now—I'm really not suicidal like that. I would definitely go to the emergency room if I needed to. I wouldn't try to hurt myself. I'm not planning anything.

Patients who have suffered the turmoil and humiliations of schizophrenia for years are often depressed, discouraged, and at risk for suicide. How to manage this risk in the context of the patient's and clinician's joint efforts for the patient to build a stable life is a recurring theme in outpatient treatment. While the clinician does not wish to leave a seriously suicidal patient without sufficient supervision, hospitalization is disruptive to the life the patient has tried to build, and many patients resist rehospitalizations because they have unpleasant memories of past stays and view hospitalization as a sign of failure. Family, community residence staff, and staff of day programs and rehabilitation facilities may share this bias, as might a therapist, especially if he or she equates hospitalization with a failure as a healer. This bias complicates assessment of the patient's ability to continue in outpatient settings, particularly when there is a possibility that the patient is concealing distress out of reluctance to return to the hospital. The nature of the patient's current alliance with the therapist, the state of the transference, and the current stresses in the patient's life all affect this assessment process. Input from other agencies working with the individual may prove useful.

For example, consider the person who, in the midst of a psychotic transference, believes the therapist to be exceedingly powerful and homosexually interested in the patient. Such a patient might well seek suicide to protect himself, feeling there is no safe haven from this powerful figure. The same patient, having a sexual delusional belief about his boss and a relatively nonconflicted positive transference to the therapist, might not require hospitalization, because he could discuss in therapy his ideas about his boss.

Using the system of hypothesis building and attending to the patient's subjective experience and the way it informs the treatment partnership, as outlined in the first section of this book, we will try to show how this orientation caused the therapist to decide to see Maryann for an extra session, at which time he hospitalized her. Though on the face of it, his rationale for this decision might not appear obvious, we will try to show

how, in following the schema outlined in the earlier chapters, the therapist arrived at this particular set of interventions.

History

First, Maryann's history as known to the clinician at this time. Maryann was a 32-year-old woman with a B.A. who had initially developed clear symptoms of schizophrenia in the course of her first post-college employment. At that time, she developed religious preoccupations and believed she was possessed by the devil. Soon Maryann was hospitalized by her anxious parents. After a short stay and treatment with phenothiazines, she left the hospital—prematurely because she felt overmedicated—and gradually began to work again part time. Her medication was gradually tapered by her outpatient psychiatrist, who saw her monthly to check on her symptoms. Maryann was off medication within a year of this first hospitalization and supposedly symptom-free; it later seemed likely that she continued covertly to have religious and paranoid delusions.

A few months after stopping all medications, Maryann once again became terrified and distraught and locked herself in her room out of fear. She was hospitalized for what turned out to be a six-month stay, because even as her pacing, agitation, and reports of delusions and hallucinations abated, she continued to engage in risky behaviors while out on passes, such as picking up men in disreputable bars. The focus in this hospitalization was to help Maryann to "seal over" (1) her psychosis by putting it behind her rather than by trying to understand it, since Maryann's interest in recognizing her illness and learning about situations that caused her to develop symptoms appeared to be limited. Nonetheless, Maryann was not felt to be stable enough to leave the hospital until an extended period of inpatient treatment with increasing passes into the community had taken place. Since Maryann always seemed to get into some kind of trouble as discharge plans to home were made, a decision was taken to refer her to a residential treatment center from which she could look for work outside a protected setting. In contrast to the case described in chapter 7 (in which the hospital staff insisted on a discharge plan which separated patient and family), Maryann and her family had decided this was the best plan during a period of family work, and although they missed each other, the separation seemed manageable.

Maryann did well, eventually holding a job and returning to her hobbies of sewing and hiking. She was maintained on chlorpromazine. But two years after her hospital discharge, she again had difficulty concentrating and began to miss work, and she felt she must return home. When she did so, she felt better for awhile and worked part time while angering her parents with her attitude of entitlement and apparent laziness. She returned to drinking and contracted pneumonia, during which her physician temporarily discontinued her psychotropic medication. Home alone and physically ill, Maryann's delusional ideas flourished. She stayed up all night playing loud music, until, enraged, but with no way to know how delusional Maryann was, her parents attempted to get her to move out of the house. When she became belligerent, they took her to the hospital.

This was to be a short-term stay; Maryann quickly began to behave more appropriately. Her parents expressed their inability to have her live at home, and Maryann seemed to accept this. While she continued to refer to the suicidal ideation she had experienced prior to admission, she reassured staff that she was in control when they asked her about suicidal impulses. But following an upsetting group therapy session, Maryann badly cut her wrists with a broken piece of plastic, necessitating an emergency room visit.

This was the beginning of another long-term hospitalization, this time with an added psychotherapy focus in which Maryann was encouraged to explore her feelings about her illness and the possible relationships between her delusions and other symptoms and her emotional reactions. This recommendation for exploratory psychotherapy was made because Maryann had begun to express curiosity about what was happening to her and a motivation to improve her relationships. Also, long trials of supportive treatment aimed at sealing over had failed to make major changes in her illness and the management of her symptoms. While psychotherapy was very difficult for her, given her grandiose wish to claim she already understood everything about herself, Maryann did develop a psychotherapy relationship and gained some insights into some of her feelings about her family, especially those that repeatedly led her to want to be at home and then behave in a way that made remaining there impossible. She was discharged to a day hospital and halfway house and to psychotherapy three times a week. Her medications controlled some of her anxiety and delusions, although she remained somewhat delusional throughout many adequate trials of various medications.

At this time, Maryann spoke of high expectations for herself but complained about the demands of the halfway house, the day program, and psychotherapy and did not seem to see that her difficulties there implied a need to lower her sights. She continued to be paranoid, grandiose, and irritable when under any stress. Her religious beliefs could be seen alternately as delusional symptoms of her illness or as an adaptive response to the many disappointments and humiliations of her illness. She spoke of her conviction that God had some reason for asking her to suffer from schizophrenia and that it was her role to undergo this suffering until some unrevealed time in the future.

In her halfway house, Maryann followed the rules but hated the group meetings and the need to take turns with cleaning chores. She presented the same picture at the day program, indicating in a variety of ways that she considered herself above the other clients and, at the same time, that the responsibilities and groups were a terrible burden because of her constant distress. In both settings, Maryann was initially successful in making staff believe she was much less fragile than she in fact was.

To Hospitalize or Not to Hospitalize

The Therapist's Model

At the time of the phone call and session described above, the therapist already had a set of hypotheses about Maryann's experience of herself, the therapy, the therapist, the day hospital and halfway house, and other significant elements of her life. In the first part of this book, we presented a model for conceptualizing schizophrenia and a series of foci for gathering data to use in the assessment of a patient's subjective experience in order to maximize the development of a therapeutic collaboration. This model was used with Maryann.

Physiological Substrate ("Primary" Disturbances)

The therapist knew that the biological substrate of Maryann's illness was quite severe, since she had several schizophrenic relatives and had been ill with many severe symptoms for several years. This meant that all of Maryann's accomplishments had to be viewed against the background of the severe disturbance with which she struggled daily. Maryann experienced constant mistrust and anticipatory anxiety of getting into trouble because other people might suddenly mistreat and provoke her or attack her physically without reason. Her baseline level of anxiety was so high that she almost never read or went to movies because she would be distracted by her fears, not to mention by the vivid fantasies the material might evoke, and thus was unable to concentrate.

"Secondary" Disturbances with Probable Physiological Basis

At times of change, loss, or higher expectations from others, Maryann regularly developed dermatitis, although she believed this to be due in part to her high consumption of sugar. She also became physically anxious and restless prior to recognizing that she might be having an emotional reaction. Her sleep varied with her psychological life, and she was subject to nightmares, which suggested that her physical self was poorly protected from the vicissitudes of her emotional reactions. While she rarely hallucinated, she had many grandiose and paranoid delusions and overvalued ideas, and managing to act appropriately in spite of these used a great deal of time and energy. Maryann's available range of affect was relatively normal, but she was frequently enraged, worried, and discouraged, and her fears and suspiciousness limited her sense of humor. She was very vulnerable to intense depression and despair at her setbacks, and, although she denied that losses or rejections had much of an impact on her, her increased anxiety and sleeplessness at such times suggested otherwise.

Psychologically Mediated Responses to the Core Physiological Deficits. Subjective Experience

Interaction with the Environment. Management of her environment (see Table 2.1) included a variety of manifest communications and a form of idiosyncratic relatedness characterized by control. Maryann's behaviors included arrogance, a sense of entitlement, and widespread complaining about her struggles and her mistreatment by others. Obviously, she could be suspicious and paranoid. Because it was so important for her to see herself as good, it was very difficult for her to allow herself to become aware of being angry unless she felt completely justified by others' real or imagined mistreatment. As a result, those she dealt with daily tended to experience her as passively aggressive or rude and self-centered, lacking in awareness of her impact on others—one of her forms of idiosyncratic relatedness. Maryann viewed others in extreme, need-gratifying terms, according to whether they made her feel comfortable or uncomfortable. She was quite contemptuous, although at times she tried to hide this attitude with clinging behavior, which also irritated others. The manifest communication of these behaviors was "Let me see myself as good; I can't bear to think I might be responsible for some of the bad things that happen to me."

Quality of Patient's Experience. These manifest communications and idiosyncratic, rigid ways of dealing with others implied, to her therapist, a particular set of subjective experiences and view of herself. He hypothesized Maryann's view of herself to be that of a special person being misunderstood and burdened by an insensitive world, which was unaware of or unwilling to acknowledge her special gifts and the fact that she was chosen to suffer.

This view of herself and her task in life represented a sustaining experience for her. She saw herself proudly as struggling on despite her misfortunes. She felt irrevocably different from others in her specialness and suffering (which supported weak self-object differentiation) and, because of this, commanding their help and respect (allowing for the possibility of relatedness). It was important for her to see herself as totally good and right in her actions, and she also believed that she had a detailed and complete psychological understanding of herself and others.

As noted, Maryann's belief that she was special and deserving of comfort and support made it possible for her to live with the disability of her illness: This was a sustaining experience for her. Her narcissistic, entitled stance warded off the terrible humiliation that would have come with a less denying approach. After all, hadn't God selected her to endure incredible suffering? Most importantly, although she mistrusted others, with the above-outlined view of herself and others to sustain her, Maryann continued to seek human contact as part of her conviction that she was deserving of special attention, a conscious goal dispite her belief that she was so different from other people.

However, Maryann's fantasy life and sustaining experiences included more work-oriented elements. If she won the lottery, she said, she would want to buy the kind of expensive computer equipment that would enable her to have her own business. (Of course, the idea of the lottery posed ticklish problems for Maryann. If, indeed, she was chosen above others for special attention from God, why resort to a lottery at all? Wouldn't there be divine intervention? Maryann struggled with this problem, and each time she lost, announced that it was one more test for her. On another level, Maryann was testing the therapist's sensitivity and timing, waiting for him to challenge her with "If you're so special, how come you lost?") Other, overtly hostile fantasies of wishing to kill her grandfather, which had been present as obsessional thoughts though never acted upon when she was in the hospital, suggested that Maryann continued to have sadistic fantasies along with the ones she was willing to share.

Under the heading of psychological continuity, clarity, and what have been traditionally called ego strengths, Maryann had been able to get an education and to work intermittently, and she maintained faith in herself despite setbacks, even if at times this confidence showed itself as grandiose delusions. This kind of optimism and grandiosity served as an adaptive response to Maryann's sense of being invaded, controlled, humiliated, and exploited by others.

In terms of other ego functions, Maryann's capacity to maintain her stimulus barrier and self-object differentiation was fragile. She was very sensitive to other people, watching them carefully and trying to analyze what they were thinking of her. But she always found them disappointing and her interactions frustrating, while others felt she was excessively demanding. She had to use contempt for others and an inflated view of herself to support self-object differentiation—that is, she could see her identity as separate from others by seeing herself as special.

Concerns. A major implication of the manifest communications, forms of idiosyncratic relatedness, and quality of subjective experience outlined for Maryann was that control was a major theme or preoccupation for her. She carefully hid her fear that others were going to manipulate her and sustained her fragile autonomy through arrogance and contempt.

She was better able to tolerate contact with others than many persons with such severe illnesses and actually sought some contact, although, of course, she readily became suspicious and felt that others expected too much of her or wanted her to grovel in return for their attention. Her conception of her own and others' limitations was minimal, and in this context, she experienced little conscious conflict about her manner of adapting to her illness, since it was essential for her to believe that she was capable and in control and that she had made the best choices possible. (In fact, the choices had been made for her.) Actually, for her even to consider this question of limitations was impossible, since she experienced herself as fighting for her life, using her beliefs in the only way she knew. Any alternative viewpoint threatened to destroy her entire system of adaptation. Thus, her major priority, that which took up the bulk of her attention and energy, was her denial of her illness. The only evidence of any benign conflict about this priority was the fact that, rather than completely refusing treatment as might be consistent with her stated views, Maryann did allow herself to see a therapist and to attend a day program and live at a halfway house, and she was very responsible about taking her medication.

The Therapeutic Alliance

All of these hypotheses about Maryann's experience informed the therapist in considering how Maryann would feel about being in therapy and how best to form an alliance with her. The therapist saw Maryann as a frightened person longing for contact but fearing it, while fighting to contain intense drives and fantasies that threatened to overwhelm her. But for Maryann herself, a traditional view of psychotherapy was nearly impossible. To be understood by a therapist was tantamount to inviting invasion and manipulative control. It meant admitting she really needed another human being, who would only disappoint, frustrate, and hurt her. It meant acknowledging that she was not fully in control of her own life and that she was ill. To her, this implied that she was weak, that she was not special in the ways she believed, that she needed help in managing her life and understanding herself. It meant allowing the possibility that she was not always correct in her perceptions and choices. Despite her wishes for friends, Maryann often felt that it was preferable to be omnipotent and lonely than to be painfully involved with people.

As noted above, Maryann's preferred mode of relating was to seek contact while maintaining control by arming herself against rebuff with contempt and devaluation. People who treated her as special and who could tolerate her passive-aggressive behaviors were the most likely to remain in touch with her, and sometimes her clinging behavior evoked impulses in others to take care of her in this way. Still, she was bound to feel alienated and paranoid in therapy.

How to offer psychotherapy to such an individual? The therapist's goal was to help Maryann become more flexible in her understanding of herself and others through a stronger sense of her identity and her self-other boundaries. He hoped that greater understanding of the internal pressures that drove her would enable Maryann to feel greater confidence in her ability to control herself so that she could make more adaptive, less self-destructive choices.

In order to offer therapy to Maryann in a way that she could tolerate, the therapist considered Maryann's priorities and sustaining experiences as described above, with their associated demands on him and the rest of the environment. He realized that Maryann was able to manage to be in therapy by viewing it as something imposed from the outside: It had been recommended by the hospital staff, and some kind of therapy was required by her halfway house. The therapist had to be willing to accept temporarily a role that allowed Maryann to maintain her denial of illness while she attended therapy appointments. She often told the therapist that as soon as she was on her own, she would "drop" him. She allowed him in her life as a friendly audience to her discussions of her daily experiences and her complaints, her hopes and dreams and her understanding of herself and others. He could also be used, in her mind, to bear witness to her specialness and suffering.

From this perspective, it was not necessary to challenge Maryann's rationale for being in therapy as long as she continued to attend sessions. The therapist could accept that for some time, his role was to be a somewhat devalued audience who was to step in to do the "dirty work" when necessary. Maryann was willing to have a therapist if it meant that there was someone else to take her part or try to explain her troublesome behaviors when she episodically alienated the staff at the day hospital or halfway house. In "allowing" him to "front" for her, she had found a way to accept help without losing face. The therapist also seemed willing to listen to how angry she was and even encouraged her to talk about her sadistic fantasies as long as she made it clear she wouldn't act on them, and sometimes doing this led Maryann to have fewer of her painful ideas of reference. Although she didn't acknowledge this, sometimes she felt the therapy gave her some relief.

In the first part of this book, we articulated the principle of establishing what the patient *can* and *cannot* do *at this time*. Using that principle and incorporating that information into a treatment, the therapist's initial technique was to support the idea that Maryann's inner life was special and private and that she could refuse to share this with the therapist unless it bore on the issue of suicide. He supported the idea that it was normal for Maryann's thoughts and dreams to be sources of pleasure for her (as one of her few sustaining experiences and thus important for the therapist to pay attention to) and that it was immaterial if the pleasurable thoughts were delusional, unless the thoughts caused her to act in ways that caused trouble in her life. Even then, the therapist was sensitive to preserving her narcissism, referring to such episodes as ones in which "there would be a serious difference of opinion between you and others, who, because of their way of understanding things, could end up causing you grief." He thus sought to regularly reinforce the distinction between inner and outer reality, between thought and action.

The therapist knew that Maryann's picture of herself as especially good and talented and able to understand herself and others was crucial to maintaining an otherwise very fragile sense of self-esteem and safety. At the same time, she felt very sensitive and experienced what others would see as ordinary demands of life as hugely burdensome expectations. While it was important to her to believe in her capacity to have close, warm relationships, she felt painfully dependent on authority figures and regularly imagined that they intended to humiliate or exploit her. Thus, the therapist tolerated her devaluation of him and of the therapy, as long as certain other conditions were met, since this devaluation defended her against her terrible fear of needing him. He insisted that she keep him fully informed about her suicidal thoughts and feelings, and she had always agreed to this and understood that otherwise he couldn't be her therapist.

The therapist also monitored his countertransference constantly. Sometimes, he felt the need to retaliate against Maryann's contempt and dismissal of him—retaliation that usually took the form of a wish to ruthlessly expose the depth of Maryann's (denied) need for him. Then he would realize that implicit in Maryann's expressed devaluation were other feelings that were hard for the therapist to tolerate at the time, such as her sense of despair and longing for him.

Thus, the therapist accepted Maryann's verbal denial and minimization of her illness as long as she indicated otherwise by her behavior, attending day hospital programs and psychotherapy sessions and agreeing to live in a supervised residence. To some extent, he accepted her paranoid transference, challenging it only when it intruded into the basic arrangements of the therapy—that is, the agreement that Maryann would be honest about suicidal feelings and other potentially dangerous impulses. He was aware that Maryann experienced change as a total revolution in her sense of identity, which would leave her feeling more empty, lonely, and insecure. Maryann's delusions were precious to her because they meant that she was special. To admit that they were only the symptoms of an illness would mean viewing herself as a person who had not accomplished much in conventional terms, although her accomplishment in living with an illness as severe as hers was considerable. Any revision in the perspective brought to these beliefs had to be undertaken slowly and respectfully because of this implication. Furthermore, Maryann's delusions were old, familiar parts of her personality by now (2). She needed to have attractive, alternative views of herself, and transformed views of her symptoms to allow her to keep her self-esteem in place before she could surrender any of her delusions and grandiose thoughts. For example, she needed to transform her delusions of grandeur into pleasant daydreams that were understandable and justifiable given her difficult life.

Maryann's habit of occasionally missing appointments was understood by the therapist in terms of her difficulty in accepting therapy. Her missing appointments was one of her mechanisms for maintaining a sense of herself as spearate from the therapist, reminding herself that she was in control and that she did not need him so much. The missed sessions were discussed in these terms, the therapist empathizing with Maryann's experience of the sessions as quite tiring at times while reiterating his need to know that she was not missing an appointment because of suicidal plans or feelings. Maryann usually noted when she called to cancel that she was "doing ok" but just didn't feel like coming to the appointment.

Maryann was terrified to say how little she trusted and how much she feared the therapist, often preferring to stay away. This was part of her devaluing and paranoid attitude toward the therapist. It was very important for her that the therapist have no reason to think that he was important to her. She saw him because she "had" to, and on a nice day, it was pleasant to walk to his office and tell him about her dreams and thoughts and the events of the day and how terrible her life was, always with the assurance that she could stop telling him something at any time. Within that context of idiosyncratic relatedness, Maryann was actually doing a great deal of therapeutic work towards shoring up her self-boundaries and understanding more about her paranoid delusions and how they arose in everyday life, despite her claim that she already understood everything about herself.

Delusional Systems

The problem of understanding the meaning of religion to Maryann is an example of the way in which the therapist was always trying to balance the need to be aware of the extent of Maryann's pathology and its impact on her functioning with the adaptive value of many of Maryann's behaviors and beliefs, even though these might seem pathological to an observer. This perspective on the patient's behaviors was crucial to understanding her attempts to function while maintaining some level of self-esteem and freedom from pain. As we noted in chapter 1, understanding the adaptive attempts in symptoms, or apparent symptoms, can lead to ways to deepen the therapeutic alliance.

Maryann's delusions about the devil seemed to have faded with the remission of her acute phase of illness. She gradually developed a set of beliefs focused on her religious position as a "born again" Christian. Most of her beliefs and practices were those of others in such sects. She watched Christian TV programs, listened to the speakers give advice about how to understand suffering, and felt that God had forgiven her for her sins.

At times, however, Maryann would make comments that implied a certain level of magical if not delusional thinking in the context of her religious beliefs. Further inquiry confirmed the impression that Maryann continued to have, or perhaps had redeveloped, religious delusions, although she limited discussion of these to the therapy. The therapist's first reaction was uneasiness and anxiety about the fact that Maryann was so clearly still psychotic, and he found himself toying with the idea of trying to find a reason that would seem plausible to Maryann to raise her medication; certainly the idea of increasing medication to suppress what to her were important religious beliefs would not appear to her a helpful step. He then began to try to assess whether Maryann's functioning was deteriorating in any way that would suggest that the religious delusions were but one sign of increasing illness. Eventually, he began to see that in telling him more about her religious ideas, Maryann was indicating greater trust in and closeness to him. When he expressed interest in her thoughts, with less anxiety about the morbidity implied by the symptoms she was revealing, Maryann also began to mention her own concern that she keep her religious feelings and beliefs in balance in her life—because she recalled the terrifying religious delusions and hallucinations that had tormented her in acute phases of her illness. She distinguished these from her beliefs in her specialness and in God's forgiveness and special plans for her. Thus, by not insisting on his priorities in this area, by appreciating the sustaining function of these ideas to Maryann, the therapist helped her to arrive at greater clarity about her inner versus outer experiences.

In the best circumstances, Maryann was able to discuss openly her difficulty talking about her religious feelings with the therapist, and this became a way to discuss more general psychological and transference issues:

M: You know, basically I'm worried that all this psychological stuff is really in conflict with my belief in God, so I don't like to tell you about it.

T: Do you wonder what I'm thinking, or how I'll react maybe?

M: Well, I assume you think I'm just crazy, or just wrong.

T: It sounds like you're thinking I would criticize you for beliefs which are very important for you, as if I couldn't accept you as a person any more.

M: Maybe that's because I don't really accept you as a person or see you as human at all—it's very hard for me, I usually just see you as a professional, as if you're not a member of the human race.

At the point Maryann and her therapist had reached when the issue of rehospitalization arose again, Maryann's relationship with her therapist could be described as one of denied dependence and conscious suspiciousness, which she generally chose to conceal from the therapist. The therapist repeatedly tried to enable Maryann to discuss her paranoid reactions to him and the circumstances under which they arose or were exacerbated, and she had gained some insight into the fact that her anger at being ill for so long and the idea that she needed the therapist contributed to her paranoid thoughts. Another major theme of the work was the slow transformation of what had been terrifying but magical delusions into pleasurable thoughts and fantasies Maryann felt to be under her control. She began to see that her inner life could add to the richness of her experience of life and that confronting this life would not necessarily make her need hospitalization. Nonetheless, there was a sense of loss as she came to see certain grandiose beliefs as delusions that had interfered with her life in the past. It should be stressed that this process occurred in a gradual and subtle way as the therapist simply encouraged Maryann to talk about what it had felt like, for example, to believe she was possessed by and then in a battle with the devil.

Note the progression: In the most primitive and regressed form, the devil had inhabited Maryann, directing her. Her ego-boundary porosity was metaphorically expressed through this image of being taken over. At a later point, Maryann, with clearer self-object differentiation, was in a struggle with an outside force—the devil outside. Both were delusions, yet the latter spoke to a higher level of ego integration and self-object differentiation.

The therapist did not suggest that Maryann's beliefs were delusional or confront her with reality or try to educate her about reality as long as her beliefs were not interfering with her responsibilities. When her narcissism got her into trouble, because others found her "lazy," he empathized with how hard it was to feel so unable to work and yet have to meet the demands of the rehabilitation program. Maryann would then decide on her own to make a greater effort. "Confronting" Maryann's narcissism as immature or unrealistic would have been dealing Maryann another narcissistic blow at a time in her life when she did not feel capable of tolerating any further blows at all.

Crisis and Rehospitalization

The therapist viewed the incident outlined at the beginning of this chapter as a crisis because the issue of rehospitalization was so sensitive for Maryann at a narcissistic level. The most conservative move, to immediately rehospitalize Maryann when she began to talk at all about suicide, was obvious and safe from many perspectives. However, frequent hospital stays, even if safe in the short run, threatened to add to her depression and demoralization in the long run. If she could manage a severe depressive episode without going into a hospital, this would enhance her confidence in herself (and in her therapist and other staff with whom she worked). Of course, the risk of repercussions in asking too much of Maryann at this point was considerable, and asking Maryann directly about her tolerance level in any area of functioning threatened her fragile self-esteem.

How, then, to understand what the patient was feeling and telling the therapist in the material presented at the beginning of the chapter? Her message that the therapist "could" call her was as direct a request for contact as she could muster, suggesting either than she was not desperate but would like to talk or that she was in distress but was feeling unwilling, perhaps due to paranoid fears or embarrassment about her need, to request help more clearly. Her depression and absences due to some minor physical illness were recurring events at this time; the absences became more frequent.

The most disturbing piece of data was Maryann's statement that she had been upset by the movie about a romantic involvement between a patient and therapist. The therapist knew that Maryann was sufficiently aware of his interest in her dreams and fantasies to know that this comment about her distress was an important message to him. Maryann's idea about her distress—that it was because in this movie the doctor stops being a doctor because of his infatuation with a patient—suggested that she was feeling that he could be unreliable—and needy like her. More ominously, it suggested that she thought he could be psychotic. Since the major plot of the movie, though not mentioned by Maryann, dealt with a therapist who fell in love with a patient and then devoted his life to her in a very overinvolved way, the idea that Maryann was developing a delusional erotic transference came readily to mind. That is, Maryann might have been imagining things about the therapeutic relationship that were making it very hard for her to be honest, since she might be imagining that the therapist was not only untrustworthy but also in love with her. This would imply that he was having problems maintaining boundaries and was psychotic and in need of help himself, which perhaps he was going to demand from her. Coupled with Maryann's conscious complaint that she felt alienated, these issues suggested that she was in more trouble than she was letting on but also that she felt that to ask for help was dangerous.

Hence the therapist's offer of an earlier session the following day, which constituted a response to the covert urgency in Maryann's message, while avoiding her usual complaint that she didn't feel like coming to therapy after a long day at the day program. The therapist offered, rather than waiting for Maryann to ask, because he knew that she needed to see herself as strong—not as the sort of person who would ever ask for an extra session from her devalued therapist, whose role was to beg to take care of her. Since she generally expected him to make the overtures in her treatment, it did not seem that this action would appear excessively seductive or make the situation worse. From a different perspective, it might have been that, through the movie reference, Maryann was indicating that she was coming to see something about the therapist's vulnerability and humanness. In this context, Maryann's former adaptation failed, leaving her momentarily at greater risk, much as a hermit crab is more vulnerable during the transition from one shell to another. In this light, Maryann's crisis was less a relapse-under-pressure than a crisis of development—a kind of growing pain.

The psychotherapy session the following day summarized the therapist's dilemma. It was important for Maryann to minimize her dependency needs in order to continue to feel good about herself and to avoid feeling humiliated, discouraged, and suicidal. It was important for her to know that she did not have to tell her therapist every detail of her precious inner life and risk the feeling that he was intruding and taking over her identity. The therapist knew that she could keep the severity of her suicidal impulses secret from him. However, if he took the most conservative position and insisted on hospitalizing her against her protestations, and if he did so in error about the seriousness of her self-destructive tendencies, damage would have been done to Maryann's fragile sense of autonomy. She may have felt that the therapist was more concerned with controlling her than with fostering her ability to manage

290 Working with the Person with Schizophrenia

her own life, despite his previous efforts to maximize her autonomy. Her view of him as a unique person with whom she had a useful relationship could have collapsed. She could have discounted him as an ally in her struggles, becoming even more paranoid and less likely to be honest in the future about her suicidal thoughts.

In the material that led to the question about whether or not Maryann should go into a hospital, Maryann had introduced a new religious theme, that of judgment day—although if this represented a change from her usual religious concerns it was a subtle one. Despite her denial of any suicide plan or death wish in connection with this, knowing that she often used her religious beliefs to guide her daily life and reassure herself, the therapist again felt worried. This is an example of how therapists become the repository for the histories that they and their patients share and of how therapists must use this history when their patients' ability to do so is in question.

To recapitulate, at this point the therapist had the following evidence regarding the degree of Maryann's suicide risk:

1. She was in somewhat more distress than usual, as indicated by her missing more sessions and asking (indirectly) that he call her.

2. Her usual complaints of feeling alienated and unsupported and her annoyance at the therapist were more in evidence.

3. Her religious concerns were taking a direction that suggested increased concern with death: the day of judgment.

4. When asked in a detailed way about the level of her suicide intent, Maryann denied a plan and stated that she felt in control of these thoughts, which were similar to those she had experienced intermittently for years. She appeared to be able to participate seriously in the therapist's inquiry into her suicidal risk.

5. Her history also included a serious suicide attempt while in the hospital at a time when she was denying that she had a plan to hurt herself.

6. There was reason to think that Maryann's experience of the therapist was more severely distorted than usual and that, in particular, she may have been having severe paranoid delusions about him. She thus may have felt more mistrustful than usual or even that she had to act a certain way to prevent him from becoming psychotic. This hypothesis, if true, meant that all of Maryann's statements to the therapist had to be seen to be affected by her current beliefs about the therapist, which may

have included the belief that she could not trust him and had to protect him, perhaps by hiding her self-destructive tendencies from him out of fear of his possible reaction.

At this point, while there was evidence for concern and continued monitoring, the indications for hospitalization were not definite, especially given the risks for the patient's long-term prognosis that could result from an unnecessary hospitalization.

With some patients, it would be enough at this point for therapists to request a commitment that their patients ask for help from available community staff or the local emergency room if their suicidal impulses mounted and for the therapists to warn day hospital and halfway house staff and enlist their help in continuing to monitor patients' conditions between therapy appointments. Many such programs have ready access to inpatient services and could have hospitalized Maryann if the need arose.

In a similar situation, it is sometimes possible to involve a willing and available family in providing the supervision and constant company that the hospital provides, while the patient continues psychotherapy and the therapist also meets with patient and family to discuss daily management questions. If a family has sufficient resources to provide supervision, daily contacts with the therapist, and some low stress activities, such a plan is often very valuable to both patient and family. The family learns about the patient's illness and strengths and weaknesses and about his or her subjective experiences in a very intense way, which, in turn, can help them manage future crises and make long-term plans for the patient. The patient and family are spared the disruption and probable stigma of a psychiatric hospital stay, and the patient always benefits from the concrete signs of love and support that the family's effort represents, although this may also induce guilt in a depressed patient. However, such an effort is not always within the family's resources of time and money and emotional stamina, and it is not feasible with a patient who may become violently assaultive or suicidal or attempt to run away when acutely psychotic or with one who has physical conditions or a medication regime that requires constant medical monitoring.

It is very important that the clinician be able to accurately assess a family's capacity to participate in such a plan of family supervision and support and its possible ramifications. For example, it is not useful to suggest such an option where the family is already drained from years of trying to manage a disruptive member at home or where overwhelming family guilt and depression will be evoked by the close obeservation of the family member's acute symptoms. It is especially dangerous if the family's motivation is primarly expiation—that is, if they feel in some fundamental way responsible for the illness and therefore must make amends. Such circumstances reinforce the patient's sadism, leading him or her to further regression.

To return to Maryann's situation and the decision to hospitalize her at this point. The option of family supervision was not feasible since Maryann lived at some distance from her parents. She might have been able to make some use of day hospital and halfway house staff, although she tended to remain aloof from the possibility of indicating any need for their support.

The therapist's decision was to see Maryann for another session the next day and to urge hospitalization at that point. He felt that it was too risky to assume that Maryann was able to be entirely honest with him, given his suspicion that she was more paranoid about him than usual. He also was not convinced that Maryann would be able to face what she viewed as the humiliation of asking halfway house staff for emergency help if she became overwhelmed with suicidal feelings; he thought it more likely she would first engage in some kind of self-destructive act and then inform staff, at which point little discussion (and therefore little humiliation) would be required. He also knew that staff usually felt that Maryann needed hospitalization at times when her functioning had overtly deteriorated more and that at present, since there was little change, they might have felt that he was overreacting.

Somewhat to his surprise, Maryann rather quickly agreed to go into the hospital and used his telephone to make her arrangements. During the rest of that session, she openly expressed, with a sense of relief, her fears about the therapist changing and the fact that she had begun thinking about local buildings from which she might jump. She was able to reveal these critical developments to her therapist only after she knew that she was going into the hospital, only when she felt safe with his understanding of how he was seeing her at this time, only when she knew that he was still capable of protecting both of them from the potentially disruptive consequences of her paranoia.

Impact of the Hospital on Outpatient Treatment

It is not only the patient who may view rehospitalization as indicating failure. The therapist must contend with the conventional view that she or he has "failed" to keep the patient out of the hospital and often also struggles with countertransference feelings around this issue. The therapist can anticipate an interruption in the therapeutic alliance and the continuity of the work even if contact with the hospitalized patient is carefully maintained.

Furthermore, in many hospital settings, the assumption of hospital staff is the conventional one: that the outpatient therapist has failed and is somehow incompetent and that what is needed is new medication, a new type of therapy, a new therapist. The patient's wish to avoid all consideration of his or her contribution to the rehospitalization and the mixed feelings about the therapist who could not effect magical cure but who had the sense to put the patient in a safe place are reinforced by any tendency the hospital staff has to see the hospital as good and the outpatient therapist as bad. This support for the patient's tendency to categorize people as either all good or all bad is particularly likely to occur in teaching hospitals, where the trainee staff are relatively inexperienced in dealing with the myriad emotional complexities of such a situation and may need to defend against feelings of intimidation by criticizing the outsider. In the worst scenario, the outpatient therapist is dismissed from the minds of inpatient staff as if no longer of any significance in a form of devaluation and denial that parallels the patient's fantasy of forgetting about all ambivalent feelings and starting fresh in a newer and more perfect world—to be "born again," in Maryann's terms.

The therapist's rationale for hospitalizing Maryann was that she needed to be able to talk more about emerging paranoid fears of him, lest the treatment founder and lest she enact some related fantasy that might involve trying to kill herself. Since, despite their joint efforts, she was not able to sustain such discussions in their outpatient sessions (except to tell him indirectly, by reference to the movie, that she thought he was crazy), he decided to guarantee safety and reduce stress with the possibility of talking to other people about her feelings for him.

In his contacts with Maryann and hospital staff after admission, the therapist suggested to Maryann that it was natural that she feel more comfortable with her hospital therapist, who was not associated in her mind with the difficulties of her daily life in the community as he was. He recommended that Maryann's hospital doctor encourage her to talk about her feelings about his decision to hospitalize her, her disappointments and dissatisfaction and mistrust of him, and how she felt about the prospect of returning to treatment with him. In this case, the trainee assigned to Maryann was not threatened or rendered defensive by the need to perform this role with a patient hospitalized by a senior clinician, and the hospitalization went well once this focus was established. Maryann reflected on some concrete alternatives developing in her day hospital and halfway house treatment and met with her outpatient therapist several times before discharge, during which meetings the therapist was able to satisfy himself that she had a less distorted view of him and would be able to sustain her involvement in therapy. Considering how essential the appearance of autonomy was for this patient, it is safe to assume that the therapist's willingness and even support for Maryann's seeing someone else were reassuring to that part of her that felt in danger of being invaded.

THE PSYCHOTHERAPIST, REHABILITATION, AND COMMUNITY AGENCIES

Individuals who suffer from schizophrenia and who are fortunate enough to be able to live in the community very often need extensive and enduring community services. Living in a halfway house or other community residence and attending a day hospital may be part of a plan for rehabilitation endorsed by clinicians. How individual therapists deal with this community system and the staff members who see much more of the patient, albeit in a very different setting than a therapy session, has a major impact on how patients will fare in community living. Some therapists have traditionally avoided contact with outside agencies, fearing this would "contaminate" the treatment.

Rehabilitation facilities are not designed primarily to address the subjective experience of individuals with schizophrenia. Where appropriate, a plan for outpatient care will allow patients to have psychotherapists with whom they can discuss their subjective feelings, their inner reality, while the other parts of their treatment will focus on how they manage external reality. The residence or day program represents the demands of conventional reality, although somewhat modulated. These programs provide a bridge to the demands of an ordinary job or living situation. The psychotherapy goal is to enable patients to develop their own abilities to cope with unusual internal states that stem from psychological conflicts and deficits. The combined focus on external and internal realities, in our view, results in more stable improvements in functioning in community life than either approach taken separately.

While the individual may at times prefer the atmosphere of therapy because of the careful, intense attention that can be paid to his or her every nuance of feeling, it is important that the therapist implicitly or explicitly support the importance of learning to manage everyday life with its myriad disappointments, as in the following example:

> One woman, a college graduate but ill and marginally functional for many years, claimed that the program staff spoke to her and generally treated her as if she were a "brain-damaged moron." Her therapist, who had been present with her at staff conferences where this was evident, agreed with her perception but suggested that there were reasons he could think of for staff doing this. He empathized with her rage and hurt, but further implied that even if it wasn't fair for staff to behave in this way, she needed to find a way to deal with them since they were an important part of her life. She could, for example, demonstrate her competence. As patient and therapist discussed ways to do this, the patient became frightened. Eventually she was able to see her own role in her interactions with staff—her fear of appearing effective and, therefore, in her mind, of being abandoned. Once again, the principle that guided the therapist's stance was to appreciate the patient's experience and to recognize the limits she placed on herself, while trusting that eventually the patient would transcend her defensiveness. Thus, the initial formulation, "They are at fault," gradually shifted to "I have a part in this."

Often it will seem to the patient and sometimes to the therapist that rehabilitation staff are insufficiently "understanding" of the patient's limitations. However, the patient must learn to deal with people who are not "understanding"—who are simply concerned with getting a job done or maintaining public order. The schizophrenic individual may need the psychotherapist's help to understand the impact he or she has on others and to take responsibility for this. For instance:

One man came to therapy bitterly complaining about having been kept back from a scheduled job interview by the intervention of day program staff. Further exploration of the situation revealed that he had appeared at the day program before the interview in disheveled clothes and unshaven. The staff had served a protective function by making him cancel his appointment. In the therapy, discussion focused on why he had needed to set up this situation and end up angry at staff, rather than feeling able to directly state his fear that he was not ready to go to work part time. In this case, the therapist's attention to the experience of the patient in feeling angry and in creating the situation that led to his anger led to an important piece of information about functioning, which the patient was urged to share with his program.

At other times, the schizophrenic individual is unable to make his position clear to the staff. The therapist may then need to serve as ombudsman, clarifying to the community service organization how, from the patient's perspective, his or her actions were necessary and even adaptive. The therapist in such situations is in a tricky position, because he or she is vulnerable to countertransference needs to lecture the staff of the treating facility. At the same time, the staff may view the therapist and his or her information with suspicion, concerned lest the patient be "excused" from living in the "real world."

Maryann presented a particular type of problem for the staff members at her halfway house and day hospital program. On the one hand, her long history of illness made it clear that she must be suffering from a severe form of schizophrenia. On the other hand, because of the methods she used to deal with her illness, Maryann's presentation of herself tended to make people forget this.

In her rehabilitation program, Maryann's presentation was that she was very capable and that she had little need for the aspects of the program that stressed interpersonal relationships: how to deal with criticism at work; how to be assertive; how to get along with other clients better. As noted above, to maintain her self-esteem it was necessary for Maryann to believe that she did not have problems in these areas. Instead, she believed that she had problems resulting from the stresses other people created by expecting her to attend the program regularly and to participate in the groups that discussed relationships. Thus, her overt behavior was that of a complainer who could not be bothered to participate on the level requested by the program staff. She seemed to prefer to use the day program as a place to drop in and socialize rather than as a major step in her transition from an inpatient setting to full independence, which was the kind of goal the staff had in mind.

Because Maryann was uncomfortable acknowledging to herself that she became enraged by others' demands, she also behaved provocatively as one way to express her annoyance. She often broke minor rules and would interrupt staff conferences if she felt she needed something. At the same time, she was only marginally adequate in her performance in the work section of the program, although she was very boastful of how hard she worked and how competent she was. These behaviors tended to cause staff to think of Maryann as narcissistic and lazy, while, in fact, she was using these behaviors to deny her neediness and her fears of being invaded psychologically. Maryann was actually fairly successful at hiding the degree of her grandiosity, paranoia, ideas of reference, and the like, but the cost was greatly reduced efficiency in carrying out assignments and the tasks of daily life. By not revealing her internally experienced symptoms and limiting her behavioral ones to lessened productivity and interpersonal failures, she supported her self-esteem but failed to keep staff informed of how many psychiatric symptoms she still had.

While it was often possible for the staff to see Maryann's overt obnoxiousness as part of her illness, at times her entitled attitude and arrogant behavior led professionals to perceive her in terms of a common misconception about persons with schizophrenia. That is, they forgot how fragile Maryann was and how her behaviors stemmed from needs to protect herself from the ravages of her illness; they saw her as not very sick but lazy instead. This led to periodic difficulties and requests for consultation from the therapist.

Knowing how best to respond to such requests depends on a complex understanding of the situation. In Maryann's case, it was not enough to simply remind the staff of her fragility; it was also important for them to feel that the therapist appreciated the predictable frustration they experienced in working with Maryann. In addition, patients may arrange to have rehabilitation staff contact their therapists in order to communicate something to them that patients cannot express directly. For example, a patient may act out sexually in a day program at a time when she wants to talk about sexual impulses with the therapist but cannot begin to do so. Likewise, while a patient is verbally reporting no problem carrying out work assignments, he may want to let the therapist know that he is having difficulty, although he cannot bring this up directly in sessions. In Maryann's case, sometimes she needed to be reminded of the therapist's concern for her and willingness to "take care" of her in some way, as in his "going out of his way" to talk to halfway house staff. As should be clear from our discussion, we view this kind of contact in this kind of case as a necessary part of the psychotherapy.

Agency staff also may not have a clear idea of what the therapist's goal is with a schizophrenic client, or may have fantasies about what goes on in therapy that will make them more or less able to collaborate with the individual therapist in the treatment. The idea that therapy is a luxury where the patient is encouraged to wallow in fantasy material, while the rehabilitation staff have to manage the client's daily problem behaviors and reluctance to work, interferes with optimal collaboration among professionals working with the schizophrenic individual. Indeed, at worst, the staff may tend to view the therapist as encouraging the patient's regression at their expense. "He gets the glory while we have to clean up the mess" is a common attitude of program staff regarding psychotherapists.

In the case under discussion in this chapter, the therapist had goals interrelated with those of the day program and residence. One goal of psychotherapy was that Maryann would become more able to rely on her capacity to separate inner from outer reality and would thereby be able to use available help more constructively and less defensively as she felt less threatened and intruded upon by others. Another goal was to foster Maryann's autonomy as much as possible, so that eventually she could manage her life with fewer outside interventions. Therefore, the therapist tried to let Maryann manage her external life as much as it seemed safe to rely on her judgment or when it was clear that she was able to get good advice from others, such as program staff. Therapy sessions often focused on how Maryann could understand and deal with the paranoid projection of her anger or the fear of psychological invasion that prevented her from making good use of the help offered by program staff. The existence of these programs, in fact, was what made outpatient psychotherapy possible for an individual like Maryann. If Maryann was in a network of programs that could help her manage her external life, the psychotherapy could be used to help her with her internal, emotional life, so that over time she would have more psychological resources and could take over more of the day to day management of her own life. Maryann also needed opportunities to be with other people and to learn more about getting along with them, despite her assertions to the contrary, and she needed the vocational rehabilitation aspect of the work so she could be productive again.

The therapist tried to let Maryann manage her interactions with the program staff without his intervention as much as possible. In fact, consistent with her use of the therapy, Maryann often idealized the program staff and devalued the therapist since he rarely gave advice or assisted with concrete problems in her life, as other staff did. When problems arose at the residence or day program, however, Maryann sometimes needed the therapist's intervention, although she feared feeling dependent on him. She was afraid, for example, that he would exact humiliating expressions of gratitude from her as payment.

In such cases, the therapist would meet with the program staff or consult by telephone. He would also try to minimize the way in which this kind of intervention cast him as an authority figure by discussing with Maryann ahead of time what she would like him to do or say. At this stage of the treatment, Maryann was usually reluctant to involve herself very far in such discussions and preferred to have the therapist take responsibility. Therefore, they would work out some specific things for him to say and then agree that he would use his best judgment about further matters that might arise. Maryann was not able to tolerate being present at all such joint discussions, since the necessary mention of the severity of her symptoms humiliated her. The net effect of his intervention in these situations was to gratify some of Maryann's dependency needs without making a point of doing so and, usually, to smooth the way for better relations between Maryann and the treatment staff. While reminding staff of how ill Maryann was, the therapist also reminded staff of his awareness of how frustrating and irritating Maryann could be and, further, noted for them the psychological functions this behavior served for Maryann. In reporting to Maryann a summary of the contact, he would also remind her of the need to learn to follow rules in life, even if they seemed unfair or silly, simply as a matter of self-protection, of avoiding trouble.

In hospitalizing Maryann, the therapist encouraged her to make her own arrangements as far as possible, but he also informed the residence and day hospital staff of his decision and reasoning. He urged her to maintain contact with them during her hospital stay and to be responsible about arranging her return to these programs and made sure the inpatient hospital staff knew whom to contact at the agencies.

SUMMARY

We have seen in this chapter how the principles we have outlined can inform outpatient treatment involving community agencies and the issue of rehospitalizations for a chronically suicidal patient. Maryann presented arrogant behaviors and entitled attitudes that served to obscure her dependency needs. A grandiose view of herself as having a special relationship with God represented the sustaining experience upon which her self-esteem rested. Similarly, her paranoid and contemptuous stance toward important people in her life, a form of idiosyncratic relatedness, revealed that control and autonomy were major preoccupations. These led her to the central priority of minimizing her illness.

In order to form a treatment partnership with Maryann, her therapist had to utilize this information about her to decide in what role he could offer himself to her in terms of his hypotheses about what she could and could not do at this time. The solution was to allow her to devalue the therapy and be secretive and paranoid as long as she maintained a basic contract to be honest about suicidal impulses and responsible about sessions, the day program, and medication. The therapist's interactions with the community agencies were dictated by his understanding of Maryann's subjective experience, and rehospitalization was indicated when the therapist came to believe that Maryann was temporarily unable to carry out the contract upon which the partnership was based and was therefore at risk for suicide despite her denials.

7

The Case of Roger: Outpatient Psychotherapy—From Apathy to Community Involvement

In work with inaccessible patients, there are times when it is necessary to relinquish one or more elements of the usual psychiatric stance in the service of establishing an ambience of trust and curiosity and thereby gaining entry into the patient's inner world. In this case history, it quickly became clear to the therapist that the patient, having accumulated over twenty years of experience with mental health professionals, was impatient with and intolerant of the customary methods of clinical inquiry. He presented with a diagnosis of schizoaffective disorder with prominent negative symptoms, including profound apathy and indifference to any of his former interests and a thoroughgoing aversion to clinical interventions oriented toward improvement. The therapist put aside her commitment to significant elements of the usual clinical posture in the hopes of finding a residue of aliveness in this man, who appeared to have abandoned his belief in the possibility of meaningful recovery.

For patients who have not improved with standard treatment, this story illustrates the importance of identifying a path that these patients are willing to follow, even when, for as long as two years in this case, there is little reason—other than a tenacious belief in the unconfirmed possibility of an eventual benevolent outcome—to continue the work of psychotherapy. The story also indicates the importance of respecting the patient's priorities—in this case, the patient's need to preserve some semblance of dignity by supporting a personal system of beliefs that, although delusional by all ordinary standards, had the effect of keeping alive a *raison d'être* when all the usual sources of meaning had long since dried up.

It may also be useful to note that the writing of this story has been taken up somewhat in the manner of an experiment. The majority of the account, up to "Learning to Use the New Paradigm," was written during the thirtieth month of the work. The remainder of the story was written nine months later and therefore constitutes a follow-up. Thus, the validity of themes first identified in the third year of the work, which have to do with a reformulation of the phasic nature of the illness, can be checked against subsequent events.

BEGINNINGS OF THE WORK

The First Encounter

The circumstances of the therapist's first encounter with Roger may be significant in the evolution of subsequent events. During the summer of 1984, at the suggestion of friends who had found some value in consulting with the therapist about their mentally ill daughter, Roger's parents consulted regarding his status then. He had been readmitted for a seventh psychiatric hospital stay some two months earlier. At first responsive to care in a short-term unit, he was subsequently transferred to an intermediate-stay unit, where the staff soon came to the conclusion that his interests would be best served if he left the confines of the parental home, taking up residence in a psychiatric halfway house. The parents were told of this conclusion and, with some difficulty, persuaded to support the recommendation. In a subsequent meeting led by the unit social worker involving Roger and his parents, Roger exploded in a fury, directed mostly toward his mother, when both parents appeared to side with the staff on the halfway house issue. Immediately following the meeting, he became suicidally depressed and inaccessible. Shortly, he proclaimed he was interested only in the plan to go to a very long-term hospital in which he would live out the rest of his short life. He avoided all activities. He would not permit visits from the family. He complied with medication, which had been increased following the bitter confrontation, and had, as a result, developed a persistent and very uncomfortable tremor of the Parkinsonian type.

At this point the parents requested a consultation with the therapist in an effort to reassess the current treatment plan. While not a unique occurrence, their son's bitter rejection of them differed in its persistence and intensity and in his simultaneous rejection of both parents. They were alarmed at the development of severe suicidal thinking and Roger's total lack of interest in any plan, even the plan of returning home with them.

At first Roger rejected out of hand the parents' request that he permit a visit from their consultant, and it appeared likely that the therapist's only role would be as a consultant to the family. The possibility of direct therapeutic work with Roger came only later. At this point, the therapist reasoned that Roger most certainly viewed her as an extension of his parents and that Roger was already suffering from a diminished sense of personal control over his circumstances. She thus recommended that the parents accede to Roger's refusal to see the therapist and inform him that the therapist had specifically made that recommendation. If the patient was going to think of the therapist in any way, the therapist wanted to be viewed as someone who took seriously his desires, including his desire not to be intruded on by his parents' agents.

Following a month-long vacation, the therapist learned from the parents that Roger had reconsidered and was now willing to permit the therapist to visit him. The first visit was characterized by two prominent manifestations of his condition. First, he presented with a continuous tremor, so severe that he managed to smoke a cigarette only by bracing the hand holding the cigarette at the wrist with his other hand. Roger offered the observation that the tremor was induced by haloperidol, which by then he was taking in large doses, and the therapist agreed, indicating that the tremor would in all likelihood diminish when the dose was reduced. Second, he appeared to have no interest in anything. It would be more accurate to say that Roger went to some lengths to make sure that the therapist knew that he was in no way interested in activity, in involvement, in return to life in the community and that indeed the only plan for a future that had any salience for him was for him to live out his life at a long-term hospital doing as little as possible.[a] He asked whether the therapist thought a hospital would take him on if he wanted to do so little. The therapist indicated she was pretty sure that most places would want some sort of commitment on his part to a goal of recovery and eventual discharge, suggesting all the same that he could still investigate and perhaps sell the hospital on the idea that he had a unique, special need to be left alone and that the usual expectation of involvement would actually be counterproductive in his case. The therapist also pieced together enough historical information to form the impression, which she shared with him, that his condition appeared to have a fluctuating course and that, although at present he thought of the future only in terms of a long stay in a long-term hospital, the time might come when he would find himself thinking of doing something with his life. At the end of the consultation interview, to the therapist's surprise (she was still grateful that the patient had permitted her to visit on this one occasion), Roger asked if she would be coming back to see him again. He did not seem to be asking the therapist to return, nor was there a hint that he desired to meet with her again. Rather, his manner was more one of seeking disinterestedly to discover whether her role as consultant called for subsequent visits. The therapist indicated that, although she had no plan to do so, it was possible that she might have reason to visit after meeting again with his parents.

In the next consultation with the parents, the therapist recommended that they withdraw their endorsement of the half-way house plan. The recommendation had been introduced by the hospital staff in a manner that completely ignored the patient's preferences in the matter of where he was to live and what he was likely to want to do with and for himself. Moreover, his family's endorsement had left him feeling abandoned by them. This neglect of the patient's priorities is, of course, an all too common aspect of contemporary hospital treatment. It is likely that, on the basis of their observations of Roger's interaction with other people in the unit, together with their correct assessment of the extent of his inability to care for himself in an independent apartment arrangement, the staff recognized that he required a supervised living arrangement as a step in regaining a niche among his peers. However, in the current era of brief hospital treatment, the staff of inpatient units are nearly always confronted with the institutional priority of identifying a disposition that will lead to an early discharge while at the same time meeting accepted standards for decent aftercare planning. In these circumstances—and especially when, as in this case, the patient has little or no interest in developing a plan that can be immediately put into effect—the patient's priorities rarely remain primary. The family is commonly recruited by the staff in an effort to gain the widest possible support for the plan, with the result that the patient's experience is one of being treated like cargo by the staff and being betrayed by the family.

In this meeting, the parents informed the therapist that Roger had shared with them a desire to have her undertake his ongoing care. Apparently, he had discovered, following the therapist's meeting with him, that the Austen Riggs Center, his preferred long-term hospital, did require a higher level of participation than he was prepared to commit to.

Following the decision not to pursue the Riggs option, Roger appeared to become less desperate but not less apathetic. For their part, the parents were quite eager to foster a connection between Roger and the therapist, having decided on the basis of their contact with the therapist and the alleviation of Roger's desperation following the therapist's visit that she was going to be a good influence on their son. So, in response to this request for a visit, mediated to an unknown extent by the parents' own attitudes toward the therapist, she agreed to visit Roger again on the hospital unit, with a view toward determining whether they might work together following his discharge.

The Patient Engages His New Therapist

If the first visit was characterized by suffering and apathy, the second was given more to understanding and optimism. Upon the therapist's arrival on the unit, Roger asked if they could walk outside, explaining without prompting that he had noticed in the past few days that he felt better if he arranged to get off the unit each day. As before, he was still refusing all off-unit activities and his only way of getting off the unit was to go for a walk. He had been able to do this only when staff was available to accompany him, and he appeared to be taking this opportunity to get a walk in on the day of the therapist's visit by asking if the therapist would be that staff person. The therapist agreed, noting silently that the plan to walk in order to feel better stood in some contrast to the global negation of interests in the first visit. Roger then took the therapist on a brisk walk of a large portion of the hospital grounds, during which, from the very beginning of their time together, he poured out his psychiatric history. He did not wait for the therapist to interview him, take a history, or otherwise start up a conversation. He appeared to anticipate that this was where the inquiry was meant to go on that day, since they were considering the possibility of the therapist's taking on his care. He could easily be considered a "veteran" of psychiatric treatment, and his expectation that the therapist would take a history presumably grew from the conduct of other psychiatrists in his own past experience.

The Patient Sets Forth His Paradigm

What was most striking about this historical sojourn was the way in which Roger charted the course of his condition. He noted a fairly predictable pattern of phases, which he had already come to call by name:

- Phase 1, the phase he was currently in, was characterized by a complete absense of vitality, imagination, desire to do anything, or any anticipations of any sort of favorable future thought, action, or event.
- Phase 2 was characterized by the presence of a desire to do things and to get back into life, but with some limitations in terms of being able to do those things.
- Phase 3 was characterized by the best of functioning, representing what he could do when everything was working just right.

The patient allowed that he had been in phase 3 on very few occasions in recent times. He indicated that the transitions between phase 1 and phase 2 that he had observed over the years were always related to one or another external event—something that in his view just happened to him, always from the outside, without any explicit, intentional, proactive contribution on his part. Furthermore, phase 1 was in all respects a state of mind that was highly undesirable, having nothing good about it and representing pure illness, a state in which he waited for that extrinsic something to happen that would transport him into phase 2. He indicated that all the bones of his face, if not his whole body, were shattered in phase 1; he had no spine, and all his features were sunken. Phase 2 was not much better, being characterized only by his desire to live without the capacity to live. By his reckoning, through the years he had spent a maximum of six months continuously in phase 2 before falling again into phase 1, and this was not a sufficiently long time to form the basis of a life that was satisfying enough to sustain him through the much longer phase 1 periods. Phase 3 was the only state in which he had any active interest, and, according to his calculations, he had spent only a few hours in phase 3 in all his life. By implication, then, he had spent very little time living at the level at which, in his view, most people spent most of their lives, and which was the only state that justified being alive. He asserted that, upon entry to the hospital, he had been in phase

2 and that the confrontation over the halfway house plan and the subsequent increase in haloperidol had triggered a switch to phase 1.

Since the therapist knew by this time that some clinicians believed that Roger had a bipolar affective disorder, she wondered aloud with him whether this set of phases might in some way be a manifestation of that condition. With polite annoyance, the patient dismissed this idea out of hand, asserting that this state had nothing to do with mania and emphasizing that it was not depression he felt but a complete and irreversible disintegration of his bones. The bones of his skull were actually shattered. What did that have to do with depression? Furthermore, he rejected out of hand the therapist's next suggestion that they might inquire as to what he had contributed—perhaps without being aware of having done so—or could contribute toward triggering that sought-after transition to phase 2. Insisting that the therapist did not understand his condition (and this insistence had the flavor of his wanting the therapist to get it right) he reiterated the specific events—the breakup of a love relationship, being fired from a job—that had, in his view, incontestably triggered transitions from phase 1 to phase 2.

It seemed clear that in order to create a bridge to her new patient, the therapist would have to relinquish certain procedures commonly employed in her work with patients, including psychiatric diagnostic inquiries, discussions about the stress-diathesis model regarding the timing of changes in mental state, and questions and interpretation in the conduct of the interview. She sat on a bench in the hospital's formal gardens, shivering in the early autumn twilight, while Roger paced back and forth, smoking one cigarette after another, recounting the events of his ten-year experience with illness and institutions, detailing especially the external events that were known to produce a transition to phase 2. The therapist acknowledged that his was a very complicated condition and that she could only assure her new patient of her commitment to understanding the patient's experience of the condition as best she could and that no guarantees beyond that assurance could be made. On this basis, after another two weeks of hospital care, the twice-weekly office work began.

THE INTERIM PERIOD

The bulk of the next twenty-seven months consisted of preliminaries, a period that has been called "the long gray middle" (1) of psychotherapy with patients who have schizophrenia. We will chronicle this period to give some flavor of the interval and to build a basis for references that will be made during the period of reformulation to be described in the following section.

Failure and Apathy

The therapist's last encounter with Roger before discharge served to underscore the significance of personal failure in Roger's inner life. The therapist came to see him for the third time, fresh from having read Zelin et al.'s paper on sustaining fantasies (2). Unlike his behavior the second contact, Roger was very flat, lacking in spontaneity, although not avoidant in his presentation. Intrigued by the importance of the idea of sustaining fantasies in patients with schizophrenia, the therapist asked him how he managed to cope with the difficulties of being ill. The patient looked at her blankly for a moment and then smiled his first smile, at which the therapist immediately declared her curiosity as to the inner workings behind such an unexpected turn of affect. The patient explained freely that he had just had a thought, in response to the therapist's question, of the downfall of his best friend, a man with whom he had spent many years, the two of them often being down and out together. Recently this man's life had taken a turn for the better: He was working. Roger was quick to point out that the job was in a family business and that his friend was pulling down a paycheck while doing nothing, so this job didn't really count. But his friend had also recently gotten engaged. Roger could still remember times when the friend had lost it all after a period of good luck, and it was this remembrance, together with the anticipation of yet another failure, that had brought him a moment of satisfaction. While this interchange arose from the therapist's interest in the patient's sustaining fantasies, his smile sustained her during the prolonged emotional deadness that dominated the first three months of office work. It is just such small "leaks of aliveness" that the therapist must identify in work with very unresponsive patients.

The evidence of vitality serves to anchor the therapist against the ever-present danger of sliding into deadness with the patient. It also points to the kinds of priorities, the aspects of life that are of interest to the patient, around which the alliance will ultimately be forged.

Session after session, he entered the office, always on time, and just sat, often motionless for several minutes, always staring at the therapist, with no indication of fear and more with a countenance that suggested he was drinking in the therapist or perhaps waiting for her to add something, to say something to get things going. Yet, when the therapist would mutter something or ask after his thoughts, he would, after a long delay[b] respond monosyllabically, only to continue staring emptily. The therapist had the distinct sense that she was alone in her discomfort and that Roger was both comfortable in his remoteness and unobservant of her unrest with it. At no time did the therapist find herself concluding, after due consideration, that the patient was attempting to provoke her distress or taking any pleasure in it. He was quite simply blank: There was nobody home. Reasoning that he might be overmedicated, the therapist lowered and ultimately discontinued thiothixene, which he had been given at discharge from hospital, supplanting this medication with chlorpromazine, at the patient's request, for use at bedtime. Even through his torpor, Roger was quite insistent at this time (and on many subsequent occasions) that he did not require antipsychotic medications because he was not a schizophrenic. He claimed to benefit from chlorpromazine solely for its soporific effects. When this change of medications proved ineffective in alleviating his blankness, the therapist mused with him that he might be actively numbing out, in the manner described by McGlashan in his discussion of aphanisis—that is, he might be seeking to avoid his pain with numbness. (3) The patient brushed this suggestion aside without any apparent feeling.

First Evidence of Aliveness: Working for the CIA

In the third month of office work, Roger opened the next part of the interim period with a most unexpected disclosure, which we will recount as much as possible as a story, rather than as history of illness in the usual clinical sense. This way of reporting the data reflects the ambience in the room: During the entire interim period, the therapist worked hard to retain a state of listening in which she could accept the veracity of her patient's reports and decline the temptation to adopt a diagnostic posture.[c]

Roger disclosed that he had once been recruited by the CIA and that he might still be under their surveillance now or at any time in the future. He was careful to preface this disclosure with the information that he had not shared this secret with other therapists for fear of being discredited. In that moment, the preface was of greater interest than the disclosure. It affirmed that, although he was still presenting himself as having no interest in anything and although he looked psychologically inert, the patient did want something from the therapist. He wanted affirmation, or at least the absence of disaffirmation. He wanted to bring the therapist in on his secret occupation without at the same time triggering a typical clinical response. The therapist was to be his psychiatric lawyer and a partner in the vindication of his pride and dignity. He would reveal the details of his experiences with the CIA, and he would seek affirmation that, far from being schizophrenic, he was indeed an important person, an agent in that most clandestine of security organizations.

The story of the CIA's entry into Roger's life began eighteen months prior to his first encounter with the therapist. Following discharge from another psychiatric hospital, he returned to his apartment in New York City, living alone and eagerly anticipating a period during which he would rebuild his life. He had just been triggered out of phase 1 into phase 2 by the breakup of a love relationship that began in the hospital. After a period of more than eight months in hospital, during which he had fully expected to live in hospitals for the rest of his life, he had begun to feel something for this woman, who was also a patient at the hospital. He was still in phase 1, despite his increasing longing for her, until she left the hospital and then immediately broke off contact with him. At the precise moment of that break, he felt lighter and was thrust into phase 2. Soon he was able and even eager to leave the hospital and to rebuild his life. This apparent paradox—a loss evoking an increase in vitality—suggested to the therapist that anticipation of failure served on some occasions as the trigger for a retreat to complete psychic numbing, a theme that would surface much later when the therapist would prescribe temporary numbing as a method of coping with anticipatory anxiety and ultimately as a means of preventing drastic and prolonged periods of complete inaccessibility.

Now, back in the city and living alone, in the absence of all former psychiatric symptoms, he noted what sounded to him like a beeping noise in or around the apartment. Though he thought nothing of it at first, soon he was drawn to locate the source and found to his dismay that the sound was emanating from the floor of his bathroom and appeared over the course of a few days to move from the floor up into the walls. It quickly became apparent to him that this was the work of the CIA, their way of making contact with him and of inducing him into a role as an informer. He had spent time a year earlier with some "heavy political types" and was now convinced that the CIA had identified him as someone who knew something of importance to the future of the presidency. He knew, without having to think too much about it, that Reagan's presidency was on the line and that he held information that, when revealed, would bring Reagan down. Believing that CIA agents were listening in, he played with them, telling them everything that came to his mind from those former heavy political times. He teased them and ridiculed them for not knowing what he knew. And then he noted that when they were especially pleased with some disclosure, they would crank up the volume of the beeper or turn on a prolonged b-e-e-e-e-p response. The beeper would always respond to a revelation. Soon Roger was transformed, like a rat pressing a lever to get a pleasure jolt, into a person who would tell things he knew just to get a response from the agents.

At some point in this string of conversations, the CIA began to play with Roger, acknowledging him with a beep on some occasions and withholding acknowledgment on others. After the regularity of the earlier conversations, the shift to a more sporadic reply sequence was disconcerting. Roger eventually decided to force the issue by removing the beeper from the wall. He obtained a hammer and proceeded to rip out a large portion of the bathroom wall. To his surprise, he was unable to locate the beeper. This development was so frustrating that it triggered a burst of activity and aggressive behavior that, in short, brought him to the attention of others in the building and led to a series of short hospital stays. Even while he was in the hospital, he received two communications referring to the CIA. On one occasion, another patient rushed up to him in an agitated state and fell to the floor blurting out, "He's protected by the CIA!" On another occasion, a second patient came up to him in the manner of a messenger and said in a low voice, "From now on, you won't hear sounds."

If the first of these communications served to affirm his status vis-à-vis the CIA, the second prepared him for what was to come. Following his discharge and up to the present time, they had not communicated with him again through the use of a beeper or other audible device. Instead, he would only hear clicks in the walls, sounds that to any other observer would seem like the natural noises one hears in an old building, but that to Roger, prepared as he had been by the time in his apartment and by the messenger, were certainly evidence of the ongoing interest of the CIA in him and his information.

Validation of the Patient's Experience

During the period of these conversations with the CIA, Roger heard from friends on two separate occasions. One friend, a woman he had known for some years, heard the sound of the beeper, remarking, "What was that?" The other friend, on hearing it during a phone conversation, asked, "Are you wired?" In both cases, he responded so as to conceal what was happening.

These two reports were critical in the therapist's early relationship with Roger, inasmuch as they suggested a unique if disorienting (for a psychotherapist) perspective. Two friends had given external validation to an experience that otherwise would lead a reasonable listener to conclude that he had been hallucinating. In telling of their validations, he appeared to be trying to establish that he was not hallucinating and seemed intent on gaining an affirmation for this conclusion from the therapist. Appealing to the part of him that was able to muster evidence and specifically to take an evidentiary orientation to an unusual experience, the therapist took the position that, while this was a most implausible occurrence, she was not prepared to dismiss it as hallucinatory since he was reporting that two other individuals had verified the presence of an actual sound.

Decline and Reentry to the Hospital

Eight months after treatment began, the sessions had become virtually dominated by Roger's descriptions of his most recent interactions with the CIA. They were now tampering with the lighting in his bedroom, on one occasion making a bedside light go on for no apparent reason. He became increasingly distraught and irritable during this time, often loud and verbally threatening toward the therapist in sessions, and describing a rise in hostile interactions with his parents. The therapist began to sense that he might be losing control and wondered whether all the discussion about the CIA might in some way be contributing to his anger.

The situation did get out of control. In the ninth month of the work, for the first time ever, Roger punched his mother and then assaulted his father, setting in motion an involuntary commitment to the hospital coordinated by the therapist. During the first part of his stay in the hospital, he was loud and abusive toward the staff, refused to see his parents, and fired the therapist, again viewing her as the agent of his parents. After four weeks on a strict room care plan, while being treated with chlorpromazine and then with chlorpromazine and lithium carbonate,[d] he calmed down, reopened contact with the parents, and then asked to see the therapist, a week before his scheduled discharge, with a view toward deciding whether he would rehire her or find another.

As with the encounter ten months earlier, Roger asked that this meeting be conducted on the grounds of the hospital. While retracing some of the same ground covered in their first walk, he shared his sense of betrayal upon learning that the therapist had participated in his commitment to the hospital. The therapist affirmed Roger's reservations about her, spelling out the extent of her involvement in his return to hospital and directly confirming that she had strongly recommended commitment in several conversations with his father immediately after the assault on his mother and again, two days later, after the assault on his father. She further indicated that, although the patient was free to tell her about his gripes toward his parents, he should not have expected the therapist to look on as a witness to his efforts to punish them with physical abuse. The therapist suggested that he carefully consider whether he wanted to work with her again and that he consider alternative therapists. She emphasized that, should he elect to rehire her, she would be pleased to resume the work, provided they had an understanding that no physical abuse would be tolerated. Indeed, control of his anger would be an important goal of any future work. Toward the end of this meeting, the patient indicated that he would think about what the therapist had said and let her know his decision in a day or two. He called the next day to ask for an appointment, at which point the therapist reiterated the requirement of abstaining from violence, which he acknowledged and accepted. From that point on, there were no further episodes of loss of control.

Getting Through Hard Times: The Wonderful CIA

Throughout the following six months, as the therapist listened to Roger relate his discontents about the banality of his life, she noted that his interest in the CIA fluctuated. There were long stretches of weeks during which he would hardly mention the CIA and when the therapist came to believe that he had put aside his interest in them. Then he would tell the therapist that the CIA was back again. Because of the turmoil of the summer and its apparent connection with the rising preoccupation with the CIA, each rise in his interest in the CIA was now associated, for the therapist, with a certain amount of anticipatory anxiety. Would he again lose control? Could the relationship survive another forced hospital stay? Instead, each increase in interest in the CIA was followed, within two to three weeks, by a waning of that interest.

The fluctuation in Roger's involvement with the CIA began to look like an endogenous cycle until, on one occasion, it came close on the heels of a potentially stressful event. One day, twelve months into the work, he told the therapist that he had received a call from a woman he had dated some years earlier. She would soon be driving through his area and wanted to drop in just for old times' sake. He had consented to the visit, but, in a session between the call and the visit he voiced fears about two consequences of attempting to act like a normal person at this time. First, he feared that he might not remember how to act in ordinary social situations and that he might reveal too much of his psychiatric troubles, causing this woman to be repulsed by him and by his demeanor. At the same time, he feared that he might be able to pass for normal, in which case she might want to see him again. He did not think he was up to resuming ordinary social contacts, especially those that might move in an amorous direction.

At the next session, it appeared that his second fear had come to pass. The woman visited, and they had a good time talking about their lives in the years since their former relationship. At the end of the afternoon, she asked him to call her, which meant to him that she was interested in reactivating the relationship. In the very next session, his interest in the CIA returned with marked vigor. He told the therapist that he had gone home, entered the bathroom, and literally commanded their attention, shouting out, "Where is the CIA?" whereupon they replied with a series of clicks in the bathroom wall. He then carried on a long conversation with them through the night. There was no mention, either by Roger or the therapist, of the possibility of a connection between the woman's visit and the return of the CIA. It was clearly premature to advance that idea. He would perceive it as a direct assault on his status as a valued government informer. At this time of declining self-esteem, such an interpretation would be like pouring acid into his wounds.

A NEW DEVELOPMENT

Looking Forward to the CIA's Return

Therapist and patient were now able to agree that, at least on some occasions, Roger was willing to actively seek out the CIA and that on these occasions, he was interested in their companionship, perhaps as a buffer against the fear of social rejection and loss of self-respect. To this date, although the correlation between a real or anticipated social rejection and the return of the CIA had often seemed compelling to the therapist, Roger had never been willing or able to confirm such a connection directly. He had consistently appeared to experience the therapist's musings about such a connection as an assault on the veracity of the CIA's interest in him. These were separate events, having nothing whatever to do with each other. He was, nevertheless, willing to confirm the therapist's observation that he often sought out the CIA actively and that he looked forward to his conversations with the agents behind the walls, signifying as they did a future time in which the nature of their interest in him would be revealed.

This type of observation stands in contrast to the more conventional interpretative intervention commonly made in the context of delusion formation. Typically, the therapist strives to make his or her patient aware of the defensive function of a delusion. However, when the state of the alliance does not yet permit the patient to replace the defensive benefits of a delusion with an involvement with the therapist or when the patient has not yet formed gratifying real relationships, interpretations that further this aim carry the risk of prematurely disabling the patient's capacity to cope with isolation. In this setting, the preferred intervention is one that leaves delusion formation intact while permitting other work to be accomplished. At this point in the work with Roger, the therapist's priority was to obtain his endorsement for two representations that would come into use repeatedly as the treatment progressed: first, she wanted the patient's endorsement for describing him as an active agent—one who recruits and dismisses delusional companions at will; second, she sought his consent to describe him as exercising this capacity in the service of buffering himself against excesses of loneliness and insignificance. Thus, the therapist elected to leave the delusion intact, in exchange for Roger's agreement that he valued and actively sought human involvement and personal significance.

The Reappearance of Real-Object Hunger

Not until the fourteenth month of treatment did Roger begin to show evidence of an interest in being with people. His loneliness for people came as an abrupt departure from the musings about his role in the CIA that had so completely dominated the work in the previous nine months. He was alone at home. His parents had departed to spend the holidays in Florida. At 4:30 A.M. on Christmas Eve, he placed an emergency call and begged the therapist to get him out of the house. He asked the therapist to arrange a stay at a hospital. This development was more disorienting than all the months of dialogue about the CIA, since this was the first time in her tenure that Roger sought entry to a hospital and the first evidence that he wanted something other than isolation and reverie.

The therapist reasoned that it was essential to respond materially to the patient's desire, rather than attempting to retain him in the community with a crisis intervention. The critical elements in her decision were the observations that, despite his opposition to institutional controls, the patient was giving evidence of loneliness and had issued a clear request for a specific service. Treating the patient in the community at this juncture—the therapist's preferred response in such circumstances—would have required her to ignore these developments. Overcoming her surprise and moving in opposition to her standard response, the therapist asked the patient which hospital he preferred, arranged for his admission on an emergency basis, and went to the patient's home just as the sun was rising to escort him to the hospital.

The patient and an affectionate mongrel by the name of Paddy, greeted the therapist at the door. Roger then revealed that in his parents' absence he had been playing with the wish that they would die, only to find himself swept into the conviction that the whole family—both parents and both sisters—had actually died in a plane crash. He presented this idea gravely as a fact and appeared quite frightened for his future. The prospect of being surrounded by people, even in an institution, had become very attractive in the aftermath of this family tragedy, and he eagerly prepared for the trip to the hospital. On the way out, he turned back and remarked, "I can't go on like this, living in the woods with a dog." Then, thinking perhaps how lonely he had become, he insisted on bringing Paddy with him, asserting that she would die of loneliness if left behind.

Taking Control of Coming and Going

So began Roger's first elective hospital stay in the three years since the appearance of the CIA. He stayed for a month and asked the therapist to visit him twice a week on the unit. There was no talk of the CIA. Uncharacteristically, he joined in the activities of the unit. He talked to the staff. He befriended two male fellow patients. When the time came for discharge planning, he told the therapist in a worried voice that he was afraid that the staff would again decide that he should go to a halfway house. He wanted to avoid this development by leaving, even though he was not, in the staff's view and by his own estimate, entirely ready for discharge.

This was a moment of opportunity. Throughout the entire period of his psychosis, Roger's arrivals to and departures from hospitals had been occasions of humiliation. He was brought in against his will. He left when the staff decided he was ready. He had little to say about his comings and goings. Now again, the staff was indeed moving in the direction of recommendations that Roger could not endorse, including referral to day treatment and placement in a supervised residence. This time, he had revealed a capacity to initiate hospital treatment appropriately. It was essential to acknowledge his evolving clinical judgement. The therapist elected to endorse a departure on his own schedule and to his preferred destination, aiming in this action to enable her patient to recapture a portion of his lost dignity. Additionally, this was a time to prepare for possible future elective hospital stays, affirming his use of the hospital as a temporary asylum. There would be an unusual twist, of course. Hospitals commonly function as a refuge from the stresses of life. In his case, the hospital could become a refuge from the unique stresses of self-enforced isolation and its attendant loneliness.

The Search for a Social Niche

At the first office session following his return home, Roger noted the appearance of depression. To his surprise, he was missing the friends he had made and the total immersion in the life of the unit. He was lonely. One could almost say that he was lonely again, except that in no prior session, during the earlier parts of the interim period, did he speak of being lonely. Rather, he had been either disparaging of contact with other people or fearful of the demands to relate that emerged or would emerge if he had elected to spend time with others. Now he was noticing the absence of the companionship of the unit. He reminisced about a time, before the onset of his psychotic experiences, when he had yearned for involvement and had often been in the company of others. The therapist was able to remind him of his statement about "living in the woods with a dog" and to suggest, without his dismissing the suggestion, that his loneliness heralded a shift in his priorities. The life of self-enforced reclusiveness was not all of his life. He could begin thinking about reinvolving himself with people.

In the context of this development, Roger began to connect with others again. He established contact with one of the people he had met in the unit, a former cleric. Over the course of a week or two, they spoke several times by phone, but he demurred on meeting face-to-face. For some weeks, the therapist thought she had seen the end of this little burst of aliveness and fully expected that Roger would soon return to his relationship to the CIA. However, as winter turned to spring, the yearning to be with others resurfaced, this time in the form of an interest in working again: If he was to have a woman, he must have an occupation, so he would work. He spoke in several sessions in the spring of his former occupation of some months as a real estate broker. Seeking to affirm the value of thinking of himself as a person who works when well enough to do so, the therapist encouraged him to consider taking up real estate again and to begin by reading the real estate listings for half an hour each day. Soon he was reading listings, making calls, going to see properties, all from the position of becoming a private investor. He found a friend of the family with whom he could work as an investing partner and started reading about real estate appraisal. He was on his way.

Then, in the eighteenth month of treatment, the crash came. In a session in May, he recounted with considerable discouragement his utter confusion over an apparently simple appraisal formula. Unable to comprehend the mathematics involved, he said to himself, "You're not a credible man, Roger!" and swept the whole real estate business aside. He was headed for a retreat. He referred to himself as having been at phase 2 for a period of a week or two, exhilarated that he was again interested in having a life, believing that he also had a future. Now he wanted only to plunge into phase 1 again and to forget that he had ever wanted anything.

At first the therapist found herself invested in holding on to the momentum gained in the time since Christmas. He had come so far. Must all of this be lost just because on the first try he couldn't master the formula? The therapist knew better than to encourage him to go back to the beginning, but the therapist did so anyway, suggesting that he return in his involvement to the original half-hour of reading listings. But Roger would have none of it: It was stupid of him to think that he could do real estate, that he could have a life, that he could have a woman. Observing the full force of his commitment to receding to phase 1, the therapist quickly switched, by the next session, to a complete endorsement of retreat. His priority was the avoidance of the humiliation of being a witness to his own inability to do simple things that he had once, in his recollection, done effortlessly. The effort to become involved was producing only an assault on his pride, with no appreciable compensations. It was premature (at the least) to support a partial retreat.

To this point in the interim period, the therapist had had little contact with the family. Now it became apparent that they were distressed about the retreat that was under way. Roger informed her, in the next session, that his father was encouraging him to stay involved in real estate, and this pressure was complicating life for him. The therapist considered this an indication for a direct intervention, the aim of which was to protect Roger's right to resign, to preserve for him the dignity of resting up after an exhausting effort to get his life moving again. Roger accepted the therapist's offer for a joint meeting with him and his father to discuss the need for retreat. In that meeting, it quickly became clear that the parents had seen real improvement in Roger's morale and in his behavior and hygiene during the real estate period and could not see the loss of this interest as anything but a backward move. For her part, the therapist was concerned that, without support for temporary time-out, Roger would have to produce more compelling evidence of infirmity in behavior that would quash their sense of optimism but would at the same time trigger a full-blown "crackup" with a very prolonged period of indifference, such as the one that had dominated the first fourteen months of treatment. Aiming for a shorter and less self-destroying retreat, the therapist recommended to the father that the family see this as an obligatory period of recuperation, perhaps to be followed by yet another period of activity and reinvolvement. Turning to Roger, the therapist recommended that he take to bed and surrender the business of real estate completely. Anticipating that Roger might feel demoralized by the therapist's support for the retreat, the therapist wondered openly with him, in his father's presence, whether he felt discouraged. He reported instead some relief. In the following session, he shared his gratitude for the therapist's role as a protector.

There followed a period of four weeks during which Roger was apathetic and disinterested, but there was no full-scale return of his CIA musings. Then, just as abruptly as it had disappeared, his loneliness returned in the fifth week of his retreat. This time, informed perhaps by the failure to move toward employment, his yearning took the form of a reconsideration of the idea of going to a long-term hospital to live. But in contrast to his talk about this idea in the very first interview, when he represented a long-term hospital stay as a way to avoid involvement, he now thought of it as a place to be with people without the performance demands of the world of work. He spoke fondly of an earlier hospital stay in which the companionship of other patients was the salutary ingredient. He asked the therapist to check out specific institutions that he had heard of as decent long-term places. He wanted to know what the average length of stay was in these places, remarking that he wanted to know "whether I can stay as long as I need to."

The search was on for a place in which he could be with people while continuing to be inactive. This may not sound like much of an advance over his original interest in long-term inpatient care, but the novel ingredient was his interest in involvement with others. His loneliness of the winter had survived the onslaught of his failure at work. He still wanted something instead of nothing. The therapist endorsed the plan and made calls to several hospitals, asking directors of admissions specifically about the length of stay and the quality of the other patients— how much they would be interested in companionship and so forth. After each call, she related her findings to Roger, functioning at this time as a consultant to a client, returning from her fact-finding mission of the week and constantly ready to go next in the direction of her client's interest, always representing him to the offices of admissions as a fellow interested in a restorative long stay. During this period, she felt more like a headhunter or a matchmaker than like a therapist.

Distinctly absent from open discourse at this time was the possible impact on Roger of his leaving the immediate area and thus ceasing regular, twice-weekly meetings with the therapist. It was certainly on her mind at each session that she would miss him. But there was no evidence coming directly or indirectly from Roger that the relationship with the therapist was central or indispensable. Indeed, they were agreed that it was time for him to make a change from his life "in the woods" and that, given the persistence of his yearnings to be with people and his still-thorough disinclination to move to a halfway house, he had to seek out a hospital environment. They both knew that, as much as they talked of the possibility of occasional trips back into the area, any move to a hospital would substantially interrupt their work together. All the same, the priority was finding a social niche that offered real companionship with real people. Their relationship would be subordinated to that goal.

In the nineteenth month of treatment, Roger identified the Austen Riggs Center as the place to go. The period between application and interview was devoted to a review of the developments leading up to the application and the goals for his stay there. There was some talk between therapist and patient about finding a way to continue their meetings, but the therapist indicated to Roger that this would be something to discuss at a time when he became clear that he wanted to stay at Riggs. He

324 Working with the Person with Schizophrenia

asked if the therapist would continue to work with him upon his return
some years hence, and the therapist assured him that she would continue
to be available to him at any point in the indefinite future. He openly
acknowledged the therapist's role as his principal friend during the prior
eighteen months. Nevertheless, he stressed, his life in the suburbs was
devoid of contact with real friends, a state of affairs that had finally
become intolerable. He spoke of this concern in the admission interview
at Riggs and was admitted there five days later.

Throughout the period of the patient's search for a more social setting, the therapist communicated implicitly her understanding that the
treatment relationship, although important, was not sufficient to sustain
the patient and did not, by itself, offer an adequate context for the
patient's social recovery. She actively supported the patient's efforts to
assess each setting, functioning more like a case manager linking the
patient to resources than like a therapist encouraging a focus on change
of self. Likes so many other aspects of the treatment of this patient, this
orientation was a direct outgrowth of the therapist's recognition of and
respect for the patient's priorities. He was not interested in psychotherapy. Indeed, he scolded the therapist on each occasion when she assumed
an interpretive stance. Rather, he struggled to find a way to reenter the
world of real people from a position of severe negativism regarding his
prospects for a successful comeback. Supporting his search, even though
it would bring their work to a halt, was her way of promoting the
patient's movement toward his avowed goal. To discourage the search,
by emphasizing internal change, would have been to disaffirm to the
patient the importance and believability of that goal.

The stay at Riggs lasted all of two weeks. Immediately on arriving at
home, he called the therapist for an appointment and arrived at her
office the next day looking amused and saying, "Well, I'm all better and
I'm going to get married!" And although this was obviously said in
humor, it was also his first reference to marriage. Upon arriving at the
Center, he had discovered that there were too many isolated people,
leading him to conclude, almost immediately, that the place would not
afford him the kind of companionship he required. In that first return
session, he asked the therapist to refer him instead to a day program,
suggesting that his search for a more companionable niche was still an
active goal. He ended the next session, three days later, pointing to the
air conditioner and remarking that it was going on and off in a manner

reminiscent of his former CIA times and indicating further that over the intervening weekend he had been "thinking about talking to the CIA out of loneliness."

If the stay at Riggs was abbreviated, Roger's involvement in a local day program was shorter still. He was accepted and began and left the program all within eight days. In a conference with the day program staff, the therapist learned that during his four days in the program he had been very restless, had trouble concentrating, and started his first men's group meeting by asking whether it was possible to get AIDS from oral sex. When the recommendation had been made that he take additional medication,[e] he had refused and subsequently intruded angrily into a staff meeting to say that he was going to talk to the therapist about the medication issue, but that if she agreed with the recommendation, he would fire her once again.

In spite of its brevity, the day program stay turned out to be a catalyst for a course of events that served as an important precedent for later developments. The session began with Roger's very vocal criticism of the day program. He was contentious toward the therapist as she attempted to discuss the issue of his disruptiveness. Suspecting that he had experienced the recommendation for an increase in medication as an assault on his integrity, but also knowing that, unless he agreed to this measure, he would certainly be asked to leave the program, the therapist suggested two possible remedies to his emerging unsteadiness. The first would be an increase in medication. She opened a discussion about medication, hoping that he would consider this proposal. He appeared to be unraveling in the face of increased interaction with people in the program, and an increase in neuroleptic medication was a rational response, if his disruptiveness was seen as a manifestation of physiological stimulus overflow. However, the therapist talked around this idea, representing it merely as a possibility. She stopped short of advancing it as a recommendation since, even while she was saying the words, the patient was drawing breath to reject it out of hand and perhaps to fulfill his threat to fire her.

The second remedy would be a voluntary return to phase 1. The therapist alluded to the time, three months earlier, when he had forcefully withdrawn from his real estate activities, plunging from phase 2 into phase 1, and suggested he consider using the same strategy now. At that time, the crash had seemed desperate and impulsive, not at all part of a plan. The therapist's only role had been as a witness to the inevitable. Now, just slightly before the patient began another plunge (but at a point when another plunge appeared inevitable), she recommended an elective return to phase 1, transforming what would otherwise have been a desperate man's solitary act into the decision of a team acting strategically to preserve his dignity. She represented it as a strategy for dealing with the challenge of getting too much contact with people too quickly. If it worked—if he did it in time—he would not lose much time, thereby enabling them to continue the search for companionship.

To the therapist's relief, Roger accepted the latter recommendation, appearing able to see this as a positive step. At the same time he alluded to the difficulty of acknowledging another defeat, saying, "The pain is awesome and nearly overtakes me." There followed, in this session and the next, a discussion about the importance of dignity, in which it became clear that, as disappointing as it was to lose the companionship promised by participation in the day program and as loathsome as a return to phase 1 might be, it was better to go that route than to participate in being induced into patienthood by accepting more medication. He gave his notice to the day program and commenced his first prescribed retreat. In these sessions, Roger also reported that he was actively inviting the CIA back into his life. Taking a chance, the therapist remarked that objectivity must be subordinated to dignity and that right now the CIA served the purpose of promoting his dignity. He did not confirm the embedded interpretation; nor did he object to the inference.

After canceling the next two sessions, saying by phone that he was too ill to come in, Roger appeared much improved and claimed to be feeling better at the next two sessions. By the fourteenth day following the discussion about medication, he was able to push through the bad feelings, take a shower, and get dressed. He was still in phase 1, but at least his irritable over-arousal had come to an end, and by the end of another two weeks, he was again complaining of depression, boredom, and loneliness. He ruminated openly about his bitterness at being excluded from the family business. For a brief interval of a few days, he was open, for the first time, to a suggestion from the therapist that he consider a training program. He phoned the day program, asking whether he could arrange a volunteer job if he were to return. And by the thirtieth day, his interest in finding a refuge from loneliness was active again.

From the twenty-third to the twenty-sixth months, Roger was actively engaged in a search, coaching the therapist in her role as his placement counselor on how to approach the hospitals in which he took an interest. In serial fashion, he assessed Four Winds Hospital, the Institute for Living, and the Menninger Foundation. In each case, it appeared that the pressure to improve was likely to be unacceptably high, outweighing the potential benefits of the companionship of other patients. Late in the twenty-fourth month, the therapist explained that a significant limitation of these and all other institutions was that most hospitals were now under increasing pressure to demonstrate active, goal-oriented treatment. This may have had a certain consciousness-raising effect on Roger, because, within a week, he asked about non-medical residential placements, including Gould Farm and Spring Lake Ranch. These settings stood in contrast to hospitals in that they usually were not characterized by the pressures of active treatment and typically had a more low-keyed orientation toward progress. At the patient's direction, the therapist contacted the admissions office at Gould Farm, ascertaining that the Farm had a long enough length of stay. However, there was a requirement for regular participation in the work of the Farm for upwards of six hours a day. The discussion of his preparedness to sustain this level of activity continued on and off for the next three months. During this interval, he applied to the Farm and asked the therapist to send a strongly supportive letter of recommendation. Shortly after this decision was reached, the patient called the therapist one day, from the family's winter home in Florida, saying he would be back in three weeks. He had decided to take a vacation, to try his hand at cruising the social clubs and discos of Miami for a while in search of new friends.

By the beginning of the active psychotherapeutic phase to be described in the next section, the patient had considered and rejected nearly all of the programs—all of the hospitals, day programs, and rehabilitation centers—that he and the therapist had together been able to propose as potential resources in his avowed search for companionship. Within a week of entering the active psychotherapeutic phase, he also rejected and was rejected by Gould Farm, the last of the alternatives investigated, and then entered new ground.

In reviewing the prolonged pretherapeutic interval, the outstanding features of the work were:

1. The patient's movement from a state of continuous, extreme apathy and anhedonia to a state of yearning for real human companionship;
2. The therapist's willingness to subordinate the continuity of the therapeutic relationship to the patient's need for real relationships;
3. The therapist's movement toward increasing acceptance of and comfort with the primitive defenses of delusion formation and apathetic disengagement;
4. Subordination of the reality principle to the patient's avowed priority of retaining his dignity and avoiding experiences that led to further humiliation;
5. The patient's acceptance of the therapist's injunction against physical abuse;
6. The therapist's acceptance of the patient's expressed unwillingness to subject himself to conventional interpretive psychotherapy;
7. The emergence of a spirit of collaboration and teamwork;
8. Identification of the mutually agreed-upon goal of adding to the patient's quality of life in ways that mattered to the patient; and
9. Subordination of the goal of improved social functioning to the goal of preserving the patient's self-respect.

Patient and therapist were brought together in their frustration at failing to find a setting that afforded the patient an opportunity to build real relationships and attain the companionship that he had come to desire. That shared frustration set the stage for the work of the next treatment period. By default, he had next to work on his capacity to engage flexibly in and then disengage from whatever social involvements were available to him, forging a social style that simultaneously took into account his object hunger, his very considerable narcissistic vulnerabilities, and his tendency toward stimulus overflow and affective flooding in the context of social involvement.

A NEW PARADIGM: PHASIC INSTABILITY REDEFINED

Twenty-seven months from the outset of the work, Roger began to show what turned out to be a persistent interest in mapping the transitions between the phases of his condition that he had identified in the second interview. For six weeks, this interest became central in the treatment, serving as the basis for active psychotherapeutic interventions aimed at offering a new and more enabling paradigm through which to understand the dramatic fluctuations that patient and therapist had witnessed throughout the treatment to date. During the long interim period, the patient had regained the courage and the capacity to want involvements with other people. But rather than leading to an increased ability to be with others, his new-found ability to yearn had given birth to a renewed dread of participation: He could plunge into life, taking up a pursuit or searching for other people to be with, but he had not yet learned how to cope with the virtual flood of affects that accompanied the involvements he was able to begin. He alternated between involvement and withdrawal, between aliveness and deadness. He saw no way to be alive without being overwhelmed, and the specter of another crackup triggered by too much involvement was, in his view, never more than a step away and could easily lead to another years-long loss of vitality.

Now, also for the first time, he revealed a belief that he might learn how to prevent breakdowns—those states of mind that followed a transition from phase 2 to phase 1 or from phase 3 to phase 1. In the first conversation on this topic, building on the concepts of humiliation and demoralization as developed in the interim period, the therapist described him as going into a power dive when he met up with the smallest frustration in a task that was too much for him. She suggested that he had no forgiveness for himself even when he was experiencing a mild break. Atypically, Roger confirmed this formulation, acknowledging his inability to forgive himself for not being "king of the hill." At the next session Roger, again uncharacteristically, reported a dream, in which he was falling through a trap door at the family business, only to have the salesmen there leave him hanging, dangling at the edge of the trap door. He then turned to a review of events in a previous treatment program, revealing that he simply could not absorb as truth the representation, offered by a former therapist, that he did not want to get better. The therapist shared with the patient her own sense, born of their two and a half years together (and of the real estate caper of the previous spring in particular), that the former therapist may have missed an invisible but very real limitation, namely his tendency to panic when he was feeling things strongly. This limitation was behind his reluctance to move ahead. But in the absence of recognition of this panic by the therapist, he had created a more obvious malady (and here the therapist was repeating and incorporating a view discussed a year earlier)—namely a psychosis—as a way of compelling the staff of the program to the view that he was genuinely incapable of moving ahead. In this conversation, the therapist asserted for the first time that the patient had a very real impairment—which they agreed to refer to as a "panic disorder"—that had been manifest in relationships and possibly in work settings as well. Even though it contained an assumption of deficit, Roger appeared to accept the formulation, in sharp contrast to all previous times when the therapist had advanced such ideas.

At the next session, Roger began immediately by asking the therapist to tell him more about panic disorder. Together, they elaborated a model in which an event triggers a state of terror—to which, the therapist again asserted, with no objection from Roger, the patient is exceptionally vulnerable. Indeed, now feeling more confident that they were on new ground and that she could go further, since Roger was not rejecting the stress-diathesis model, the therapist claimed that this was his primary vulnerability, to which he responded by entering, defensively and adaptively, into something more recognizable to us—namely, a crackup or psychotic break. There was still no objection from the patient. Going on, the therapist suggested that his occasional use of various substances—benzodiazepines, heroin, alcohol—was an attempt to rid himself of the terror, but that, since these were often proscribed or unavailable to him, he had evolved a capacity for psychic numbing and the erection of an enforced invalidism as his preferred response to the experience of terror. The therapist then suggested the use of the new antianxiety agent buspirone as a possible buffer against this terror. Since he was also nearing the time to visit Gould Farm, the therapist forewarned the patient of the possibility that going to the Farm could evoke this terror.

The next session was cancelled due to a major snowstorm. He came into the following session looking wrecked, with a furtive, vigilant glance, reminiscent of the glance of those hallucinating, and readily confirming that he had used cocaine the night before for the first time in a month. Spontaneously, he attributed this lapse to missing the daily company of his parents, who had by this time been away in Florida for a week. He said nothing about the visit to Gould Farm the next day. At the next session, he indicated he had not liked the Farm and then quickly refocused on the breakdown process. At his suggestion, the therapist took careful notes on the elements of the process that were known to them, as it had occurred in the time since its onset in 1975. Following this session, the therapist was off on a winter vacation for a week.

At the next session, Roger immediately started in again on the break-down process. He looked and smelled good, was clean shaven, and was dressed casually but well, much like an upper middle-class, thirty-year old banker on the weekend. In this conversation, building on his apparent acceptance of the concept of deficit, the therapist advanced the notion that panic increased his need for rest, which was greater than that of other people, and suggested that he think about allowing himself to enter a state of mind, which they could call phase 2.1, or even phase 2.01, in which he would be more open than at phase 1 and yet would not expect himself to be in any way active. This was clearly a novel thought to Roger, and his first reaction was not one of curiosity. Nor, however, did he conclude, as he had so many times before, that for the therapist to invent something like this, something about his condition that did not come from him, meant that she did not understand him at all. The therapist talked fast about the advantages of his permitting himself to rest and catch his breath from the depletion caused by social involvement, without at the same time suffering the loss of dignity that he had always found waiting for him whenever he resorted to a transition into phase 1 as a way to get the needed rest. With a lot of talk from the therapist, he appeared able to accept that she had described something unknown to him about his condition. He did not incorporate the idea in this session, but he left without completely rejecting the idea.

In the next session, Roger announced that, during the last session, during all of their talk about finding a way to stay at phase 2.1 or 2.01 and while he had been insisting that under no circumstances was he at anything higher than 1.9, he was actually—he had later realized—at phase 3. The next day, after a night of no chlorpromazine and no sleep, he had become frightened, had taken some chlorpromazine, and had become aware of a strong impulse "to reenter the mental patient role" [the patient's own words]. He then revealed that when he really wanted to dive into phase 1, he would wear old, very ill fitting, and mismatched clothes, dressing to look like a mental patient. He went on to describe how, later in that same day, he had nearly gone in the direction of the mental patient, nearly giving in to a small but notable impulse to wear an old "mental patient sweater." The therapist asked whether he was saying that he had actually fought with such an impulse? Yes. And he had resisted the impulse? Yes. The therapist indicated to him very matter-of-factly, right there and then, that this was new ground, that he had never reported fighting off that sort of impulse. How different this was from last spring, when, as he headed into phase 1 because of the failure to do a real estate formula, there was no stopping him and no indication that any internal struggle could be going on around the impulse to fall into phase 1. The patient then recounted that on the following morning he had awakened quite uncertain whether he would find himself moving toward phase 1 or phase 3 and had seen himself going toward phase 1, only to find that on the very next day he arrived by some unknown path in phase 2.6! Roger himself remarked that this was a most unusual event, since on virtually all other occasions when he had gone from phase 3 to phase 1, he had ended up spending months to years in phase 1 before moving out to phase 2 again. The therapist asked him to consider at least the possibility that this kind of short-term variability had important positive implications and drew three graphs depicting increasing degrees of variability—and mobility—and at the same time increasing access to phase 3.

The therapist was working here to challenge the patient's fundamental, rigid assumption that phase 3 should be a permanent status and that a person existing in a full state of aliveness does not require rest (i.e., phase 1) of any kind.

Roger started the next session by focusing on the breakdown process, indicating further that he was glad that they were finally attending to this. He went on to describe two models of processes that could be making contributions to the breakdown. First, there was a self-induced numbing process, through which he shut down his mind and entered more or less deliberately and intentionally into the mental patient role. Second, there was a process of being overwhelmed by terror and by the events that evoked or could be expected to evoke terror. The therapist observed that these two models appeared to be incompatible or contradictory, but that they could both be making contributions to the breakdown process. She noticed at one point, while he talked about all these things, that, for the first time, he was talking from the point of view that there might be some possibility of a moderate, compromising lifestyle in which he might be able to live with a limitation like panic disorder. This was the first time that the patient had given voice, on his own, to the idea of limitations and to the idea of being able to adapt to a lifestyle that took those limitations into account. The therapist recalled and recounted a scene in *The Right Stuff* in which Charles Yaeger takes the X-15 so high that it conks out and crashes, describing this as a metaphor for his trouble. By likening him to a famous and courageous man, while alluding to the dangers of exceeding the limitations of one's "equipment," the therapist was preparing a frame of reference that, if incorporated by the patient, would enable him to protect his dignity when coming up against his own limits.

Choosing to Move Between Phases

In the next session, the patient again talked exclusively about the breakdown process. This was beginning to feel to the therapist like a regular bill of fare now; she no longer wondered whether he would permit her to take a growth-oriented stance. In this session, he seemed to hear her, almost for the first time, on the concept of the reversibility of movement between the phases. He remarked that being able to move from phase 3 to phase 1 to phase 2 to phase 1 to phase 2 and so forth was a new idea and allowed that it was worth exploring further.

Roger did not appear for the next session. During the hour, the therapist called the house and found that Roger had forgotten the appointment and that he was disappointed because there was something he wanted to discuss. Reasoning that this was his way of asking for an extra session, the therapist found time to see him the next day, when he indicated that he wanted to try tranylcypromine, "to see if I can stabilize myself at phase 2." In discussing the use of this medication, they reviewed his experience at another hospital, when tranylcypromine had been used to treat depression because he was claiming to be extremely suicidal. He now revealed that he had not been at all suicidal at that time and that he had claimed to be so only to see to it that he stayed in the hospital for a long time. His hospital doctor had turned to the use of tranylcypromine at this point, along with a neuroleptic, resulting in a severe toxic reaction. The therapist reviewed very carefully the dietary restrictions, including the absolute restriction against the use of cocaine.

In the next session, they again broke new ground as the patient told the therapist that he was accepting the validity of the idea of being able to shift between phase 1 and phase 2. In this context, and because it appeared that his interest in evoking a shift was mainly centered on the ability to shift up, the therapist asked him how he was doing at shifting down from phase 2 to phase 1. Roger indicated that he had real trouble doing this because he would lose face, a report suggesting that, for the moment, the idea of an underlying deficit was not operative. The therapist replied emphatically that, in her view, he was entitled[f] to shift from phase 2 to phase 1 any time he wanted and that he could do so with dignity, because it took such tremendous courage for him to make any attempt at all to go from phase 1 to phase 2 in the face of an unforgettable string of breakdowns and their consequent humiliations. He started on tranylcypromine that week.

At the time of the next session, Roger called saying that, on an impulse, he had decided to go to Florida again to join his parents. He was taking the tranylcypromine, along with enough chlorpromazine to guarantee good sleep, and observed that he might be feeling a little bit better.

In summarizing the developments of this part of the work, we see this as a period when the patient's emerging interest in others led him to confront his illness from a new perspective. Now, for the first time, he endorsed the concept of self-regulation and certain ideas critical to the development of coping skills relevant to his social needs and commensurate with his known vulnerabilities. He gave at least provisional credence to the following theses:

1. Moving between involvement and disengagement is normative and therefore respectable.
2. Rest is a necessary preparation for and sequel to active involvement with people.
3. I require more rest per unit of activity than others because I have a proneness to panic anxiety that is not shared by other people.
4. If I rest as soon as I become aware of the need, I am less likely to get stuck in the resting state for a long time.
5. The capacity to move toward involvement after a period of rest requires that I learn to cue in to my actual readiness for involvement, rather than relying on general societal injunctions about when I should be ready for involvement.

LEARNING TO USE THE NEW PARADIGM

As indicated at the beginning of this chapter, the majority of the material to this point was written contemporaneously with the developments described in the previous section. We will now chronicle subsequent developments in the treatment that are relevant to reformulating the phasic nature of the illness. Of special interest in this section is the interplay between the patient's yearnings for involvement, his efforts to make social contact, shifts between the three characteristic states of mind, and preoccupations with the CIA. Heretofore, each time the patient retreated to phase 1, he experienced a decrease in the very relational skills he hoped to regain and, in the absence of competing evidence of his real value to real people, exposed himself to a relentless barrage of depreciatory and intensely humiliating global self-representations. Thus, each effort to recover his capacity to be alive ended in failure and, of greater long-term consequence, further decreased his capacity to anticipate pleasurable outcomes from future strivings. The result was a self-enforced apathy that had all the markings of the negative syndrome, punctuated by occasional bursts of excessive and undirected activation.

Beginning in the twenty-eighth month of treatment, the therapist strove to foster the development of the patient's capacity to move electively and with dignity between phase 1 and phase 2. She conceived of phase 1 as a recuperative and preparatory state, a psychological "home base" from which the patient could make exploratory moves into phase 2, which she saw as the state that supported involvement and participation with real objects. She believed the patient's capacity for involvement would be strengthened through practice and repetition, provided patient and therapist devised ways to avert the adverse effects of prolonged withdrawal.

The first opportunity to practice the new orientation occurred during the patient's trip to Florida, noted above. Ten days into the trip, he phoned the therapist to say that he had spent most of his time in phase 2, going out every night to discotheques. He was, however, concerned because the day before he did not get dressed and did not shave, which suggested to him that he was sliding back into phase 1. She recommended that he think of those behaviors as examples of the kind of temporary regression to phase 1 that they had been talking about recently. He immediately confirmed that she might be right. He added that he was finding it hard to carry on conversations with women, which the therapist suggested was to be expected because he was out of practice and because his mind would keep defensively shutting down on him until it saw that no terrible things would happen when he ventured forth. Five days later, he returned from Florida looking confident and relaxed, clean-shaven, tanned, wearing a blue blazer and boat shoes. The therapist concluded provisionally that on this occasion her efforts to represent his retreat favorably had prevented the usual cycle of withdrawal and humiliation.

Using the Hospital as a Social Club

Within two weeks of his return home, the patient asked for admission to the hospital, having become discouraged by the isolation of "life in the woods" without his parents and with no access to other people. In contrast to all previous admissions, this hospital stay seemed barely justifiable, occurring in the absence of crisis or deterioration. Indeed, when the therapist visited him on the unit the day after his admission, she found him actively in conversation with a female patient. The therapist made note of this development, emphasizing in an accepting way that Roger was using the hospital as a social club. They joked about the fact that he had come to the hospital this time with his best clothes, almost as if he were headed for a stay at a resort. Five days later, he was optimistic about having come into the hospital electively and ready to socialize and even allowed that his presence was valued by some other patients. He spoke of his desire to have a girlfriend—someone to hold hands with and sit beside and watch television with, nothing more complicated than that. He was conflicted about going home. Much as he was ready to go after less than a week in hospital, he had become interested in a very attractive female patient who had showed open disappointment on learning of his plan to leave the unit. The therapist supported the idea of his remaining in the hospital a bit longer, representing this as an opportunity for him to drink in some contact of a kind that he had not had in a long time. She validated the patient's view that, if presented with the choice between medication and a kiss as treatment for depression, most people would benefit more from the kiss treatment.

Beginnings of Satisfying Relationships with Women

He did stay, spending hours in the presence of this woman, later revealing with unqualified pleasure that they had had some good physical contact, some brief moments of kissing and hand-holding while in the unit. After returning home a week later, Roger called this woman daily and went out on several dates with her after her discharge. He spoke of a future and of a developing relationship with her for two weeks thereafter, indicating that he was living at phase 2 plus. In a few days, however, he was openly ambivalent about the relationship, revealing that, although he wanted a girlfriend, some sexual release, and some companionship, she was not the right person for him. He then broke off with her when, on several conversations, she did not seem totally supportive of his complaints about his parents. Three weeks later, he reported a dream in which he was married, and in the discussion that followed, the therapist took a developmental perspective:

R: At first I didn't like being married, but then I got used to it.
T: See? You're practicing, even in your dreams!
R: But then a girl named Linda Love came along and murdered both of us.
T: So you're conflicted. Consider the possibility that you are getting ready for something. Not in any dramatic way, but gradually.

The matter-of-fact optimism of the therapist's responses in this interchange was an important element of her continuing efforts to compete with the patient's tendency to negate positive developments. Furthermore, the focus of the dream interpretation was in keeping with the priority of providing the patient with ways in which to experience himself as being like other people. Rather than open an inquiry regarding the source of the self-destructive element embodied in Linda Love, she chose to emphasize how ordinary, how normal it is to feel conflicted when opening up a new line of development.

In the next session, Roger noted that, in contrast to all previous relationships in which he had grown to care about a woman, he had not felt smothered by this woman. He allowed that, while this was probably because the relationship hadn't lasted long enough for it to happen, it might also be because of some maturational move. To these optimistic remarks, the therapist responded by pointing again to the favorable implications of his having had a marriage dream. In the very next session Roger was pessimistic, reminiscing about the beepers and the CIA. He seemed pressured to do something with his life, to try to get a job, and yet fully anticipated that he would fail. The therapist placed his discouragement in the context of his yearning for a woman, pointing out that he wanted to have a girlfriend but felt he could not keep up his end of a relationship.

Beginning a Productive Involvement with Day Treatment

During this same hospital stay, Roger accepted a referral to a day treatment program situated in his old neighborhood in the city. His willingness to enter this program was linked to his desire to get back to his apartment in the city. He preferred living by himself to living with his parents, but did not know what he would do with his time. In this context, the therapist suggested that he consider this particular day program, which she had visited informally several months earlier on his behalf. His initial reaction, while negative, did not stop him from attending. Within a short time, he had made several friends in the program and was regularly meeting with them for dinner after hours. The therapist placed this development in the context of Roger's strivings over the previous fifteen months to find some companionship, deemphasizing the extent to which he would otherwise have been adversely affected by being more involved in the role of a psychiatric patient than ever before.

The connection to peers at the day program came under intense pressure early in the sixth month of his day program stay and the thirty-fifth month of treatment, in the face of an unanticipated invitation from a former female acquaintance. Since there had been little affection, it would be overstating their relationship to describe her as a girlfriend. There had been, however, some very satisfying sex, and now he was anticipating the possibility of a physical encounter. In this context Roger reported feeling the urge to go into phase 1, in anticipation of failure on the upcoming date. The therapist discussed the need for him to accept the regressive push as a legitimate way to forestall a drastic collapse. At a session two days later, when Roger reported he had canceled the date and now claimed to be cracking up, the therapist insisted that, in point of fact, he was constructively running for cover.

There followed a profoundly intense and confrontational discussion in which the therapist was able to distinguish two parts of the patient: a vulnerable part that struggled to be involved and retreated when overwhelmed, and a vicious, punitive, perfectionistic part that was a prime cause of the self-shaming that led to extensive, prolonged demoralization of psychotic proportions. Roger accepted this formulation and the idea that his experience in a drug rehabilitation program had amplified the latter to his detriment. The therapist gave him a prescription for lorazepam, recommending that he use up to 4 milligrams per day to treat his panic anxiety. The patient felt that if he went to the program in his present state of mind, he would surely lose face with his peers, making a fool of himself and destroying the good will that he recognized as existing there for him. The therapist offered to call the staff to validate his temporary retreat from the program, provided that the patient also contract the staff directly to explain the need for a temporary absence. Roger gladly agreed to this intervention and remained out of the program for a total of five weeks. By the end of the first week, he had rebounded substantially, playing rock music and recruiting the CIA toward the end of mending his self-esteem. He was able to say, both at home and in session, that he was not leading the worst possible life and was able to agree that the big problem generating the suicidality was his vicious superego. He indicated that he was thinking of going back to the day program. The therapist cautioned him not to go back too soon and suggested that he should remain out until he had regained his yearning to be with others. Four weeks later, he returned to the program.

Considering a Move to a Halfway House

In addition to the movement toward increased social contact, two months after joining the day treatment program, Roger began to voice an interest in leaving home. Since he continued to have real doubts about his capacity to manage life by himself, he volunteered one day, in the thirty-second month of treatment, that he was considering making application to a halfway house in the city. He found it difficult to consider this option in the light of the intense conflict that had emerged three years earlier between himself and his parents over the issue of the hospital staff's recommendation: Going to a halfway house would be like admitting that they and his parents were correct. Thus, he discussed the idea of a halfway house in the context of the increasing conflict and resentment he was experiencing in his relationship with his father. He could not continue to live under the same roof with the man. The therapist encouraged him to decide the question solely on the basis of its place in his long-term effort to find a more companionable niche for himself.

DISCUSSION

By the time Roger introduced the idea of moving to a halfway house, he and the therapist had come full circle. They began their work in the context of a dramatic worsening in his clinical state, apparently evoked by the hospital staff's recommendation, endorsed by the family, that he live in a halfway house. He was violently opposed to the recommendation, to the indignities of life as a supervised mental patient. Now Roger was placing the idea on the agenda for their work. From this point forward, the sessions were characterized increasingly by the patient's direct expressions of loneliness and narcissistic injury and by the therapist's rejoinders that his isolation was no longer serving him and that he must, in due time, find a living situation that, while according him some dignity, included peers with whom he could find some meaningful companionship. The work continued to be punctuated by occasional "visits" from the CIA, and he was still haunted by the beeper experience, convinced that at least this was a real event. But by the thirty-eighth month of treatment, even while he would not altogether relinquish the hope of having a role in "their" plans and even while he would not permit the therapist to assume an interpretive stance, Roger was able himself to give the interpretation that, whatever "their" plans, the CIA represented for him a possible way out of the unbearable sense of insignificance that his life had taken on.

Despite these continuing ruminations, the patient was able to make use of the flexibility of the new paradigm in orienting himself toward involvements with peers. The high point came in the thirty-sixth month of treatment and represented clear evidence of his increasing capacity to cue in to the signs of overload and retreat momentarily. In a group at the day program, Roger confronted another patient about being cliquish and arrogant and was in turn confronted by other group members about his own obnoxious ways. He left the program feeling shaky, observed that he was afraid to listen to music on the way home (a familiar sign of an impending breakdown), went out to dinner with his parents and a friend, took some lorazepam to curb the anxiety, and then, recalling recent times when crackups had been short-lived, found that instead of wanting to crack and retreat, he wanted to go out dancing. He went to a local discotheque, approached a woman standing by herself, danced, broke a sweat, bought some drinks for himself and the woman, stayed with her, kissed a little, then kissed more in earnest, asked her home, "gave it the old college try," and weathered her refusal. He went home, felt truly tired, and slept without dreams, or at least without dreams that he could recall, and awoke in a state of serenity the next morning. In session, he reported feeling proud of himself and optimistic, having taken more responsibility for himself than in years and having weathered a rejection with more resilience than he thought he had.

This case demonstrates how a therapist, taking an interest in identifying the patient's priorities and then incorporating those priorities into her approach, was able to establish an active collaboration with the patient in the service of eventual, incremental increases in the patient's flexibility in managing interpersonal relationships. The patient presented with extreme sensitivity to emotional contact and, at the same time, with profound injury to his self-esteem emanating from the continual flow of evidence of deficiencies in his capacity to perform ordinary tasks and functions up to conventional standards. He used psychic numbing to attenuate his interest in involvements and, simultaneously, as a way to diminish his capacity to experience the pain of his situation. Yet his continuing object hunger led him to undertake, at first in delusional ways, and then later in more realistic ways, to create satisfying involvements with people. He had evolved a model of his condition that incorporated the numbing process on one end of a spectrum and desired forms of aliveness on the other. After many years of experience with a range of therapists and modalities, he had little patience with conventional diagnostic and psychotherapeutic frameworks. He specifically disallowed the use of the diagnosis of schizophrenia or any of the paradigms that are commonly in use in the understanding and treatment of schizophrenia. He would not permit the therapist to assume an interpretive stance.

The therapist's stance demonstrates how the framework described in this book, when brought to bear on a complex clinical reality, leads to the gradual unfolding of an increasingly detailed understanding of the interplay between a patient's conflicts and deficits. If, out of disgust, the patient spurned conventional psychiatric frameworks, at least he offered one of his own. As baffling and uncomfortable as working within that framework might have been, the therapist recognized immediately that the goal of establishing an alliance required that she learn to do so. As she demonstrated respect for and curiosity about his paradigm, the patient was increasingly willing to reveal his central priorities—overcoming loneliness, being admired by people whose opinion he valued, and above all, protecting his dignity against the onslaught of his own and others' realization of his infirmities. Armed with a better understanding of the ways in which these principles organized his inner life and his behavior, she was able to offer modifications of the patient's model of illness that modestly enhanced his capacity to enter into involvements with selected peers while enabling him to buffer himself against the risk of the massive collapse of self-esteem that had commonly occurred in the past and that had uniformly led to complete inaccessibility and psychosis. Building on the therapist's apparent acceptance of his priorities, the patient was able to reveal that, far from being a passive victim, he was actively regulating his mental state in accord with the extent of sensory and emotional flooding he was experiencing. While herself seeing this regulatory process as a response to deficient stimulus barrier functioning, to the patient she responded more concretely and within his paradigm by recommending the use of psychic numbing (which he was already doing by going into phase 1 in his paradigm) as a means to achieve rest between involvements. While the therapist recognized the need for this coping device, she increasingly saw that its use triggered a catastrophic form of demoralization. The patient harbored an idealized view of manhood in which such rest was not permissible and was therefore the occasion for deep self-stigmatization. While keeping alive in the dialogue his needs for companionship and respect, she offered him a soothing and dignified orientation by normalizing the need for intervals of recuperation between periods of involvement. Operating within his own paradigm modified by this orientation, the patient was able to increase his capacity to both enter into and adaptively retreat from involvements with desired objects. The modest successes he experienced in socialization enabled him to accept the therapist's representations of him as having a vulnerability to intense interpersonal interaction. Eventually, the patient began to talk about moving from the parental home to a supervised community residence, in which access to peers would be enhanced, and hinted at the possibility of eventually relinquishing a valued delusion. The work with the patient continues, centering on working through the loss of his valued capacity to socialize at will, the acceptance of illness-related limitations, and the formation of a realistic life structure.

To summarize, the work with this patient demonstrates the process, through the initial and intermediate phases of treatment, of identifying the patient's own priorities and shaping and reshaping a treatment strategy that is extensively customized to those priorities. Conventional clinical methods of interviewing, observation, case formulation, and intervention were considerably modified and, in some ways, put aside in the service of developing the kind of relatedness that the patient would accept. The progress permitted through this method of working, while modest, has brought this patient to a state of mind, attitude toward illness, and degree of social involvement he could not otherwise attain.

8

Beyond Psychoeducation: Raising Family Consciousness About the Priorities of People with Schizophrenia

Work with families of the mentally ill has been transformed in the last decade in ways that are both favorable and problematic for clinicians treating the most seriously mentally ill patients. Before the mid-1970s, the prevailing clinical orientations to the family were based on interpersonal theories of the pathogenesis of schizophrenia (1–5) that shared a common emphasis on family interaction as an essential element in the pathogenesis of schizophrenia. Emerging from and consonant with a distinctly American belief in the primacy of environmental influences in human personality development, these theories possessed such powerful apparent validity that they were quickly adopted as fundamental clinical tenets, dominating family therapy with hospitalized patients. Families often complained that encounters with clinicians working under the assumptions espoused by these theories were guilt-invoking and did not help the family to understand or accommodate to the behavior of the ill family member (6).

By the late 1970s, the whole group of family interaction theories of schizophrenia had fallen into disfavor as a result of three interacting forces. First, no compelling, internally coherent, and comprehensive body of empirical evidence had been developed to confirm any of the specific hypotheses (7–8). Second, biological paradigms began to gain the ascendancy in models of schizophrenia, beginning with the discovery that phenothiazines had specific effects on the symptoms of schizophrenia—symptoms that had heretofore been seen as manifestations of interpersonal operations within the family. The biological revolution went on to yield increasingly cogent and empirically based models for the principal manifestations of the disorder. Third, the trend away from lifelong institutional care had thrust clinicians into direct contact with the fami-

347

lies of their patients to a degree unparalleled during the era of asylum treatment. As patients moved from hospital-based to predominantly community-based care, families came to accept an increasingly central role in supporting patients. The increased burden experienced by families led many to seek more contact with clinicians and to ask for less blame-invoking, more information-providing methods of working with families.

The work of the British group at the Maudsley Institute of Psychiatry led the way toward a form of family therapy that overcame, at least partially, the limitations of the previous paradigm. Beginning in the early 1970s, this group demonstrated a strong correlation between certain family attitudes and short-term morbidity (as measured by relapse rates) from schizophrenia (9–10). Patients discharged from hospital treatment fared best among relatives who showed high tolerance for the patient's lack of everyday conversation and detachment from family life.

Subsequent studies by other groups, designed to test the effects of family interventions aimed at promoting understanding of illness and tolerance of illness-related behavior, have shown that families can acquire more tolerant ways of relating to the patient with schizophrenia, with attendant declines in short-term morbidity for the patient (11–12). Because of their emphasis on family education about schizophrenia, these approaches are often referred to as "psychoeducational" programs. (Although these programs frequently have a broader scope than this term implies, we will use the term here.) Families find information about the nature of schizophrenia useful in understanding the behavior of the patient, the treatments applied, and the prospects for the future. In addition, specialized training in problem-solving everyday family situations helps family members cope with the behavioral and communicational ambiguities and variations in functioning that are inherent in the illness.

While the psychoeducational family programs have, on balance, produced more affirmative orientations to the families of patients with schizophrenia, among treating clinicians, certain difficulties have become apparent as these approaches have increased in popularity. Foremost among the difficulties is that, while many families now understand the aspects of schizophrenia that arise from disorders of the brain, manifestations of the illness that arise from the patient's personal reactions to symptoms, to functional disability, and to loss of vital connections to others are not always satisfactorily dealt with in psychoeducational programs and are not well recognized, understood, or accepted by families. In this chapter, we will focus on difficulties presented by this programmatic gap as they relate to the tasks of treatment within the framework developed in earlier chapters.

A clinical example will illustrate the dilemma now commonly encountered in work with families of individuals with schizophrenia.

> A 26-year-old man with schizophrenia was hospitalized for the sixth time for increasing delusions, disorganization, irritability, and socially inappropriate behavior. While receiving neuroleptic medication and participating in the hospital milieu, his psychotic symptoms abated significantly. At this point, his father, a professional man who had consistently denied that the son had ever been ill or required medication to remain well, began to pressure the son to come home and return to college. The son's condition in the hospital unit worsened, with a return of delusional ideation, including the delusion that he was not his father's son but rather was the son of a well-known rock star. The patient's mother, who had openly acknowledged for several years that her son had a serious mental illness, describing the condition as an imbalance of brain chemistry, asked that the son be placed on higher doses of neuroleptic medication. Clinicians working with the son became aware that father and mother, operating from divergent perspectives, shared a diminished understanding that the son's conflict about the father's renewed expectations was contributing to the recent clinical exacerbation. During a family session in which this linkage was identified to the parents, the son, in a rare moment of clarity, was able to reveal that he did not believe he could function in school because of the effects of schizophrenia on concentration and reading. He declared that he wanted nothing more than to take his medication and return to farm life. He knew from recent and past experiences that such a life offered considerable satisfaction. He turned to his father and pleaded with him to accept that he had schizophrenia and needed medication to stay well and asked that he be allowed to return to living on a farm.

The son's clinical exacerbation can be seen in part as an attempt to teach his father about the illness and remind him of its impact on his functioning, all in the service of gaining support for discharge to a setting in which he could function adaptively. For his part, the father had not yet developed a way of coping with the impact of the son's illness on his own image of himself as father and on his dreams for his son's future. He had not yet mourned the loss of the idealized son. His priorities demanded that the son return to a life structure that was normative for his age peers. For her part, the mother had not recognized the son's active contribution to his clinical state. In her view, the illness and the son's regressed behavior were simply the results of a brain disorder. To her, the conflict between father and son was no more than a distressing sidelight; the correct approach was an increase in psychotropic medication.

While psychoeducational programs have gone a long way toward alleviating families of the guilt that is commonly an adverse effect of psychodynamic family orientations and while family members are increasingly cognizant of the biological side of schizophrenia, many do not appreciate the extent to which the symptoms and the course of the illness are shaped by the patient's own priorities—his or her goals and aspirations, fears of deficient performance, grief and rage over lost functional capacity. Increased emphasis on the biological aspects of schizophrenia may occlude recognition of these human reactions to the illness. Without substantive modification, the current psychoeducational orientation falls short of promoting specific, individualized family understanding of the patient's personal reactions to his or her predicament. Failing to give sufficient weight to the patient's priorities and to the likelihood of conflicting priorities within the patient, family members have no perspective through which to give meaning to some of the most prominent clinical manifestations of schizophrenia in the open community. They are often left baffled and confused by these behaviors, at at loss to connect empathically with the ill member's predicament.

BEHAVIORS FAMILIES FIND DIFFICULT TO UNDERSTAND

Three examples, representing frequent relatives' complaints about patient behavior that we believe represent personal reactions to illness rather than primary manifestations of schizophrenia, serve to illustrate this problem.

Noncompliance with Psychotropic Medication

Families often have great difficulty comprehending noncompliance with psychotropic medication, especially when, as in the case described below, the patient shows significant improvement with the use of medication.

During an intake interview, the mother of a 29-year-old man with schizophrenia recounted the patient's life history in great detail, emphasizing how, for thirteen years, she had sought at great personal sacrifice, any and all forms of treatment that might be of help to him. She had no life apart from her efforts to help him, and yet no treatment that was applied seemed to offer benefit. Then three years ago, the patient was given a trial of depot neuroleptic. He showed a decrease in delusions, a virtually complete remission from thought disorder that had been so severe as to be described as "word salad," and ceased his use of abusive, foul language. He was in the best clinical state that she had seen in all the time of his illness and was discharged home. However, he refused to permit the continuation of the depot neuroleptic and within three months suffered a recurrence of symptoms. Now, three years later, she described herself as shut off from her son, no longer allowing herself to care about him, and on some occasions saying openly to his clinicians that it would be better for him to be dead rather than continue on in this state.

As long as the patient was ill with no remedy in sight, this mother was able to accept his condition and freely subordinated her own life to the endless pursuit of a remedy. With the arrival of an effective treatment, she lost her capacity to be sympathetic to his predicament. She regarded his refusal to take medication as willful and unnecessary, became angry, and withdrew. She lacked a perspective through which to understand this behavior as a manifestation of his struggle to preserve autonomy or to ward off psychic deadness.

This vignette exemplifies typical situations that end in an impasse when psychoeducational interventions that do not draw on specific knowledge about the patient's internal world are used. Resolving such an impasse requires careful attention to the creation of an unusual and highly individualized form of family empathy—that is, empathy for the patient's preference for a specific delusional world view. To accomplish this goal in the case described above, the family therapist would first make an alliance with the mother's own disappointment related to the loss of a normal son, communicating understanding and acceptance of the mother's frustration and sense of loss. Going further, the family therapist would access, either directly or through consultation with the patient's individual therapist, knowledge about the experiences the patient was prioritizing by refusing medication and, ideally, some understanding of the patient's own sense of conflict and frustration in the matter of taking medication. The latter knowledge could help the mother to appreciate that there is an active struggle taking place entirely *within* the patient and therefore outside of the mother's experience—a struggle that is analogous to the observable (to the mother) one between mother and son, in which she completely favors the use of medication, while her son is totally opposed to it. In this case, individual work with the patient revealed that, in response to a series of rejections by women, the patient had developed the highly erotized view of himself as a man of "fatal charms," by which he meant that he was the center of desire of many women who, should they come into contact with him, would die. Such information allowed the family therapist, working in concert with the patient's individual therapist, to facilitate the mother's capacity to empathize with her son's dilemma and, in the process, to appreciate that taking medication meant losing the capacity to keep alive his sense of importance, however delusional. Given access to this information, the mother could appreciate how disconfirming conventional social encounters had often been for her son and how unappealing such encounters would be in the future, unless supplemented by a special and sustaining (even if delusional) sense of importance. Finally, she was helped to see that this delusional elaboration was not entirely a safe haven for the son, since his perception was colored by the conviction that ultimately women would leave him. Detailed and highly individualized parallels were then identified—between the son's need for hope (of being desired) and the mother's need for hope (of recovery)—that furthered the development of maternal empathy. Of equal importance, the family therapist then highlighted the nature of their very different orientations toward medication: The mother saw it as a solution to the son's frightening and demoralizing (for her) behavioral disorganization, whereas for the son it interfered with necessary (for him) access to a self-affirming inner world. A conventional family therapy intervention, coaching the mother to refrain from struggling with him about medication, was then invoked, creating a more neutral interpersonal field and thereby preparing the son, in individual and family sessions, to identify, reveal directly to mother, and resolve his own internal conflict about compliance with medication.

Rejection of Rehabilitation Treatment Programs

Many family members are aware that, following a remission of symptoms with psychotropic medication, the most productive work of treatment is built around the goal of promoting recovery of interpersonal, social, and vocational functioning. Psychoeducational interventions provide an understanding of the patient's needs during the immediate postpsychotic phase, during which increased activity, especially increased social interaction, may interfere with convalescence and provoke a return of psychotic symptoms. However, many family members find themselves at a loss to understand why the patient will not participate in low-stress activities that are recommended by treating clinicians during the convalescent phase. Not uncommonly, if family members express their reasonable concerns to the patient's clinician persistently enough, the clinician may, unconsciously, raise his or her own expectations for the patient. Experiencing this shift as the clinician's disappointment, the patient, in turn, may respond with anger, fear, or demoralization, while the family may take the clinician's increased expectations as confirmation of the validity of their own excessive expectations, as evidence that the patient could have been more functional all along. This in turn may trigger family resentment toward the patient for not having been more active. A vicious downward spiral then ensues.

Disruptive Behavior Directed Toward Family Members

As patients with schizophrenia spend more time living in the open community, some families are increasingly exposed to abusive, threatening behavior. Families often ask clinicians how to deal with this problem, manifesting a belief that it constitutes evidence of a return of the primary symptoms of the illness and just as often revealing that they are permitting burdensome levels of disruption of family life. While the psychoeducational orientation usually includes specific family guidance for limiting abusive behavior, little attention is given to its psychodynamic basis. The result is that families often move to stop the abuse without possessing an understanding of the behavior that would enable them to do so with empathy. Families lose patience with this manifestation of the illness and cease supportive interaction with the patient. These problems typify the limitations of existing psychoeducational programs in fostering family understanding of the human reactions to illness that underlie many manifestations of schizophrenia.

PROMOTING FAMILY EMPATHY FOR THE PATIENT'S DILEMMA

In attempting to address the problems posed above, we have found it useful to conduct a form of sensitivity training for the families of individuals with schizophrenia as a part of a comprehensive package of services provided within a psychoeducational frame of reference. The following presentation is excerpted from a workshop given to families of people with schizophrenia. Modeled after the Survival Skills Workshop developed by Anderson, Hogarty, and Reiss (12), the workshop begins with a description of the clinical manifestations of schizophrenia, the inner experiences of the illness as reported by patients, and the prevailing treatments for schizophrenia. The final section of our workshop, which goes beyond the usual psychoeducational workshop, centers on experiences of narcissistic injury as experienced by people with schizophrenia who are attempting to reintegrate into society. Structured as a guided fantasy, its goal is to increase the family's realization that, despite the biological roots of the disorder, the course of illness and much of the day-to-day behavior of the patient are driven by the patient's struggle to maintain self-esteem in the face of his or her attempts to regain a niche in a community of peers. We report this section here substantially as it is presented in the family workshop. In the discussion to follow, general principles are elucidated that are relevant to work with families aimed at enhancing family sensitivity to the human side of the illness.

The Humiliation Workbook

Workshop Leader: For the next few minutes, I'm going to ask you to come with me into the experience of people who have fallen ill with schizophrenia. I should tell you at t e outset that, walking with me on this path and identifying with the position of an ill person, may be disagreeable, even painful in some m asure. I offer the exercise neverthe- less, believing that there is a great deal of truth here, and that no matter how painful, this truth ultimately promotes the well-being of people suffering from schizophrenia.

For the sake of illustration, I will ask you to follow the story of a man named Bill (not his real name). As we set out, Bill is 28, has been ill for ten years, was living in a halfway house and attending a day treatment program until he was rehospitalized a week ago. Just before entering the hospital, Bill was due to be transferred from day treatment to a rehabili- tation program, in which he would start a transitional job. It would have been a simple assembly job, but it would have been a way for him to get going after a decade away from the job market.

Bill never made the transfer to the rehabilitation program because, two days after agreeing to enter the program, he secretly discontinued all his medication. Within ten days, he was too disorganized to remain in a community residence. When I visited him in the hospital shortly after admission, he revealed, with a wide smile of immense pleasure, that he stopped the medications as an experiment—to establish once and for all whether he really needed it. I noticed that on the wall of his room he had hung a drawing completed in high school. It was a smiling, full- faced picture of himself. Above the face was the inscription "Bill Turner for President." I learned that Bill had used this poster during an actual campaign for the presidency of his high school class. I was immediately struck by the contrast between this image and another that he had given me a few months earlier to hang in my office: That drawing shows an unshaven, unkempt man hunkered down in a cluster of garbage cans on a city street corner.

It doesn't take a master clinician to realize that these two images speak for the two sides of a central life conflict that Bill was living out. His dilemma, like the dilemma of thousands of other young men and women afflicted with a psychiatric illness that does not go away and that leaves the sufferer partially disabled, is as follows: *After coming to believe, on the basis of his cumulative childhood and adolescent experi-ence, that he is going to become a citizen, perhaps even an important citizen, he finds that he has become a mental patient instead.* Profession-als can point optimistically to the evidence of recoveries in the long-term outcome studies, and some know from direct personal experience of patients who were once brought low by schizophrenia and have gone on to recover. However, Bill did not have access to these sources of opti-mism. In fact, there was no evidence directly available to *him* that he would ever have a life that he would want to be a part of. That is not to say that Bill will always be incapacitated or that he will always require protection and supervision. Rather, it is an acknowledgement of his experience—of long and seemingly endless stretches of time ahead in which he will exist more as a mental patient than as a citizen. And with this anticipation, it is no wonder that, by surreptitiously rejecting drug treatment, he chose to return himself to the status of an institutionalized mental patient rather than suffer the larger blows to pride that would come with being, in his view, a substandard citizen: Being insane was less of an attack on his self-respect than being well this way—as an employee in a sheltered workshop.

Wounds to the Self

Now I'd like to ask you to enter into Bill's position and imagine that it is you who are caught on the horns of his dilemma. Imagine yourself realizing that soon after you went off your medication, you lost control of your mind:

- You couldn't control your behavior anymore.
- You did things that you are now ashamed of. You're not sure you can live with the realization that you did those things.

Imagine realizing that even though you are better now, your mind doesn't seem the same:

- You cannot think as straight or as sharply now as you did ten years ago. You don't seem to be able to remember things very well anymore, even very simple things.
- Most of the time, you are too exhausted to do very much of anything anymore. Nearly everything you try to do leads to boredom or failure.

Even thinking about undertaking a new activity leaves you confused or exhausted.

- You wonder what has become of the person you once were, and you wonder if you will ever be that person again. Sometimes it seems as though all you have left of that person is a memory; you're not sure you even want to hold onto the memory, but you're terrified of losing it.

Now, staying with that position, imagine yourself as seen by others after you went off your medication. Imagine realizing that, when you stopped your medication, other people noticed that you were "losing it." Imagine realizing that people treat you as if you were an invalid:

- They speak slowly to you or loudly, as if you were retarded or deaf.
- When you do some really simple thing—like taking out the garbage or taking a shower—your family rejoices, as if what you had done were a major accomplishment.
- People avoid you as they would a leper, as if they could catch what you have if they stayed around you too long.
- When you reveal your unusual experiences to ordinary people, they get frightened or offended. When you reveal them to professionals, they tell you that you have something called symptoms.

Judging from the reactions of the people—the ordinary people and the clinicians—whom you encounter in the course of your days living in the community, you have ceased to be a desirable, valued member of that community.

Imagine realizing that, with increasing frequency, your old friends can't seem to find time for you:

- The people who do make time for you are people whom you think of as more ill than you are.
- You sometimes wish they would leave you alone, because you are embarrassed to be seen in public with someone who looks mentally ill.

Imagine realizing that even when you are putting in a maximal effort, nothing that you do and nothing that you produce evokes pride or pleasure in your family. Imagine realizing that in all likelihood your life will never turn out the way you thought it would:

- Other people do not appear to take your dreams and your plans for the future seriously.
- When you ask if you will ever be okay again, people fall silent, look away, and change the subject.

In the course of your days in the community, you have daily experiences that remind you of who you might have been if not for the illness and other experiences that suggest a bleak, disaffirming future:

- You wait on a street corner for the minibus that will take you to your day hospital program. On the opposite corner, you see boys and girls talking and laughing, waiting for another bus to take them to your former high school.
- You listen to your doctor encouraging you to take a job stapling plastic bags shut—a job that in your most desperate dreams you never imagined would be a part of your life.

As if all this were not enough, you are also more or less continuously confronted by the loss of your personal sovereignty. You do not have control over your own thoughts, your own feelings, your movements, whom you choose to spend time with, whom you live with. In short, your life is no longer your own:

- Every day you go to the day program, you pass the hospital. You remember that you were forced bodily into that place. People you trusted called in the police in response to your expressed desire to take to the road for a while.
- When you walk in the city, you see other people going to work or walking with their friends. You realize that you do not have their mobility. You can't imagine that you ever will have their mobility.
- You watch other people making decisions for you as if you were 6 years old. They care about you. This you know. But they make plans for your life without even thinking that you might have opinions or preferences of your own.
- When you talk to the staff in the day program about your life, which you feel is going nowhere, you realize that their lives are going just fine.

It doesn't mean that their lives are really going fine. But from the perspective of a person suffering from the disabling effects of schizophrenia, clinicians' lives are just wonderful.

Protecting Yourself Against Wounds

Now I want you to hold onto Bill's perspective for a while longer and think about what you might do if you were in his position. In this part of the exercise, I'm going to be describing behavior that we have all been taught to think of as *symptoms of schizophrenia*. But I'm suggesting that at least some of these behaviors are better thought of as the external manifestations of certain *strategies used by patients to insure the survival of the self.* Think for a moment about how you might try to cope with the injury to your self-respect and how you would respond to the loss of a desirable personal future. You might make an attempt on your life, of course, for your daily experience has become an endless string of assaults on your will to endure. But more likely than that, or at least long before taking that route, you will do other things.

Blame and Recrimination

You will ruminate about your current existence, reviewing all that has happened to you and concluding that someone, maybe some specific person or persons, is at fault for this endless series of humiliations:

- You search your past in a blameful reverie. You remember some things that your mother—or your father or other people—did to you a long time ago. You conclude that they made you sick. You plan ways to get even with them.
- You set out to give your very successful kid brother, who is now the pride of the family, a hard time. You think up ways to embarrass him in front of his friends. You sidle up to his fiancée, knowing that she can tell you haven't had a bath in weeks. You notice your brother's discomfort, and you are pleased that he does not challenge you.

Noticing the pleasure in these moments, you begin to devote part of every day to thinking up ways to get even with other people:

- You think up ways of behaving that produce discomfort in your doctor and in the day hospital staff.
- You focus your vengefulness especially on anyone who presumes to make recommendations as to how you can improve your life.

Numbing Out

Vengeance may diminish your pain. But you pay a price inasmuch as you realize you are hurting people who care about you. So you explore other ways of killing your pain:

- You discover that when you have a drink, you don't feel much of anything for a while. So you take to drinking a couple of beers every time you anticipate a humiliating encounter. And then you drink to stop yourself from even thinking about the possibility of humiliating encounters.
- You take to experimenting with drugs, like speed and downers, to see if they will shut out the agony.
- You notice that sometimes, even without drugs or alcohol, you are able to shut down the parts of your mind that remember the past and dream about the future. You are not quite sure how you're doing this, but the main thing is that when you stop your mind from thinking, you also succeed in stopping the pain.
- You realize that it is *wanting things* that causes the pain. You put this observation to work in your daily life, killing off any and all former interests and declining to become interested in anything new. You learn to live by a new version of an old maxim. The new maxim is "No gain, no pain."
- You avoid any ongoing activity that might remind you of who you would have been if not for the illness. You certainly do not let anyone talk you into going to a rehabilitation program.

Handling Loneliness Through Withdrawal and Anonymity

Whether through the use of drugs or alcohol or just by having learned to numb out, you now are able to abolish a great many of the experiences of humiliation that were your daily bill of fare. Certain problems become apparent, though. You notice that you are often lonely for some sort of companionship. You are still attracted to the opposite sex. You still look forward to conversation with a friend, even if it's just small talk. You notice that you look forward to seeing *certain people*. In spite of yourself, you have become attached to them, and yet you know that any one of these people can—at any moment, without any warning, and without in any way wanting to hurt you—become a source of injury.

- You take to staying home from the places where you run into the people you like the most. You stay away from the day hospital. You take to your room.
- You decide to go on the road, moving from place to place, reasoning that if you can just get into an anonymous, nomadic life-style you will succeed in getting the best of this apparently automatic tendency to get attached to people.

Repudiating Conventional Reality

And if, after all this, you are still in pain, there are yet other ways to shield yourself against the humiliation, ways that involve not only letting go of involvement with other people but also relinquishing your commitment to what we call reality. You will be drawn to these ways of coping because, in the final analysis, truth and accuracy and realistic thinking are only useful so long as they lead to some degree of reward in the moment, or at least point to the possibility of future reward:

- You stop taking your medicines, realizing that they are maintaining your sanity.
- Once off the medicines, you are too confused to think the thoughts that are the source of your pain.
- You find yourself thinking that you have become all-powerful or famous, and you come to prefer these dreams to "reality," even though others seem to think that these beliefs are evidence of illness.
- You make believe you are secretly a member of a powerful organization, like the CIA or the FBI. You fill your days with fantasies of daring missions.
- You realize that you are no longer on earth, but now reside secretly in a satellite, circling the globe, in complete control of everything below.
- You make believe that you are not ill, convincing yourself that you are just fine and that it is everyone else, and especially your adversaries, who require psychiatric attention. You try to convince them to go for help.
- You convince yourself that, although you were once ill, you are all better now.
- You ignore any evidence of continuing impairments, and you repudiate observations made by others, who in their helpfulness, seek to convince you that you are still a mental patient.

- You convince yourself that you have some condition less dreadful than the one you are supposed to have. If you are said to have schizophrenia, you seek evidence that it is really manic-depressive illness or alcoholism.
- You take to behaving like a bad person so that nobody, including you yourself, can notice how impaired you are.
- You enter a timeless reverie, remembering former times when life was good to you. You even invent remembrances of things that never actually occurred. Through these remembrances, you are able to believe that you were *somebody* before you became a *nobody*.

In these ways, and in a myriad of others, you do your best to survive the onslaught of the many moments of injury to your dignity that are yours by reason of your presence in and access to the open community. You learn first and foremost to protect your soul from annihilation. You do things in the service of that goal that others cannot understand and do not support. You do these things on the premise that sanity without dignity, without a sense of being valued, is no bargain. You are telling your family and any others who encourage you to stay out of the hospital and to get better that the price you are paying for what they call community care is greater than you can bear.

Principles Derived from the Humiliation Workbook

Now, if you can disengage from the exercise, I'd like to comment on some of the principles that can be derived from work with patients who tell us, directly and indirectly, about the injuries to the self that are theirs because they attempt to return to useful lives. First and foremost, we must address the principle of *recoverability*. Not so long ago, it was preposterous to think that most people with schizophrenia could get better. We must underscore at this juncture how much the beliefs of the psychiatric profession—beliefs about the outcome of schizophrenia—have been challenged by recent scientific studies of the long-term course of schizophrenia. Just in the last five years, it has become clear that most of the expectations we were taught to have for our seriously ill patients were unduly pessimistic. All of these studies report that between one-half and two-thirds of patients with very severe and prolonged schizophrenic illnesses experience complete recoveries or very marked improvement when provided with access to decent housing and community services over long enough periods of time.

Yet the time frame of these studies is an issue for some people, who observe that the studies took in observations over periods of twenty to thirty years and say that is too long for people with schizophrenia and for their families to be expected to wait for improvement. Indeed, the time until recovery begins is often very long, but it should be noted that all the long-term outcome studies employed clinical treatment methods that were available in the 1950s and 1960s. In the intervening years, we have learned a few things about drug treatment and psychosocial programming that increase the prospects for social recovery. All the same, there are still large numbers of people who, despite their efforts and our own, will continue to exist more as mental patients than as citizens. So, we cannot ethically proceed as if there were the promise of recovery in all cases.

Then we are faced with the need for a definition of *recovery* as applied to prolonged mental illness. In this context, recovery is not just a matter of leaving one's condition behind. Rather, I prefer to think of recovery as meaning the *rebuilding of a life* and of *meaningful and rewarding involvements* in particular. It is from this vantage point that we can most readily comprehend the reluctance of many people with schizophrenia to participate willingly in conventional forms of community treatment. While we succeed with these treatments in removing symptoms, we do not at the same time do very well at restoring the person to a niche that provides access to evidence of his or her importance and to a sense of belonging somewhere to somebody.

This brings us directly to a third principle, which is the phenomenon of *interindividual variability,* or, more plainly, the notable differences in the paths taken by different people in rebuilding their lives. Many patients mount a recovery in some domains of functioning while continuing to manifest limitations in others. Many, for example, are up and about—working, living with family or friends—even though they continue to experience the primary symptoms of their illness. This should not surprise us, for people who have schizophrenia are as varied as everyone else in their basic humanity. We see individuality manifesting itself in the paths people choose in the face of any adversity, including that presented by schizophrenia. There is great need for respect for *individual preferences* in our work with people with schizophrenia. In

1974, the psychiatrist Aaron Lazare recommended that each patient be asked, as one element of our efforts to develop a treatment plan, "How would you like to be treated?" He called the approach implied by the question the "customer approach to patienthood" (13), forecasting the emergence of the current era, in which a patient shops for the most attractive path, for the program or activity that is most affirmative of his or her basic human dignity.

"Bill, how would you like to be treated here? What do you think will work best for you?" For a variety of reasons, we do not often get useful answers immediately in response to such questions. People who are veterans of the mental health system are used to being regimented and having their individual preferences ignored or disaffirmed. At best, they are simply not prepared for this form of curiosity from clinicians. At worst, they are wary of such an inquiry, taking it as just one more attempt at diagnosis or as a set-up for frustration or disappointment. We should not be surprised that the veteran decides it is best to be circumspect and replies in an uninformative manner. We must be prepared to ask the question repeatedly and to affirm preferences that the patient elects to reveal to us, no matter how outlandish they may at first appear. We must be on the lookout for indirect evidence, for clues that point toward preferences. We must show the patient our attempts to guess how he or she prefers to be treated, ready to be told that we got it wrong, but representing by the act of guessing openly and in front of the patient that we genuinely want to discover his or her opinions so that we may take them seriously.

Finally, there is the importance of *dignity* as a basic principle for program development. Life for those with persistent psychiatric impairments is replete with opportunities for injury to the soul and offers very few balancing opportunities for dignified and rewarding involvements. In these circumstances, apathy and despair are the obvious, ordinary, reasonable choices of the afflicted. I recall now one young man, a veteran of eight relapses and as many hospital stays, who announced in a day program case conference, "I'd rather not go to these activities." And after a moment, as if to explain himself, he added, "I think of myself as being in justifiable retirement." Then there is the woman whose sole genuine satisfaction was, for some time, her sexual encounters with several men and who eventually contracted a form of venereal disease not easily treated. Her evident distress in the face of this disease led me to inquire whether she was thinking of its implications for the future. She replied in a low, desperate voice, "I have no future. I have no future."

The tragedy of this situation is that, with enough imagination and enough public commitment, much of the injury can be avoided. Not that we could altogether abolish the injury. Schizophrenia damages the sufferer's dreams in some ways that have little to do with the attitudes of others or with the availability of countervailing positive involvements. But we can do better at providing access to circumstances that promote quality of life.

Above all, there is the need for a *dignified place to live*. Too often, we deliver people with schizophrenia into the very worst of physical settings. There was a time when we could get by with this practice, because the people we sent to such places had lived for so long in the regimentation of large institutions that they jumped at the chance to live anywhere in the open community. Increasingly, however, the vast majority of the mentally ill have not lived for decades in institutions. Consequently, they do not know how to be grateful for a niche in a slum neighborhood. They spurn the very same quarters that the previous generation clung to. The new generation rejects excessive constraints on their movements. They take to the road if they experience too much regimentation, too much loss of sovereignty. They do so even at the expense of losing access to services they need.

Second, there is the need for access to *activity that makes a contribution to the life of the community*—not a contribution to a large, impersonal world, but to a community of persons known to the patient and about whom he has come to care. One young man, living in a state hospital and still many years away from returning to the open community, said to his parents, "What I need is someone to take care of!" He was giving voice to the need to be valued. People suffering from schizophrenia are capable of contributing to the communities in which they reside, if only we can think of their sometimes short and inconstant workdays as having value. Too often, we impose timetables for improvement on such persons that make participation in treatment programs untenable for them.

Third, there is the need for *contact with persons who can legitimately claim to have recovered*, people who were once incapacitated by schizophrenia but who now are up and about, having recovered their capacity for involvement and made a life for themselves. In virtually all other walks of life, you will find readily at hand graduates or alumni, people who have been where you are and who have gone on to better things. Not so with former patients. The public fear and revulsion attached to the condition are so intense that practically as soon as a person recovers a niche among the citizenry, he or she ceases all contact with those still suffering with the illness. Some courageous formerly ill men and women maintain a degree of public visibility, remaining accessible to those still down and out with the illness. But most people with schizophrenia will go through a lifetime without ever having access to such a person. Without this kind of personal testimonial, without a living, breathing, credible example, all our statistics about recovery are for naught. When we find ways to provide access to former sufferers, those still suffering have reason to believe in the future and can sustain hope of better times ahead, even in their darkest moments.

And finally, there is great need for *respite* from time to time. It is clear from day-to-day clinical work that one does not proceed straightforwardly from illness to recovery. The path is virtually always characterized by advances and retreats, even under the most optimal of circumstances. In the present era, in which care in the open community is the prevailing orientation, an accumulation of wounds to the self sufficiently weighs down the recovering patient from time to time, so that he or she asks for refuge from life in that open community. Without our support for the legitimacy of refuge, without occasional, brief access to refuge, the weary and demoralized patient will achieve it just the same, through an aggravation of the illness and its symptoms, in the form of a major relapse. Just this week, the man who described himself as being in justifiable retirement decided, after two years of isolation, to risk coming around to a day program and daring to hold hands there with a woman, also a veteran. Feeling the pressure very directly and anticipating yet another humiliation, he exclaimed in my office, "I'm dying for another breakdown!" He may yet seek refuge from this newfound aliveness and its attendant risks. And if he does, I will immediately endorse his elective and presumably brief return to his favorite hospital unit. There, he will smoke cigarettes and tell jokes. He will hide out from the risks of wanting things and yearning for contact. His desire to hold hands again, to reach out for some life, will return in short order because, through the use of brief respite, he will have averted a more massive and more prolonged regression. And when his desire does return, he will ask to go home and to go back to that day program and to that girl. He will have learned to make use of what we call "regression in the service of the ego." He will have learned, as we do, to take a vacation to avoid burn-out. Together, the two of us will have learned how to cycle between rest and involvement and through this cycling to keep alive the long-term movement toward rebuilding a life of belonging.

Thank you for your attention.

Discussion of the Humiliation Workbook

We have presented this excerpt from our model workshop in an attempt to illustrate one way that clinicians treating individuals with schizophrenia can work to increase families' understanding of patients' priorities having to do with self-esteem regulation. Central to the presentation is the primacy of the risk of narcissistic injury among patients who are attempting to recover a niche in the community. Far from being simply manifestations of schizophrenia, such frequently observable phenomena as noncompliance with medication, rejection of therapeutic and rehabilitation treatments, and disruption of family life are seen as the external representations of the patient's struggle to maintain some semblance of dignity in the face of disaffirmation, stigmatization, and exposure to failure in the open community. Working from within the perspective offered in the workshop, we are able to respond to the mother who was at a loss to understand her son's rejection of depot neuroleptic that her son is attempting to ward off a neuroleptic-induced loss of a treasured sustaining fantasy. Going further, we can suggest that, in time, he may come to appreciate the value of medication, provided some affirmative real experiences with women can be made available to him through which he can achieve a sense of being valued. In his case, a community nurse was assigned to make frequent visits to his home following discharge. At first, he preferred to think of her as his English teacher, and only after six months was he able to acknowledge that she was a nurse. He rejected all medications for many months following discharge, but finally, through active coaching from the nurse, he was able to agree to take medication temporarily during a relapse and thus to avoid a return to hospital treatment. More than the avoidance of hospitalization, however, it was the ready access to the nurse as a community-based companion that made it possible for him to accept medication. Additionally, he chose to resume medication on his own terms, so that, for the first time in thirteen years of illness, he could experience medication as something within his control rather than seeing it as the emblem of his subjugation.

To the family of the patient represented by Bill Turner, we were able to say that he required a longer stay in hospital treatment, preparing him through repeated confrontation with his deficits to accept his status as a mental patient and thus eventually for a more stable reinvolvement in community life. "Bill" stayed on a special long-term unit for patients with schizophrenia for eighteen months and was then discharged to live with his family while continuing with day treatment. One year following discharge, he was working part time in a bakery, his first sustained employment since the onset of the illness.

To families who present questions regarding violence and abuse, we are able to point to the theme of vengeance as a primary coping device for patients who cannot bear the damage to their self-esteem evoked by the confrontation with well siblings and other family members not affected by the illness. In no way does this perspective suggest that the patient's behavior should be tolerated. But it does offer families a way to view the agony that drives the patient under some circumstances to turn against loved ones. We are reminded of the comment of a recovered patient who, on hearing the presentation, wrote to us that it was the first time she felt truly understood and offered the observation that, in her experience working with formerly mentally ill people, those who fight often have the best prospects for the future.

COUNTERPOINT: THE FAMILY'S PRIORITIES

In this chapter, we have attempted to describe some methods of working with families that promote empathy for the person with schizophrenia. In the course of their work, family therapists universally become witnesses to another aspect of these situations—the priorities of individual family members and of the family as a whole. These priorities, as they become known to the family therapist and to other clinicians who spend time interacting with family members in the course of their work with the patient, represent an important counterpoint to the focus on the patient's priorities. We will end this chapter with a brief discussion of this aspect of the work, which has been described more fully elsewhere (14).

In work directed toward teaching families about schizophrenia, it is common to observe that one or more members of the family are not prepared to accept the information provided in psychoeducational programs. These family members, who often stay away from formal psychoeducational programs because they reject outright the basic assumption that the patient is ill and requires psychiatric treatment, become involved, albeit reluctantly, in interactions with front-line clinicians. For this group of family members, acceptance of illness constitutes a too-painful assault on their own sense of dignity, on their own identity as parents, or on their internalized representations of the ill member. It is our observation that many family members, perhaps the majority, begin with a very extensive denial of illness, which then gives way to recognition and acceptance only with repeated exposures to the extremes of disorganization and more often only when they begin to perceive some hope of recovery. For these relatives, the clinician's task is to work diligently to preserve the family's capacity to envision an alternative, more hopeful future, even when, or perhaps especially when, the current clinical picture looks thoroughly bleak. Thus, rather than making repeated attempts to break through the family's denial of illness, the clinician seeks to find in the patient's current behavior evidence observable to the family that the patient is more than an illness, that he or she continues to have a soul, continues to dream about and look for satisfaction in daily life, and still has some determination to become a whole person again. By giving voice to the family's wish for recovery, by keeping alive in the mind of the family the possibilities for an eventual recovery, the clinician can at times create an alliance with the family through which some accommodation, some recognition of illness, and some collaboration with clinicians is allowable. A final example illustrates the role of the family therapist as an interpreter of the favorable aspects of a patient's symptoms:

> The family of a 25-year-old man with schizophrenia, who had led an isolated life in another city, denied the extent of his illness for many years, believing that he suffered from a borderline personality disorder. At one point, the patient was arrested for an attempted rape that took place in broad daylight and that oc-

curred, by the patient's subsequent account, in response to an auditory hallucination in which he heard a woman's voice saying, "Take me, take me." During the ensuing months, while the family was still absorbing the implications of the attack for their son's future, the therapist was able to interpret the act as the first indication of the son's wish for a relationship with a woman. Up until this point, despite their espoused belief that the son did not have schizophrenia, the parents had never given evidence that they thought of him as a man who might want the companionship of a woman. The therapist referred frequently in the ensuing two years to this incident, confronting the family not so much with his illness as with his aliveness. Gradually, the parents began to talk in family meetings about his loneliness and his attraction to women as indications of his underlying health, and the patient, who was present in many of these meetings was, in this way, a witness to his being talked about and thought of by his parents as a sexual being in a constructive sense. A year later, he met a woman in a local day hospital program and began dating her. The family was concerned about this liaison because they did not favor their son developing a romantic relationship with a mental patient, fully expecting, at this time, that he would one day meet a normal girl and get married. However, the therapist reminded them that there was a time when the idea of any relationship with any woman seemed out of the question to this young man and challenged them to affirm the developing relationship. Three years later, the mother sent the therapist, who was no longer working with the family, an announcement of the marriage of the young man to this same woman, signifying her acceptance of both the legitimacy of the son's status as a mental patient and his movement toward recovery.

Left to their own devices, this family would have remained so focused on the dangerousness of the son's behavior that they would have avoided altogether the subject of his sexuality, hoping to discourage him from any further acts of violence. In this way, crucial evidence of his vitality, of his strivings, even his psychotic strivings, would have gone unnoticed. Perhaps the result would have been a repetition of the attack, thereby moving him closer to a career as a mentally ill offender. Additionally, though, the parents would have persisted in their denial of his illness, for there was no basis in the attack, as perceived by them, on which to assemble the hope for an acceptable future that was the crucial ingredient in their acceptance of the illness in the present. The therapist's representation of the son as a person who yearned for the company of a woman broke open a new line of thought, constituting the basis for the family's seeing him once again in hopeful terms.

In conclusion, while the task of the clinician who relates to the patient's family members includes, in part, promoting an appreciation of the patient's priorities and how these become manifest in observable behavior, the clinician soon discovers that family members have their own legitimate priorities that profoundly shape the extent and quality of their participation in the work with the patient. If schizophrenia is frightening and if life in the face of the illness often seems unbearable to the patient, it is equally true that the illness and the attendant loss of function in the patient represent a crisis of major proportion to the family. Family responses to schizophrenia, including some responses that are helpful to the patient and others that interfere with the patient's attempts to cope constructively with the illness, are central to the course of the disorder over time. A full appreciation of the family's experience of schizophrenia, which is beyond the scope of this book, prepares the clinician to work at the interface between patient and family in ways that maximize the likelihood of restoring the patient's capacity for productive social and vocational involvements in community life.

Notes

INTRODUCTION

a. We do not mean to imply that the clinician will endorse actions that are harmful to self or others. On the contrary, the aim in such circumstances is to contain or mediate against harm while at the same time conveying an understanding of the intent of the patient's contemplated action as well as the clinician's own intent in providing containment.

1. A MODEL FOR UNDERSTANDING SCHIZOPHRENIA

a. An important corollary is that the caregiver's response to these behaviors, often characterized by confusion, anger, fear, or withdrawal, can compound the patient's difficulty with relatedness and communication.

b. Indeed, we shall see, the patterns of adaptation in schizophrenic individuals do appear to follow comprehensible and expectable courses, consistent with the principles of psychodynamics and cognitive theories. It is the consequences of this process of adaptation, which are so disabling and defeating to the schizophrenic individual, that we intend to study, and, ultimately, to treat.

c. The manner in which treatments are "applied"—that is, the way in which the clinician presents the treatment to the patient and the discussions that go on around it—are crucial to the effectiveness of the treatment. It is not a simple matter to apply somatic treatments in work with schizophrenic patients because of the way in which they perceive the treatment process and their interaction with the clinician.

d. For example, an extremely paranoid, angry male was asked to head the ward's task force, petitioning the hospital to allow the ward to have a pool table. His demanding, litiginous stance, fueled by his belief that figures in authority were inherently malevolent, made him a powerful, albeit at times eccentric, spokesperson. At the same time, he was forming an alliance with the ward through this activity.

e. This distinction is related to a classic controversy in the area of schizophrenic phenomenology—whether the patient simply suffers from a "deficit" in perception and cognition or is "in conflict" about his view of the world. Our model allows for a putative physiologic role, but asserts the importance, and indeed the essential contribution, of psychological responses to the illness. Thus, we see that the patient's conviction about a delusional view of self and/ or others is, in part, and significantly, motivated and sustained by his difficulty in tolerating the psychological alternative: confronting the disturbed nature of his experience, and the fact of his illness, of which he is, in spite of the delusion, aware—though that awareness includes doubt.

The delusion is an alternative view that "satisfies" the individual's psychological priorities. The unconscious mind is, in some sense, aware of its conflicting representations of reality. The delusional view can then be said to be at odds with the individual's rational view of experience. We do not fully understand how or why the conscious mind selects one or the other view. We do know that such conflict can be identified and that patients can, over time, change the way they interpret events, even in the face of ongoing psychotic stimuli.

2. UNDERSTANDING THE SUBJECTIVE EXPERIENCE OF THE PERSON WITH SCHIZOPHRENIA

a. The length and complexity of this comment illustrates the principle that "giving advice" cannot be thought of as straightforward and simple. Advice may still be given, but the complexity of the patient's experience of the advice must be anticipated.

3. FROM UNDERSTANDING TO ACTION: THE ALLIANCE
AND THE TREATMENT PROGRAM

a. How remarkable that we wish to insulate patients from the ritual of trial and failure through which learning proceeds and with which we all struggle daily! What is more, the activity coordinator's remarks repeat the common error of asserting authority where reflection and recommendation based on experience would suffice. This tendency is quite common in health care settings for a variety of reasons: Patients are infrequently grateful or complimentary to staff members and usually (defensively due to their unconscious frustration or shame) demean the activities and other interventions offered them; in addition, most hospitals—and ironically psychiatric hospitals and departments are no exception—are remiss in their efforts to sustain morale among health care workers, who in our experience have been generally competent, caring, overworked, underpaid, and unappreciated. The staff members' frustration and lack of control (and insecurity about the value of their work) is then expressed in authoritarian responses.

4. THE MAN WITH A BUG IN HIS BRAIN: AN INITIAL INTERVIEW

a. Many patients, by contrast, present such bizarre or primitive attitudes or reactions that the clinician lacks access to analogs within him- or herself (perhaps, because they would be too threatening), making it more difficult for the clinician to find common ground with the patient and therefore making it harder to identify ways to be helpful.
b. For example, in the case alluded to in chapter 1, the clinician refused to devote his time to defending the patient against the CIA. He and the patient could, however, both agree that the patient's sense of being unjustly treated was an issue worthy of their collaboration.
c. Naturally, the patient's attitude toward involvement is far more complex than the interviewer's comments suggest. The interviewer is not here addressing the patient's ambivalence about contact, only that part of the patient that, as he has indicated, wishes to be involved.

7. THE CASE OF ROGER: OUTPATIENT PSYCHOTHERAPY—
FROM APATHY TO COMMUNITY INVOLVEMENT

a. The patient had been investigating his options while in the hospital, mostly by talking with fellow patients who had been to other institutions or had heard about them from others who had been there.

b. The delays were long enough to set the therapist to wondering whether this was psychomotor retardation and thereby evidence of depression.

c. The therapist often referred openly to her struggle to listen without prejudice. She would say, "This is where a real psychiatrist would say to you . . ." She would tell him how difficult, how disorienting, and even how frightening it was to absorb his story without the protection accorded by the usual psychiatric perspective.

d. The patient covertly discontinued the use of lithium carbonate in about the eighteenth month of therapy, having insisted from the beginning that it never had had any appreciable effect on his condition.

e. He was, by this time, taking chlorpromazine on a self-directed basis, using sleep disturbance as the target symptom, with an average daily dose of 400 mg. per day at bedtime. All efforts to educate him as to the benefits of dopamine blockade for overstimulation had been met with a wall of irritable denial: He did not have an illness; all he required was something to promote a good night's sleep, and chlorpromazine was good for that purpose.

f. The patient echoed this sentiment at several points as the work proceeded. On one occasion a year later he declared, "I earn the food that I eat, just by being able to bite it!"

References and
Suggested Readings

This is not intended to be an exhaustive reference list. We have selected a few illustrative articles that can be used as guides to further exploration. Some chapters have references, some have suggested readings, and some have both. The former are used either to substantiate the text or to acknowledge a source. Suggested readings are included to illuminate or extend what has been presented.

In addition, there is a brief list of general references that offer excellent overviews of some of the main themes of the book. It is our hope that, by making this list concise, we encourage readers to pursue the references.

CHAPTER REFERENCES AND SUGGESTED READINGS

Introduction

References

1. Rothman, D. J. *The discovery of the asylum: Social order and disorder in the new republic.* Boston: Little, Brown and Company, 1971.

2. Chamberlin, J. *On our own: Patient-controlled alternatives to the mental health system.* New York: McGraw-Hill, 1978.
3. Estroff, S. E. *Making it crazy: An ethnography of psychiatric clients in an American community.* Berkeley: University of California Press, 1981.
4. Runions, J., and R. Prudo. Problem behaviours encountered by families living with a schizophrenic member. *Canadian Journal of Psychiatry* 28 (1983):382–86.
5. Van Putten, T. Why do schizophrenic patients refuse to take their medications? *Archives of General Psychiatry* 31 (1974):67–72.
6. Marder, S. R. Low and conventional-dose maintenance therapy with Fluphenazine Decanoate. *Archives of General Psychiatry* 44 (1987):518–21.
7. Carpenter, W., and D. Heinrichs. Targeted medication strategies. *Schizophrenia Bulletin* 9, 4 (1982):533–42.
8. Herz, M., H. Szymanski, and J. Simon. Intermittent dose strategies. *American Journal of Psychiatry* 39 (1982):918–22.
9. Kane, J., G. Honigfeld, J. Singer, and H. Meltzer. Clozapine for the treatment-resistant schizophrenic. *Archives of General Psychiatry* 45 (1988):789–97.
10. Blackwell, B. The drug defaulter. *Clinical Pharmacology and Therapeutics* 13 (1972):841–48.
11. Strauss, J. S., W. T. Carpenter, and J. Bartko. The diagnosis and understanding of schizophrenia: Part III. Speculations on the processes that underlie schizophrenic signs and symptoms. *Schizophrenia Bulletin* 11 (1974):61–75.
12. Andreasen, N. C. Negative symptoms in schizophrenia: Definition and reliability. *Archives of General Psychiatry* 39 (1982):784–88.
13. Crow, T. J. Two syndromes in schizophrenia? *Trends in Neurosciences* 5 (1982):351–54.
14. Crow, T. J. Positive and negative schizophrenic symptoms and the role of dopamine. *British Journal of Psychiatry* 139 (1981):251–54.
15. Mackay, A. V. Positive and negative schizophrenic symptoms and the role of dopamine: I. *British Journal of Psychiatry* 137 (1980):379–86.
16. Angrist, B., J. Rotrosen, and S. Gershon. Differential effects of amphetamine and neuroleptics on negative vs. positive symptoms in schizophrenia. *Psychopharmacology* 72 (1980):17–19.
17. Andreasen, N. C., S. A. Olsen, J. W. Dennert, and M. R. Smith. Ventricular enlargement in schizophrenia: Relationship to positive and negative symptoms. *American Journal of Psychiatry* 139 (1982):297–302.
18. Allen, H. A. Dichotic monitoring and focused versus divided attention in schizophrenia. *British Journal of Clinical Psychology* 21 (1982):205–12.
19. Frieswyk, S. H., J. G. Allen, D. B. Colson, L. Coyne, G. O. Gabbard, L. Horwitz, and G. E. Newsom. Therapeutic alliance: Its place as a process and outcome variable in dynamic psychotherapy research. *Journal of Consulting and Clinical Psychology* 54, 1 (1986):32–38.

20. Hartley, D. Research on the therapeutic alliance in psychotherapy. *American Psychiatric Association Annual Review* 4 (1985):532–49.
21. Horowitz, M. J., and C. Marmar. The therapeutic alliance with difficult patients. *American Psychiatric Association Annual Review* 4 (1985):573–85.
22. Allen, J. Therapeutic alliance and long-term hospital treatment outcome. *Comprehensive Psychiatry* 26 (1985):187–94.
23. Greenson, R. R., and M. Wexler. The non-transference relationship in the psychoanalytic situation. *International Journal of Psycho-Analysis* 50 (1969):27–39.
24. Pious, W. L. A hypothesis about the nature of schizophrenic behavior. *Psychotherapy of the psychoses*, A. Burton, ed. New York: Basic Books, 1961. Pp. 43–68.
25. Donlon, P., and K. Blacker. Clinical recognition of early schizophrenic decompensation. *Diseases of the Nervous System* 36, 6 (1975):323–27.
26. Freeman, T. The pre-psychotic phase and its reconstruction in schizophrenic and paranoiac psychoses. *International Journal of Psycho-Analysis* 62 (1981):447–53.
27. Docherty, J. P., and D. P. Van Kammen, et al. Stages of onset of schizophrenic psychosis. *American Journal of Psychiatry* 135 (1978):4.
28. Andreasen, N. C. *The broken brain: The biological revolution in psychiatry.* New York: Harper and Row, 1985.
29. Crow, T. J. The continuum of psychosis and its implication for the structure of the gene. *British Journal of Psychiatry* 149 (1986):419–29.
30. Andreasen, N. C., and S. Olsen. Negative vs. positive schizophrenia. *Archives of General Psychiatry* 39 (1982):789–94.
31. Lewine, R. R., L. Fogg, and H. Y. Meltzer. Assessment of negative and positive symptoms in schizophrenia. *Schizophrenia Bulletin* 9 (1983):368–76.
32. Kay, S. R., L. A. Opler, and A. Fiszbein. Significance of positive and negative syndromes in chronic schizophrenia. *British Journal of Psychiatry* 149 (1986):439–48.
33. Frank, A. F., J. G. Gunderson, and B. Gomes-Schwartz. The psychotherapy of schizophrenia: Patient and therapist factors related to continuance. *Psychotherapy* 24, 3 (1987):392–403.
34. Lin, I. F., R. Spiga, and W. Fortsch. Insight and adherence to medication in chronic schizophrenics. *Journal of Clinical Psychiatry* 40, 10 (1979):430–32.
35. Barr, M. A. Homogeneous groups with acutely psychotic schizophrenics. *Group* 10, 1 (1986):7–12.
36. Pao, P. *Schizophrenic disorders: Theory and treatment from a psychodynamic point of view.* New York: International Universities Press, 1979.
37. Carpenter, W. T., and D. W. Heinrichs. Treatment relevant subtypes of schizophrenia. *Journal of Nervous and Mental Disease* 169 (1981):113–19.

1. A Model for Understanding Schizophrenia

References

1. Wallace, E. R. What is truth?: Some philosophical contributions to psychiatric issues. *American Journal of Psychiatry* 145, 2 (1988):137–47.
2. Faust, D., and R. A. Miner. The empiricist and his new clothes: DSM-III in perspective. *American Journal of Psychiatry* 143 (1986):962–67.
3. Crow, T. J. Positive and negative schizophrenic symptoms and the role of dopamine. *British Journal of Psychiatry* 137 (1980):383–86.
4. Crow, T. J. Molecular pathology of schizophrenia: More than one disease process? *British Medical Journal* 280 (1980):1–9.
5. Andreasen, N. C., and S. Olsen. Negative vs. positive schizophrenia: Definition and validation. *Archives of General Psychiatry* 39 (1982):789–94.
6. Jackson, J. H. *Selected writings,* J. Taylor, Jr., ed. London: Hodder and Stoughton, Ltd., 1931.
7. Johnson, E. C., et al. Mechanism of the antipsychotic effect in the treatment of acute schizophrenia. *Lancet* 1 (1978):848–51.
8. Wing, J. K. Psychosocial factors affecting the long term course of schizophrenia. *Psychosocial treatment of schizophrenia,* J. Strauss, W. Boker, and H. D. Brenner, eds. Toronto: Hans Huber, 1987.
9. Carpenter, W. T. Approaches to knowledge and understanding of schizophrenia. *Schizophrenia Bulletin* 13 (1987):1–8.
10. Ciompi, L. Toward a coherent multidimensional understanding and therapy of schizophrenia: Converging new concepts. *Psychosocial treatment of schizophrenia,* J. Strauss, W. Boker, and H. D. Brenner, eds. Toronto: Hans Huber, 1987.
11. Opler, L. A., et al. Positive and negative syndromes in chronic schizophrenia in patients. *The Journal of Nervous and Mental Disease* 172 (1984):317–25.
12. Levin, S.: Frontal lobe dysfunctions in schizophrenia-II: Impairments of psychological and brain functions. *Journal of Psychiatric Research* 18 (1984):57–72.
13. Weinberger, D. R., et al. Physiologic dysfunction of dorsolateral prefrontal cortex in schizophrenia I: Regional cerebral blood flow evidence. *Archives of General Psychiatry* 43 (1986):114–25.
14. Goldberg, T. E., et al. Further evidence for dementia of the prefrontal type of schizophrenia? *Archives of General Psychiatry* 44 (1987):1008–14.
15. Chaika, E. Thought disorder or speech disorder in schizophrenia? *Schizophrenia Bulletin* 8 (1982):587–91.
16. Crosson, B., and C. W. Hughes. Role of the thalmus in language: Is it related to schizophrenic thought disorder? *Schizophrenia Bulletin* 13 (1987):605–21.
17. Freedman, R., et al. Neurobiologic studies of sensory gating in schizophrenia. *Schizophrenia Bulletin* 13 (1987):669–77.

18. Patterson, T. Studies toward the subcortical pathogenesis of schizophrenia. *Schizophrenia Bulletin* 13 (1987):555–76.
19. Holzman, P. Recent studies of psychophysiology in schizophrenia. *Schizophrenia Bulletin* 13 (1987):49–75.
20. Nasrallah, H. A., and D. R. Weinberger. *The neurology of schizophrenia.* New York: Elsevier Science, 1986.
21. Harding, C. M., et al. Vermont longitudinal study of persons with severe mental illness (Parts I and II). *American Journal of Psychiatry* 144 (1987):718–35.
22. Kraepelin, E. *Dementia praecox and paraphrenia.* Huntington: Robert E. Krieger, 1971.
23. Bleuler, E. *Dementia praecox or the group of schizophrenias.* New York: International Universities Press, 1950.
24. Brenner, H. D. On the importance of cognitive disorders in treatment and rehabilitation. *Psychosocial treatment of schizophrenia,* J. Strauss, W. Boker, and H. D. Brenner, eds. Toronto: Hans Huber, 1987.
25. Weinberger, D. R. Implications of normal brain development for the pathogenesis of schizophrenia. *Archives of General Psychiatry* 44 (1987):660–69.
26. Michels, R., and J. O. Cavenar, Jr., eds. *Psychiatry.* Philadelphia: Lippincott, 1987. Vol. 1, pp. 14–26; vol. 3, pp. 3–8.
27. Rifkin, A., ed. *Schizophrenia and affective disorders: Biology and drug treatment.* Boston: Wright, 1983.
28. Andreasen, N. *The broken brain: The biological revolution in psychiatry.* New York: Harper and Row, 1985.
29. Karown, F., et al. Preliminary evidence of reduced combined output of dopamine and its metabolites in chronic schizophrenia. *Archives of General Psychiatry* 44 (1987):604–7.
30. Sandler, M. The dopamine hypothesis revisited. *The biological basis of schizophrenia,* G. Hemmings and W. Hemmings, eds. Baltimore: University Park Press, 1978. Pp. 79–85.
31. Ingvar, D. H., and Franzen. Distribution of cerebral activity in chronic schizophrenia. *Lancet* 2 (1974):1484–86.
32. Jaskiw, G. E., et al. Medial prefrontal cortex lesions in the rat. Abstract, New Research Section, American Psychiatric Association Annual Meeting Proceedings. May 1988.
33. Grossberg, S., and G. Stone. Neural dynamics of word recognition and recall: Attentional priming, learning and resonance. *Psychological Review* 93 (1986):46–74.
34. Oke, A. F., and R. N. Abrams. Elevated thalamic dopamine: Possible link to sensory dysfunctions in schizophrenia. *Schizophrenia Bulletin* 13 (1987):589–604.
35. Lishman, W. A. *Organic psychiatry.* Oxford: Blackwell Scientific, 1987.
36. MacLean, P. D. A triune concept of the brain and behavior. Lecture I.

382 *References and Suggested Readings*

Man's reptilian and limbic inheritance. Lecture II. Man's limbic brain and the psychoses. *The Hincks Memorial Lectures,* T. Boag and D. Campbell, eds. Toronto: University of Toronto Press, 1973.

37. Falloon, I., D. C. Watt, and M. Shepard. The social outcome of patients in a trial of long-term continuation therapy in schizophrenia: Pimozide vs. Fluphenazine. *Psychological Medicine* 9 (1978):265–74.
38. Marder, S. R., et al. Low and conventional-dose maintenance therapy with fluphenozine decanoate. *Archives of General Psychiatry* 44 (1987):518–21.
39. Siris, S. G., et al. Adjunctive imipramine in the treatment of post psychotic depression. *Archives of General Psychiatry* 44 (1987):533–39.
40. Hirsch, S. R., A. G. Jolley, R. Manchanda, and A. McRink. Early intervention medication as an alternative to continuous depot treatment in schizophrenia: Preliminary report. *Psychosocial treatment of schizophrenia,* J. Strauss, W. Boker, and H. D. Brenner, eds. Toronto: Hans Huber, 1987.
41. Docherty, J. P., D. P. Van Kammen, S. G. Siris, and S. R. Marder. Stages of onset of schizophrenic psychosis. *American Journal of Psychiatry* 135 (1978):420–26.
42. Lacan, J. The case of Aimee, or self-punitive paranoia. *The clinical roots of the schizophrenia concept,* J. Cutting and M. Shepherd, eds. Cambridge: Cambridge University Press, 1987. Pp. 213–226.
43. Rogers, R. W., and C. R. Mewborn. Fear appeals and attitude change: Effects of a threat's noxiousness, probability of occurrence, and the efficacy of coping responses. *Journal of Personality and Social Psychology* 34 (1976):54–61.
44. Rippetoe, P. A., and R. W. Robers. Effects of components of protection-motivation theory on adaptive and maladaptive coping with a health threat. *Journal of Personality and Social Psychology* 52 (1987):596–604.
45. Clum, G. A., et al. Information and locus of control as factors in the outcome of surgery. *Psychological Reports* 45 (1979):867–73.
46. Poll, I. B., et al. Locus of control and adjustment to chronic hemodialyses. *Psychological Medicine* 10 (1980):153–57.
47. Miller, S. M., et al. Preference for control and the coronary prone behavior pattern: "I'd rather do it myself." *Journal of Personality and Social Psychology* 49 (1985):492–99.
48. Nowack, K., et al. Coronary-prone behavior, locus of control and anxiety. *Psychological Reports* 47 (1980):359–64.
49. Rotter, J. B. Generalized expectancies for internal versus external control of reinforcement. *Psychological Monographs* 80, 1, no. 609 (1966).

2. Understanding the Subjective Experience of the Person with Schizophrenia

References

1. Bowers, M. *Retreat from sanity: The structure of emerging psychosis.* Baltimore: Penguin Books, 1974.

2. Freedman, B. The subjective experience of perceptual and cognitive disturbances in schizophrenia. *Archives of General Psychiatry* 30 (1979):333–40.

3. Johnson, D. Representation of the internal world in catatonic schizophrenia. *Psychiatry* 47 (1984):299–314.

4. Landes, D., and F. Mettler. *Varieties of psychopathological experience.* New York: Holt, Reinhart and Winston, 1964.

5. Morgan, R. Conversations with chronic schizophrenic patients. *British Journal of Psychiatry* 134 (1979):187–94.

6. Reed, G. *The psychology of anomalous experience.* London: Hutchinson, 1972.

7. Sechehaye, M. *Autobiography of a schizophrenic girl.* New York: New American Library, 1970.

8. Mahler, M. S. *On human symbiosis and the vicissitudes of individuation.* New York: International Universities Press, 1968.

9. Schultz, C. The contribution of the concept of self-representation-object-representation differentiation to the understanding of the schizophrenias. *NIMH* 3 (1980):453–70.

10. Feinstein, D. The symbiotic block. *International Journal of Psychoanalytic Psychotherapy* 6 (1977):131–44.

11. Lichtenberg, J. The development of the sense of self. *Journal of the American Psychoanalytic Association* 23 (1975):453–84.

12. Bion, W. Differentiation of the psychotic from the non-psychotic personalities. *International Journal of Psycho-analysis* 38 (1957):266–75.

13. Hatan, M. The importance of the non-psychotic part of the personality in schizophrenia. *International Journal of Psychoanalysis* 35 (1954):119–28.

14. White, R. The experience of efficacy in schizophrenia. *Psychiatry* 28 (1965):199–211.

15. Davie, J. Observations on some defensive aspects of delusion formation. *British Journal of Medical Psychology* 36 (1963):67–74.

16. Cassimatis, E. G. The "False self": Existential and therapeutic issues. *International Review of Psycho-analysis* 11 (1984):69–77.

17. Beavers, W. Schizophrenia and despair. *Comprehensive Psychiatry* 13 (1972):561–72.

18. Sandler, J. The background of safety. *International Journal of Psychoanalysis* 41 (1960):352–56.

19. Burnham, D., A. Gladstone, and R. Gibson. *Schizophrenia and the need-fear dilemma.* New York: International Universities Press, 1969.

20. Modell, A. *Object love and reality.* New York: International Universities Press, 1968.

21. Searles, H. The schizophrenic individual's experience of his world. *Psychiatry* 30 (1967):119–31.

22. Winnicott, D. W. The capacity to be alone. *International Journal of Psychoanalysis* 39 (1958):416–20.

3. From Understanding to Action: The Alliance and the Treatment Program

References

1. Selzer, M. A., M. Carsky, B. Gilbert, W. Weiss, M. Klein, and S. Wagner. The shared field: A precursor stage in the development of a psychotherapeutic alliance with the hospitalized chronic schizophrenic patient. *Psychiatry* 47 (1984):324–32.
2. Selzer, M. A. Preparing the chronic schizophrenic for exploratory psychotherapy: The role of hospitalization. *Psychiatry* 46 (1983):303–11.
3. Brown, L. J. A short-term hospital program preparing borderline and schizophrenic patients for intensive psychotherapy. *Psychiatry* 44 (1981):327–36.
4. Volkan, V. The introjection of an identification with the therapist as an ego-building aspect in the treatment of schizophrenia. *British Journal of Medical Psychology* 41 (1968):369–80.
5. Lidz, T. The developing guidelines to the psychotherapy of schizophrenia. *Psychotherapy of schizophrenia*, J. Strauss, M. Bowers, T. Downey, et al., eds. New York: Plenum, 1980. Pp. 217–26.
6. Boyer, L. B. Office treatment of schizophrenic patients: The use of psychoanalytic treatment with few parameters. *Psychoanalytic treatment of schizophrenic, borderline, and characterologic disorders*. L. B. Boyer, P. L. Giovacchini, eds. New York: Jason Aronson, 1980. Pp. 129–70.
7. Schulz, C. G. An individualized psychotherapeutic approach with the schizophrenic patient. *Schizophrenia Bulletin* 13 (1975):46–69.
8. Kohut, H. The analysis of the self. New York: International Universities Press, 1971.
9. Selzer, M. A., H. W. Koenigsberg, and O. F. Kernberg. The initial contract in the treatment of borderline patients. *American Journal of Psychiatry* 144 (1987):927–30.
10. Benedetti, G. Individual psychotherapy of schizophrenia. *Schizophrenia Bulletin* 6 (1980):633–38.
11. Frosch, J., J. Gunderson, R. Weiss, and A. Frank. Therapists who treat schizophrenic patients. *Psychosocial intervention in schizophrenia: An international view*, H. Stierlin, L. C. Wynne, and M. Wirsching, eds. New York: Springer-Verlag, 1983.
12. Schulz, C. G. Self and object differentiation as a measure of change in psychotherapy. *Psychotherapy of schizophrenia*, J. G. Gunderson and L. R. Mosher, eds. New York: Jason Aronson, 1975. Pp. 305–16.
13. Searles, H. F. Psychoanalytic therapy with schizophrenic patients in a private practice context. *Countertransference and related subjects: Selected papers*. New York: International Universities Press, 1979. Pp. 582–602.
14. Feinsilver, D. B., and J. G. Gunderson. Psychotherapy of schizophrenia: Is it indicated? *Schizophrenia Bulletin* 6 (1980):11–23.

15. Grinspoon, L., J. Ewalt, and R. Shader. *Schizophrenia: Pharmacotherapy and psychotherapy.* Baltimore: Williams and Wilkins, 1972.
16. Gunderson, J., A. Frank, H. Katz, M. Vannicelli, J. P. Frisch, and P. H. Knapp. Effects of psychotherapy in schizophrenia II: Comparative outcome of two forms of treatment. *Schizophrenia Bulletin* 10 (1984):564–99.
17. Klerman, G. L. Ideology and science in the individual psychotherapy of schozophrenia. *Schizophrenia Bulletin* 10 (1984):608–12.
18. Rosenfeld, H. Notes on the psychoanalytic treatment of psychotic states. *Long term treatments of psychotic states,* C. Chiland ed. New York: Human Sciences Press, 1977. Pp. 202–16.
19. Will, O. A. Schizophrenia: The problem of origins. *The origins of schizophrenia,* J. Romasin, ed. Amsterdam: Excerpta Medica, 1967. Pp. 214–27.
20. Anthony, W. J., and R. P. Liberman. The practice of psychiatric rehabilitation. *Schizophrenia Bulletin* 12 (1986):542–59.
21. Frey, W. D. Functional assessment in the 80's: A conceptual enigma, a technical challenge. *Functional assessment in rehabilitation,* A. Halpern and M. Fuhrer, eds. New York: Brooke, 1984. Pp. 11–43.
22. Presly, A. J., A. B. Gribb, and D. Semple. Predictors of successful rehabilitation in long stay patients. *Acta Psychiatrica Scandinavica* 66 (1982):83–88.
23. Carpenter, W. T., and D. W. Heinricks. Early intervention, time-limited, targeted pharmacotherapy of schizophrenia. *Schizophrenia Bulletin* 9 (1983):533–43.
24. Falloon, I., and R. Liberman. Interactions between drugs and psychosocial therapy in schizophrenia. *Schizophrenia Bulletin* 9 (1983): 543–55.
25. Hogarty, G. E., N. R. Schooler, R. Ubrich, F. Mussare, P. Ferro and E. Herron. Fluphenazine and social therapy in the aftercare of schizophrenic patients. *Archives of General Psychiatry* 36 (1979):1283–95.
26. Anderson, C. M., G. E. Hogarty, and D. J. Reiss. Family treatment of adult schizophrenic patients. *Schizophrenia Bulletin* 6 (1980):490–506.
27. Greenley, I. R. Familial expectations, post-hospital adjustment and the societal reaction perspective on mental illness. *Journal of Health and Social Behaviour* 20 (1975):217–27.
28. Vaughn, C. E., and J. P. Leff. The influences of family and social factors on the course of psychiatric illness. *British Journal of Psychiatry* 129 (1976):125–37.
29. Vaughn, C. E., and J. P. Leff. The measurement of expressed emotion in the families of psychiatric patients. *British Journal of Social and Clinical Psychology* 15 (1976):157–65.
30. Leff, J. P., L. Kuipers, R. Berkowitz and D. Sturgeon. A controlled trial of social intervention in the families of schizophrenic patients: Two year follow-up. *British Journal of Psychiatry* 146 (1985):594–600.
31. Leff, J. P., L. Kuipers, R. Berkowitz, C. E. Vaughn, and D. Sturgeon. Life

events, relatives' expressed emotion and maintenance neuroleptics in schizophrenic relapse. *Psychological Medicine* 13 (1983):799–806.

32. Goldstein, M. J., and A. M. Strachan. The impact of family intervention programs on family communication and the short-term course of schizophrenia. *Treatment of schizophrenia: Family assessment and intervention*, M. J. Goldstein, I. Hand, and K. Hahlweg, eds. Heidelberg: Springer-Verlag, 1986. Pp. 185–92.

33. Giovacchini, P. C. Countertransference with primitive mental states. *Countertransference: The therapist's contribution to therapeutic situation*, L. Epstein and H. Feiner, eds. New York: Jason Aronson, 1983. Pp. 235–67.

34. Grinberg, L. On a specific aspect of countertransference due to the patient's projective identification. *International Journal of Psycho-analysis* 43 (1962):436–40.

35. Searles, H. The schizophrenic's vulnerability to the therapist's unconscious processes. *Journal of Nervous and Mental Disease* 12 (1958):247–62.

36. Winnicott, D. W. Hate in the countertransference. *Collected Papers*. New York: Basic Books, 1958. Pp. 229–42.

5. The Case of Sharon: A Hospital Stay Involving Noncompliance, Violence, and Staff Conflict

References

1. Selzer, M. Preparing the chronic schizophrenic for exploratory psychotherapy: The role of hospitalization. *Psychiatry* 46 (1983):303–11.

2. Schwartz, D. Aspects of schizophrenic regression. *Psychotherapy of Schizophrenia*. Amsterdam: Excerpta Medica, 1979. Pp. 79–87.

3. Searles, H. *Countertransference and related subjects*. New York: International Universities Press, 1979.

4. Gunderson, J. Patient-therapist matching: A research evaluation. *American Journal of Psychiatry* 135, 10 (1978):1193–97.

5. Auerhahn, N., and M. Moskowitz. Merger fantasies in individual inpatient therapy with schizophrenic patients. *Psychoanalytic Psychology* 1, 2 (1984):131–48.

6. Feinsilver, D., and B. Y. Yates. Combined use of psychotherapy and drugs in chronic, treatment-resistant schizophrenic patients. *Journal of Nervous and Mental Disease* 172, 3 (1984):133–39.

7. Kernberg, O. *Object relations theory and clinical psychoanalysis*. New York: Jason Aronson, 1976.

8. Munich, R., M. Carsky, and A. Appelbaum. The role and structure of long-term hospitalization: Chronic schizophrenia. *The Psychiatric Hospital* 16, 4 (1985):161–69.

9. Ogden, T. Projective identification in hospital treatment. *Bulletin of the Menninger Clinic* 45, 4 (1981):317–33.

10. Schulz, C. Technique with schizophrenic patients. *Psychoanalytic Inquiry* 3, 1 (1983):105–24.

11. Selzer, M., M. Carsky, B. Gilbert, W. Weiss, M. Klein and S. Wagner. The shared field: A precursor stage in the development of a therapeutic alliance with the hospitalized chronic schizophrenic patient. *Psychiatry* 47, 4 (1984):324–32.

6. The Case of Maryann: Psychotherapy and Community Management, Rehabilitation, and Rehospitalization

References

1. McGlashan, T., J. Docherty, and S. Siris. Integrative and sealing-over recoveries from schizophrenia: Distinguishing case studies. *Psychiatry* 39 (1976):325–38.
2. Searles, H. Phases of patient-therapist interaction in the psychotherapy of chronic schizophrenia. 1961. *Collected papers on schizophrenia and related subjects.* New York: International Universities Press, 1965. Pp. 521–59.

Suggested Readings

Goering, P. N., and S. K. Stylianos. Exploring the helping relationship between the schizophrenic client and rehabilitation therapist. *American Journal of Orthopsychiatry* 58, 2 (1988):271–80.
Roberts, R. The outpatient treatment of schizophrenia: An integrated and comprehensive management-oriented approach. *Psychiatric Quarterly* 52 (1984):91–112.
Strauss, J. S., and W. T. Carpenter. *Schizophrenia.* New York: Plenum, 1981.
Wing, J. K. The management of schizophrenia in the community. *Research in the schizophrenic disorders: The Stanley R. Dean Award Lectures*, R. Cancro and S. R. Dean, eds. New York: Spectrum, 1985. Vol. 2, pp. 113–54.
Wing, J. K., and B. Morris, eds. *Handbook of psychiatric rehabilitation practice.* Oxford: Oxford University Press, 1981.

7. The Case of Roger: Outpatient Psychotherapy— From Apathy to Community Involvement

References

1. C. C. Beels. Personal communication, 1974.
2. Zelin, M. L., S. B. Bernstein, C. Heijn, R. M. Jampel, P. G. Myerson, G. Adler, D. H. Bule, Jr., and A. M. Rizutto. The sustaining fantasy questionnaire: Measurement of sustaining functions of fantasies in psychiatric inpatients. *Journal of Personality Assessment* 47 (1983):427–39.
3. McGlashan, T. H. Aphanisis: The syndrome of pseudo-depression in chronic schizophrenia. *Schizophrenia Bulletin* 8, 1 (1982):118–33.

Suggested Readings

Cassel, E. J. The nature of suffering and the goals of medicine. *New England Journal of Medicine* 306 (1982):639–45.

Josephs, L. Witness to tragedy: A self-psychological approach to the treatment of schizophrenia. *Bulletin of the Menninger Clinic* 52 (1988):134–45.

Venables, P., and J. F. Wing. Levels of arousal and the subclassification of schizophrenia. *Archives of General Psychiatry* 7 (1962):114–19.

Wynne, L. C. A phase-oriented approach to treatment with schizophrenics and their families. *Family therapy in schizophrenia*, W. R. McFarlane, ed. New York: Guilford Press, 1983. Pp. 251–65.

8. Beyond Psychoeducation: Raising Family Consciousness About the Priorities of People with Schizophrenia

References

1. Bateson, G., D. D. Jackson, J. Haley, and J. Weakland. Toward a theory of schizophrenia. *Behavioral Sciences* 1 (1956):251–64.
2. Bowen, M. A family concept of schizophrenia. *The etiology of schizophrenia*, D. D. Jackson, ed. New York: Basic Books, 1960.
3. Lidz, T., A. R. Cornelison, D. Terry, and S. Fleck. Intrafamilial environment of the schizophrenic patient. VI. The transmission of irrationality. *Archives of Neurology and Psychiatry* 79 (1958):305–16.
4. Wynne, L. C., I. Ryckoff, J. Day, and S. Hirsch. Pseudo-mutality in the family relations of schizophrenics. *Psychiatry* 21 (1958):205–20.
5. Singer, M. T., and L. C. Wynne. Communication styles in parents of normals, neurotics and schizophrenics. *Psychiatric Research Reports* 20 (1966):25–38.
6. Terkelsen, K. G. Schizophrenia and the family: II. Adverse effects of family therapy. *Family Process* 22 (1983):191–200.
7. Hirsch, S. R., and J. P. Leff, *Abnormalities in parents and schizophrenics: A review of the literature and an investigation of communication defects and deviances.* London: Oxford University Press, 1975.
8. Leff, J. P. Developments in family treatment of schizophrenia. *Psychiatric Quarterly* 51 (1979):216–32.
9. Brown, C. W., J. L. T. Birley, and J. K. Wing. Influence of family life on the course of schizophrenic disorders: A replication. *British Journal of Psychiatry* 121 (1972):241–58.
10. Vaughn, C. E., and J. P. Leff. The influence of family and social factors on the course of psychiatric illness: A comparison of schizophrenic and depressed neurotic patients. *British Journal of Psychiatry* 129 (1976):125–37.
11. Falloon, I. R. H., J. L. Boyd, and C. W. McGill. *Family care of schizophrenia.* New York: Guilford Press, 1984.
12. Anderson, C. M., G. E. Hogarty, and D. J. Reiss. *Schizophrenia in the family.* New York: Guilford Press, 1986.

13. Lazare, A., S. Eisenthal, and L. Wasserman. The customer approach to patienthood: Attending to patient requests in a walk-in clinic. *Archives of General Psychiatry* 32 (1975):553-58.
14. Terkelsen, K. G. Evolution of family responses to mental illness through time. *Families of the mentally ill*, A. B. Hatfield and H. Lefley, eds. New York: Guilford Press, 1987.

GENERAL REFERENCES

Anderson, C. M., G. E. Hogarty, and D. J. Reiss. *Schizophrenia and the family*. New York: Guilford Press, 1986.

Black, B. J. *Work and mental illness: Transitions to employment*. Baltimore: Johns Hopkins University Press, 1988.

Bowers, M. B. *Retreat from sanity: The structure of emerging psychosis*. New York: Human Sciences Press, 1974.

Ciardiello, J. A., and M. D. Bell. *Vocational rehabilitation of persons with prolonged psychiatric disorders*. Baltimore: Johns Hopkins University Press, 1988.

Falloon, I. R., J. L. Boyd, and C. W. McGill. *Family care of schizophrenia*. New York: Guilford Press, 1984

Freeman, T. *The psychoanalyst and psychiatry*. New Haven: Yale University Press, 1988.

Hafner, H., W. Gattaz, and W. Janzarik, eds. *Search for the causes of schizophrenia*. Berlin: Springer-Verlag, 1987.

Sechehaye, M. *Autobiography of a schizophrenic girl*. New York: Grune and Stratton, 1951.

Strauss, J. S., and W. T. Carpenter. *Schizophrenia*. New York: Plenum, 1981.

Wing, J. K., and G. W. Brown. *Institutionalism and schizophrenia*. Cambridge: Cambridge University Press, 1970.

Index

Adaptive intent of patient's beliefs and actions, 5, 6, 14, 35, 45, 46, 47, 51; empathy for, 96; expressed in delusions, 32–33, 361–62; identifying, with the patient, 32, 60; and manifest communication, 78, 80, 81; and social withdrawal, 38, 39, 45, 47, 360–61

Affect, 125, 226–27; and countertransference, 246; and relatedness, 70; restricted, 38

Affective flooding, 328, 329, 342

Age of onset, 41

Aggression, 38, 178; and boundary disturbances, 85; distance created by, 103; and manifest communication, 80–81. *See also* Violence

Agitation, 18, 38–39

Alcohol and drugs, 330, 360

Aliveness, 310–14, 320, 329, 332, 341;

absence of, 2; and treatment alliance, 6. *See also* Vitality, loss of

Allies, potential, 200

Amotivation, 12, 38, 39; and boundary disturbances, 85; and demoralization, 57, 60; and interaction of physiology and psychology, 43, 45; and psychological discontinuity, 93–94; and treatment alliance, 19, 23; and treatment program, 160–65

Anderson, C. M., 354

Andraesen, N., 37

Anger, 8, 39, 51–53, 133, 134, 161, 178, 226, 227, 241, 315; in resigned patients, 162, 164, 165

Anhedonia, 39, 328; and demoralization, 57, 60

Antidepressants, 24, 250–51

Antipsychotic medication. *See* Medication